D1553655

The Future of the History of Economics

The Future of the History of Economics

Annual Supplement to Volume 34
History of Political Economy

Edited by E. Roy Weintraub

Duke University Press
Durham and London 2002

Contents

Will Economics Ever Have a Past Again?   1
E. ROY WEINTRAUB

Part 1. North American Issues

Sitting on a Log with Adam Smith: The Future of the History
of Economic Thought at the Liberal Arts Colleges   17
BRADLEY W. BATEMAN

Graduate Studies in the History of Economic Thought   35
TED GAYER

The History of Economics as a Subdiscipline: The Role of the History
of Economics Society Meetings   62
JOHN B. DAVIS

Part 2. International Issues

The Future of the History of Economic Thought in Britain   79
ROGER E. BACKHOUSE

Economics as History of Economics: The Italian Case in Retrospect   98
MARIA CRISTINA MARCUZZO AND ANNALISA ROSSELLI

The Present Situation of the History of Economic Thought
in France   110
GHISLAIN DELEPLACE

Reflections on the Past and Current State of the History of Economic
Thought in Germany   125
BERTRAM SCHEFOLD

The History of Economic Thought in Spain and Portugal:
A Brief Survey   137
JOSÉ LUÍS CARDOSO

A Brief History of History of Economic Thought Teaching in the
Netherlands   148
ALBERT JOLINK AND MARK BLAUG

The History of Economic Thought in Australia and New Zealand   154
JOHN LODEWIJKS

History of Economics in Japan: A Turning Point   165
AIKO IKEO

Part 3. Publication and Research

The Future of Publication in the History of Economic Thought:
The View from *HOPE*   179
CRAUFURD D. GOODWIN

Heaven Can Wait: Gatekeeping in an Age of Uncertainty,
Innovation, and Commercialization   190
STEVEN G. MEDEMA, JOSÉ LUÍS CARDOSO, AND
JOHN LODEWIJKS

Coming Together: History of Economics as History of Science   208
MARGARET SCHABAS

A Hunger for Narrative: Writing Lives in the History of Economic
Thought   226
EVELYN L. FORGET

Surfing the Past: The Role of the Internet in the Future of the
History of Economics   245
ROSS EMMETT

Part 4. The Next Generation

Confusion and "Interstanding": A Figured Account of Hope   263
MATTHIAS KLAES

The Interesting Narrative of a Duke-Trained Historian of Economics, from Prospectus to Ph.D. to Profession; or, How I Learned to Love Weintraub and Start Worrying   272
STEPHEN MEARDON

So You Want to Be a Historian of Economics? Reflections of a Recent Recruit   284
ESTHER-MIRJAM SENT

Once and Future Historians: Notes from Graduate Training in Economics   298
DEREK S. BROWN AND SHAUNA SAUNDERS

Reflections on the Tales of the Next Generation   309
EVELYN L. FORGET

Part 5. Heterodox Traditions

History of Economic Thought in the Post-Keynesian Tradition   319
SHEILA C. DOW

The Use and Abuse of the History of Economic Thought within the Austrian School of Economics   337
PETER J. BOETTKE

The Marxist Tradition in the History of Economics   361
ANTHONY BREWER

Afterword

A Pall along the Watchtower: On Leaving the *HOPE* Conference   378
PHILIP MIROWSKI

Contributors   391

Index   397

Will Economics Ever Have a Past Again?

E. Roy Weintraub

> The sciences are unique among creative disciplines in the extent to which
> they cut themselves off from their past, substituting for it a systematic
> reconstruction. . . . Such reconstruction is a precondition for the
> cumulative image of scientific development familiar from science
> textbooks, but it badly misrepresents the past.
> —Thomas Kuhn, *The Road since Structure* (1987)

From the curricula they construct, economists apparently regard the history of economics as a subdisciplinary field within economics, symmetric as a subfield with labor economics, public finance, or economic development. Indeed, that perspective is instantiated in the *Journal of Economic Literature* subject classification system. Based on their pedagogy, economists appear to believe that one studies core subjects to become socialized as an economist; then one masters several fields of specialization for teaching purposes; and finally one selects a problem in one of those fields in which to become a specialist as a scholar or researcher.

This argument parallels economists' ideas of what goes on in, say, mathematics, where basic work in algebra, analysis, and topology is thought to define the core training, which is followed by work in fields

I wish to thank, without implicating them in its argument, Neil De Marchi and Craufurd Goodwin for commenting on this piece. Despite the rumors of an agenda-setting, reward-constructing, blacklist-producing "Duke Cabal," the fact is that the three of us ride off, disagreeing, in usually different directions. That understood, my intellectual esteem, moral regard, and warm sense of personal colleagueship for them both cannot go unremarked here.

like algebraic number theory or Lie groups. Economists likewise believe that core work in mechanics (quantum, classical, statistical) and electromagnetism is followed by fieldwork in solid-state condensed matter or elementary particles.

Yet in neither mathematics nor physics does history have a place. While history of mathematics is occasionally found in undergraduate programs in mathematics, the history of physics (like the history of chemistry) is more usually taught in the department of history, possibly cross-listed in physics (or chemistry) if the scientists can bring themselves to offer credit for that which they consider to be nonscience. Of course, what is true in mathematics and physics and chemistry is now true in economics as well. Whereas once upon a time the history of economics was a required core course for economists, no longer is that so. But more to the point, in doctoral training programs in nearly all North American universities, the history of economics is not even a field course, and this is increasingly true in doctoral programs in Europe and the antipodes as well.

Despite this fact, History of Economics Society (HES) and European Society for the History of Economic Thought (ESHET) presidential and distinguished fellow addresses employ a rhetoric of good health concerning the subdiscipline of the history of economics. Believing that this cheerfulness masked some real structural problems for the field, I began in 1999 to organize a group of scholars to consider the state of the history of economics as a discipline in the new millennium. The occasion for this review was the annual *HOPE* conference, in this case the *HOPE* 2001 conference, held (fittingly) in the Millennium Hotel just off the Duke campus in Durham, North Carolina, 27–29 April 2001. The conference was sufficiently animated that the discussions were continued in a closed mail-list through eh.net over the next few months.

The conference call did not circumscribe approaches to assessing the health of the subdiscipline, for there are a variety of ways to gauge this. Nevertheless, three main paths seemed to present themselves. The first is essentialist. If when considering how the subdiscipline fits into the larger disciplinary whole as a cognitive enterprise one finds that its health is essential to the health of the larger economics, then it follows that the subdiscipline must be maintained in a healthy way if economics is to prosper. That philosophical or theoretical move produces arguments that travel along specific lines. For instance, one may argue that since economics is a historical discipline (the essentialist move), not a scientific one, cutting economics off from historical argumentation is logically incoherent. Alternatively, one may argue that economics is a scientific discipline (the essentialist move), but that the best ways to do science themselves are contested, and so the most successful gambits of science in the past must be known in order to provide exemplars for better current and future practice. This kind of health assessment forces the argument that the history of economics has to play an important role in the field of economics and in the training of economists.[1]

Second, as an alternative, one can explore measures of a discipline's actual—not ideal—health, where those appropriate measures could be variously faculty lines, new Ph.D. entrants, number of journals, attendance at annual meetings, funding for conferences, courses taught, and so on. This sociological framework for the discussion would assess health according to the increase or decrease of one, several, most, or all of the constructed metrics.

And third, for us as historians, it is natural to assess subdisciplinary health historically. Such a discussion would engage with the local and contingent circumstances of the evolution of the history of economics by reconstructing its context, or several contexts, in a thick and interesting narrative, perhaps in various voices. Philip Mirowski, who served with William Barber and Mark Blaug as a roving conference commentator, pointed out that despite the future-looking conference call, it was curious that the conferees did not utilize historians' tools to take the measure of the subdiscipline's health. That is, the historian's craft could perhaps have produced an account of the health of the subdiscipline with chapters like "Changes in the Undergraduate Economics Curriculum in England and Scotland: 1945–90" or "Changing Perspectives on History: The Consequences of Letting the Quantitative GRE Determine Who Gets an Ivy League Economics Ph.D." or "Follow the Money: The Effect of the National Science Foundation Funding Patterns on Economics Graduate Education, 1958–88." This, though, is not that book. My own suspicion is that historians of economics are generally unaccustomed to doing such historical work, so that complex, self-reflexive studies are difficult at best, and self-serving at worst, usually confirming a position defined in advance of evidence.

---

1. Probably the best recent statement of this argument was developed by Warren Samuels (1997). But see the earlier piece by Bradley Bateman (1992) and, more recently, the article by Mark Blaug (2001).

Thus the conferees' arguments actually followed two tracks, essentialist and sociological, only sometimes connecting one with the other. Essentialism itself took two primary forms, one of which was historiographic, reflecting alternative ways to write histories of economics. The second essentialist line concerned heterodox traditions. That is, the historical enterprise was, because it was essential to those crafts' rhetorical strategies, healthy within those heterodox traditions.

Although the millennial historiographic issues were the subject of the 2000 HES meetings in Vancouver, the record of which appeared in the *Journal of the History of Economic Thought* (*JHET*) in June 2001, they also concerned the *HOPE* 2001 conferees, although less in the papers than in the discussions that tracked the presentations. The reason for this is simple: the discussions that the conference sought to develop about the health of the subdiscipline seemed to require participants to testify to the relevance of that health. Such testimony ordinarily took the form of a background or implicit commentary that "the health of the history of economics is important because . . . " Significantly, however, the conference did not address the issue that if most economists regard the history of economics as unimportant, perhaps historians of economics should respond with something other than, "They're wrong, and we should try to convince them of their error." In other words, what the conference lacked was a discussion along the lines of, "Suppose (as nearly all economists will argue) that the history of economics as a subdiscipline, as it is constituted today, *is not and cannot be made to be* important for the education of economists: discuss the implications of this for historians of economics." I believe that this nondiscussion is connected to a fundamental historiographic problem.

In his recent book *On the Methodology of Economics and the Formalist Revolution* the distinguished methodologist Terence Hutchison (2000, 11) makes the following argument:

I agree, therefore, wholeheartedly with Colander's formulation of a main aim of methodological discourse as that of commenting on, and criticizing, the theorizing of economists, and explaining why what they are doing does not, and cannot, achieve results of the interest and relevance which they are apparently claiming or aiming at (often simply because conclusions of relevance and interest cannot follow from the assumptions, explicit or inexplicit, on which their theories are based: which are so seriously oversimplified as to mislead profoundly if applied to the actual economic world).

If one comes to the history of economics out of a concern that economics is misguided in some fundamental ways, out of a concern that contemporary economics somehow misses what is important about economic life and economic argumentation, one form that criticism may take is quite direct: one criticizes the way economics is done on the basis of some argument or other about the right way to do it, measuring current practice against transcendental standards.

In such a case, the economist will oftentimes turn to history because of a belief that, while current practice may not meet reasonable standards, at least at some point in the past economics as a practice was consistent with the canons of good economic argumentation. Indeed, if there were no past (positive) evidence of acceptable work, it would be very difficult to derive any sense of what would (normatively) constitute acceptable work in economics. Without some past exemplar, all one could argue would be that standards, transcendental or immanent, come from other forms of scholarly practice—physics, chemistry, biology, and so on—and that those standards ought be applied to an economics that has never come up to the mark.

If one does not want to hold economics to the standards of chemistry and physics though, modern failures must be based on wrong turns taken in the past. This is the argument of Hutchison, who has been quite clear in his belief that what he refers to as formalism has sidetracked economics from its appropriate concern with real phenomena and empirical testing of economic models.

It is not necessary here to take issue with Hutchison.[2]

Rather, I will simply point out that critics such as Hutchison employ the history of economics in a particular fashion, one that structures how they will "do" history: for such scholars, historical writing is shaped by the methodologist's belief that present-day economics is a mess. Critical work in the history of economics will thus examine current economics to see how it got (at some point in the past) to be as bad as it is. This kind of history will often begin with current issues in economics and push the historical argument back in time to recover some kind of bifurcation,

---

2. As I have done elsewhere, by arguing that Hutchison is simply misguided in many respects regarding his ideals on formalism (Weintraub 2001).

some place in the past when the road not taken would have been the better one.

Notice what Hutchison's argument requires of a historian. First, it requires that a historian not do economics the way many economists do it, as an exercise in Whiggish triumphalism. Paul Samuelson's Whig history would appear ruled out of court by Hutchison's argument, since whatever his belief about present work in economics, Samuelson would hardly suggest that it is misguided and on the wrong track. For economists imbued with the idea of progress, Hutchison is giving a very different set of instructions on how to interpret the past; he is asking economists to seek in the past a source of the degeneration that characterizes current research activity.

Suppose historians of economics were to take this advice. I submit that the history of economics would soon stand in the same relation to economics as creationism does to evolutionary biology. "They will be held in contempt" is too weak a forecast of the position of a small band of outsiders that sets itself up to criticize the fundamental analyses of a dominant scientific elite. If most economists understand the history of economics as an attack on mainstream economics, they will be hostile to the subdiscipline and its claims on common resources of faculty positions and students' time.

As the historian Ted Porter (1992, 235) has noted:

Technical history, after all, has often served an apologetic function. This, I must emphasize, is by now greatly attenuated in historical studies of natural science. I regret to add that history as legitimation is still very strong in the history of economics. And this, I think, may be the decisive reason why historical work on recent economics has made so little impression on a generation of historians who insist on their autonomy from science. Unfortunately, many historians of economics are so completely socialized as economists, and so little as historians, that the genre of historical study is not fully distinct from that of the review essay. The review essay surveys a field and assigns credit, almost always on the assumption that knowledge is steadily progressing. Far too much history of economics, still, aims to extend the review back twenty or fifty years by presenting the ideas of the economist on some modern question. The precursor, long dismissed as a category mistake in history of science, is still alive and well in economics, and this is almost inevitable so long as history of economics is written to meet the standards and presuppositions of ahistorical economists.

Porter's comments present a different set of problems from Hutchison's for the history of economics. Porter argues that histories of economics have been too much shaped by the concerns of economists. That is, historians of economics have been socialized as economists, and consequently their understanding of what constitutes a historical discussion is based on their interest in either legitimizing modern economics, by uncovering what has led to the present, or uncovering the errors of the past that the present theories and analyses rectify. Economists who are most interested in doing applied economics today—that is, nearly all economists writing research papers in North American institutions—have no interest whatsoever in historical reconstruction. They are concerned with how the present science has succeeded where the past science had failed. What Porter is arguing then is that the concern with current economic practice is a poor structure in which to do historical reconstructions.

Suppose historians of economics were to take Porter's advice and stop writing histories based on the "presuppositions of ahistorical economists." The audience then would become, I suspect, scholars writing in the history of science and science studies. And as a subdiscipline, the history of economics would likely become even less interesting to economists than it is now, if that is possible.

Hutchison subverts historians of economics who appear content with economics, at least economics as it stands today, while Porter subverts economists who write history out of an "economics" interest. Now, most economists would appear, broadly speaking, to be practitioners of the neoclassical variety or, in smaller numbers, heterodox critics of that tradition. Thus taking Porter and Hutchison together, we are forced to conclude that few economists can reasonably take an interest in, let alone construct, a historical argument worth reading. The task is to carve out a space between the different parts excised by Porter and Hutchison.

How much is left, and what kind of historical craft can be built upon it? The papers delivered by Margaret Schabas, Evelyn Forget, and Ross Emmett (in the so-called All-Canada Session) made connections between the history of economics and other traditions. In her essay, Margaret Schabas revisits her 1992 suggestion that historians of economics should break away from the economics discipline and join forces with historians of science. She reemphasizes that the historiographic standards of our subdiscipline need to reflect that connection, although the institutional arrangement should be whatever can be worked out to the advantage of individual scholars in particular places. After all, economics departments pay us more than history departments would. Evelyn Forget argues that biography as a genre is increasingly employed in a variety of studies and that autobiography—the autobiographical turn, as it has been called—is increasingly employed in theoretical work in a wide range of disciplines. Her question about the employment of biography and autobiography in the subdiscipline opens a set of questions for new connections. Ross Emmett, in an examination of the new world of information services in which historical scholarship finds a place, explored for the conferees the possibilities and problems that this new world has opened up. His attention to the emerging conflicts concerning intellectual property rights produced a near explosion at the conference as individuals were apprised of the difficulties that electronic access creates in the concept of authorship and ownership. That on-line access to journals means that authors' works will be formed and reformed by the copyright owners and publishers presents some complex issues for scholars in all disciplines, but some especially troublesome ones for those using archival material. As archival material is put on-line, it will be increasingly difficult for historians of economics to make use of those materials in the same way as they had in the past. Access will be easier, but utilization may very well be significantly more difficult.

A second essentialist line, concerning the history of economics and heterodox traditions, was developed more optimistically in the essays. As the contributions of Sheila Dow, Peter Boettke, and Anthony Brewer made clear, heterodox economics and the traditions of heterodox economics utilize historical argumentation in ways quite different from the practices of neoclassical economists. That is, the rhetoric of the heterodox traditions, how individuals argue and persuade one another, involves appeal to historical argument and older texts in ways that neoclassical economists find outside their ken. Indeed, the historical approach was called intrinsic to heterodox argumentation in the sense that game theorists would not appeal to a point of interpretation in *The Theory of Games and Economic Behavior* in order to assess the merits of a particular form of an auction for offshore oil leases. Consequently, the history of economics has been a big tent—and certainly the HES, HETSA, and ESHET meetings a welcome tent—for heterodox economists to present historical argumentation as part of their own economic analysis. Because of the difficult and often contentious relationship between neoclassical and heterodox traditions, the linkage of heterodox traditions to the subdiscipline of the history of economics may make it difficult for mainstream economists to encourage the growth of, let alone accept the continued existence of, the history of economics: people seldom wish to proffer food by hand to those who bite. To the extent that economics may be increasingly intolerant of heterodoxies, "big tent" history of economics may be ever more marginalized.

It needs to be recognized, though, that a number of the conferees were quite unimpressed by the strong claims made about the important role of historical reconstructions in heterodox economics. It was obvious from the noisy discussion that there is going to be no easy soothing of historiographic sensibilities by heterodox economists' claims to have uncovered better ways to do economics by re-presenting the canonical texts of Marx, Sraffa, Hayek, or Keynes. To put it bluntly, some historians at the conference believe that heterodox economics has produced very little historically interesting scholarship (Sraffa editing Ricardo to the contrary notwithstanding), nor is it likely to do so, since that is not its purpose.

The sociological track of the conference developed concerns about the institutional health of the arrangements by which the subdiscipline has organized itself. For the marginalization of our subdiscipline is quite real. My colleague Craufurd Goodwin argued me out of titling the conference—and this volume—"Does the History of Economics Have Any Future?" I allowed his optimism with respect to the answer to trump my own pessimism. That pessimism, however, is not chimerical. Conference essays by Ted Gayer and Roger Backhouse document the increasingly difficult time historians of economics are having in the United States and Great Britain in securing resources for training new entrants into the profession. In the United States, the subdiscipline, as represented in Ph.D. programs, is in near free fall, with little on the horizon to provide a safe landing. This theme is reflected in the set of essays by young members of the profession. Those by Derek Brown and Shauna Saunders, Matthias Klaes, Steve Meardon, and Esther-Mirjam Sent detail the difficulty "our young" have in defending an interest in the history of economics in graduate education and, once defended, the difficulties in finding a place to practice our craft. During the conference, this line of argument produced great consternation among older members of the subdiscipline. A few of the youngest members of the profession were told, curiously, to be more cheerful, and that there are many jobs out there for historians of economics, as long as one is not interested in teaching in North American Ph.D. programs. However, the next generation of economists are being trained in precisely those programs, and if there is no one in those programs presenting the history of economics either in courses or in model behavior for scholarship, the audience for history of economics will become quite similar to the audience for history of chemistry in chemistry departments: nil. It was also argued that this state of affairs provides some opportunities for economists with historical interests to take up positions on undergraduate faculties or in liberal arts colleges. Brad Bateman's essay points out the possibilities in this area, although the pressures on liberal arts colleges to conform to the standard of Ph.D. training in economics, as the technical discipline increasingly shapes the undergraduate experience, is quite real and appears unrelenting. Evelyn Forget's comment on that session, one of two essays I solicited after the conference, captures well the spirit of the discussions.

To be sure, the situation is not the same in all countries. Reports from Ghislain Deleplace on France, Bertram Schefold on Germany, and Cristina Marcuzzo and Annalisa Rosselli on Italy suggest that the structure of the subdiscipline, as it is institutionally embedded within the educational practices of each country, makes the issue not so much resources as cross-disciplinary activity and respect among the larger profession of economists. Aiko Ikeo argued that in Japan, historically quite different with respect to the institutions and the place of the history of economics, the subdiscipline is fairly healthy, although quite disconnected from the kinds of historiographic practices becoming more common in North America and Europe. Practice in Australia and New Zealand, as discussed by John Lodewijks, is heavily shaped by the connection of economists in those countries to the Cambridge traditions in the history of economics and may not survive with great vigor a generation past Peter Groenewegen's and Geoffrey Harcourt's retirements.

These arguments produced strong feelings at the conference associated with individuals' beliefs that they either were or were not participating in a formerly respectable but now degenerating Lakatosian research program. Although John Davis, past president of the History of Economics Society, painted a positive picture of those annual North American meetings, discussion did bring out some consequences of their inclusiveness. Does the policy of the HES to accept virtually all papers offered for presentation at its annual meeting, in a desire to encourage members of the subdiscipline, result in a low average quality? What metric could be used to assess this? Is the role of the Society to promote this inclusiveness, or is it to establish norms for peer review? The conferees were quite divided on this point, although they agreed to sign a letter to the HES encouraging it to explore new arrangements to enrich the annual meetings.

The reports from the editors of journals—Steven Medema, Craufurd Goodwin, José Luís Cardoso, John Lodewijks—generally paint a different picture from the reports on graduate training. Journal editors are quite pleased by the large number of articles crossing their desks and believe that their number is a measure of the health and vitality of the subdiscipline. Nevertheless, the difficulty of establishing the merits of the journals, because of the noninclusion of most subdisciplinary journals other than *HOPE* and *JHET* in the *Social Sciences Citation Index*, means that our journals are only weakly present in the hierarchies for citation studies and concomitant journal rankings. Thus the Research Assessment Exercise of the British Higher Education Funding Council, North American tenure review committees, and departmental or college external review teams in the United States cannot do the kinds of assessments in history of economics increasingly demanded by resource managers. And although it may be boorish to mention it, high rates of journal submissions and publications in the history of economics may mean, in the absence of any metrics, that historians of economics are producing more pages, to be read by fewer individuals, to even less effect on scholarship over time.

This is related to the question of book publication in the history of economics. We had a brief discussion at the conference about the quality of books being published in various series in the history of economics, although there was no systematic analysis of this issue. Nevertheless, at least in North American universities, historians of economics are being asked to publish articles if they wish to be promoted as economists but to publish books to satisfy scholars in the humanities that the subdiscipline is really historical. This is producing our own contribution to the movement that has been recently decried by the director of Harvard University Press, that of publishing more books of lower quality as young faculty are told the rule is one book and a book proposal for tenure, two books and a proposal for a professorship (Waters 2001). The *HOPE* 2001 conferees, however, did not pursue this set of issues. The fact that many of us were either editors or on the editorial boards of book series that often publish nearly unedited masters and doctoral dissertations at high prices may account for the silence.

What we had at the conference then was a multiple voiced examination, across countries, approaches to economics, institutional settings, and craft-commitments, of the state of our subdiscipline shaped by the kinds of perspectives *economists* bring to problems. Because this conference was the first opportunity historians of economics have had to debate the future of the subdiscipline, at least since the History of Economics Society and the *History of Political Economy* were formed as entities more than thirty years ago, the discussions were heated and convoluted. The variety of positions represented make forecasting the subdiscipline's health problematic. Moreover, the international structure of the subdiscipline is intertwined with the globalization of educational initiatives more generally, as the American fetish of evaluation is now constraining institutional behavior in the United Kingdom and elsewhere in Europe. Since research assessment is the golden shovel that digs up dollars, pounds, yen, or euros for scholarship, when economists assess the history of economics in this way there are real and increasing burdens on the subdiscipline to behave differently. The historicization of these moves, the context called globalization or Americanization,[3] was only alluded to in discussion at the conference, for the self-reflexive nature of such an activity presented real problems for the historians assembled to contextualize themselves and their own concerns. It is thus left to me as director of the conference, and editor of the volume that represents what was delivered at the conference, to share my own perspective, which is additionally reflected in the selection of essays that follow.

As the twenty-first century unfolds, it is less likely that economics will be a happy home for the history of economics. In the major American research universities, economic statistics has migrated to departments of statistics, research and teaching in economic policy are now moving to departments and schools of public policy, political economy has moved to political science departments, and management studies are migrating to departments of management and of sociology. Whether we like it or not, the internationalization of education is shaped by the practices in those universities, sooner or later. That graduate students in economics are taught using the same textbooks in the United States, China,

3. For the globalization issues with respect to economics, see Coats 1997.

Italy, and Canada simply reflects the fact that mathematics students in those countries likewise use the same mathematics texts, and the same is true for chemists and neurobiologists. Globalization is real, and higher education is, like Hollywood and rock music, mostly made in America. The age of the contemplative economist-scholar, at home equally among classical languages, the history of ideas, and mathematical theory, has passed. For the subdisciplinary community in which, for a variety of reasons, I find myself at home (Weintraub 2002, chap. 8), there are going to be interesting challenges to face over the coming decades. They were well articulated by Margaret Schabas and her commentators in 1992[4] and reprised at this conference. Namely, with which larger scholarly communities will the history of economics share permeable boundaries: economics, history, literature, philosophy, sociology, science studies? Closure was not achieved, however, as every one of these fields was endorsed by at least two of the *HOPE* 2001 conferees. Thus one could be optimistic that the history of economics will turn out to be a robust field as it is nurtured and tied to so many interesting communities. Alternatively, perhaps one should be pessimistic that the history of economics has no real loving home.

For me, were a single scale of optimist = 10 and pessimist = 0 to represent the possible perspectives on the future of the subdiscipline of economics called the history of economics, 3 would be my upper bound.

References

Bateman, Bradley. 1992. The Education of Economists: A Different Perspective. *Journal of Economic Literature* 30.3:1491–95.

Blaug, Mark. 2001. No History of Ideas, Please, We're Economists. *Journal of Economic Perspectives* 15.1:145–65.

Coats, A. W. 1997. *The Post-1945 Internationalization of Economics*. Durham, N.C.: Duke University Press.

Hutchison, Terence. 2000. *On the Methodology of Economics and the Formalist Revolution*. Cheltenham, U.K.: Edward Elgar.

Porter, Ted M. 1992. Comment on Schabas. *HOPE* 24.1:235.

Samuels, W. J. 1997. The Work of Historians of Economic Thought. In *Research in the History of Economic Thought and Methodology*, edited by W. J. Samuels and J. E. Biddle. London: JAI Press.

---

4. See the multiple perspectives evoked in the *HOPE* minisymposium built around Schabas 1992.

Schabas, Margaret. 1992. Breaking Away: History of Economics as History of Science. *HOPE* 24.1:187–203.

Waters, Lindsay. 2001. Rescue Tenure from the Tyranny of the Monograph. *Chronicle of Higher Education* 47:B7.

Weintraub, E. Roy. 2001. Review of *On the Methodology of Economics and the Formalist Revolution* by Terence Hutchison. *History of Economics Review* 33 (winter): 128–29.

———. 2002. *How Economics Became a Mathematical Science.* Durham, N.C.: Duke University Press.

Part 1

North American Issues

Sitting on a Log with Adam Smith: The Future of the History of Economic Thought at the Liberal Arts Colleges

Bradley W. Bateman

> The question may have arisen in your minds, Why do reasonable people studying economics attach some importance to the history of the subject? Well, the history of the subject is not necessarily important to you in professional life, unless you aspire to teach the subject matter later on.
> —Lionel Robbins, *A History of Economic Thought: The LSE Lectures* (1998)

When economists ask if a subdiscipline has a future, you can almost be sure that they mean, "Does it have a future as a field on the 'cutting edge' of research?" The question is not an idle one. Only twenty years ago, the field of development economics was being eulogized in many quarters. And until the fall of the Berlin Wall, the subdiscipline of comparative systems was a largely moribund field, not yet transformed into the alluring new field of "transition economics." Subdisciplines *do* rise and fall.

What economists mean when they talk about the vitality of a subdiscipline is captured nicely in Paul Krugman's book *Development, Geography, and Economic Theory* (1995), in which he argues that fields in which the theorists cannot (or do not) work in the dominant mathematical discourses suffer neglect and disregard. He explains that both

I would like to thank Patti Dale for her help in compiling the data on course offerings at liberal arts colleges. I would also like to thank Ruth Grant, Bill Barber, Derek Brown, Shauna Saunders, Laura Welp, Trey Reasonover, David Nathan, Philip Holroyd, Steve Meardon, Steve Medema, and Roy Weintraub for their comments on earlier drafts of the essay. All the remaining errors are mine alone.

economic development and economic geography, despite their importance, languished after midcentury because their questions were not being framed in the dominant economic models of the late twentieth century.

Without citing all the literature, it is no surprise that in a world in
which subdiscipline success depends on this kind of formula, the history
of economic thought has suffered a perpetual crisis of self-confidence
during the last fifty years. For many years, for instance, the odds were
better than 50 percent that the topic of the presidential address at the
History of Economics Society annual meeting would be a defense of the
subdiscipline.[1]

Note, however, that all of the kinds of thinking about the subdisciplines of economics that I have described so far depend solely on research for their understanding of what constitutes success and survival.
Without at all denigrating the importance of research, it is nonetheless
possible to frame the success and future of a subdiscipline in other
terms.[2]

A Success Story: The History of Economic
Thought at the Liberal Arts Colleges

If you want to see an active and vital practice of the history of economic
thought, you need to look no further than the hundreds of small liberal
arts colleges in the United States. These colleges, unique to the American educational system, are focused on the education of undergraduate students; by all indications the economics faculty at these schools
think that teaching the history of economic thought is an important enterprise.[3] Seventeen of the top twenty liberal arts colleges in the *U.S. News
& World Report*'s annual rankings (fall 2000) list at least one course in
the history of economic thought in their course catalogs, and fourteen of
them offer the course regularly (see appendix 1). In Minnesota and Ohio,
two states with a large and diverse set of small liberal arts colleges, 80
percent of the liberal arts colleges list the history of economic thought in
their course catalogs, and 70 percent of them offer the course regularly

1. See Barber 1990 for an example of this genre and a review of the previous literature.
2. In fact, I will make an explicit argument in favor of research later in this essay, but only
after I have tried to establish alternative criteria for the success of a subdiscipline.
3. The only self-described liberal arts college of which I am aware outside the United States
is Augustana University College in Canada.

(see appendix 2). Not surprisingly, a large number of the jobs advertised every year in the field are at the small liberal arts colleges.[4]

So just what are these small liberal arts colleges? And why are they teaching a subject that so many people fear is irrelevant or even dying? Because the audience for this essay is international, it seems worthwhile to step back and answer these questions, if only briefly, so that the phenomenon of the history of economic thought's success at the liberal arts colleges can be better understood.

What Is a Liberal Arts College?

Of the more than 3,000 colleges and universities in the United States today, 212 are formally classified by the Carnegie Foundation as liberal arts colleges.[5] This relatively small number is deceiving, however. One reason is that these colleges are widely seen as among the best places in America to receive an undergraduate education, and so they are influential in shaping undergraduate education at a majority of all other colleges and universities where undergraduate education is the primary goal. Another related reason is that while many schools are not formally classified as liberal arts colleges, they began as liberal arts colleges and still offer an undergraduate education that follows the model of the liberal arts colleges.[6]

The small liberal arts colleges owe their enduring status in American higher education to many historical contingencies (that we cannot explore in the space available here); but clearly they are the beneficiaries of a certain mythology that arises from their association with the ancient Greek and Roman traditions of liberal education.[7] In a new nation, with a short colonial past, the imprimatur of Greek antiquity undoubtedly gave

4. Within the last five years, Williams, Bryn Mawr, Grinnell, DePauw, Trinity (Texas), and Colby have advertised positions in the history of economic thought.

5. See www.carnegiefoundation.org/Classification/classification.htm.

6. I will argue later that what is said in this essay about the liberal arts college is true for almost all public, four-year universities that do not have graduate programs. In 1987, there were 540 colleges classified by the Carnegie Foundation as "liberal arts colleges." About 320 were removed last year to a broader category because they offered more than 40 percent of their degrees in fields outside the traditional liberal arts (e.g., in business administration or physical therapy). In the traditional liberal arts departments at these 320 colleges, there will have been little or no change in the course offerings as a result of this formal reclassification.

7. The classic treatment of the history of the liberal arts college in America is Rudolph 1962. More recently, the winter 1999 issue of *Daedalus*, titled *Distinctively American: The Residential Liberal Arts College*, is devoted entirely to this topic. The essay by Hugh Hawkins

these small, struggling colleges, which were created by the hundreds on the western frontier, a patina of authority that would have been otherwise difficult to attain.[8]

And the patina effect should not be overlooked, for the small liberal arts colleges drew much more explicitly from the *idea* of liberal education than they did from its original *content*. There was no effort to build a curriculum around the trivium and quadrivium, which comprised the seven traditional subjects of classical liberal education. Instead, the purpose of these colleges was to train "free men" through "education for freedom," and if the centerpiece of that education was four years of Latin and Greek, that was because these languages were necessary for reading the Bible, which for the Protestant founders of these colleges was *the* text for freedom. The explicit purpose of these small frontier colleges was to prepare a student either for ministry or for effective citizenship as a good "person in the pews."

This self-understanding lasted into the second half of the nineteenth century and was only seriously shaken in the last two decades of that century. Even then, "Greek, Latin, and Christianity" defined one of the small handful of tracks available for students at these colleges. The twentieth century, however, brought several waves of change and redefinition for the small liberal arts colleges as they faced first the rise of the larger research university and then the creation of mass-produced higher education to accommodate the baby boomers.[9] Without too much exaggeration, it is fair to say that what emerged in the second half of the twentieth century was a small cadre of secularized, private colleges that offered small class size and a broadly defined curriculum that did not include professional courses such as engineering or business education.[10]

(1999) in that volume serves as the best recent treatment of the evolution of the liberal arts college identity.

8. Bateman 2001 contains a longer discussion of the history of liberal education as it pertains to contemporary economic education.

9. See Hawkins 1999 for an excellent short history of the American liberal arts college. George Marsden's (1994) history of the research universities provides the best background to the secularizing forces that were to sweep through the liberal arts colleges as the research universities became their important rivals. See also Reuben 1996.

10. The "nonprofessional" nature of the liberal arts college education also extends to the idea (common throughout American higher education) that students only take about a quarter of their course work in the area in which they "major" or specialize. Thus, for instance, an economics major will do work in the humanities and natural sciences en route to her or his degree.

Why Does the History of Economic Thought
Succeed at the Liberal Arts Colleges?

Briefly, then, we have established what the liberal arts colleges are and that they are the sites of an impressive success for the history of economic thought. The question remains, "Why is this the case?"

Here, I am afraid, the answers must be speculative. I am the graduate of a small liberal arts college, I work at a small liberal arts college, and I have written before about their economics curricula (Bateman 1992, 2001). In short, I have considerable personal experience of the thing about which I write. Thus, all the usual disclaimers apply, in spades. At any rate, I have in mind that there might be several reasons for the continuing vitality of the history of economic thought at these schools.

Inertia

It could be that the teaching of the history of economic thought has held up at the liberal arts colleges because it is part of a traditional curriculum there. The subject was, after all, widely taught fifty years ago, and perhaps it has held on at these schools because they are out of the research mainstream and so have clung to their older curricula. This cannot be the case, however, since the departments at liberal arts colleges in all disciplines engage in constant and vigorous curriculum revision. It would be difficult to find a liberal arts college that does not have regular, outside evaluations of its departments; holding onto old curricula for inertial or conservative reasons simply is not an option in this scenario. It is true that they had the history of economics in their course lists fifty years ago, and that they have it there today; but this will have been the result of critical reflection, not inertia.

An Atmosphere of Intellectual Curiosity

For lack of a better term, I would say that the combined intellectual curiosity of the students and faculty at the small liberal arts colleges lends very much to the continued teaching of our subject there. Now, of course, intellectual curiosity comes in many forms. One could just as easily argue that the unit root literature is driven by intellectual curiosity as one could that it drives the literature of the history of economic thought. But there is a particular kind of intellectual curiosity in the students who are first entering the discipline. As apprentices, they are likely to have a broad and fundamental curiosity about why economists ask the questions they do and why they answer them the way they do. They wonder who Adam Smith was, and they are curious to know what Karl Marx said. Likewise, generally speaking, the faculty who end up spending their careers at small liberal arts colleges teaching undergraduates are the kind of people who are curious to know how economics unfolded and where the important turns in the substance and style of the discipline took place.

The history of ideas is a large part of the "education for freedom" at every liberal arts college, and, thus, the intellectual curiosity that supports the presence of the history of economic thought at these schools is in some ways a facet of what it means to be at one of them.

The Nature of the Employment at a Liberal Arts College

In the many advertisements for economists at liberal arts colleges listed in the *Job Openings for Economists*, it is not unusual to find a line that reads something to the effect of, "Applicants should be willing to teach in an interdisciplinary course required of all sophomores," or "The successful applicant will teach regularly in a team-taught interdisciplinary course in the humanities and social sciences." Forget for a moment the terror (or disdain) that such an advertisement must strike in the heart of a young Ph.D. who believes that happiness (or success) consists of publishing at least two articles a year for the next six years in the *Journal of Political Economy* and *Econometrica*. For the lucky applicant who lands such a job, the future involves a world in which they will teach with colleagues from English, classics, and philosophy, on equal terms, the ideas that have shaped human history. It does not matter too much if they were ill prepared for the task in their graduate education; few of their colleagues in other disciplines were any better prepared. But the newly hired economists will have to face the challenge, and they will suddenly find themselves immersed in intellectual history: studying it and teaching it. In all likelihood, they will end up loving it.

The Vision of Teaching at a Small
Liberal Arts College

The distinctive teaching environment at the small liberal arts colleges also lends to the continued vitality of the history of economic thought there. One reason for this has to do with the explicit understanding that the professor will work closely with each student to develop his or her skills in writing, discussion, and critical thinking. It is no secret, for instance, that the teaching of writing is in a poor state at most large research universities. The *Chronicle of Higher Education*, which serves as the primary site for advertising university positions in the United States, has experienced an explosion of ads in the last three years for positions at newly created "centers for teaching, learning, and writing" at the large research universities. We do not have these centers at the small liberal arts colleges because we already do this work. And as it turns out, there are few places in an economics department where it is easier to teach a writing course than in the history of economic thought.[11]

My point here goes beyond simple questions of the pedagogy of teaching basic skills to students, however. When you spend many hours involved in your students' lives and when you engage with them in a regular dialogue about your discipline, it seems impossible to avoid discussion about the meaning and implications of what they are studying. Because the normal course of a class in intermediate microeconomic theory can only allow so much room for this kind of "meta-reflection" before you are forced to abandon large pieces of your syllabus, it is always nice to be able to point students to a course that is centered around the question of how economic ideas have developed and changed through time. I do not mean to say that meta-reflection does not take place across the economics curriculum at the small liberal arts colleges; my point is rather that because it is a frequent part of what we encounter in the classroom there, it makes sense to take advantage of the division of labor and to preserve a place in the curriculum where this kind of work can be pursued in greater depth.

11. Cohen and Spencer 1993 contains a good discussion of "writing across the curriculum" in the economics major and illustrates how the history of economic thought course can be used as a "designated writing course."

Careers and Liberal Education

It is a myth of liberal education that it is not "about" getting a job or starting a career. This mythology arises, of course, from the ancient Greek and Roman definitions of a "free man" as someone who did not have to work for a living, or someone who did not have a trade. Thus, liberal education was for these free (*liberalis*) men. This idea has some good currency in the liberal arts colleges themselves, where it is often said that we teach our students for the pure pleasure of learning, or that our curricula are not "polluted" with professional training.

As is the case with all myths, there is some basis in reality for this one. We do expect our students to follow their intellectual curiosity, and we do not teach much that can be defined as "preprofessional" in the sense of engineering or business. Nonetheless, it is impossible to ask students to pay the very high tuition charged at most small liberal arts colleges without also having in sight that they will *work* for a living when they leave. In the sense in which the ancient Greeks and Romans used the word, our students are *not* free. Not many of them are, anyway.

As the fates would have it, however, we have not had to change our curricula to make our students employable. The things that we teach—critical thinking, analytical acumen, how to write and speak well—are the very keys to success in an economy increasingly defined by the flow of information and the ability to work with others in small teams to analyze that information. If you picture yourself having seven careers in your lifetime, rather than as a cog that needs to get a place as quickly as possible on the wheel on which you will spin for the rest of your life, a liberal education is exactly what you need. In the last decade, the proof of this has been in the pudding as we have seen growing numbers of our students hired into consulting, financial management, and high-tech firms at salaries that are not much below our own. And those who choose not to follow these paths usually do so because they are trekking off to medical school, law school, or some other professional graduate program. So, in fact, we are engaged in quite an elaborate preprofessional education at the liberal arts schools.

But why would this militate for having the history of economic thought in our curricula? The answer here has to do with the alternative, which is to throw out the history of economic thought to teach a more narrowly defined, highly mathematized, theoretical curriculum. This, at any rate, is the only alternative that has been mooted publicly, and it is the rather obvious alternative if we return to my opening point that the subdisciplines are defined by many in the discipline by how far along the theoretical spectrum they can be located (see Kasper et al. 1991). But what would be the purpose of abandoning the history of economic thought and teaching more real analysis and advanced game theory? The only purpose would be to better prepare our students for doing graduate work in economics. But fewer than 5 percent of our students will pursue that path.

For the rest of our students, the extra theory that could supplant the history of economic thought in the curriculum is just not necessary to anything that that they will do in their lives. It is not necessary in consulting, it is not necessary in banking or finance, it is not necessary in the law, and it is not necessary in management, social work, or medicine. Our students leave us and take some of the best jobs available in the American economy, and they do it without being forced through whatever is in the current first-year graduate core in the economics departments of the top research universities. Employers appear to want students who think critically, analyze well, write clearly, and speak articulately. Professional schools appear to want exactly the same thing. But no one who takes our students after graduation is suggesting to us that we teach them more cutting-edge theory.[12] The value added to an undergraduate economics education by a course in the history of economic thought is higher than the value added by a course in advanced topology for the simple reason that 95 percent of our graduates will not do advanced research in the discipline. Instead, they must use the rudimentary insights of economics in their everyday jobs outside academe.

Sitting on a Log with Adam Smith

The long and the short of what I have said about the success of the history of economic thought at the small liberal arts colleges could be summarized by paraphrasing an old definition of American liberal education. In 1871, James Garfield, who was about to be nominated for the American presidency, was attending a Williams College alumni banquet when the discussion turned to the question of whether Williams was falling behind the times. In arguing that there was no reason to suppose that this was the case, Garfield responded, "The ideal college is Mark Hopkins

12. No one, that is, except for the Ph.D. programs in economics.

at one end of a log and a student on the other" (Rudolph 1962, 243). Hopkins was a fabled teacher at Williams who had written the standard early-nineteenth-century textbook on the evidences of Christianity.

In much the same spirit, many of the economists today at small liberal arts colleges would probably agree, "The ideal undergraduate economics education includes Adam Smith sitting on one end of a log and the student sitting on the other end." In saying this, I do not mean to suggest that the economists at the small liberal arts colleges undervalue the rest of the economics curriculum, or that they would consider the history of the discipline a substitute for learning all the other parts of the discipline taught in a standard undergraduate curriculum, such as intermediate micro, intermediate macro, and econometrics. Quite to the contrary, we merely believe that the probability of producing really good economists increases when students understand the origin of the ideas they learned in those standard classes. The students' ability to use those ideas critically and apply them well is likely to increase if they have knowledge of the give and take that produced them. Once they are immersed in the narrative of the discipline, as opposed to the mere acquisition of technical skills, they are better able to reason and use what they have learned.

Is There a Future for the History of Economic Thought at the Liberal Arts Colleges?

So far, all this sounds quite nice. Or I hope it does. We teach undergraduates all the rudiments of thinking like an economist, and we believe that *one important piece* of that education is learning the history of economic thought. But is there a cloud on the horizon that would threaten to change this picture?

In the short run, I think that the answer is clearly, "No." The recent demand by top colleges to hire people in the area, and the figures on the number of liberal arts colleges that are offering the subject on a regular basis, suggest that there is no reason to suspect any significant change in the next five to ten years. In fact, given the frequency with which the subject is taught regularly at the small liberal arts colleges; and given the fact that many people who have active research programs in the area are employed at liberal arts colleges; and given the likelihood that many of these active researchers have fifteen to twenty years left in their (tenured) careers, it seems safe to expect that things are not likely to change in the intermediate term.

So what about the long run? If you read the essays by Ted Gayer and by Derek Brown and Shauna Saunders in this volume, the long run does not look promising. Gayer reports that virtually no top graduate program in economics now even offers its students classes in the history of economic thought. Brown and Saunders report a sad tale of the status of the history of economic thought at the only top-twenty program that *regularly* offers the field.

Unfortunately, the graduate programs seem even more hell-bent than they were twenty years ago to produce only one kind of graduate, and that graduate, as Gayer shows, is not introduced to the history of economic thought. Thus, the questions become whether the courses can still be staffed and whether there will still be people in the liberal arts college departments who believe that the subject has a place in the curriculum.

The answer to these two questions is not at all obvious, and it leads us to a set of possible outcomes, some of which are already familiar to those who work in the field. One of these is what we might label the Schabas option, so called after Margaret Schabas, whose essay "Breaking Away" was the focus of a minisymposium in *HOPE* several years ago on the subject of whether the future of the discipline might not be in departments other than economics. Such an option is not unimaginable, especially given the proliferation of new graduate programs in "economics and philosophy." It may just be that the reflective, ethical, and historical parts of what used to be economics may be splitting off into a separate area and that cutting-edge theory will become the sole concern of the department that keeps the name *economics*.[13] In the liberal arts colleges, this will be harder to bring about because their small size does not allow for the easy creation of new departments; but some move of this type is not unimaginable.

Nor is the move that I hear discussed more openly each year. More and more people seem to believe that economics is destined to be replaced in the undergraduate curriculum by a new discipline called "policy studies" or "political economy." Most of the small liberal arts colleges already have a major, a minor, or a concentration in this area, and increasingly there is talk about the possibility of people from the graduate programs in economics teaching undergraduates only by virtue of showing that they deserve a niche in "policy studies." If this is the future,

13. Kaufman 2000 provides an excellent case study of how a subdiscipline can evolve out of economics and surprisingly quickly become an independent discipline that no one remembers as being a part of what constitutes economics.

then my crystal ball is too clouded to reveal the role the history of economic thought might have at the liberal arts colleges. Adam Smith and
Karl Marx still seem like important people to have sit on the log with
the students, if this is the future shape of the social sciences at the liberal
arts colleges, but that is an idea that may not be obvious to others.

Yet another option is that because the turnover at the liberal arts colleges is slow and gradual, economics department faculty will not change
their fundamental commitment to teaching the history of economic
thought. That is to say, it is possible that the people who slowly trickle
into the liberal arts colleges will adapt to their situation there and then
decide that the history of economic thought is a part of the curriculum
that deserves to stay unchanged. These same people may change some
things, such as reorienting the intermediate microeconomics course more
toward game theory, and they may leave other things unchanged, such
as the history of economic thought. As they develop their careers at liberal arts colleges, and as their human capital in cutting-edge theory is
quickly depreciated, they may see more value in our subdiscipline than
they were trained to suppose that it might have.

Why Leave Things to Chance?

No good historian would think that the future is subject to his or her
whims and desires, but I nonetheless find myself coming to the end of
my essay believing that I need to do more than leave you with this set of
three hypothetical futures: the Schabas option, the policy studies option,
and the muddling along option.

Before I go on to make my own argument for the future, let me briefly
note that much of what I have already said about economics education
at the liberal arts colleges, and what I will say in conclusion, are applicable not just to the liberal arts colleges, but to the entire group of colleges
and universities that teach primarily to undergraduates. This means the
"regional" colleges and universities, such as Drake, Bradley, or Elon. It
means the large state schools like Northern Illinois University or South-
west Missouri State that are primarily undergraduate institutions. Ironically, it may even apply to some of the top research universities, such
as the University of Texas at Austin or Princeton, where there is a growing practice of hiring a faculty (separate from the high-caliber research
faculty) to teach solely to undergraduates.

At *any* college or university where the economics department's primary goal is teaching undergraduates, there is a growing divide between what they do and what is done at the research universities. One place is training people to enter the world of work and to go on for training in the law, management, or medicine. The other place is reproducing people like themselves. Ten years ago, when the American Economic Association commissioned the Committee on Graduate Education in Economics (COGEE), they were worried by the fact that many traditional employers of new Ph.D.s were no longer hiring them. One area that they did not explore, however, was the employability of their graduates in educational institutions that teach undergraduates. In that one area, they felt secure that they themselves set the agenda for the terms of employment.

But this is no longer the case. On the one hand, there is the growing move toward the creation of new areas in the undergraduate curriculum that I identified above. If students begin to gravitate to policy studies (a fine place to prepare for many of the jobs that new graduates actually take) or to "philosophy and economics" (a wonderful preparation for law school), there will be a falling demand for new Ph.D.s at all the institutions that teach primarily undergraduates. On the other hand, there is growing pressure at all large universities, private and public, for undergraduate education that is focused on the teaching of critical thinking, writing, and speaking. Frankly, few Ph.D. programs now pay any attention whatsoever to preparing people to teach. Thus, I believe that there will be growing pressure to think about how graduate programs are preparing their students to teach undergraduates.

And with this in mind, I believe that it behooves the economics profession to examine what it does to prepare people to teach undergraduates. That is, they should start with a clean slate and ask themselves what undergraduate departments do and then ask themselves how they can prepare people to work in that environment, as opposed to how well they are preparing them to teach graduate students at another research institution. They would find that there is no need to reproduce the first-year graduate core for undergraduates in order to make them employable or well rounded.[14] I have assiduously tried to avoid saying in this essay that cutting-edge theory is useless or undesirable. That is *not* my point. But its value does not lie in the education of undergraduates. New Ph.D.s

---

14. The argument against having the first-year graduate theory core included in the undergraduate curriculum is made at greater length in Bateman 1992.

in economics who take jobs where they are paid to teach undergraduates need to be able to design courses in which they teach the skills of writing well, speaking well, and analyzing data (and arguments) critically. What I am accusing most Ph.D. programs of is ignoring what is necessary to prepare their graduates to provide good undergraduate education in economics.[15] What we need is a new kind of graduate education that prepares new graduates to do the jobs that they are hired to do: teaching undergraduates.

Any good undergraduate program needs, for instance, to have economists on their faculty in applied areas. These economists will be able to teach their students how to apply theory to data, how to use econometric techniques, and what the basic institutions are that define the markets in their field. They will also be able to teach students how to formulate an argument, how to write a good paper, how to edit a friend's paper, and how to present material in front of their peers. In other words, they will be able to teach students to do the things that they might be asked to do as a research assistant at the Federal Reserve or the Congressional Budget Office. What graduate programs now consciously prepare students for the work of teaching these many skills?

If those who develop curricula for graduate programs asked themselves the root and branch questions about preparing people to teach undergraduates, they would undoubtedly realize that they could do a much better job. I have every confidence that they would also find they need to be preparing their graduates for teaching the history of economic thought. Thus, they would find that they need to offer a field in the area so that their students could be prepared for this part of their job. The graduate departments might even find that the course work in this area is an excellent site for preparing students for some of the other things they need to do, such as teaching writing.

This is not a utopian dream. In fact, from where I sit, it is a very pragmatic piece of advice that I offer to my colleagues in the graduate programs to help them help themselves before they find themselves out of

---

15. I hasten to add that my colleagues at Grinnell report that the disconnection I am describing between graduate education and the needs of those who teach undergraduates is the same in almost all disciplines today: in the humanities, the social sciences, and the natural sciences. It seems a universal that those who teach in graduate programs see it as lesser work to teach at an undergraduate institution and disdain anything that would involve preparing people for such work.

the business of preparing people for academic careers teaching under-graduates.

A Final Word on Research

I have so far avoided completely the issue of research in the history of economic thought. Because I started the essay by wanting to avoid a definition of success that depends on productivity in cutting-edge research and have spent the body of my essay trying to argue for a definition of success that depends on the successful education of undergraduates, I set research to one side. But what about research?

If my argument is followed through to its conclusion—that there should be at least some graduate programs that teach people to teach economics to undergraduates—and if I am correct that the history of economic thought should be a part of such an education, then it follows that a small number of Ph.D. programs should be preparing the people who will teach the history of economic thought to the aspiring Ph.D.s. This might not be a large number of schools, but someone needs to be prepared to prepare the teachers. Graduate students such as Derek Brown and Shauna Saunders (contributors to this volume) should not have to hide their interest in the history of economic thought for fear of marking themselves as fools or knaves who don't "get it" and are wasting their graduate educations.

The bigger picture here will not be any different than it is in an applied area like labor economics. Not only will the graduate teachers at the research universities publish; so, too, will the people whom they educate and send off to teach at the undergraduate institutions. Thus, the teachers at the research universities had better be good enough to teach their graduate students how to do publishable research. For despite all my paeans to the importance and the joy of teaching, the simple fact is that few people today at the liberal arts colleges "just teach." Most of them are also publishing researchers (albeit often in applied areas, and rarely in theory). While the students are sitting on a log with Adam Smith, their professors are usually not far away, under a tree with their laptops open, trying to revise an essay they are working on.

Thus, not only should the graduate programs be teaching people to teach the history of economic thought, they should also be teaching them to do research in the area. As in any field, the two enterprises are inseparable.

Appendix 1 The Elite Liberal Arts Colleges

Liberal arts colleges in the top twenty of the *U.S. News and World Report* (2000) rankings that list the history of economic thought in their course catalogs and teach it regularly:

Barnard College	Middlebury College
Bates College	Pomona College
Bryn Mawr College	Smith College
Carleton College	Vassar College
Colby College	Wellesley College
Colgate University	Wesleyan University
Grinnell College	Williams College

Liberal arts colleges in the top twenty of the *U.S. News and World Report* (2000) rankings that list the history of economic thought in their course catalogs but are not teaching it regularly:

Bowdoin College
Claremont McKenna College
Washington & Lee University

Liberal arts colleges in the top twenty of the *U.S. News and World Report* (2000) rankings that do not list the history of economic thought in their course catalogs:

Amherst College
Haverford College
Swarthmore College

Appendix 2 Liberal Arts Colleges in Minnesota and Ohio

To construct these lists, I considered all schools in the Carnegie Foundation's list of 212 liberal arts colleges. I did *not* include the colleges listed in appendix 1 that are in Ohio (none) or Minnesota (Carleton).

Minnesota

Liberal arts colleges in Minnesota that list the history of economic thought in their course catalogs and teach it regularly:

St. Benedict's/St. John's University
Gustavus Adolphus College
St. Olaf College

Liberal arts colleges in Minnesota that do not list the history of economic thought in their course catalogs:

Concordia College
Hamline University
Macalester College

Ohio

Liberal arts colleges in Ohio that list the history of economic thought in their course catalogs and teach it regularly:

Antioch College   Kenyon College
College of Wooster   Oberlin College
Denison University   Wittenberg College
Hiram College

Liberal arts colleges in Ohio that list the history of economic thought in their course catalogs but are not teaching it regularly:

Ohio Wesleyan University

References

Barber, William J. 1990. Does Scholarship in the History of Economic Thought Have a Useful Future? *Journal of the History of Economic Thought* 12.2:110–23.

Bateman, Bradley W. 1992. The Education of Economists: A Different Perspective. *Journal of Economic Literature* 30.3:1491–95.

———. 2001. The Skills of Freedom: The Liberal Education of William J. Barber. In *Historians of Economics and Economic Thought: The Construction of Disciplinary Memory*, edited by Steven Medema and Warren Samuels. London: Routledge.

Cohen, Avi J., and J. Spencer. 1993. Using Writing across the Curriculum in Economics: Is Taking the Plunge Worth It? *Journal of Economic Education* 24.3:219–30.

Hawkins, Hugh. 1999. The Making of the Liberal Arts College Identity. *Daedalus* 128.1:1–26.

Kasper, Hirschel, et al. 1991. The Education of Economists: From Undergraduate to
Graduate Study. *Journal of Economic Literature* 29.3:1088–1109.

Kaufman, Bruce E. 2000. Personnel/Human Resources Management: Its Roots as
Applied Economics. In *Toward a History of Applied Economics*, edited by Roger
Backhouse and Jeff Biddle. *HOPE* 32 (supplement): 229–56.

Krugman, Paul. 1995. *Development, Geography, and Economic Theory.* Cambridge:
MIT Press.

Marsden, George. 1994. *The Soul of the American University: From Protestant Establishment to Established Nonbelief.* Oxford: Oxford University Press.

Reuben, Julie. 1996. *The Making of the Modern University: Intellectual Transforma
tion and the Marginalization of Morality.* Chicago: University of Chicago Press.

Rudolph, Frederick. 1962. *The American College and University: A History.* New
York: Vintage.

Graduate Studies in the History of Economic Thought

Ted Gayer

If the current curriculum in graduate economics programs is any indicator, then the economics community finds the history of economic thought (hereafter HET) of limited or no relevance in the training of the next generation of professional economists. Almost no Ph.D. programs require HET as part of their core curriculum, and a relatively limited number of programs offer field courses (or even electives) in HET. The virtual absence of HET within the Ph.D. core and field curriculum should come as little surprise, as a downward trend in interest in doctoral-level HET courses was signaled by H. R. Bowen (1953) in his report on graduate education in economics and was reaffirmed more than ten years later in D. F. Gordon's (1965) study of the state of HET.

I leave it to the reader to decide whether the current level of Ph.D. education in HET is satisfactory. My hands-off approach to this normative claim reflects my own ambivalence. As a graduate student, I was drawn to HET as a partial balm for the (not uncommon) malaise of being a first-year Ph.D. student. HET also offered, at Duke, three collegial professors generous with their time and eager to discuss and foster any of my intellectual pursuits. But these don't present clear arguments for advocating that more departmental resources should be devoted to increasing the presence of HET within graduate programs. There is little demand for HET in the job market, and unless one is explicitly hired to

I am grateful for the helpful comments provided by Roy Weintraub, Shauna Saunders, Rachel Lurie, three anonymous referees, and the participants of the 2001 *HOPE* conference.

do HET research, there is little consideration given to such research in tenure decisions (which is not the case for other fields).

While I'm uncertain if (and how vigorously) the status quo should be fought against, one could make the case for either (or both) of two strategies for increasing the prominence of HET in graduate programs: promote the teaching of HET within existing core courses (something that apparently is currently nonexistent), or advocate for more field and elective HET courses.[1] I think the former strategy has a greater potential for success for primarily two reasons. First, I agree with Derek Brown and Shauna Saunders (this volume) that the job market demonstrates little demand for HET field specialists, which makes graduate faculty reluctant to substitute away from other specialties in order to offer more HET courses and also makes graduate students disinclined to choose HET as a research interest. Second, there is some evidence of a desire within the economics community to improve the breadth of understanding of economics within the core graduate curriculum, which could make graduate faculty amenable to teaching historiographic tools within core courses. This desire was represented in the report of the state of graduate education commissioned by the American Economic Association (Krueger et al. 1991) and in the conversations that A. Klamer and D. Colander (1990) had with graduate economics students in the mid-1980s.

The main focus of this essay is to present the current state of HET within Ph.D. economics programs and to point out any indications of potential demand for HET training within graduate programs, particularly within the core curriculum. When I set out to collect information about the state of HET, I felt it was best to hear from those people most directly involved with Ph.D. economics programs. I sent two separate questionnaires: one to chairs of economics departments that offer graduate-level HET courses, and another to HET professors within these departments. What follows is a description of what I learned from a sample of department chairs and from another sample of HET professors.

The evidence suggests that there is currently little training of Ph.D. students in core or field HET courses, and there is little indication that more will occur anytime soon. Indeed, given the small number of junior HET faculty and the small number of recent placements of HET job

---

1. Another option, which I don't discuss in this essay, is that HET should follow the advice of Margaret Schabas (1992) and break away from economics departments to find homes within the history of science.

market candidates at Ph.D. programs, one sees at best a steady state of low levels of Ph.D. training in HET in the foreseeable future.

Perhaps a bit of optimistic news for historians of economic thought is that there is a small pocket of programs that place a relatively greater focus on HET. These programs tend to emphasize political economy as part of their degree requirements and use HET to supplement the teaching of political economy. And while I didn't ask about undergraduate education in the questionnaires, some respondents did suggest that undergraduate HET courses are an important part of the undergraduate curriculum of the programs, as well as the undergraduate curriculum at other non-Ph.D.-granting programs in which they hope to place their students. Presumably, these undergraduate programs find teachers for these HET courses in the few programs that provide field courses in HET, although there is little evidence of this from my survey responses. However, my survey does indicate that some professors migrate toward HET after receiving their Ph.D., and—as one would expect given the greater demand for HET teaching in undergraduate programs—anecdotal evidence suggests that this occurs more frequently among professors in non-Ph.D.-granting programs.

While the surveys hardly leave one feeling sanguine about the current state of HET in graduate programs, there may yet be some room for HET to fill existing gaps within the Ph.D. core curriculum. These gaps were well described in the American Economic Association's Commission on Graduate Education in Economics (COGEE). Among other things, the commission discussed a need to improve graduate students' knowledge of economic institutions and real-world economic problems, it lamented the narrowness of the current core curriculum, and it advocated a greater emphasis on fostering students' creativity and improving their writing and communication skills (Krueger et al. 1991).[2] However, nowhere in the report did this commission recommend more HET courses for graduate students; instead, its emphasis was on supplementing the teaching of techniques within the core courses with greater instruction of the workings of institutions and real-world economic problems and the ways in which economists have addressed these problems.

2. The concerns of COGEE were remarkably similar to the concerns reported in Bowen 1953 about the state of graduate education in midcentury. Bowen worried that graduate students "become so completely preoccupied with technicalities that they have little time or energy to acquire the kind of historic, philosophical, and institutional breadth which would give them perspective and judgment" (4).

In their conversations with Ph.D. economics students in the mid-1980s, Klamer and Colander (1990, 170) also found that students desired "more ideas, more policy relevance, more discussion of the fundamental assumptions, and more serious consideration of alternative approaches." Albeit limited, the COGEE report and the conversations with the graduate students (not to mention my own graduate school experience) suggest some demand for historical inquiry as part of the standard economics toolkit. This presents an opening for graduate professors who can teach the core theory courses while also providing some historiographic education.

Questionnaire 1

My first goal was to survey the department chairs of all U.S. economics Ph.D. programs that have recently offered HET classes for their doctoral students to gauge the degree to which doctoral students are exposed to HET. I started with a list of 162 Ph.D. programs obtained from *Peterson's Graduate Programs in the Humanities, Arts, and Social Sciences, 2000*.[3] By examining the programs' Web sites and by calling some of the programs directly, I was able to determine that ninety-one of these programs have not recently offered any graduate courses in HET.

On 12 October 2000, I sent the chairs of the other seventy-one programs a brief questionnaire about the role of HET in their Ph.D. programs.[4] On 8 January 2001, I re-sent the same questionnaire to those chairs who had yet to return the original questionnaire. In order to obtain a high response rate, the questionnaire was brief. It consisted of a few questions about HET courses and seminars within the department, a few questions about the Ph.D. programs, and a few evaluative and speculative questions about the role of HET in graduate education. Appendix 1 contains a copy of the questionnaire.

The total response rate was an exceptionally high sixty-one out of seventy-one (see table 1).[5] Of these sixty-one respondents, thirty-two said that their department had offered a doctoral-level class in HET in the past five years. Table 1 lists the seventy-one programs that were sent a questionnaire. The first column of table 1 indicates the sixty-one schools that

3. The list is available at http://www.albany.edu/econ/eco_phds.html.
4. When in doubt, I assumed the program qualified for the survey.
5. Not included in this number is the response by the chair who mailed back the questionnaire with an attached note reading, "Too much work for too little pay."

responded to the questionnaire. In the second column of table 1, the non-italicized entries indicate which thirty-two of the schools that responded offered HET courses in the past five years. The italicized entries indicate whether or not a program that did not respond to the survey currently offers an HET course. The information for the nonresponding programs is less precise, since it was obtained through a search of the programs' Web pages.

The final column of table 1 contains the 1998 *U.S. News and World Report* ranking of the Ph.D. programs, for those programs that were ranked.[6] I only included the ranking for those programs that have offered Ph.D. HET courses in the past five years. Based on the ranking of economics departments by the *U.S. News and World Report*, most of the top programs do not offer doctoral-level classes in HET. Only thirteen programs of the top sixty-two have offered any Ph.D. HET courses in the past five years. Among the top twenty programs, only four programs (Harvard, Stanford, Columbia, and Duke) have offered any doctoral-level HET courses in the past five years. However, according to Stanford's department chair, the HET professor at Stanford recently left, and they now "have no one on our faculty keen to teach a course on the subject." At Harvard and Columbia, the doctoral-level HET courses are offered only irregularly. That leaves Duke as the only top-twenty program that has regularly scheduled HET courses for Ph.D. students.

There are four more programs among the top thirty (New York University, University of Virginia, University of North Carolina at Chapel Hill, and University of California at Davis) that have offered doctoral-level HET courses in the past five years. However, the University of North Carolina at Chapel Hill no longer offers Ph.D. HET courses, and the other three only offer them irregularly.

The other five programs among the top sixty-two that offer doctoral-level HET courses are Michigan State University, Washington University in St. Louis, University of Southern California, Syracuse University, and George Mason University. Each of these programs currently requires its Ph.D. students to take an HET course, although Syracuse allows the students to substitute other courses to fulfill the requirement.

The remainder of this section discusses the characteristics of the thirty-two departments that responded to the survey. This omits the six

6. *U.S. News and World Report* ranked the top sixty-two economics programs.

Table 1   Survey Response and Universities that Recently Offered Ph.D. HET Courses

School Name	Responded to Survey	Course in Last 5 Years	Ranking
American University	Yes	Yes	
Arizona State University	Yes	No	
Boston College	Yes	No	
Boston University	No	*No*	
CUNY Graduate School	Yes	No	
Clemson University	Yes	No	
Colorado State University	Yes	Yes	
Columbia University	Yes	Yes	14
Duke University	Yes	Yes	19
Florida International University	Yes	Yes	
Florida State University	Yes	Yes	
Fordham University	Yes	No	
George Mason University	No	*Yes*	62
George Washington University	Yes	Yes	
Georgia State University	Yes	Yes	
Harvard University	Yes	Yes	1
Howard University	Yes	Yes	
Indiana University	Yes	No	
Iowa State University	No	*No*	
Kansas State University	No	*No*	
Lehigh University	Yes	Yes	
Louisiana State University	Yes	No	
Michigan State University	Yes	Yes	34
New School University	Yes	Yes	
NYU (Economics)	Yes	Yes	21
North Carolina State University	Yes	No	
Northern Illinois University	No	*Yes*	
Oklahoma State University	Yes	Yes	
Oregon State University	Yes	Yes	
Penn St. University	Yes	No	
Purdue University	Yes	No	
Stanford University	Yes	Yes	1
SUNY-Binghamton	Yes	No	
SUNY-Stony Brook	Yes	No	
Syracuse University	Yes	Yes	57
Texas A&M University	Yes	No	
University of Alabama	No	*Yes*	
University of Arkansas	Yes	No	
University of California, Berkeley	Yes	No	
University of California, Davis	Yes	Yes	30

Table 1   continued

School Name	Responded to Survey	Course in Last 5 Years	Ranking
University of California, LA	No	*No*	
University of California, Riverside	Yes	Yes	
University of Connecticut	Yes	Yes	
University of Houston	Yes	No	
University of Illinois at Urbana-Champaign	Yes	No	
University of Iowa	Yes	No	
University of Kansas	Yes	No	
University of Kentucky	Yes	Yes	
University of Maryland, College Park	Yes	No	
University of Massachusetts, Amherst	Yes	Yes	
University of Miami	Yes	No	
University of Mississippi	No	*Yes*	
University of Missouri, Columbia	Yes	No	
University of Nebraska, Lincoln	Yes	Yes	
University of New Hampshire	No	*Yes*	
University of New Mexico	Yes	No	
University of New Orleans	Yes	No	
University of North Carolina, Chapel Hill	Yes	Yes	29
University of Notre Dame	Yes	Yes	
University of Southern California	Yes	Yes	44
University of Tennessee, Knoxville	Yes	Yes	
University of Utah	No	*Yes*	
University of Virginia	Yes	Yes	25
University of Washington	Yes	No	
University of Wisconsin, Milwaukee	Yes	No	
Virginia Tech University	Yes	No	
Washington State University	Yes	No	
Washington University in St. Louis	Yes	Yes	34
Western Michigan University	Yes	Yes	
West Virginia University	Yes	Yes	
Yale University	Yes	No	
Total	61	32 (*38*)	

Notes: The italicized entries in the second column are for non-responding programs. I obtained this information from a search of the department's Web page. The rankings are from the *U.S. News and World Report* (1998); Harvard and Stanford tied for the top ranking in the report. The rankings column is conditional on the program having offered a Ph.D.-level HET course in the past five years.

departments in which the chair did not respond to the survey yet (according to their Web pages) currently offer doctoral-level HET courses. Two of these departments (University of Utah and University of New Hampshire) offer required core courses in HET.

Information about the HET Courses

Table 2 again lists the departmental rankings for the thirty-two respondents, as well as some information about the HET courses offered at the programs. Of the programs in the top sixty-two, only Harvard University (ranked first), the University of Virginia (ranked twenty-fifth), the University of North Carolina at Chapel Hill (ranked twenty-ninth), the University of California at Davis (ranked thirtieth), Michigan State University (ranked thirty-fourth), and Syracuse University (ranked fifty-seventh) have offered required core courses in HET in the past five years.

While the survey question asked if the HET courses were "required core courses," it should be noted that, given the departments' Web information on required courses and the information provided by the HET professors within the department, some chairs designated the HET courses as "required core courses" when in fact they are not required. For example, Harvard University last offered "Critical Perspectives in Economic Theory" in the spring of 1999, and this course is not found on Harvard's on-line "Requirements of the Graduate Program in Economics." Other programs, such as the University of Virginia, require students to take either an HET course (they can choose between "Foundations of Modern Economic Thought" and "Seminars in the History of Economic Thought") or a course in economic history. Given the evidence from the second-round survey, students tend to choose the latter. The University of California at Davis also allows students to choose between HET and economic history, with the economic history course offered much more frequently than the HET course. For Syracuse University's Ph.D. program, students must fulfill a "breadth requirement," in which "one course must be taken either in history of economic thought, when offered, or in courses that may be offered in the future, such as economic history, scientific methods, philosophy of science, or other courses that the department may designate." There is some indication that the department may drop the course in the near future. Finally, the University of North Carolina at Chapel Hill dropped the core HET course in December 1998.

Table 2 Department Chairs' Responses about HET Courses

School Name	U.S. News Ranking	Core	Field	Elective	Preliminary Exam	Field Exam	Seminar
American University		Yes	Yes	Yes	No	Yes	No
Colorado State University		No	Yes	No	No	Yes	Yes
Columbia University	14	No	No	Yes	No	No	No
Duke University	19	No	Yes	Yes	No	Yes	Yes
Florida International University		Yes	No	No	No	No	No
Florida State University		Yes	No	No	No	No	No
George Washington University		No	No	No	No	No	No
Georgia State University		Yes	No	Yes	Yes	No	No
Harvard University	1	Yes	No	No	No	Paper	No
Howard University		Yes	No	No	No	No	No
Lehigh University		Yes	No	No	No	No	Yes
Michigan State University	34	Yes	Yes	Yes	No	Yes	Yes
New School University		No	Yes	Yes	No	Yes	Yes
NYU (Economics)	21	No	No	Yes	No	No	No
Oklahoma State University		Yes	No	No	No	No	Yes
Oregon State University		Yes	No	No	No	No	No
Stanford University	1	No	No	No	No	No	No
Syracuse University	57	Yes	No	No	No	No	Yes
University of California, Davis	30	Yes	No	No	No	No	Yes
University of California, Riverside		Yes	No	No	No	No	Yes
University of Connecticut		Yes	No	No	Yes	No	Yes
University of Kentucky		No	No	Yes	No	No	Yes
University of Massachusetts, Amherst		No	Yes	Yes	No	Yes	No
University of Nebraska, Lincoln		Yes	No	No	No	No	No
University of North Carolina, Chapel Hill	29	< 12/98	No	No	No	No	No

Table 2   continued

School Name	U.S. News Ranking	Core	Field	Elective	Preliminary Exam	Field Exam	Seminar
University of Notre Dame		Yes	No	No	No	No	Yes
University of Southern California		No	No	Yes	No	No	Yes
University of Tennessee, Knoxville		Yes	No	No	No	Yes	No
University of Virginia	25	Yes	No	No	No	No	No
Washington University in St. Louis	34	No	No	Yes	No	No	No
Western Michigan University		No	No	No	No	No	Yes
West Virginia University		No	No	No	No	No	No
Total		18	6	11	2	7	14

The evidence therefore suggests that very few of the Ph.D. students in the top sixty-two programs are required to take an HET course as part of their degree. This has not always been the case. In his survey of thirty graduate institutions approximately fifty years ago, Bowen (1953, 115) found that 49 percent of the programs required their doctoral students to take HET. However, Bowen did caution that the popularity of HET is being "partially displaced" due to "competition with other new and more technical fields." Yet twelve years later, Gordon (1965, 120) surveyed the forty largest graduate departments in the United States and Canada and found that HET "appears to be persisting quite tenaciously in the face of declining popularity."

Outside of the top sixty-two programs there are thirteen programs that offer HET as a required core course. Other programs, such as Colorado State University, New School University, and University of Massachusetts at Amherst, require a course in political economy and also offer a selection of HET field and elective classes.

According to the department chairs, only two programs in the nation (Georgia State University and the University of Connecticut) have "HET [as] part of the preliminary/qualifying exams for Ph.D. graduate students," and only seven programs offer a field exam in HET (although one chair indicated that they offer a field paper in HET in lieu of an exam). Fourteen of the programs offer seminars in HET, but six of these indicated that such seminars are infrequent, for a want of either interest or HET presenters.

Information about the Students

Table 3 lists some information about the students in the thirty-two programs that have offered HET courses in recent years. These programs average approximately fifty-eight Ph.D. students. In order to gauge the training of the next generation of HET professors, I asked the chairs, "How many Ph.D. students [in the past five years] went on the job market as historians of economic thought (either as their primary or secondary field specialty)?" I also asked them to provide the "names and job placement" of each of these students. These were the most time-intensive questions on the questionnaire, and my hunch is that they therefore provide the least accurate responses. The answers to the first question were often rough estimates, and the names and job placement were frequently not provided. Conditional on these caveats, the responses indicate that in the past five years these programs have yielded a total of forty-five Ph.D. job candidates with either a primary or secondary field specialty in HET.[7] Yet there is a large variance among the schools. Only ten of the programs placed any HET students on the job market in the past five years, and more than half of the candidates came from New School University and the University of Massachusetts at Amherst. It is unclear whether chairs of these two departments distinguished between HET and political economy when listing the recent job candidates. There is little one can say about the placement of these HET candidates since the response rate for this question was low. Of the nineteen job placements listed, most were at small state schools or at liberal arts colleges, and about one-third of the academic placements were for nontenure-track jobs. Therefore, it seems that Ph.D. economics programs are not training many new historians of economic thought, and even fewer HET Ph.D. students wind up with tenure-track jobs at Ph.D.-granting programs.

---

7. I asked the same question in the questionnaire I later sent to HET professors. Department chairs and HET professors were in perfect agreement when there were no job market HET candidates. Occasionally, the HET professors reported slightly fewer HET job market candidates than did the department chair.

Table 3   Department Chairs' Responses about Ph.D. Students

School Name	Number of Students	HET Job Market Candidates in Past 5 Years
American University	70	0
Colorado State University	56	5
Columbia University	125	0
Duke University	78	4
Florida International University	20	0
Florida State University	30	0
George Washington University	55	1
Georgia State University	50	0
Harvard University	150	0
Howard University	20	0
Lehigh University	20	0
Michigan State University	75	2
New School University	50	13
NYU (Economics)	118	0
Oklahoma State University	35	0
Oregon State University	15	0
Stanford University	130	0
Syracuse University	60	0
University of California, Davis	75	0
University of California, Riverside	45	4
University of Connecticut	50	0
University of Kentucky	30	0
University of Massachusetts, Amherst	90	10
University of Nebraska, Lincoln	20	0
University of North Carolina, Chapel Hill	76	1
University of Notre Dame	42	4
University of Southern California	60	0
University of Tennessee, Knoxville	35	1
University of Virginia	60	0
Washington University in St. Louis	60	0
Western Michigan University	25	0
West Virginia University	40	0
Mean	*58.28*	*1.41*
Standard deviation	*34.62*	*3.08*

Evaluative/Speculative Responses

I posed three evaluative or speculative questions in the final part of the questionnaire. Table 4 presents information on the responses to these questions. The first question was, "Do you think an understanding of HET can substantially contribute to a modern economist's training?" The responses to this question may offer some encouragement to historians of economics. Twenty-six of the thirty-two department chairs indicated that HET could substantially contribute to a modern economist's training.

The next question asked what the chair believes is "the optimal number of HET course offerings." Admittedly, this question leaves out mention of a budget constraint and does not indicate which social welfare function one should be optimizing over (my intention being to allow the chairs to project their own constraints and social welfare function). Most department chairs (of the thirty-two departments that have recently offered Ph.D. HET courses) indicated that one HET course offering is optimal.

The final question was whether the department intended to add or subtract courses in HET in the near future. Twenty-four of the respondents said there was no plan to either add or subtract HET courses, although in practice many of these departments only offered HET courses sporadically. One department chair indicated that the program plans to subtract an HET course in the near future. Three other chairs indicated that the department is considering subtracting an HET course in the near future. Only one chair indicated that the program is considering adding an HET course in the near future. The programs that indicated they would not add HET courses in the near future frequently cited "more pressing needs" or "limited resource constraints."

Thus, while the COGEE report debated technique versus substance and depth versus breadth and suggested that graduate education might gain from more substance and breadth, the departmental chairs believe that more graduate HET courses is not optimal, ostensibly because they think HET courses don't achieve the COGEE goals (although perhaps because they disagree with the COGEE goals altogether). However, given that most chairs think that an understanding of HET can substantially contribute to a modern economist's training, there might be demand to incorporate some HET education within other courses (perhaps even the core courses).

Table 4 Department Chairs' Responses to Evaluative/Speculative Questions Concerning HET

School Name	Contribution	Optimal Number	Add, Subtract, or Same
American University	Yes	3	Same
Colorado State University	Yes	Depends	Same
Columbia University	Yes	1	Same
Duke University	Yes	NA	Same
Florida International University	Yes	0–1	Same
Florida State University	Yes	1	Same
George Washington University	No	0	Same
Georgia State University	No	1	Same
Harvard University	Yes	2	Same
Howard University	Yes	1	Same
Lehigh University	Yes	1	Same
Michigan State University	Yes	1	Perhaps subtract
New School University	Yes	1–2	Add
NYU (Economics)	Yes	1	Same
Oklahoma State University	Yes	At least 1	Perhaps subtract
Oregon State University	Yes	1	Same
Stanford University	No	NA	Same
Syracuse University	Yes	1	Same
University of California, Davis	Yes	2–4	Same
University of California, Riverside	Yes	2	Possibly add
University of Connecticut	Yes	1	Same
University of Kentucky	Yes	1	Same
University of Massachusetts, Amherst	Yes	1–2	Same
University of Nebraska, Lincoln	Yes	1	Same
University of North Carolina, Chapel Hill	NA	0	Same
University of Notre Dame	Yes	2	NA
University of Southern California	No	1	NA
University of Tennessee, Knoxville	Yes	1	Subtract
University of Virginia	No	1	Perhaps subtract
Washington University in St. Louis	Yes	1	Same
Western Michigan University	Yes	1	Same
West Virginia University	Yes	1	Same

Questionnaire 2

As part of my survey of the department chairs, I asked them to provide the names of faculty members (if any) that have recently taught doctoral-level HET in the department. This yielded a list of forty HET professors from twenty-seven different universities.[8] On 7 January 2001, I sent these forty faculty members a questionnaire about the role of HET in their department. This questionnaire was more extensive than the one sent to the department chairs, and consequently, the response rate was lower. It consisted of questions about HET courses offered in the department, questions about the respondent's career and the role that HET has played in that career, questions about the Ph.D. students, and evaluative and speculative questions concerning HET. The total response rate was twenty-one out of forty.[9] Because a few of the respondents requested that their replies remain anonymous, in the remainder of this section I present summary information about the responses without individual identifying information.

Information about the HET Professors

The sample consists of one retired (but still teaching) professor, seventeen full professors, two associate professors, and one assistant professor. When one also considers the sparse number of recent Ph.D. job candidates with an HET background, the implication is that there will be a rather small next generation of HET professors in doctorate-granting programs. On average, the sample of HET professors received their Ph.D. degrees twenty-six years ago (with a standard deviation of ten years).

It is important to keep in mind that this sample consists only of HET professors who teach at programs that offer doctoral-level HET courses. There are other people with doctorates in economics who specialize in HET but do not teach doctoral-level HET courses. For example, in the

---

8. Two of the departments from the first-round questionnaire were excluded from the second questionnaire because the first-round responses were sent in too late. Two other departments from the first-round questionnaire were excluded from the second round because the HET professor had either retired or left the department (and there were no other HET professors remaining within the department).

9. This total does not include the response from one faculty member who has been retired for the past five years, so was unable to provide the information requested.

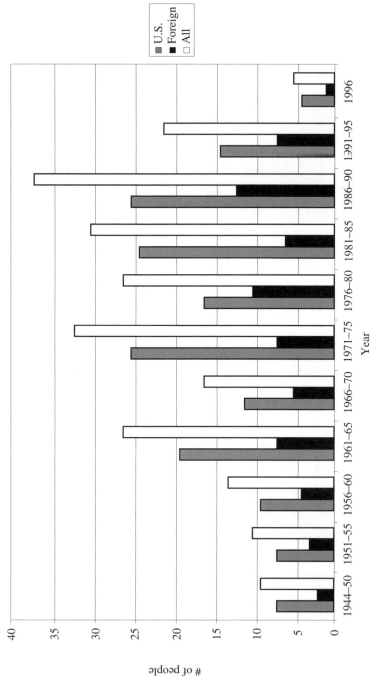

Figure 1   Number of AEA Members Who Specialize in HET, by Year of Ph.D. Completion, as of 1997

1997 American Economic Association (AEA) on-line membership survey, there were 225 people who listed B0 (Schools of Economic Thought and Methodology: General), B1 (HET through 1925), B2 (HET since 1925), or B3 (HET: Individuals) as one of their specializations.[10] This number excludes students, those who are retired, and those who do not have a doctoral or equivalent degree.

Figure 1 gives the distribution of these AEA members who specialize in HET by their year of Ph.D. completion. The modal ranges for Ph.D. completion for those working in the United States are 1971–75 and 1986–90 (whereas the modal range for the respondents to my survey was 1971–75). There are very few recent Ph.D.s (i.e., completed since 1991) working in HET, which is consistent with my survey evidence that few programs are offering doctoral-level HET courses. However, this could also suggest that an interest in HET tends to develop later in one's career. Also, it is important to keep in mind that the numbers in figure 1 are in absolute terms. The decline in HET specialization of recent Ph.D.s is more pronounced when one considers that there were many more economics doctorates granted in the 1990s than in previous decades. For example, according to Siegfried and Stock 1999, there were 20 percent more doctorates awarded in economics in 1996 than in 1977, and there were 17 percent more doctorates awarded in economics in 1996 than in 1986.

The HET professors in my survey have also stayed primarily at the same university for much of their career. On average, they have been at their current university for 90 percent (standard deviation 16 percent) of the years since receiving their Ph.D. degree.[11] Only less than half of the sample (48 percent) indicated that they were hired by their current program "in part to fulfill a need to teach and do research in HET." Again, this is consistent with the hypothesis that many HET professors become interested in the field later in their academic careers.

Exactly half of the respondents listed HET as a "primary research field of interest." Thirty percent of the respondents listed HET as a "minor field of interest." Two respondents "have an interest in HET, but do

---

10. I thank Roy Weintraub for collecting this information on HET specialization among AEA members.

11. I coded those who have been at their current university since before they received their Ph.D. degree as being there 100 percent of their career.

not conduct any research in the field." One respondent expressed an "interest in particular topics in HET, but not in the field as a field."[12]

The respondents listed a range of HET research interests, including heterodox economics, Marxian political economy, classical economics, Adam Smith, Alfred Marshall, Frank Knight, twentieth-century economics, science studies approaches to HET, and institutional economics. The respondents' list of "other research fields of interest" was also diverse, with little overlap. A cursory comparison with the *JEL* classification codes indicates that most areas of economics are covered within the interests of the sample of respondents. The only possible gaps are "Health, Education, and Welfare," "Industrial Organization," "Business Administration and Business Economics," "Agricultural and Natural Resource Economics," and "Urban, Rural, and Regional Economics." Three people listed comparative economic systems as a field of interest. Two others listed macroeconomics. The rest include, among others, public finance, public choice, microeconomic theory, law and economics, empirical labor economics, economic history, economic education, international political economy, general equilibrium theory, social and economic history, banking regulation, trade, computational economics, and methodology.

Information about the HET Courses and the HET Students

The sample of HET professors provided a list of forty-one undergraduate and graduate HET courses that they have taught in the past five years. Table 5 lists the names of these courses and the corresponding universities. Most of the courses are listed under a fairly broad title, such as "History of Economic Thought." However, not all "History of Economic Thought" classes cover the same periods. The most common division is before and after the late nineteenth century. Others concentrate on the twentieth century or specifically on the post–World War II era. One seminar is dedicated solely to Adam Smith.

Other course titles suggest more specialized topics. These include two courses offered at the New School University: "Marx, Keynes, and Kalecki" and "Smith, Ricardo, and Sraffa." Duke University and Harvard University each offer courses on Keynes. Other course titles include "Economics in the Bloomsbury Group," "The Uses of Economics,"

---

12. Another respondent apparently misunderstood the question and instead explained the role of HET classes within the department.

Table 5   HET Professors' Course Offerings

School Name	Course
Colorado State University	Evolution of Economic Thought
Colorado State University	Recent Economic Thought
Colorado State University	History of Economic Thought
Colorado State University	Political Economy II
Barnard College	History of Economic Thought
Duke University	John Maynard Keynes
Duke University	Modern Economic Thought
Duke University	Economic Science Studies
Duke University	The Bloomsbury Group
Duke University	History of Economic Thought
Duke University	Economics in the Bloomsbury Group
Duke University	The Uses of Economics
Duke University	Adam Smith and the System of Natural Liberty
Duke University	Economics, Society, and Morality in 18th Century Thought
Florida State University	History of Economic Ideas
Harvard University	Keynes and the 20th Century
Michigan State University	Economic Thought I (Undergraduate)
Michigan State University	Economic Thought II (Undergraduate)
Michigan State University	Economic Thought I (Graduate)
Michigan State University	Economic Thought II (Graduate)
Michigan State University	History of Economic Thought
New School University	Marx, Keynes, & Kalecki
New School University	Smith, Ricardo, & Sraffa
New School University	Historical Foundations of Political Economy
Oregon State University	History of Economic Thought
Syracuse University	History of Economic Thought
Syracuse University	History of Economic Thought
University of California, Riverside	History of Economic Theory & Methodology
University of Connecticut	History of Economic Thought
University of Connecticut	Topics in Economic History & Thought
University of Connecticut	History of Economic Thought before 1890
University of Connecticut	History of Economic Thought after 1890
University of Massachusetts, Amherst	History of Economic Thought
University of Nebraska, Lincoln	History of Economic Thought
University of Notre Dame	History of Economic Thought in the Context of Intellectual History
University of Notre Dame	Economics & Philosophy
University of Notre Dame	Seminar in Methodology & History of Economic Thought

Table 5 continued

School Name	Course
University of Notre Dame	History of Economic Thought & Methodology
University of Virginia	Seminar in the History of Economic Thought
University of Virginia	Seminar in the History of Economic Thought
Western Michigan University	History of Economic Thought

"Economics and Philosophy," and "Historical Foundations of Political Economy."

For each course, the respondent was asked to indicate whether the course "covers (at least in part) methodological issues and whether it covers (at least in part) the history or philosophy of science." Of the thirty-four responses about methodology, twenty-seven indicated that the course covered some methodological issues. Only eighteen courses of thirty-two responses indicated that the course covered some history or philosophy of science. From the syllabi that some of the professors submitted with their questionnaire, it appears the common practice is to cover methodology or the philosophy of science as part of the introductory section of the course.

According to the HET professors of the sixteen programs represented in this sample, six of the programs offer doctoral-level HET courses at least once a year. Four of the programs offer doctoral-level HET courses exactly once a year, and five more offer them less than once a year.[13] The average number of Ph.D. students that typically enroll in these HET courses is 9.5.[14] However, there is a rather large standard deviation of 5.6. Much of this is due to the New School University, which reported that twenty-five students typically enroll in each HET course.

Seven of the respondents indicated that some Ph.D. students interested in HET have taken related courses in other departments. However, many of the respondents qualified their response by suggesting that it is not a common occurrence. Six respondents indicated that Ph.D. students have taken classes in the history department, and five indicated that Ph.D. students have taken classes in the philosophy department. The other departments are political science (two), history of philosophy

13. One respondent did not answer this question. Where two professors of the same program provided different estimates, I took the average of the two.

14. Again, where two professors in the same program disagreed, I took the average of their answers.

(one), history of psychology (one), English (one), anthropology (one), and literature (one).

Evaluative/Speculative Responses

I posed six evaluative/speculative questions to the HET professors. The first three questions asked how they perceive the views of their colleagues with respect to the importance of HET. The first question asked whether the respondent thinks that his or her "departmental colleagues view your interest in HET positively, negatively, or neutrally." For the most part, the respondents think their colleagues hold a neutral to positive view of their interest in HET. Seven respondents indicated a positive response and seven indicated a neutral response. The remainder included one negative response, two negative-to-neutral responses, and three mixed responses.[15]

I then asked whether the HET professor thinks that his or her department "views HET as an important part of the Ph.D. graduate curriculum." The answers suggest a fairly even split. Eight respondents indicated that they believe their colleagues view HET as an important part of the graduate curriculum. One of these eight qualified his remarks by indicating the support was "precarious." Seven other respondents said that their colleagues do not view HET as an important part of the Ph.D. graduate curriculum. Four other respondents said the views were mixed. Another indicated that HET was not viewed as an important part of the curriculum, but that political economy was viewed as important.[16] Given that the sample consists of professors in those few programs that offer doctoral-level courses in HET, it is particularly striking that about half of the sample believes that their colleagues do not think HET is an important part of the Ph.D. curriculum.

My next goal was to see whether current "departmental attitudes toward HET [have] changed significantly over the past 5–10 years." Eleven of the respondents believe that the attitudes are unchanged. Seven respondents, however, believe that their colleagues have less interest in HET today than they had in recent years. Many of these respondents cited a generational shift within their department, with the younger faculty having less interest in HET than the older faculty. For example, one

---

15. One respondent did not answer this question.
16. One respondent did not answer this question.

respondent wrote that it has "become less frequent to find junior [faculty] who have had any exposure at all." This is consistent with the earlier finding that there have been few recent Ph.D. job candidates with primary or secondary fields in HET. It is also consistent with figure 1, which indicates that there are very few recent Ph.D.s specializing in HET. Only two respondents believe that there has been an increase in interest in HET in their department in recent years.[17] This generational divide is nothing new: thirty-six years ago, Gordon (1965, 120) reported that 63 percent of his survey respondents "indicated that they believe the younger economists would be less inclined than older ones to replace faculty in [HET]."

I then posed the same question to the HET professors that I earlier posed to the department chairs; namely, whether the professor thinks that the department "intends to add or subtract courses in HET from the curriculum in the near future." There seems to be much agreement between the HET professors and the department chairs. Sixteen of the HET professors indicated that there were no plans to add or subtract HET courses. This includes one respondent who answered "unlikely to add." Four of the respondents indicated that their department might subtract an HET course in the near future. One respondent summed up his opinion on the matter by saying "over my dead body."

The other question to the department chairs that I also posed to the HET professors was what he or she thinks "is the optimal number of HET course offerings." Perhaps not surprisingly, the HET professors believe that the optimal number of HET courses is slightly greater than what the department chairs believe it to be. Seven respondents thought one course was optimal, three respondents thought two courses were optimal, and four respondents thought three or more were optimal.[18]

Perhaps the greatest unanimity occurred in the final question, which asked whether the respondent thought "it better to offer HET in other departments instead of within the economics department." Nineteen out of twenty-one of the respondents thought that HET should not be offered in other departments, and three of these responses were emphatic.[19] One

---

17. One respondent did not answer this question.

18. The "three or more" category includes those who felt that "many" was optimal. Three respondents did not answer this question.

19. By "emphatic," I mean that the response was either underlined or followed by an exclamation point. Included among these nineteen responses was one person who stated "probably not."

other respondent felt HET should be offered in other departments only if there were no other HET option. And another respondent indicated that he might migrate to science studies over the next decade.

Conclusion

The survey responses suggest that most current Ph.D. students are not exposed to any HET. This is particularly true among the top Ph.D. programs, which more frequently place their Ph.D. students in tenure-track jobs in Ph.D.-granting programs. There are a few programs (such as New School University, University of Massachusetts at Amherst, Colorado State University, University of Notre Dame, and University of California at Riverside) that do place relatively greater emphasis on HET, frequently within the context of political economy. While these programs have had job market candidates with backgrounds in HET, there is little evidence that they are placing them at tenure-track jobs in Ph.D.-granting programs.

An even smaller number of other programs (such as Duke University and Michigan State) take the intermediate position of not offering HET as a central part of their curriculum but instead offering a few courses for those few Ph.D. students interested in pursuing the field. These programs average about one job market candidate every few years with a background in HET, although few of these candidates go to Ph.D.-granting programs. And given the graduate student experiences represented by Brown and Saunders (this volume), one sees little reason to expect an increase in HET interest among Ph.D. students. Apparently, the few programs that offer fields in HET fulfill the demand for qualified instructors of undergraduate HET courses. It is unclear whether the field offerings of HET have reached a steady state or whether there is a downward trend taking place in which a dearth of Ph.D. students obtaining training in HET results in the absence of a next generation of faculty members qualified to teach HET. Possibly acting against such a downward trend is the migration of some current professors toward a greater interest in HET after they obtain their doctorates.

I have not addressed here whether this virtual nonexistence of graduate-level interest in HET should be resisted or accepted. I see little reason to expect an increase in demand for HET field courses. Nonetheless, I do think there is some potential demand for HET education in the core curriculum. The virtual absence of HET within the core curriculum is somewhat alarming when one considers that the role of the core is to transmit to students the essential body of knowledge that defines what it means to be an economist. While nearly forty years apart, the two official studies of the economics profession conducted under the auspices of the AEA shared the overriding concern that graduate programs place too much emphasis on technique relative to knowledge of institutions, real-world problems, and a breadth of understanding of the discipline. Among other things, the COGEE report advocated that "course work should also convey to students a broad sense of the questions with which the discipline has been concerned, and how successful it has been at addressing those questions" (Krueger et al. 1991, 1048). This view was also reflected in my survey of department chairs, a large majority of whom felt that HET "can substantially contribute to a modern economist's training." Nevertheless, it is incorrect to read the COGEE report as a call for more graduate courses in HET, for no such call was made; nor do the chairs in my survey indicate a greater demand for HET graduate courses. Indeed, the COGEE report emphasized that the core curriculum should "acquaint students with theoretical and statistical tools that will be used in dissertation writing and in their subsequent professional careers" (1044), and it should be taught by "persons who are skilled in the techniques of economics" (1046). Thus, within the toolkit that contains Lagrangian multipliers, CES production functions, comparative statics, dynamic programming, and the Slutsky equation (among others), there is also some room for core-course faculty to include tools of historiographic inquiry. The goal then should be to equip these professors with a working knowledge of such tools.

Appendix 1 Questionnaire 1 (Department Chairs)

The History of Economic Thought (HET) in Ph.D. Economics Programs

I designed the following survey to take only a few minutes to complete. Should you want to expand on any question, feel free to write on the back of this page or to add additional pages. Please return this survey in the enclosed stamped envelope at your earliest convenience. Thank you.

Questions about the History of Economics (HET) Course(s):

- In the past five years, has the department offered a class in HET for Ph.D. students? [YES/NO]
- If so, what are the course names and instructor names for these Ph.D. HET courses?
- Are the HET courses required core courses, field courses, or electives for the Ph.D. students?
- Is HET part of the preliminary/qualifying exams for Ph.D. graduate students? [YES/NO]
- Is there a field exam in HET? [YES/NO]
- Does the department ever offer seminars (with guest speakers) in HET? [YES/NO]

Questions about the Students:

- Approximately how many Ph.D. students are enrolled in the graduate economics program?
- In the past five years, how many Ph.D. students went on the job market as historians of economic thought (either as their primary or secondary field specialty)?
- Ph.D. students' names and job placement?

Evaluative/Speculative Questions:

- Do you think an understanding of HET can substantially contribute to a modern economist's training? [YES/NO]
- What do you think is the optimal number of HET course offerings?
- Does your department intend to add or subtract courses in HET to the curriculum in the near future?

Appendix 2 Questionnaire 2 (HET Professors)

Survey on the History of Economic Thought in Ph.D. Programs

Please return this survey in the enclosed stamped envelope as soon as possible. If you prefer, you can email it to me at gayert@socrates. berkeley.edu, or fax it to me at (510) 643–8614. Feel free to expand on any question listed below.

Your name:_____

Questions about History of Economic Thought (HET) Courses:

- What are the names of the HET courses that you have taught in your department in the past five years? For each course, please indicate whether it covers (at least in part) methodological issues and whether it covers (at least in part) the history or philosophy of science. Please also indicate the time periods covered in each course and the names of textbooks used, if any. Feel free to include a copy of the syllabi with this survey.
- How frequently are HET courses for Ph.D. students offered in your department?
- How many economics Ph.D. graduate students typically enroll in these courses?
- Please name the current departmental staff members other than yourself who teach Ph.D. HET courses. Please indicate if they are core or adjunct faculty.

Questions about You:

- What is your professorial rank?
- Where and when did you receive your Ph.D.?
- What year did you start working at your current institution?
- Did your department hire you in part to fulfill a need to teach and do research in HET?
- Which of the following best describes your interest in HET? (Circle one.)
  1. HET is my primary research field of interest.
  2. HET is a minor research field of interest.
  3. I have an interest in HET, but do not conduct any research in the field.
  4. Other (please explain):
- If you have published in the field of HET, how would you categorize your HET research?
- What, if any, are your other research fields of interest?

Questions about the Ph.D. Students:

- Have graduate students interested in HET taken related courses in other departments (e.g., history department)? If so, what were the departments?
- In the past five years, have Ph.D. students gone on the market as historians of economic thought (either as their primary or secondary field specialty)? If so, please list their names and initial job placement.

Evaluative and Speculative Questions concerning HET

- Do you think that your departmental colleagues view your interest in HET positively, negatively, or neutrally?
- Do you think your department views HET as an important part of the Ph.D. graduate curriculum?
- Have departmental attitudes toward HET changed significantly over the past 5–10 years? If so, how?
- Do you think your department intends to add or subtract courses in HET from the curriculum in the near future?
- What do you think is the optimal number of HET course offerings?
- Do you think it better to offer HET in other departments instead of within the economics department?

References

Bowen, H. R. 1953. Graduate Education in Economics. *American Economic Review* 43.4:1–223.

Gordon, D. F. 1965. The Contribution of the History of Economic Thought to the Understanding of Economic Theory, Economic History, and the History of Economic Policy. *American Economic Review* 55.1/2:119–27.

Klamer, A., and D. Colander. 1990. *The Making of an Economist.* Boulder, Colo.: Westview Press.

Krueger, A. O., et al. 1991. Report of the Commission on Graduate Education in Economics. *Journal of Economic Literature* 22.3:1035–53.

Schabas, M. 1992. Breaking Away: History of Economics as History of Science. *HOPE* 24.1:187–203.

Siegfried, J. J., and W. A. Stock. 1999. The Labor Market for New Ph.D. Economists. *Journal of Economic Perspectives* 13.3:115–34.

The History of Economics as a Subdiscipline: The Role of the History of Economics Society Meetings

John B. Davis

My focus in this essay is on how the annual meetings of the History of Economics Society (HES) have contributed to making the history of economics a relatively independent subdiscipline within the field of economics over the last quarter century. I do not attempt to decide whether the history of economics becoming an independent subdiscipline has strengthened or weakened the subject as a domain of investigation within economics as a whole. Arguments can be made for both conclusions. Rather, my main emphasis is on how social factors—specifically academic social factors—have helped bring about a change in the character and practice of the history of economics in this period, particularly through the medium of the meetings.

Because it was academics who undertook these efforts, and because their efforts were rooted in their own professional concerns as individuals competing for positions and resources in college and university programs, the change in the nature and practice of the history of economics can be characterized as an academic professionalization of the field. In this regard, I follow the lead of A. W. Coats (e.g., 1993, 1998), who has argued that economists in general, historically lacking an identifiable professional status, have sought to create one through a variety of means. This is true of historians of economics as well. The regular meetings of

I am indebted to Roy Weintraub, an anonymous referee, and those attending the 2001 *HOPE* conference for helpful comments on this essay.

the HES have been an important means to this end in the history of economics in the last quarter century.

The list of academic social factors I judge to have been important to this process of academic professionalization of the history of economics are:

1. The publication of history of economics specialty journals.
2. The organization of history of economics associations and societies.
3. The holding of regular scholarly association meetings apart from general economics meetings.
4. The holding of regular scholarly association meetings in conjunction with general economics meetings.
5. The inclusion of the history of economics in scholarly classification systems (e.g., the *Journal of Economic Literature*, the *Social Science Citation Index*, *Current Contents*, and *Historical Abstracts*).
6. The existence of college and university instruction and doctoral supervision dedicated expressly to the field.
7. The ability of individual academics to credential themselves for promotion and salary purposes by work done in the field.
8. The availability of book publishing opportunities with major publishers for scholars in the field.
9. The identification of special library collections.
10. Dissemination and sharing of information about the field (such as in newsletters, bulletins, and, more recently, electronic lists).

Clearly these factors have operated in varying degrees and in interaction with one another in professionalizing the history of economics. My main focus is on the HES meetings, but I also make reference to connections between the meetings and specialty journal publication, as well as to connections between the meetings and academics credentialing themselves through work in the field, in order to give a fuller account of the role of the meetings.

One reason the HES meetings have been an important part of the professionalization of the history of economics is that they have expanded the space within which historians of economics have been able to present and discuss their research. Independent conferences restricted to a single area of research within a field also make a prima facie case for treating that area of research as a distinct subdiscipline within that larger discipline. Of course, it can be argued that having independent conferences has contributed to the marginalization of the history of economics within economics by minimizing other economists' contact with the subject. This, however, has to be weighed against the limited and declining opportunities that were available to history of economics presentations in general economics meetings at the time the HES meetings began. At issue, then, is a trade-off between the increased professional activity made possible by independent conferences and a possible reduction in visibility of the field within economics as a whole. By posing but not resolving this issue, I hope to contribute to thinking about the role and nature of the HES meetings in the history of economics.

A second reason that the HES meetings have been an important part of the professionalization of the history of economics is that they supported the decision to begin publication of *History of Political Economy* (*HOPE*), the field's first specialty journal. The beginnings of the professionalization of the history of economics in North America, in fact, might be said to date from the late 1960s and early 1970s with the appearance in 1969 of *HOPE* and the founding of the HES in May 1974.[1] When *HOPE* first appeared, there was concern that publishing opportunities were disappearing for historians of economics in generalist journals (Goodwin, Spengler, and Smith 1969, 1). But it was not a foregone conclusion that the journal would be able to attract sufficient history of economic thought research to sustain it. As a new journal, *HOPE* would not have the readership and prestige of established journals, and thus there had to be other reasons for scholars to submit their work to *HOPE*. One was that a concentration of research in one location possibly heightened historians' interest in research in the field as a whole. However, the marginalization issue arises here also, since research published in specialty journals is not generally read by individuals outside the relevant field. In any event, for the meetings to make a contribution to the joint HES-*HOPE* enterprise meant that they probably had to both be held regularly and attract growing participation. This essay looks at the history of the HES meetings with this issue in mind.

1. The founding occurred at the first annual meeting at the University of North Carolina at Chapel Hill. (An exploratory meeting was held in Chicago in 1973.) The HES was not the first history of economics society. The Japanese Society for the History of Economic Thought (JSHET) was founded in 1950, and the History of Economic Thought in the United Kingdom (HET UK) group had its first meetings in 1968.

Section 1 of the essay discusses the historical organization of the meetings, and how it worked to facilitate high participation. Section 2 describes changes in the level of participation in the meetings and then looks at measures of change in the character of participation in the meetings, in terms of both individuals involved and trends in research. Section 3 turns to the current experience of history of economics scholars in colleges and universities and relates the existence of meetings in the history of economics to the issue of academics being able to credential themselves by work in the field. Section 4 offers brief conclusions.

1. The Organization of the Meetings

The founders of the HES (Robert Eagly, Frank Fetter, Craufurd Goodwin, Warren Samuels, Joseph Spengler, and Vincent Tarascio) were all academics, and not surprisingly the meetings were structured according to the needs of academics. One implication of this was that the meetings were held annually to match the cycle of the academic year. Also, since the meetings were held after or toward the end of the academic year, presentations often constituted the outcome of a year's research. *HOPE*, on the other hand, was semiannual from 1969 through 1973 and then quarterly beginning in 1974, the first year of the meetings. Once doubled in size, *HOPE* arguably depended on an increase in research activity, which could be brought about through the meetings. Thus, not only did the conferences need to occur each year, but participation at the conferences also needed to increase. While it was important that at least initially *HOPE* have a fairly high acceptance rate to reinforce interest in the journal, in the long run the quality of scholarship had to be emphasized, which implied a higher rejection rate and, consequently, required a higher submission rate. If the meetings were to be a principal means of generating interest in history of economics scholarship and ultimately submission to the journal, more scholars would need to attend the meetings. In this regard, two aspects of the organization of the meetings and their programs are worth noting.[2]

First, although the year's president-elect reviews proposals for each conference, in practice few proposals are rejected, and participation has

2. HES conferences, presidents-elect, and sites for 1974–2000 appear in table 1.

Table 1   The Twenty-Seven History of Economics Society
Conferences, Locations, and Presidents

2000	University of British Columbia, Vancouver, B.C. (John Davis)
1999	University of North Carolina, Greensboro, N.C. (Bruce Caldwell)
1998	Université du Québec à Montréal, Montréal, Québec (David Colander)
1997	College of Charleston, Charleston, S.C. (Robert Clower)
1996	University of British Columbia, Vancouver, B.C. (Malcolm Rutherford)
1995	University of Notre Dame, Notre Dame, Ind. (James P. Henderson)
1994	Babson College, Wellesley, Mass. (Laurence S. Moss)
1993	Temple University, Philadelphia, Pa. (Ingrid Rima)
1992	George Mason University, Fairfax, Va. (Karen I. Vaughn)
1991	University of Maryland, College Park, Md. (Robert F. Hébert)
1990	Washington and Lee University, Lexington, Va. (S. Todd Lowry)
1989	University of Richmond, Richmond, Va. (William J. Barber)
1988	University of Toronto, Toronto, Ont. (Donald E. Moggridge)
1987	Harvard University, Cambridge, Mass. (Donald A. Walker)
1986	Barnard College, New York, N.Y. (Abraham Hirsch)
1985	George Mason University, Fairfax, Va. (A. W. Coats)
1984	University of Pittsburgh, Pittsburgh, Pa. (Mark Perlman)
1983	University of Virginia, Charlottesville, Va. (John Whitaker)
1982	Duke University, Durham, N.C. (Martin Bronfenbrenner)
1981	Michigan State University, East Lansing, Mich. (Warren Samuels)
1980	Harvard University, Cambridge, Mass. (William D. Grampp)
1979	University of Illinois, Urbana, Ill. (Royall Brandis)
1978	University of Toronto, Toronto, Ont. (Craufurd D. Goodwin)
1977	University of California, Riverside, Calif. (Carl G. Uhr)
1976	University of Chicago, Chicago, Ill. (George J. Stigler)
1975	Harvard University, Cambridge, Mass. (Joseph J. Spengler)
1974	University of North Carolina, Chapel Hill, N.C. (Vincent J. Tarascio)

always basically been open to anyone working in the history of economics. At the same time, because proposals must actually be accepted by the president-elect, proposals for the program are still in effect accepted only upon review. This combination of openness and review has the advantage of maximizing participation while simultaneously validating participants' proposals as properly within the subdiscipline of the history of economics—a matter essential to individuals acquiring funding for travel. Yet this procedure obviously also raises questions regarding the quality of conference presentations and thus creates another trade-off, in this instance between the opportunities created for scholars in the field and the possible perception that the field produces research of uneven quality.

Second, in maximizing conference attendance, conference sessions have generally needed to include three to four relatively short presentations, rather than one or two relatively long ones. While this generates more opportunities for participants, conference sessions with shorter presentations have often been criticized as allowing insufficient time for the development and exchange of ideas. Shorter presentations also need not be as carefully prepared as longer ones. A possible offset against these disadvantages is that high levels of attendance at the conferences made possible by maximizing participation may increase informal out-of-session exchange between scholars in the field who have limited contact with one another during the academic year but can meet in large numbers at the conferences. In effect, the meetings can act as a forum at which individuals discuss plans and strategies of research. More formal, focused exchange in conference sessions, then, has to an extent been sacrificed for more extensive, informal exchange outside of sessions.

2. Change in the Level and Character of Participation in the Meetings

Measuring changes in participation in the meetings enables us to reach a number of conclusions regarding how the meetings contributed to the professionalization of the history of economics over time. I review conference programs from 1978 to 2000 to measure participation in terms of the number of presentations per conference[3] and take the number of presentations to be the best measure of participation.[4]

In table 2 one can note a steady increase in the number of presentations given at the conferences over the years. This is particularly evident when comparing the number of presentations in the first eight years of conferences (for which I have programs) with that in the last eight years.[5] For the first eight HES conferences (1978–85), the average number of presentations is slightly more than 54. For the eight conferences from 1993 through 2000, the average number of presentations is 131, nearly two-and-a-half times larger. This increase can be evaluated relative to the growth in participation in meetings in economics generally. Comparing attendance at the North American Allied Social Science Associations Meetings (ASSA) for the 1978–85 period with the 1993–2000 period used for the HES meetings, attendance increased by about 45 percent. Comparing the number of sessions over these two time periods, the increase was about 70 percent (Sikes 2001).[6] Thus participation in the HES meetings has grown relative to participation in the ASSA meetings.

3. The programs for 1978–89 are from the *History of Economics Society Bulletin*, for 1990–93 from the *Journal of the History of Economic Thought (JHET)*, and for 1994–2000 from conference programs distributed at the conferences. The programs for 1974–77 were not available. The *Bulletin* programs are drawn from after-conference summaries of the sessions for 1978 and 1979 and after-conference abstracts of papers presented for 1980–89. The *JHET* programs are all preconference provisional programs. The 1994–2000 conference-distributed programs are also preliminary programs, but they are more complete than the *JHET* provisional programs, which needed to be compiled considerably in advance of the conferences in time for publication in the spring issue of the journal. It is does not appear possible to determine how closely the programs correspond to actual participation.

4. The number of sessions per conference is a not a good measure, since presentations per session vary. The number of authors might be used, but second authors sometimes do not attend. The number of chairs and discussants is not used because presentations are more important for professionalization, and chairs and discussants are largely drawn from the ranks of presenters. Special addresses, such as distinguished speakers, presidential addresses, and other invited talks, are not included among presentations because these have been included in most conferences and consequently do not show a pattern of change over time. I do not include workshops that appear meant to provide a service, but I do include presentations in roundtables and panel discussions irrespective of whether the presenter had a primary or commenting role. Conference registrations would be a good measure of participation, but this information does not exist for most of the conferences.

5. With the exception of 1993, none of the programs for these two sets of years is an early *JHET* preliminary program, and thus the planned presentations are likely close to the actual conference presentations

6. I do not have information regarding the number of presentations at the ASSA conferences. Note that cuts in the number of sessions were imposed in 1999.

Table 2 Number of Presentations per Conference

Year	Presentations
2000	163
1999	139
1998	144
1997	109
1996	133
1995	128
1994	132
1993	103
1992	94
1991	105
1990	91
1989	57[1]
1988	120
1987	163
1986	107
1985	73
1984	56
1983	72
1982	59
1981	54
1980	40
1979	43
1978	37

1. Not all abstracts were published.

Evaluating the growth in participation in the HES meetings also suggests we consider changes in the character of participation in the meetings. If changes in the composition of participation in the meetings do not reflect changes in the composition of participation in professional meetings in economics generally, this might indicate a weakening of the history of economics as an independent subdiscipline of economics. I therefore look at changes in selected characteristics of participation across the HES meetings and compare these to changes in those same characteristics in economics generally.

A first such characteristic is international participation in the meetings. The HES originated as a North American academic society that was chartered in the United States with most of its original members from either the United States or Canada. History of economic thought research, however, had a long tradition outside of North America in Europe and Japan. Therefore, one important measure of the nature of the history of economics as an independent subdiscipline is whether participation in the meetings would expand beyond the primary involvement of individuals from North America. That is, there is an argument that unless the HES became a more international society, at least in terms of participation in its meetings, a case could always be made that the relative autonomy of the field in North America reflected its decline. A second argument is that a more international participation would increase the diversity of topics at the meetings and that this might contribute to the vitality and viability of the field.

The evidence shows that over time participation in the conference did become more international. In terms of presentations (or coauthored presentations), participation by individuals from outside North America (hereafter international participation) has risen from a low of 5 percent in 1978 to a high of 53 percent in 2000. For the eight conferences from 1978 through 1985, the average percentage of international presentations was about 19 percent. For the eight conferences from 1993 through 2000, the average percentage of international presentations was about 39 percent, more than twice as high as in the earlier period. This change, however, probably understates the extent of international participation in the meetings, since it is likely that greater numbers of individuals from outside the continent have North American affiliations today than they did at the time of the earlier meetings.

I have not attempted to determine the change in international participation in economics meetings generally across the two eight-year periods concerned, since if done in terms of the ASSA meetings it would involve significant data collection efforts. However, it can be argued that international participation in the meetings has likely increased. According to Aslanbeigui and Montecinos 1998, the proportion of economics doctorates conferred on foreign students by programs in the United States has increased from 20.5 percent in 1972 to 43 percent in 1988, and foreign students now represent over half of doctoral students in economics programs. In addition, 40 percent of doctoral students indicate an intention to leave the United States after their studies. It seems not unreasonable to suppose that some proportion of these individuals return to participate in the ASSA meetings, raising international participation in the meetings. But whether for this reason and possibly others the international ASSA participation has doubled, as has been the case with the HES meetings, cannot readily be determined.

Another change in the characteristics of participation in the meetings that can be established is the percentage of women making presentations in the meetings. In terms of presentations (or coauthored presentations) the participation of women in the meetings has risen from a low of about 3 percent in 1978 to a high of about 22 percent in 1996. But 1996 was an unusually high percentage, and the later conferences do not have a significantly higher share of presentations by women. For the eight conferences from 1978 through 1985, the average percentage of presentations by women was about 9 percent. For the eight conferences from 1993 through 2000, the average percentage of presentations by women was about 13 percent. Moreover, not only is there is no trend in the share of presentations by women across the last eight conferences, but several of the conferences in the first eight years of the meetings had shares as high as a number of the conferences in the last eight years.

In economics as a whole, however, women have increased their representation in a variety of professional activities, especially over the last decade. For example, the Committee on the Status of Women in the Economics Profession (CSWEP) reports the percentage of women in tenure-track positions at the assistant professor level and with tenure at the associate professor level in all Ph.D.-granting departments for 1993 through 1999.[7] These are individuals who are likely to be actively engaged in research and making presentations at professional meetings. In general, the percentages are somewhat higher for economics as a whole than the percentage of HES presentations by women over the same period, though in some years the reverse is the case (CSWEP 1999). How are we to interpret this difference? On the one hand, it might be said that the history of economics has failed to attract a share of women comparable to the share of women now in economics as a whole. On the other hand, it might be argued that the history of economics has been reasonably successful in attracting women given declining opportunities in colleges and universities for individuals specializing in the history of economics.

Other changes in the characteristics of participation in the HES meetings are difficult to determine on account of the limited information contained in the HES programs, problems in interpreting those programs,

7. The percentage of female untenured assistant professors rose from 20.0 to 21.6 from 1993 to 1996; the percentage of female tenured associate professors increased from 9.0 to 16.3 over that same period.

and difficulties involved in supplementing the programs with additional information about participants. For example, it would be difficult to determine changes in the age profiles of participants at the conferences because of the problem of learning participants' birth years. Age profiles would be of interest if it were thought that a rising average age of participants was a sign of declining entry into the subdiscipline. Age profiles would also be of interest if it were thought that younger participants, as more recent doctoral vintages, brought an infusion of new ideas, which would contribute to the vitality of the field and its independence as a subdiscipline. It would also be interesting to be able to track trends in the types of research presented. For example, were heterodox economists to constitute a greater share of those attending the conferences, this might support the marginalization thesis, since heterodox economists have seen their numbers reduced in most economics departments. At the same time, increased activity on the part of heterodox economists could be a sign of vitality in that the history of economics had become a highly pluralist field.

3. The Role of the Meetings in the Credentialing Process

In this section, I turn to the current experience of history of economics scholars in colleges and universities and discuss the relation between the existence of history of economics meetings and the ability of academics to credential themselves by work in the field. A real concern among historians of economics regarding the history of economics' status as a subdiscipline is the declining number of positions in the history of economics in colleges and universities. Yet while the number of such positions has decreased significantly in recent years, participation in history of economics meetings, those of both the HES and other societies, has increased significantly. In addition, the number of history of economics specialty journals and thus the number of articles published in the field has also increased significantly in the last two decades. How is this to be explained?

Whether individuals pursue history of economics research depends in part on whether they are rewarded in terms of compensation and promotion for doing so at their colleges and universities. Since publication of research is now generally the most important factor determining compensation and promotion in colleges and universities, the growth in meetings participation and specialty journal publication implies that

history of economics research is still being accepted as legitimate research in economics—at least at some institutions. Which institutions
this involves in the United States is suggested by Ted Gayer's survey
of economics graduate studies programs that include the history of economics and Bradley Bateman's study of the teaching of the history of
economics in liberal arts colleges (both in this volume). Gayer's survey
demonstrates that Ph.D. institutions in economics, with a small number
of exceptions, no longer provide instruction in the field. Bateman's study
shows that the history of economics continues to be taught in many liberal arts colleges, if on a somewhat decreased basis. Thus it appears, at
least in the United States, that the history of economics remains a legitimate area of research in economics in the latter institutions, but not
in most of the former institutions. This proposition certainly has a number of qualifications. Among these are that liberal arts colleges may be
less willing to accept history of economics research per se than other
research, that some particular kinds of history of economics research
may be less accepted than other types of research, and that individuals
can only devote a portion of their research to the history of economics.
Nonetheless, Bateman's evidence suggests a place remains for historians
of economics in liberal arts colleges.

Before turning to Ph.D. institutions, then, let me suggest one view
of how participation in meetings and publication in history of economics journals might allow individuals to credential themselves in liberal
arts institutions. The development of disciplines in terms of the proliferation of subdisciplines compartmentalizes expertise regarding work in
subdisciplines.[8] This means that individuals not in a subdiscipline give
up the right to evaluate research in it, while retaining the right to evaluate whether the subdiscipline itself is viable. This latter judgment, however, is arguably based less on the intrinsic characteristics of a given subdiscipline and more on the characteristics of subdisciplines in general,
such as whether certain standard types of professional activities (professional meetings and publication in appropriate journals) are pursued.
Given this, two things appear to indicate there are likely to be generally
positive evaluations of research in the history of economics on the part of
nonhistorians of economics. First, because economics is relatively stable as a whole, subdisciplines continue to develop, and specialization

8. For this reason, I have argued that single rankings for journals in economics are no more
appropriate than single rankings for journals in the social sciences (Davis 1998).

is increasingly characteristic of the field. This means that the willingness of outsiders to judge research in *any* subdiscipline harshly is probably declining. Second, because the history of economics is a relatively
small subdiscipline, experts for evaluating research in it are often drawn
from outside an individual's home institution. This not only reduces the
number of informed critical voices within that individual's institution but
may also produce more favorable than average outside evaluations, since
many individuals in the history of economics are concerned to protect
the subdiscipline across colleges and universities as a whole.

In Ph.D. institutions, however, this argument does not appear to apply. Since the 1980s, Ph.D.-granting economics departments have placed
heavy emphasis on departmental rankings in their evaluation of faculty
performance (Laband 1985). Departmental rankings in turn have been
determined almost exclusively in terms of faculty publications in a short
list of "core" journals (Diamond 1989), with the rankings of journals and
thus the publications in them being determined in terms of relative impact measures (Laband and Piette 1994). Since publications in history of
economics journals have low relative impact, individuals publishing in
the field are generally perceived by their colleagues as not contributing
to departmental performance. In this regard, it is arguable that historians'
commitment to relatively autonomous activities in the form of the HES
meetings and publication in specialty journals has undermined their status vis-à-vis their colleagues. In contrast to liberal arts colleges, then,
individuals in departments offering the Ph.D. find it difficult to credential themselves primarily through research and publication in the history
of economics.

This raises the concern that in the future the credentialing practices of
Ph.D. institutions could be transferred to liberal arts institutions when
new faculty are drawn from Ph.D. programs that no longer value the
history of economics. Should "core" journal publications come to play
an increasingly important role in the credentialing process in liberal arts
colleges in the future, then the HES meetings and history of economics journals might cease to play a role in academics credentialing themselves in these institutions. A similar process whereby "core" journal
standards have begun to be imposed on institutions where they formerly
did not apply has been the Research Assessment Exercise now being carried out in the United Kingdom (see Backhouse in this volume). Though
U.S. colleges and universities are not subject to the same centralization

forces as those now operating in the United Kingdom, the increasing importance of "core" journals in the two largest academic economics communities may not bode well for U.S. liberal arts institutions.

4. Concluding Remarks

The efforts taken in the late 1960s and early 1970s to establish the history of economics as a relatively independent subdiscipline within economics were motivated by a desire for additional opportunities for historians of economics. It does not seem to have been foreseen at that time that creating a separate space for the history of economics might be attended by a devaluation of the field in economics as a whole. Rather quite the opposite, the optimistic view was that establishing the field as an active, independent subject of inquiry would enhance its status in economics. Cause and effect in all this, however, remain unclear. It can be argued that establishing the history of economics as a subfield of economics contributed to its marginalization, for example, for some of the reasons discussed above, and it can also be argued that the history of economics becoming a subfield may have retarded its decline in status within economics as a whole. How one looks at this issue depends in part on how one understands the evolution of economics itself. Thus, should it be argued that the postwar emphasis on formal and mathematical argument in economics—surely a factor in contemporary disregard for the history of economics—has been driven by very strong forces intrinsic to the nature of postwar economics, then the marginalization of the history of economics within economics probably has little to do with the actions of historians of economics in professionalizing the subdiscipline.

However one looks at this issue, the concerns raised by current practices surrounding the organization and nature of the HES meetings ought still be addressed. The argument that quality of research in the history of economics may have been traded off in some degree by having meetings aimed at achieving maximum participation can be addressed by rethinking the nature of the meetings. Thus there are ways of reorganizing the meetings that might provide different opportunities for those attending. Similarly, the argument that visibility of the history of economics may have been traded in some degree for independent meetings can be addressed by rethinking the place of the meetings in the field. Thus there may exist other forums in which the history of economics can be pursued that offer new opportunities for making the case that the history of economics is relevant to economics as a whole. But whatever strategies are considered and adopted, since they are likely to be initiated by academic historians of economics rather than economists in general, they will constitute further professionalization of the history of economics as a subfield within economics. Here lies perhaps the most serious limitation to an improvement in the status of the history of economics in the future. Until economists in general come to have a higher regard for the history of their field, the history of economics is likely to remain on the margins of the field.

References

Aslanbeigui, N., and V. Montecinos. 1998. Foreign Students in U.S. Doctoral Programs. *Journal of Economic Perspectives* 12.3:171–82.

Coats, A. 1993. *The Sociology and Professionalization of Economics: British and American Economic Essays*. Vol. 2. London: Routledge.

———. 1998. Economics as a Profession. In *Handbook of Economic Methodology*, edited by J. Davis, D. Hands, and U. Mäki. Cheltenham, U.K.: Elgar.

Committee on the Status of Women in the Economics Profession (CSWEP). 1999. Annual Report. Available from www.cswep.org/Annual99.htm.

Davis, J. 1998. Problems in Using the Social Sciences Citation Index to Rank Economics Journals. *American Economist* 42.2:59–64.

Diamond, M. 1989. The Core Journals in Economics. *Current Contents* 21 (January): 4–11.

Goodwin, C., J. Spengler, and R. Smith. 1969. Avant-Propos. *HOPE* 1.1:1–4.

Laband, D. 1985. An Evaluation of Fifty "Ranked" Economics Departments by Quantity and Quality of Faculty Publications and Graduate Student Placement and Research Success. *Southern Economic Journal* 52.1:216–40.

Laband, D., and M. Piette. 1994. The Relative Impacts of Economics Journals: 1970–1990. *Journal of Economic Literature* 32.2:640–66.

Sikes, V. 2001. Allied Social Science Associations Meetings, 1976–2001. Personal communication to author.

Part 2

International Issues

The Future of the History of Economic Thought in Britain

Roger E. Backhouse

Homogenization within British Higher Education

Higher education in the United Kingdom has changed almost beyond recognition during the past twenty to thirty years.[1] Three dimensions are relevant: first, at the undergraduate level there has been a change from a system catering only to an elite toward a mass higher-education system, and the percentage of eighteen-year-olds entering higher education has risen from 7 percent in 1962 to more than 30 percent by 1994 (since when it has fluctuated between 30 and 35 percent). Second, there has been a move to what is perhaps best described as American-style graduate education and research, a trend that has been particularly marked in economics. Graduate training programs have increased their emphasis on advanced coursework centered on the "core," and theses now tend to comprise three potential journal articles rather than a substantial monograph. There has been a growing emphasis on regular publication in the best possible journals. Finally, university funding has been progressively reduced with potentially important consequences. The twin effects of the drive to attract more non–European Union (EU) students (who pay higher fees than EU students) and of declining salaries and working conditions that make academic careers unattractive for most U.K. students have led to graduate programs being filled almost exclusively with

1. These changes are discussed in more detail in Backhouse 1997, 2000.

students from outside the U.K. The "slack" that was in the system in the 1960s (staff being free of pressure to perform in ways that are acceptable to their employers) has been eliminated.

Much of this will probably sound familiar to American (and many international) readers (see Goodwin 2000). However, two things make the situation radically different. One difference concerns the extent to which the best British students no longer wish to enter academic careers (see Oswald 2000 and Machin and Oswald 2000). Very few British undergraduates obtaining first class honors degrees (around the top 5 to 10 percent of undergraduates) go on to do a Ph.D. in economics.[2] In recent years it has become customary for the top British departments to have hardly any British students in their doctoral programs. New entrants to the British economics profession, therefore, generally either do not obtain firsts or come from abroad. This might have only a positive effect, but it may be significant for the sustainability of the British profession.

The other difference between Britain and the United States is the high degree of centralization in the university system. Universities are autonomous institutions, but although a few (notably Oxford and Cambridge) have substantial endowments, and all of them raise large amounts of money from the private sector, the core of universities' funding comes from the state. Most of this is distributed through funding councils, the largest of which are the Higher Education Funding Council for England (HEFCE) and the Scottish Higher Education Funding Council (SHEFC). Starting from a situation where universities were substantially free to organize their own affairs, free of government intervention, there has been increasing pressure (via research councils) to undertake research that is seen as "relevant." The main change, however, was the introduction, in 1989, of the research assessment exercise (RAE). This involved the evaluation of research in different subject areas, one of which was "Economics and Econometrics." In each subject area, a single panel, comprising around ten academics (mostly well known in the profession and nominated by bodies such as the Royal Economic Society), assigns a grade to each university's research. The precise mechanism and criteria evolved to the current system, which grades each university on a seven-point scale: 5*, 5, 4, 3A, 3B, 2, 1.[3] These grades had a direct effect on universities' funding. The RAE solved the problem of how to allocate funds to the

2. Master's degrees are valued because they provide quantitative skills required in business, but Ph.D.s are seen as qualifying one only for academia.

3. This system is meant to preserve compatibility with the previous five-point scale.

"new" universities—the fifty polytechnics that were granted university status and brought into the same funding body as the fifty "old" universities in 1992. The price of doing this, however, is that within each subject area, a single committee is responsible for judging the whole country's research, and universities are obliged to heed the views it is believed to hold. Though supporters view the system as competitive, its structure is perhaps better described as a socialist parody of a competitive system.[4]

This is of vital importance for fields such as the history of economic thought because that assessment is based on the submission of four named publications for each member of staff deemed to be "research-active." Each subject panel evaluates these four publications per member of staff (published during the four years prior to the assessment), together with statements about the university's research and data on grants and Ph.D. numbers, to produce a grade for the university concerned.[5] This grade and the number of research-active staff enter the formula that determines funding. The result is that *all* universities are under pressure to have staff who publish work that will be ranked highly by the RAE panel. It is accepted that articles in "top" journals are prima facie evidence of quality.[6] It is widely believed that this system discriminates against unorthodox work and against fields such as the history of economic thought.[7] (Heterodox economics can earn a 3, as De Montfort managed, but there must be great doubts about whether a predominantly heterodox department would ever achieve 5 or 5*.) There is no equivalent to the U.S. liberal arts colleges.[8] The British system is much more homogeneous in that all universities are increasingly playing the same game, even though some are more successful than others.[9] The main qualification to this is that business studies is a separate panel. Many

4. I owe this phrase to Denis O'Brien. Note that it was a Conservative government, not a Labour one, that introduced the system.

5. Restricting information to four publications is intended to focus the assessment on quality rather than quantity.

6. There are no definite criteria, for subject panels use their judgment in evaluating research.

7. See Hodgson 1995 for an argument about this in the context of heterodox economics.

8. The exception to this generalization is the University of Buckingham, established in 1976, which is the only completely private university in the United Kingdom. It remains small and, because of its high fees and nonstandard academic year, recruits almost exclusively non-U.K. students.

9. A further complication is that universities choose the number of research-active staff to submit. Thus one department with twenty staff might submit all twenty and obtain level-4 funding for them all, while a comparable department might decide, strategically, to submit only ten staff and obtain level-5 for those ten.

universities decided that they would do better in the RAE by submitting their economists as part of their business school, for the business studies panel was widely believed to be softer and more eclectic in its tastes than the economics panel.[10] Several business schools are centers of heterodox economics.

After RAE was introduced it became clear that the incentives all favored research and that teaching might be being neglected. The government's response was to supplement RAE with assessments of teaching quality. This, too, evolved, and the current system (soon to be replaced because it requires an unbelievable input of resources and fails to provide potential students with real guidance about the quality of tuition they will receive) gives universities a mark out of four on each of six criteria. There have also been attempts to standardize undergraduate teaching. The aspect most relevant to this essay is the so-called benchmarking statement, which specifies what students at each level ought to be able to do. This is a national statement, drawn up by a committee appointed by the Conference of Heads of University Departments of Economics (CHUDE). This includes the statement, "The following is an indicative list of what the attainments of students might be. . . . Appreciation of the history and development of economic ideas and the differing methods of analysis that have been and are used by economists."[11] The main emphasis in the document, however, is on the ability to use and apply standard theory.[12]

The Place of History of Economic Thought (HET)

A widely held view among those involved with the subject is that these measures place academics under increasing pressure to engage in research in subjects other than HET and that HET teaching has become increasingly marginalized. To collect information on this, I circulated a questionnaire to all university departments of economics that I could identify.[13] All universities that entered staff for "economics and

10. In 1996 the number of universities submitting to the economics and econometrics panel fell from approximately one hundred to around fifty.

11. The full text is available at www.qaa.ac.uk/crntwork/benchmark/benchmarking.htm.

12. One respondent to the questionnaire discussed below sees the benchmarking statement's mention of HET as an opportunity to be taken up. Others are more pessimistic about the way it will be interpreted.

13. The questionnaire is attached as appendix 1.

Table 1   Levels and Trends in HET Teaching, by RAE Score

	RAE Score			
	5–5*	4	1–3	Other
Universities	13	19	18	n/a
Responses[1]	12 (92%)	10 (53%)	7 (39%)	16 (n/a)
Number teaching HET[2]	4 (33%)	5 (50%)	5 (71%)	7 (44%)
Number with HET staff[3]	8 (67%)	8 (80%)	6 (86%)	10 (63%)
HET up or down[4]	$0 - 7 = -7$	$3 - 3 = 0$	$1 - 3 = -2$	$3 - 1 = 2$
Number facing pressure[5]	3 (38%)	7 (88%)	3 (50%)	2 (20%)

Note: Figures include some HET staff in economic history (LSE). "Other" comprises universities where economics departments either did not enter the RAE or were submitted under another category (typically business studies).
1. Percentage of universities replying.
2. Percentage of respondents.
3. One or more staff either teaches, researches, or wishes to teach HET.
4. Number of respondents saying that HET teaching increasing (either number of students or availability of courses) minus number saying it is falling (over the past decade or so).
5. Number of universities where respondent says there is pressure not to work on HET (as percentage of universities with HET staff as defined above).

econometrics" in the 1996 RAE were included as well as any other university where I could find evidence (mostly from university Web sites) that economics was taught.[14] It is unlikely that I found every university offering the subject. The most difficult area was business schools, some of which are umbrellas that include economics, and others of which are not. Coverage of universities that did not submit to the 1996 economics RAE panel is therefore erratic. Responses include some that did not believe they had sufficient research to justify submitting to any panel, others that submitted to business studies because they believed their research would be ranked higher there, and others that are integral parts of business schools. The main results are summarized in tables 1 and 2.

The questionnaire elicited information on forty-five universities. HET was taught in twenty-one (47 percent) of these and in fourteen (48 percent) of twenty-nine universities covered by the economics and

14. The issue of HET outside economics departments is discussed later in this essay.

Table 2   Staffing Levels, by RAE Score

	RAE Score			
	5–5*	4	1–3	Other
Responding universities	12	10	7	16
Staff in economics RAE[1]	372	149	65	n/a
Staff teaching HET	8 (2%)	9 (6%)	5 (8%)	11 (n/a)
Staff interested in teaching HET[2]	10 (3%)	10 (7%)	7.5 (12%)	18.5 (n/a)
Staff researching HET as main field	8 (2%)	9.5 (6%)	7 (11%)	3 (n/a)
Staff researching HET as minor field	5 (1%)	7.5 (5%)	7 (11%)	10 (n/a)

Note: Numbers of HET staff include some in departments other than economics and hence are not part of the denominator in the percentages. There are two instance of double-counting, where HET staff have a full-time position at one university and teach part-time at another.
1. Number of staff submitted as research-active in "economics and econometrics" (note that a small number of HET staff in these institutions were submitted under other categories because they were in other departments).
2. The question did not elicit whether there are further staff qualified to teach HET but not wishing to do so (note also that this is the opinion of the respondent who may or may not have consulted the colleagues whose attitude he or she is summarizing).

econometrics RAE.[15] However, the percentage teaching HET is much lower at universities scoring high in the RAE.[16] If we make the assumption that nonrespondents are like respondents, it is possible to correct for the fact that a much higher response rate was achieved for high-scoring universities than for low-scoring ones. Doing this suggests that HET may be taught in 59 percent of those universities that submitted to the economics and econometrics RAE panel in 1996.[17]

In addition to showing that high-scoring universities are less likely to teach HET, table 1 illustrates a trend away from HET and that this has been particularly strong in high-score universities. In all other categories,

15. *Teaching* refers to courses in the subject. In Britain, Ph.D.s in economics generally follow a "one plus three" model, in which a one-year master's degree by coursework is followed by three years' research. Graduate coursework is therefore at the master's level.

16. Throughout this essay, RAE scores refer to "economics and econometrics." Universities listed under "other" may have received high scores in other research areas.

17. The sample might appear to be extremely biased because institutions with no interest in HET will be less likely to reply. I am doubtful that this is the case because it was virtually costless for people to reply that HET was not taught, whereas answering the questions if it was taught took significant time. In addition, I can immediately list a large number of nonresponding universities that do have a commitment to HET. No other calculations in this essay depend on this assumption.

there was a mixture of expansion and contraction: indeed, the net decline is accounted for entirely by universities scoring 5 and 5*.

The questionnaires yielded some encouraging signs. The first is that in addition to the predictable declines, the provision of HET teaching had expanded in some universities. In addition, several respondents reported that their colleagues valued HET and that the pressures to downgrade it were external ones. Against this, one person commented that most members of his or her department considered the subject to be a waste of time,[18] and another said that HET was regarded as a "fringe" subject. The need to make space for other fields was cited. Thus one respondent wrote, "There seems to be widespread recognition in the department of the value of teaching HET, but, when the crunch comes every year, it is sufficiently low in priority that the course is not offered." A similar response came from a department where HET was dropped in 1997: "The module had received a number of complimentary comments from one of our external examiners at the time, both for the fact that we still taught it and for the course per se. We were sorry to lose it." There were several signs of great frustration, such as the respondent who claimed that "intellectual activity of any kind is increasingly frowned upon."

Many (including several high-scoring universities) cited low student interest as a reason for the subject being discontinued or under threat: students were seen as more instrumental than they used to be. On the other hand, there were several universities where demand was buoyant.[19] Where HET was taught, it was generally at second- or final-year undergraduate level, with a few places offering it to graduate (master's) students.[20]

The response from one Scottish university explained how HET used to be considered an essential part of the curriculum, citing Aristotle's dictum that "if you wish to understand what presently exists you must

18. This was in response to the second questionnaire.

19. For example, my own course is one of the largest final-year options in the degree program, regularly attracting sixty or more students. Some choose it for positive reasons (genuine interest in the subject, a desire to broaden their education, its links with history or political science), although some choose it in the hope that they will thereby avoid mathematics, technical micro theory, and econometrics.

20. Second-year undergraduates would typically be using "intermediate" macro and micro texts (and many of them will be required to take econometrics as well) having studied introductory economics plus mathematics and statistics in their first year. Second-year courses are typically taught using calculus.

first understand the origins from which it springs."[21] The respondent then explained how the cultural and managerial environment had changed: staff were less interested in history; there was pressure on the curriculum raising the opportunity cost of teaching history; and students in a mass-education system took a more utilitarian view of their studies. The result was that "compulsory courses have all gone. History exists only as a special subject or honours option, and such courses are now taken mainly by students from the U.S.A. or the Continent."

In some new universities, the introductory principles course contained a short, compulsory HET component, followed by optional courses in subsequent years. In many cases, retirement was frequently the immediate cause of HET being discontinued. Several respondents said that the subject was safe until they retired, but that it was likely to be discontinued on their retirement. Typical responses were, "When I leave, it will disappear and no-one else will or could do it" and, "When I retire, it will only be by luck that the subject will continue, I suspect. We typically want to appoint people who publish in major journals. Few if any HET specialists would count." Marginally more positive was the reply by someone who wrote, "When I retire the department will not look for a replacement. If anyone develops an interest then I doubt the department will oppose that interest and probably encourage the putting on of a course. HET is like urban, international trade. . . . It does not have to be covered." In Oxford there is an almost unique problem—the tutorial system, whereby students are taught by college tutors, makes it difficult to offer any syllabus that requires teaching by specialists.

The final column of table 1 provides evidence on the link between this state of affairs and the RAE. It shows the percentage of institutions where the respondent considered that there was pressure not to engage in the HET.[22] Virtually all respondents who believed there was pressure cited the RAE as the main factor, several considering it almost too obvious to need saying. One respondent went so far as to say, "I have been told that my interest in HET is 'unhelpful' to my department's RAE effort" and that his teaching load had been increased and his research budget cut. Others made it clear that, in their departments, the extent of such

21. See Dow, Dow, and Hutton 2001 on the Scottish tradition, of which this attitude forms a part.
22. The questionnaire did not make it explicit whether this referred to teaching or research. However, the written responses made it clear that this was interpreted as referring to research, teaching not generally being decided by individuals.

pressure was much greater for junior staff than for senior staff. As one respondent put it, "A good HET specialist would be supported (I got a personal chair after all) but it is unlikely one would be appointed at a junior level."[23] Such a view is compatible with the large number of respondents who did not see any pressure.

An interesting feature of these results is that the tendency to report pressure not to do HET research varies with RAE score exactly as would be expected. In top departments, few staff have an interest in HET and most of those who do are sufficiently well established to do what they choose. Pressure is greatest at grade 4 level: in such departments the pressure is to get publications that will move the department from 4 to 5. There is thus pressure to get into "general journals" (interpreted as *AER, JPE, QJE, Econometrica*, etc.) rather than into HET journals that are generally assumed to be ranked lower (though there is no official ranking of journals).[24] A representative response (from a 5-ranked department) is: "No pressure not to [research in HET], but no positive incentives to do so. A strong perception . . . that HET would not attract a high RAE profile. I suspect the School would not be keen to appoint an HET specialist." In contrast, for departments with scores of 1 to 3, papers in HET journals may be seen as contributing positively to the department's score with the result that departments are happier to encourage HET research. This is, however, not always true. Respondents wrote of pressure to do "quantitative" and "mainstream" research. Someone in a 3-rated department wrote, "Quantitative/theoretical research is promoted as the real area for publication. Books are ignored!"

Even where there is no explicit pressure not to do HET research, there is evidence of indirect pressure. Several respondents referred to joint research (something encouraged by the RAE). Given the paucity of HET staff, this generally implies non-HET research. Others referred to a desire to list only policy-relevant research and only historical research that had a bearing on contemporary issues. There is also pressure to produce articles in suitable journals. One department explicitly told its staff that their personal research priorities might not coincide with those of the department and that whatever their own wishes, their first priority should be to write four journal articles. Once they had done this, they should concentrate on getting articles into better journals. Books and other types

23. This was in response to the second questionnaire.
24. There was an attempt to construct such a list, but it was not accepted by CHUDE (see Lee and Harley 1998).

88   Roger E. Backhouse

of publication more important in HET than in, say, econometrics, were
thus discouraged. Several respondents mentioned the difficulty in obtaining funding, represented by the following quotation: "There are external pressures in that it is difficult to attract external funding, and so
the time necessary for good HET research. This is very noticeable when
comparing notes with fellow HET scholars at international meetings—
non-U.K. scholars seem to have much more research time."

Table 2 shows numbers of HET staff in British universities, classified by RAE score. This shows a clear negative relationship between
RAE score and the proportion of staff actively interested in HET (either wishing to teach it or undertaking research in it). Most noticeable
is the dramatic gap between 5- or 5*-ranked departments and 4-ranked
ones. However, given that the former are on average twice as large as
the latter, this may be less significant than the difference, reported in table 1, in the proportion of institutions in which there is someone with an
interest in HET. This was 67 percent for 5- or 5*-ranked departments,
compared with 80 percent for 4-ranked departments, and 86 percent for
lower-ranked ones. This makes it clear that, at least in the very short
term, it would be possible for the provision of HET teaching to rise, if
demand were there. In the longer term, the ability to include HET in the
curriculum depends on the supply of new teachers, which takes us into
career patterns.

HET Careers

The previous section focuses, loosely, on the demand for HET in British
universities. To understand the supply, we need to know how historians
of economics are produced. The standard model, at least in the United
States, is that the supply of specialists in a field is determined by the
numbers of new Ph.D.s created in the field.[25] The result is a focus on
graduate schools offering the subject. However, while this may be true
for many fields, it is something that should be tested, especially in a field
like HET, where it is common for people to combine teaching and research in the field with work in other areas. To provide information, I
sent out a second questionnaire (appendix 2) to every U.K. academic I
could identify with an interest in HET, for whom I could find an

25. For an example of analysis based on this assumption, see Biddle 1998.

Table 3 Age Structure of Historians of Economics

Age	Number
Up to 30	3
30–40	4
40–50	8
50–60	12
60–65	2
65+	6

Table 4 Undergraduate Education of Historians

Degree	Number
Single-honors economics	12
Joint-honors economics and history[1]	7
Politics, philosophy, and economics	2
Economics and business, etc.	2
Joint honors including economics, other	8
Degree outside economics[2]	4

1. Includes economic history.
2. Includes mathematics, philosophy, politics, and modern languages with politics.

E-mail address.[26] The result was thirty-five usable replies, a response rate of around one-third.

The first thing revealed by this survey is the age of British historians of economics. The mode was fifty to sixty, with 80 percent of the sample being forty or over (see table 3).[27] Sixty-three percent are affiliated with economics departments, 17 percent with business schools, and 11 percent with history or economic history departments.[28]

26. The list included everyone who met *one* of the following criteria: have published an article in *HOPE, JHET, EJHET, HER, HEI*; be on the membership list of a society such as the HES, ESHET, or the HES newsletter; or be mentioned in a response to questionnaire 1 (which asked respondents to list everyone in their institution who either taught or researched in HET).

27. Fifty-seven percent of the sample are over the age of fifty. Because it includes retired people, this figure is not strictly comparable with figures for the age structure of university staff more generally (in which 37 percent of staff on teaching-and-research contracts are over fifty, according to an education supplement published in the *Guardian*, 2 October 2001).

28. My sampling might appear biased against people outside economics departments. In view of this I made great efforts to inquire about noneconomists with an interest in the subject whom I should contact. I was given fewer names than I expected.

Table 5   Heterodoxy/Orthodoxy of Sample of Historians of Economics
Classification

Classification	Number
Heterodox: institutionalist	6
Heterodox: post-Keynesian	4
Heterodox: Marxian	2
Heterodox: other[1]	7
Heterodox: total	19
Neoclassical	4
Other	2
Inappropriate for modern economics[2]	2
Not economist, so inappropriate	5
No response	3

1. Includes some who answered "eclectic" and others who selected more than one heterodoxy.
2. Includes one who answered, "This probably means I am neoclassical."

Tables 4 and 5 show that, although they are largely in economics departments, trained in economics, historians of economics are different
from the average economist.[29] Whereas most economics graduates study
single-honors economics, the majority of historians of economics studied economics as a joint honors degree.[30] Perhaps not surprisingly, the
largest subject paired with economics was history or economic history,[31]
followed by politics, philosophy, and economics (PPE—the main way to
study economics at Oxford) and business studies. Table 5 demonstrates
that historians of economics are predominantly heterodox in their approach to economics, 54 percent identifying themselves as heterodox.[32]

29. I considered analyzing these and other responses in relation to current age, but no clear
patterns were evident. The numbers are too small.

30. Education in England and Wales, although not in Scotland, is much more specialized
than in the United States and much of Europe. In their last year at school, students still typically
specialize in three subjects (one of which may be economics or business studies). They apply
to university to read a specific subject.

31. In Britain, unlike in the United States, economic history is generally closer to history
than to economics. See Coleman 1987 for an explanation.

32. It should be noted that the term *historian of economics* is being defined broadly in the
sense that no attempt is made to distinguish "professionals" from "amateurs." It is possible that
it may exclude some activities that respondents did not think to classify as HET, even though
they dealt with historical figures. Given that this is more likely to be true of heterodox than
of orthodox economists, it has been suggested that this will cause an understatement of the
level of HET activity. Against this, many respondents' comments made it clear that they had
considered the possibility that HET might be taught in places such as principles courses. There

Table 6   Reasons Given for Working on HET

Factor	Number
Random events	4
Pure interest	8
Economics-motivated reasons	11
History-related reasons	1
Philosophical case study	1
Interest in Marx, Keynes, or Hayek	3

Equally significant, only 11 percent wished to describe themselves as neoclassical (*Chicago*, an option on the questionnaire, drew a complete blank). *Institutionalist* probably topped the list of heterodoxies for two reasons: the label encompasses a variety of viewpoints, and some people who would generally be considered post-Keynesian opted to identify themselves with a variety of heterodoxies, thus entering the "other" heading.

The heterodox inclinations of many historians of economics are consistent with the evidence in table 6. Thirty-nine percent of respondents cited an economics-related reason for entering the field. This category included looking for explanations of economic phenomena, dissatisfaction with conventional economics, and wishing to place economic theories in a historical context. If we add those who entered to understand specific individuals (Marx, Keynes, and Hayek), the figure rises to 50 percent. The next category, pure interest in the subject, accounted for 29 percent of replies.

The remaining tables document how people got into the field. Table 7 shows a roughly equal split between those taking an HET Ph.D. and those taking a Ph.D. in another field. Table 8 illustrates two further important findings. The first is that a high proportion of respondents (37 percent) became interested in HET as undergraduates. The second is that half those responding to this question did not start writing with a view to publication until after they had finished their graduate work. In other words, many get interested in the subject very young, and a substantial

---

is also a conceptual problem of what should be counted as HET. For example, if someone teaches Milton Friedman's analysis of the Phillips Curve in a macroeconomics course, should that be considered HET? Two respondents stated that they did not work on HET—though they did work on "history of economics." They nonetheless completed the form as if I had used the phrase *history of economics*.

Table 7   Number of Ph.D.s

In HET	
Economics	12
Economic and history[1]	2
Economics and sociology	1
Not in HET	
Economics	11
Area studies	2
Philosophy	1

1. Includes economic history.

Table 8   Initial Steps in HET, by Career Stage

	When Interested?	When Writing for Publication?
Undergraduate	14	1
Postgraduate	14	15
After postgraduate work	8	16

number do not start publishing on it until later in their careers. The sample would appear almost equally divided between those following the "traditional" route of entering the field via a Ph.D. and those taking it up later on. Table 9 shows similar information, but classified by age rather than career stage.[33] This clearly correlates with the information in table 8 but emphasizes the very flat distribution of the date when people started writing with a view to publication. Almost one-fifth of the sample did not do this until they were forty-five or older. The sample revealed two people (7 percent of the total) who did not even develop an interest in the subject until after the age of fifty-five.

The remaining group of questions sought to ascertain career patterns in terms of movements in and out of the field. These responses proved difficult to classify, exhibiting a bewildering variety of patterns. The simplest patterns were "HET always main or only field" (20 percent), "HET always minor field" (29 percent), and "career in HET with spell in other field" (6 percent). A pattern that does seem to emerge, however, is for

33. Some people answered the question about age but not the one about career stage and vice versa, hence the numbers are different for both tables.

Table 9   Initial Steps in HET, by Age

	When Interested?	When Writing for Publication?
Under 25	14	6
25–35	11	9
35–45	2	7
45–55	0	4
55–65	2	1

HET to become more important as people get older.[34] This is shown in figure 1. To separate out the effects of age from those of different cohorts, the average commitment to HET (none = 0, minor field = 1, major field = 2) is plotted for four different cohorts (those currently twenty-five to forty, forty to fifty, fifty to sixty, and over sixty). All show rises with age, although with falls in either the early or mid-thirties.

The Outlook

Given the above account, it would be possible to paint a very pessimistic picture of the prospects for HET in Britain. Economics is itself under pressure, with a dearth of new British graduate students to enter the profession and staff demoralized by the twin pressures of rising workloads (student-staff ratios in some departments in the mid- to high twenties) and external monitoring of both teaching and research. Within economics, HET is under pressure. Students increasingly want vocational courses (a trend that may be accentuated as the effects of loan-funded education become clearer), government funding bodies have emphasized "relevant" research, and the RAE has placed a premium on mainstream theoretical and quantitative research. The result is that, over the past five to ten years, HET has increasingly been pushed out of the leading economics departments. These pressures spread out to lower-ranked departments competing for a place among the elite. The age profile of HET staff raises the possibility that when the generation currently in its fifties retires, the number of staff available to teach the subject will plummet,

34. This may be in part a sampling issue, for people who are no longer in HET are less likely to be included. However, the inclusion of people who have published in HET journals, even if they no longer have an interest in the subject, offsets this effect (if people replied). (One person was excluded from the sample on the basis of his reply that, although his name had once been on an HET article, he had never been in the field.)

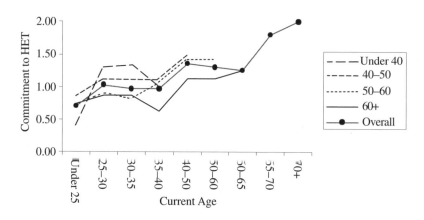

Figure 1   Career paths in HET by cohort

Note: Figure based on answers to question 8 in the questionnaire on careers (appendix 2).

and the subject will be in danger of dying out altogether. The supply of new Ph.D.s in HET is tiny, and even if there were more of them, universities would favor those working in mainstream fields.

This picture, however, is too gloomy, for several reasons. Within economics departments, there are still people who value HET, and there are places where it is expanding. Even in departments where the subject is not taught, there are economists who develop an interest in it. The sample discussed above includes a substantial proportion of people who came to the subject after they had started their careers. It is not uncommon to discover people who have been working on HET topics for years but of whom one has previously been completely unaware. It may be that the move toward more homogeneous, technical economics (assuming, of course, that it continues)[35] will make such late interest a thing of the past and that economists who wish to turn to HET will find that they simply cannot afford the necessary investment of time. Equally, however, it is possible that the desire to reflect on the subject's history may become even more urgent. Even at the top of the British profession, there remain economists who, though decidedly economists, not historians, have a keen interest in HET.[36]

35. I refrain from forecasting this. Forecasting the future of the HET conditional on the state of economics is hard enough.

36. John Sutton's (2000) work on Alfred Marshall and David Hendry's on the history of econometrics (see Hendry and Morgan 1995) come immediately to mind.

The second reason is that even if HET were to die in top economics departments, it would continue in other disciplines (even if researchers there do not think of what they do as HET). At Cambridge, HET is being abandoned in economics, but it is growing in history, where it is being introduced as part of a master's program. The Centre for History and Economics, involving economists and historians, is established outside the Faculty of Economics and Politics. At the London School of Economics there may be fewer economists committed to teach and research in HET, but the subject is alive in economic history and in philosophy (the Centre for the Study of the Natural and Social Sciences). Elsewhere there are historians who, though they may not be linked into HET networks, are committed to work on topics that lie squarely within the history of economics. There are also English scholars, philosophers, and others doing work in the field. (Currently there are several initiatives that, if successful, will create interdisciplinary networks of scholars with an interest in HET.) There are also business schools, where a much more tolerant attitude toward nonmainstream economics is to be found. Although some aspects of business school culture work against HET, some of them provide an environment where HET can develop. It is perhaps significant that of the three staff in the survey under the age of thirty, only one is in an economics department—the other two are in departments of sociology and management (equally significantly, both are from continental Europe, with British Ph.D.s supervised in departments outside economics). If HET ceases to be the preserve of economists (if it ever was) and becomes a more interdisciplinary grouping of activities, this may be a positive outcome.[37]

Appendix 1 Questionnaire on HET Teaching

Please note that responses will be read and used as the basis for a discussion, not simply calculating statistics. Hence comments, in as much detail as you care to provide, are welcome on all of the questions.

If HET is taught/researched/published by people in other departments, please either include those departments in your answers, or pass a copy of this questionnaire on to them.

---

37. It was interesting that some respondents described their research as becoming more interdisciplinary, as though this implied a movement away from HET.

1. Your name.
2. Name of institution/department.
3. Is HET taught in your institution?
4. At what levels is HET taught in your institution? (Please give approximate numbers of students for each category; is it compulsory/optional?)
5. Is HET regarded as an important/integral part of the curriculum? (If attitudes vary, comments would be welcome.)
6. Has the situation changed significantly over past 5–10 years?
7. If HET was taught in the past but is no longer taught, please give details, in particular when it stopped being taught and the reasons (lack of student demand, pressure to include new subjects, retirement of teachers, perceived lack of relevance, etc.).
8. How many staff are involved in teaching HET?
9. How many staff would have an interest in teaching HET?
10. If a main textbook is used, what is it?
11. Have there been significant changes in the HET syllabus? Please explain.
12. How many staff do research or publish in the HET?
13. Has the situation changed significantly over past 5–10 years? (Please give as much detail as you can.)
14. Are there pressures not to engage in the HET? If yes, please give as much detail as possible.
15. Are these pressures greater or less than 5–10 years ago? Please explain.
16. How do you view the future prospects for the HET in your institution (perhaps over the next 5–10 years)?

There were also questions on resources.

Appendix 2 Questionnaire on Careers

For most questions, the questionnaire included a list of options between which respondents could choose.

1. In what subject(s) was your bachelor's degree?
2. If you took a postgraduate course, in what subject(s)?
3. If you took research degrees (primarily by thesis), what was the topic?

4. At what stage in your career did you develop your initial interest in the HET?
5. At what stage in your career did you start writing with a view to publishing in HET?
6. Which of the following best describes your career in HET?
7. If you have switched fields during your career, what were the main reasons for leaving/entering HET?
8. In which of the following periods of your life did you undertake research in HET?
9. Do you expect to be working on HET in the future?
10. Is your commitment to the field likely to increase or decrease?
11. What reasons lie behind these decisions?

References

Backhouse, R. E. 1997. The Changing Character of British Economics. In *The Post-1945 Internationalization of Economics*, edited by A. W. Coats. *HOPE* 28 (supplement): 33–60.

————. 2000. Economics in Mid-Atlantic: British Economics, 1945–95. In *The Development of Economics in Western Europe since 1945*, edited by A. W. Coats. London: Routledge.

Biddle, J. 1998. Institutional Economics: A Case of Reproductive Failure. In *From Interwar Pluralism to Postwar Neoclassicism*, edited by M. Morgan and M. Rutherford. *HOPE* 30 (supplement): 108–33.

Coleman, D. C. 1987. *History and the Economic Past: An Account of the Rise and Decline of Economic History in Britain*. Oxford: Clarendon Press.

Dow, A., S. C. Dow, and A. Hutton. 2001. The Scottish Tradition in Political Economy. In *Toward a History of Applied Economics*, edited by R. Backhouse and J. Biddle. *HOPE* 32 (supplement): 177–98.

Goodwin, C. D. W. 2000. Comment: It's the Homogeneity, Stupid! *Journal of the History of Economic Thought* 22:179–84.

Hendry, David F., and Mary S. Morgan, eds. 1995. *The Foundations of Econometric Analysis*. Cambridge: Cambridge University Press.

Hodgson, G. 1995. In Which Journals Should We Publish? *European Association for Evolutionary Political Economy Newsletter* 11:6–8.

Lee, F. S., and S. Harley. 1998. Peer Review, the Research Assessment Exercise, and the Demise of Non-mainstream Economics. *Capital and Class* 66:23–51.

Machin, S., and A. Oswald. 2000. U.K. Economics and the Future Supply of Academic Economists. *Economic Journal* 110:F334–49.

Oswald, A. 2000. A Sorry State. *Economist*, 1 July, 122.

Sutton, John. 2000. *Marshall's Tendencies*. Cambridge: MIT Press.

Economics as History of Economics: The Italian Case in Retrospect

Maria Cristina Marcuzzo and Annalisa Rosselli

The history of economics or history of economic thought (HET) is not an unambiguous term; what it denotes is something not unequivocally understood regardless of context. What it means today in the United States to identify someone as a historian of economic thought or to say that an article should be classified as B (according to the *JEL* descriptors) is not necessarily what it meant some years ago in Italy and other European countries.

In this essay we look at the peculiar Italian way of doing HET, which germinated in the late 1960s, blossomed in the mid-1970s, and withered away in the early 1980s, involving people who considered themselves and were generally perceived as economists rather than historians of economic thought.

Our purpose is to make a case for the historical nature of practices and motivations in doing HET, which impinges on the much broader question of appraisal, namely, what is good or bad HET?

The question of what defines a legitimate contribution to the history of economics subdiscipline was raised by Roy Weintraub in his editorial piece for the HES list (Weintraub 1996). Legitimate membership in the community of historians of economic thought, he argued, requires a style of scholarship (use of primary sources, circumstantial evidence,

We wish to thank for their comments, without implicating them, A. Birolo, R. Faucci, A. Ginzburg, B. Ingrao, M. Lippi, A. Roncaglia, F. Vianello, R. Weintraub, and an anonymous referee.

background knowledge, and so forth) that is standard among historians, but not among economists. His conclusion was that a "good" economist is not necessarily a "good" historian of economic thought, and vice versa.

This line of argument has become increasingly popular since the 1990s,[1] being applied to criticize both mainstream and nonmainstream economists as prone to write mainly "internalist" or even "Whig" histories. It is precisely the opposite of what was held in Italy twenty-five or so years ago, namely that only economists trained in the "right" economic theory could have a full understanding of the issues involved in past theories and therefore produce "good" history of thought. In the first section we give three examples of this approach; in the second we conjecture on its origin; finally, in the last section, we air some thoughts on how the present situation may blight future prospects.

The peculiarity of the Italian case originating in the 1970s was a way of doing history of economics *as if* doing economics. The profusion of articles and books devoted to matters of interpretation (mainly of David Ricardo, Karl Marx, and John Maynard Keynes) marking that period[2]— not only in Italy, of course, but, we believe, there more than elsewhere— were meant or considered to be not exercises in doctrinal history but, rather, contributions to the production of new economic ideas.

This approach was characterized by two essential features: (1) the primary role assigned to textual exegesis; and (2) the almost exclusive attention given to the "great economists" (who did not, however, reach ten in number).

The textual exegesis approach may explain why the professional, personal, and intellectual context hardly came into the picture, while the

---

1. See, for instance, the contributions by Margaret Schabas (1992), D. Wade Hands (1994), and James P. Henderson (1996). For an evaluation of this debate, see Roncaglia 1996.

2. The number of articles by Italian authors on Ricardo, Marx, or Keynes (109) as a percentage of all the articles by Italian authors recorded in *EconLit* from 1969 to 1985 (4550) amounts to 2.4 percent. (It is worth noting that the Italian journals indexed in *EconLit* in that period included the top ten journals with the highest reputation.) This result can be compared with the percentage of articles by Italian and non-Italian authors on Ricardo, Marx, and Keynes (987) over all the articles recorded in *EconLit* in the same period (130,433), which comes to 0.7 percent. This result clearly is born out by the high percentage of articles on Ricardo, Marx, and Keynes by Italian authors in proportion to the total of articles on the same subject, that is, 11 percent, while the percentage of articles by Italian authors over all the articles recorded in *EconLit* in the same period is 3.5 percent.

"great economists" approach—perhaps in part because critical editions of the works and correspondence of the most famous authors were being made available[3]—may explain why the need or passion for archival work did not actually arise.

In the following pages we give three examples that we see as representative of this approach, and that also proved influential outside Italy. They can be characterized by the quest for ideas to use—and, indeed, for ideas to reject—as building blocks for an alternative economic theory once their original and "true" meaning had been restored.

The aim of Marco Lippi's (1979) book on Marx was to reconstruct the multifaceted role played by the theory of labor-value and thus distinguish which of its functions could be performed by other analytical tools (above all by Piero Sraffa's theory of prices) and which ought to be abandoned once and for all. The book answered the question: why is labor and no other factor chosen by Marx as "source" and "measure" of value? Lippi's argument was that the labor theory of value cannot be regarded as a theory of prices with a limited scope, holding only under circumstances too specific to have any relevance for a capitalist economy, nor were labor-values an initial approximation of the actual exchange values. The choice of labor as source of value—Lippi argued—was an expression of Marx's deep belief in a universal law of production, according to which labor is the "real social cost" and measures the difficulties that anywhere and at any time human beings have to overcome to provide for their needs (xv). This is what Lippi labeled as the "naturalism" of Marx. In a capitalist society the universal law of production manifests itself in the form of exchange values of commodities depending on the quantities of labor socially necessary for their production. Prices can only redistribute values, which is to say that they redistribute the total amount of labor supplied by the producers. This—according to Lippi—is what lies behind the famous condition of the transformation problem, namely, that the sum of prices must be equal to the sum of values.

Lippi's implication was that, once we understand that the labor theory of value has that particular function in Marx's conceptual framework, we can do without it. Other parts of Marx's theory—explanation of economic crisis and determination of prices based on technological

3. For instance, in the case of the three authors mentioned above, the eleven volumes of Ricardo's *Works and Correspondence* were published between 1951 and 1973; the thirty volumes of Keynes's *Collected Writings* were published between 1971 and 1989; and the first volumes of the Marx-Engels *Gesamtausgabe* began to be published in Italian in the early 1970s.

conditions of production—do not need the labor theory of value and thus can, and indeed should, be used for the reconstruction of an alternative economic theory.

Our second example of HET as an activity of separating the "good" from the "bad" parts in selected works of past economists is offered by Pierangelo Garegnani (1978). Garegnani praised Keynes's principle of effective demand as showing that market forces do not lead to full employment but also asserted that Keynes's argument in the *General Theory*—that saving and investment are brought into equilibrium by changes in income and not in the rate of interest—had a fundamental weakness in that it relied on expectations and uncertainty whose effects, if any, are confined to the short period. Thus Keynes's theory had to be modified so as to exclude the possibility that in the long run flexible wages might restore full employment, which is the case when the rate of interest can bring investment to equality with saving at the level of full employment income. To rule out this possibility, any relationship between investment and rate of interest must be severed. Indeed, the inverse relationship between investment and rate of interest is an expression of the marginal principle, that is, of determination of the price of a factor of production by its scarcity (344). There is no such thing as "scarce" capital—Garegnani argued—since the measurement of capital has been proved to be subject to all the theoretical difficulties brought to light by the controversy of the 1960s between the two Cambridges. Once free of its marginalist element, the principle of effective demand can become part of an alternative economic theory and find firmer grounds for extension to the long period (336).

Finally, our third example is Luigi Pasinetti (1960, 1977), who translated the relevant propositions of Ricardian theory of distribution into a few equations with the aim of facilitating understanding of the "standpoint" (Sraffa 1960, v) of classical political economy as opposed to the marginalist approach. The classical standpoint is identified with the surplus approach and interdependence between the productive sectors. However, these elements can be used as the main ingredients for an alternative economic theory only if all the ambiguities in Ricardo are eliminated and the assumptions underlying his theory clearly stated. The mathematical formulation, concise and rigorous as it proves, is a tool to this end (Pasinetti 1960, 78).

This Italian style of doing HET, as exemplified in the three cases discussed above, can be better assessed when compared with contemporary examples of textual exegesis combined with the "great economists" approach, which draws its inspiration from a different tradition altogether. For instance, in Sam Hollander's (1979, 689) work on Ricardo in particular, past theories are seen not as providing the material to build an alternative to the modern (neoclassical) economic theory, but rather as evidence of continuity in the general equilibrium tradition. The difference between the traditional American and British "Whig" approach—as exemplified by Hollander and many others—and the Italian style of doing HET in the 1970s is that for the former the past is sifted for the predecessors of modern theory and present ideas ("quest for ascendancy"), while for the latter the past is searched for what has been lost and can no longer be found in modern theory ("quest for an alternative"). Of course, motivations cannot be invoked to appraise results (the "good" reasons for which HET is practiced do not necessarily make that practice "good"). However, the quest for alternatives rather than confirmation of present truths seems to us potentially more fruitful.

At this point we would like to attempt to explain the peculiarity of the Italian case. In Italy, Marx and Sraffa were highly influential from the late 1960s to the early 1980s owing to a combination of two factors. First, Cambridge (U.K.) was the center Italian economists gravitated toward for advanced education, thanks to the reputation Cambridge-based economists—and especially the Italian émigré Piero Sraffa—enjoyed at the time. Second, the 1968 movement drew people to economics from other fields (philosophy, mathematics, physics, architecture) under the influence of Marx (1969, 15), who had promised not only to interpret the world, but to change it.

Marx and Sraffa had a message that turned out to be very important for HET: economics has not always been in the same unsatisfactory state we now see it in; good and important ideas were buried in classical political economy, "submerged and forgotten" (Sraffa 1960, v) with the advent of the marginalist revolution (or the transformation of "classical" into "vulgar" political economy, as Marx would have had it). This message was understood as a program to restore some of the ideas of the classics, freeing them from the distorted forms in which they came to us, and from their embedded errors.

The special relationship with classical political economy was asserted by Marx and by Sraffa after him with their best known and most widely read works, *Capital* and *Production of Commodities by Means of Commodities*, which in fact share the same subtitle ("Critique of Political Economy" and "Prelude to the Critique of Economic Theory"), and Sraffa's famous introduction to Ricardo's *Principles* (see Rosselli 2001).

We have further evidence of how Marx and Sraffa conceived of the special relationship with past ideas and authors. Indeed, we have two works by them that are real histories of economic thought: *Theories of Surplus Value*, which Marx wrote as the fourth volume of *Capital*, and *Lecture Notes on Advanced Theory of Value*, written by Sraffa for the course he gave in Cambridge from 1929 to 1931. Both works were left unpublished by their authors (and one still is).[4]

The main point of *Theories of Surplus Value* is the distinction Marx draws between "classical" and "vulgar" political economy, the former running from William Petty to Ricardo, the latter from the dissolution of the Ricardian school to the early 1860s.

Each economic theory—according to Marx's historical materialism—reflects the material conditions of society and, thus, given phases in capitalist development and the class struggle. Because "classical" political economy developed in a phase of incipient capitalism, it was better situated to understand its laws of motion and could therefore be science. On the contrary, "vulgar" political economy, evolving from a phase of mature capitalism, tended to hide the nature of social relations—above all the antagonism between capital and labor—and justify the existing social order, thus foregoing any possibility of being a science to become "pure apology" (Marx 1954, 24–25). So it was that history of economic thought became an exercise in seeing who came closest to a real understanding of what Marx thought to be the foundation of capitalism, namely, surplus value, as the title of his book reveals.

Turning, now, to Sraffa, his *Lecture Notes on Advanced Theory of Value* focus on the theory of value from the historical viewpoint, their main purpose being to show how the notion of cost of production was transformed from the classical school to the marginalist school, leading—as the result mainly of Alfred Marshall's work—to unification with utility and to the statement of symmetry between cost and utility. For such unification to be possible, Sraffa argued, the notion of cost of production had to undergo a scries of changes that made it unrecognizable

---

4. The "Lecture Notes" are preserved among the Sraffa Papers, D2/1, Wren Library, Trinity College, Cambridge.

in terms of the meaning ascribed to it by the classics, but comparable with utility.

Comparison between the notion of cost in Petty and the Physiocrats, on the one hand, and in Marshall, on the other, shows that while for the former authors cost is mainly food for the worker, for the latter it is the sum of "efforts and sacrifices," in abstinence or waiting and in labor required. These two notions of costs reflect different conceptions of what economics is about (the classical economists were mainly concerned with *measures*, the marginalist authors with *motives*) and gave rise to two theories of distribution, namely, two conceptions of wages and profits. One sees profits as surplus of the product and wages as necessaries, while the other considers both to be shares in the product (see Marcuzzo 2001).

Sraffa's program was to reestablish an objective as opposed to subjective value theory, as the classical authors had it, getting rid of the labor theory of value, but maintaining the dependence of prices on conditions of production and an exogeneously given distributive variable. An integral part of this antimarginalist program was to disentangle classical concepts from their current interpretations and pursue an approach to economic theory free of marginalist elements.

In the 1970s many Italian economists derived their approach to HET from Marx and Sraffa as part of a program to build an alternative economic theory. So it was that HET became synonymous with doing nonmainstream economics.

The story we have told is now a matter of the past. By the early 1980s, in Italy as elsewhere, the scene had rapidly changed, and was to change yet further as we came closer to the end of the millennium.

The approach inspired by the message and research program of Marx and Sraffa, coupled with insights by Keynes, is a legacy that a few people still treasure. In Italy work is still being done on Sraffa, Ricardo, and Keynes, and rather less on Marx. People engaged in this type of research are defenders of the tradition we have described and remain fully persuaded of the importance of doing HET as a basis for developing an alternative paradigm. They hold chairs in economics—not in HET—are active in nonmainstream economics, and have pupils and younger colleagues who are encouraged to follow their example.

However, their number is much reduced. To account for this we must bring into the picture a peculiar trait of recent Italian political history. The antiestablishment movements of the 1960s brought about many positive changes in Italian society, but some degenerated into plain disruption and terrorism. Appalled by these developments, a number of people distanced themselves from previously held views—given the dire consequences they are believed to have produced—and were thus labeled "repentant" (*pentiti*). The same term could be used to describe those economists who once drew their inspiration from the message and the research program of Marx and Sraffa and no longer do so. Once they would write reams on these authors, attend conferences, and apply for funds to carry out research on related topics, but eventually they reacted against their own formerly cherished views and sources of inspiration, "repented," and abandoned the field.

Career strategies, fashionable new locations attracting brilliant young graduates, and, above all, the change in political climate are certainly among the major factors behind the phenomenon. To these "external" factors we believe that another, "internalist" element should be added. The various exercises involved in the return to classical political economy and Keynes ended up being performed in a dogmatic fashion, new ideas emerging with difficulty, old problems still unsolved. A sense of déjà vu prevailed. The implication was not only abandonment of the Marx-Sraffa approach, but also the irrelevance of exploring past theories and authors altogether. HET ceased to be seen as a legitimate, respectable endeavor worth pursuing.

In actual fact, in some cases "repenting" simply meant changing heroes (for instance, Hayek rather than Keynes), which, in principle, leaves the importance attributed to HET unscathed. However, this may have significant implications for the future of HET. In fact, doing HET tends to be more or less appreciated according to the topic chosen (interpreting von Neumann and Hayek or writing the history of game theory has more "value" than interpreting Keynes or writing the history of classical monetary theory) and its vicinity to the present. Yet rejecting the previous sources of inspiration and granting legitimacy to ideas and authors not belonging to the previously fashionable tradition is no guarantee per se of doing better HET. Within the field itself we find the same variety in depth, in historiographic skills displayed, and in purpose as there was in the past.

The above case (changing heroes and vicinity to the present) seems to us neither the most general nor the worst as far as the future of HET in Italy is concerned. Rather, this is when the "repentant" join forces with the younger generation of economists, who possibly have never heard of the old Cambridge, struggled to get their Ph.D. in (mostly) prestigious U.S. universities, and are determined to import the same standards and contents of economics into their home universities. They are appalled by those senior colleagues who have not kept up with the subject, in turn reinforcing the latter's propensity to reject past modes and habits.

The culprit becomes HET, seen as "antique collecting," possibly a subject for social conversation but hardly a professional field in an economics department. The lack of mathematical skills often involved in doing HET reinforces the suspicion that it may attract only people with weaker intellectual abilities. In conclusion, in Italy, too, doing HET is now seen simply as not doing economics or, alternatively, doing second-rate economics.

This was the personal experience that both authors of this essay had when they came up for tenure as full professors in their economics departments, proof being required of them that they were in fact economists rather than well-established historians of economic thought. We might equally cite the editor's reply when an essay in HET was imprudently sent by one of the authors to a renowned generalist journal: "The journal is anxious to get away from the somewhat parochial and backward looking orientation which has characterised at least some papers published in the past. . . . Today we have to ask whether past positions were correct."

We would like to conclude with some more objective evidence. In Italy full, associate, and assistant professors belong to disciplinary subgroups, identified by descriptors. Each individual chooses his or her subgroup according to his or her field of research. Members of the committees for promotion and new appointments are elected among people of the same subgroup. The descriptors of economics disciplines have recently been reduced from the previous ten to the present six.[5] In December 2000, all the economists previously in the largest subgroup, P/01 (political economy), were given the option either to remain in the same subgroup or to join the P/04 subgroup (history of economic thought). At

5. These are: P/01 political economy; P/02 economic policy; P/03 public finance; P/04 history of economic thought; P/05 econometrics; P/06 applied economics.

the time of writing (September 2001) 217 full professors, 182 associate professors, and 228 assistant professors, for a total of 627 economists, belong to the P/01 subgroup. Only one full professor, one associate professor, and three assistant professors chose to join the history of economic thought subgroup, which now consists of fifteen full professors, fifteen associate professors, and twenty-one assistant professors, for a total of fifty-one individuals. The ratio between the two groups is 1:12; certainly, however, more than one out of twelve Italian economists born before 1960 have written at least one article in HET during their career, and more than one between 1969 and 1985 (either of which would qualify them for the HET subgroup), but they are not inclined to be associated with a subject that is not attracting students, resources, and academic recognition.

It is not the survival of HET that is threatened in Italy.[6] Under the present system of government funding, a minimum of resources—for research and teaching—is granted to holders of tenured positions in any discipline.[7] By contrast, the opening of new positions and promotions are conditional on the relative importance of the discipline in teaching and research, and on the academic stance of the subgroup to which it belongs.

It is our view that two lines of action should be pursued for not merely the survival but the positive growth of HET. The first course is academic distinction: we must enhance our capacity to be versed in *both* economic theory and historiographic methods. It is by combining these two skills and not simply being knowledgeable in one or the other of them that we may hope to advance the quality of our scientific results.

The second priority is academic strength: we must acquire bargaining power vis-à-vis the economists' community, as other subdisciplines have succeeded in doing (for example, economic history) to establish a central role for HET in the training and research of economists. In Italy, holders of academic positions in HET are currently divided on this very issue. On the one hand are those who favor stronger links with the community of

6. Since its foundation in 1992, membership in the AISPE (Italian Association of Historians of Economic Thought) has steadily grown, now amounting to more than 120 members. A course in HET is offered in thirty-six out of fifty-four institutions granting a first degree in economics. Moreover, there are currently four journals devoted to HET—*History of Economic Ideas*, *Il pensiero economico italiano*, *Storia del pensiero economico*, and *Il pensiero economico moderno*.

7. Unlike the situation in British and American university systems, in Italy full, associate, and assistant professorships are all tenured and state-funded positions.

economists; on the other, those who oppose this strategy as threatening their autonomy and resources.

Academic distinction and strength are not ends in themselves. What we are advocating is a thorough questioning of the present practice of doing economics, fostering the critical thinking and openness of mind that are essential to the social sciences. This critical attitude is also a means to draw attention to principles and methodologies alternative to the present set, rooted in past theories.

Are we then suggesting a return to the 1970s and the instrumental use of HET to reinstate classical political economy–with–Keynes? Clearly not, since the past does not repeat, and we have learned from our mistakes. We cannot do HET *as if* doing economics; we should make room for it as an autonomous subdiscipline with its own agenda, methods, and standards of achievement. As in the 1970s, however, we must reposition HET at the center of the battlefield of economic ideas.

References

Garegnani, Pierangelo. 1978. Notes on Consumption, Investment, and Effective Demand: I. *Cambridge Journal of Economics* 2.4:335–53.

Hands, D. Wade. 1994. The Sociology of Scientific Knowledge: Some Thoughts on the Possibilities. In *New Directions in Economic Methodology*, edited by Roger Backhouse. London: Routledge.

Henderson, James P. 1996. Whig History of Economices Is Dead. R.I.P—Now What? www2.eh.net/HE/hes_list/Editorials/Henderson.php.

Hollander, Sam. 1979. *The Economics of David Ricardo*. Toronto: University of Toronto Press.

Lippi, Marco. 1979. *Value and Naturalism in Marx*. London: NLB.

Marcuzzo, Maria Cristina. 2001. Sraffa and Cambridge Economics 1928–1931. In *Piero Sraffa's Political Economy*, edited by Terenzio Cozzi and Roberto Marchionatti. London: Routledge.

Marx, Karl. 1954. Afterword to the Second German Edition. In vol. 1 of *Capital*. London: Lawrence and Wishart.

———. 1969. *Theses on Feuerbach*. In vol. 1 of *Selected Works*, by Karl Marx and Friedrich Engels. Moscow: Progress Publishers.

Pasinetti, Luigi. 1960. A Mathematical Formulation of the Ricardian System. *Review of Economic Studies* 27:78–92.

———. 1977. *Lectures on the Theory of Production*. New York: Columbia University Press.

Roncaglia, Alessandro. 1996. Why Should Economists Study the History of Economic Thought? *European Journal of the History of Economic Thought* 3.2:296–309.

Rosselli, Annalisa. 2001. Sraffa's Edition of Ricardo's Works: Reconstruction of a Reconstruction. In *Piero Sraffa's Political Economy*, edited by Terenzio Cozzi and Roberto Marchionatti. London: Routledge.

Schabas, Margaret. 1992. Breaking Away: History of Economics as History of Science. *HOPE* 24.1:187–203.

Sraffa, Piero. 1960. *Production of Commodities by Means of Commodities*. Cambridge: Cambridge University Press.

Weintraub, Roy. 1996. What Defines a Legitimate Contribution to the Subdiscipline "History of Economics"? www2.eh.net/HE/hes_list/Editorials/weintraub.php.

The Present Situation of the History of Economic Thought in France

Ghislain Deleplace

For historical reasons, history of economic thought (hereafter HET) has been until today in France more an integral part of economics in general than a specialized subdiscipline in the field of economics or in the history of sciences and culture. There is no doubt that inherited idiosyncrasies have played a role in maintaining until now the weight of HET in the teaching and research system. But I shall argue that its present strength may also be explained by the way economics in France repudiated around 1970 its past insularity and opened itself to foreign influences. HET then developed through an active link with modern theory. Today, the threat to the future of HET is not the outcome of the lifting of barriers supposedly protecting French economics, but the consequence of a change in foreign influences. Nevertheless, some signs of hope exist, which should prevent French historians of economic thought from falling into nostalgia.

I shall first mention some facts about HET in France, before stressing which type of HET they have shaped. Finally, I shall describe the elements that sketch an uncertain future.

Some Facts about HET in France

The weight of HET in French universities has remained until today quite significant, and one should turn to long-term factors to explain that

I thank Nathalie Sigot and Mehrdad Vahabi for providing information and comments.

situation, both in the institutional environment and in the evolution of economic thinking.

The Weight of HET

The significance of this subdiscipline may be evaluated at three levels: undergraduate teaching, postgraduation and research, and the academic system.

French universities offer three national levels of graduation after two (*DEUG*), three (*licence*), and four (*maîtrise*) years. Although less than 50 percent of the students entering the universities in economics obtain the four-year degree, the programs (which, due to the national diploma, have a unified structure, but may be adapted by each university) are conceived over the four years. An inquiry made in 1999 by Association Charles Gide pour l'étude de la pensée économique (the French equivalent of HES) provides information on the teaching of HET in sixteen universities (Association Charles Gide 1999); my own investigation has raised this number to thirty-eight, out of the fifty-eight where an economics program exists. It appears that only two universities do not offer compulsory courses in HET at least once in the four-year program, and the same number offer courses during three years. On the whole, the thirty-eight universities deliver on average sixty-eight hours of courses (compulsory or not) in HET over the four-year program; 73.7 percent of them deliver more than fifty hours, and 18.4 percent deliver more than one hundred hours. The distribution of the courses over the duration of the program is given by tables 1 and 2.

These results are quite favorable to HET. The fact that its teaching is alive and well is also illustrated by the volume and variety of published textbooks in French. In two years (1999 and 2000), and in addition to the translation of the fifth edition of Blaug [1962] 1999 and to the reprinting of the classic Gide and Rist [1909] 2000 and Denis [1966] 2000, no less than ten new textbooks came out: three for intermediate and advanced courses (Béraud and Faccarello 2000, Deleplace 1999, and Etner 2000); three for introductory courses, in standard (Gnos 2000 and Montoussé 2000) or pocket (Duboeuf 1999) size; and four in pocket size on particular schools (Combemale 1999, Defalvard 2000, Poulon 2000, and Ravix 1999).

At the postgraduate level (the equivalent of the master's degree), courses in HET are usually replaced by methodology ones. But one

Table 1   Number of Years in the Four-Year Program with at Least One HET Course

	0 Years	1 Year	2 Years	3 Years	Total
Percentage of universities	5.3%	36.8%	52.6%	5.3%	100%
Total average hours over the program	0	61	76	102	68

Table 2   Existence of HET Courses at a Given Level of the Four-Year Program

	1st or 2nd Year	3rd Year	4th Year
Percentage of universities	50.0%	60.5%	47.4%
Average hours over the universities offering a course at this level	32	53	43

specific program is devoted to HET (delivered jointly by the two most important universities for economics in Paris, Paris 1 and Paris 10), and another one (at Paris 1) devoted to economic epistemology leaves much room to it. A research laboratory specialized in HET gathers twenty Paris-area academics, and in eight other laboratories in France, HET is an axis of research implemented by at least three scholars. Another structure dependent on the Centre National de la Recherche Scientifique (CNRS) sponsors a postgraduate summer school in HET and a winter one on the relation between HET and other fields of economics. The scientific society Association Charles Gide (mentioned earlier) had 110 members in 2001; it organizes a yearly conference, cosponsors the summer school, and publishes a letter and a register. Two French reviews are specialized in HET: *Cahiers d'économie politique* since 1974 (half-yearly) and *Oeconomia* since 1984.

The weight of the research in HET in the French academic system is difficult to ascertain because no systematic data for articles or doctoral dissertations in this field (or any other one) are available. It is then necessary to combine heterogeneous information. One piece of information is particularly disappointing: since its creation in 1953, the annual doctoral dissertation prize given by the Association Française de Science

Économique (AFSE) (the French equivalent of AEA) never rewarded a work in HET. Another is more encouraging: of 411 articles published between 1980 and 1990 by the generalist *Revue économique*, 32 of the 918 themes treated (3.5 percent) concerned HET in the *JEL* classification, at the fifth rank of the various fields, just behind money and finance (Jeannin 1993, 125); a special issue on the (old) classical theory of money appeared in this review in 1994. A quick overview of the more recent period shows that over the last five years (1997–2001), 12 out of 319 articles (3.8 percent) published in *Revue économique* dealt with HET; so did 22 out of 139 articles (15.8 percent) published in the other French generalist review, *Revue d'économie politique*, where a special issue on the legacy of Sraffa appeared in 1998.

An examination of academic recruitment procedures may draw mixed opinions about the weight of HET. In every discipline, university professors are in France civil servants, recruited through national competitions, and divided in two ranks: *maîtres de conférences* (associate professors) and *professeurs* (full professors). The organization of the competition for the lower rank is the same in every discipline and gives the last word to the university where the position is open. But economics has inherited from its fellow discipline law a special centralized competition to recruit most full professors, called *agrégation*, which in cases of success guarantees a lifetime position in a university. At the level of the *maîtres de conférences*, doctors in HET seem to have no difficulty obtaining their national *qualification* (while only 45 percent of all candidates in economics succeed in obtaining it), but, in the absence of systematic data, it is difficult to know whether this favorable bias also exists when the universities fill their positions. At the level of the (full) *professeurs*, one must distinguish between the *agrégation externe*, which is mostly taken by young candidates (under forty), and the *agrégation interne*, reserved to *maîtres de conférences* over forty years of age. In the first, 11 out of the 203 *professeurs* recruited in economics over the last seven sessions (1990–2002) were historians of economic thought (5.4 percent), the first of these ranking sixth out of thirty-three; in the 2002 session, a new HET specialization was opened, without affecting significantly the results: among 144 candidates applying for 33 positions, 10 enrolled in HET and 2 succeeded (6.1 percent of the positions filled). In the second category of *agrégation*, HET specialists were six (18.8 percent) out of the thirty-two economics *professeurs* promoted over the last two sessions (1998–2000),[1] the first of these ranking first out of sixteen.

The Institutional Environment of HET

Here one must take into account three factors: the first two are general and concern teaching and research in economics as in any other discipline; the third is particular to economics and concerns procedures for the recruitment of university professors

The French higher education system is split in two parts: the universities and the *grandes écoles*. If the first go back to the Middle Ages (the University of Paris was founded eight hundred years ago), the most prestigious *grandes écoles* were created around the Revolution to train civil engineers or high school teachers; since World War II, new ones appeared to train business managers or high-ranking civil servants. Access to the two systems is different: the high school diploma (*baccalauréat*) allows anyone to enter universities without selection, for a two- to four-year program of instruction. By contrast, one must stay two years in high school after the *baccalauréat* and pass a difficult examination to enter the most famous *grandes écoles* for a three-year course of study. The consequence is that the French elite is mostly reproduced through the *grandes écoles*, and that the universities are devoted to mass education, particularly since the end of the 1960s. No direct competition apparently exists between universities and *grandes écoles* for the training of economists (only business managers or statisticians are explicitly trained in some of the latter). However, the *grandes écoles* have understood that their reproduction of the elite required a training in modern economic problems; together with a long tradition of mathematical economics in the *écoles* for civil engineering, this has led them to develop economic teaching. Both aspects explain why, with very few exceptions, HET is absent from this training.

A second institutional factor is the division that exists in the public research system: on the one hand are agencies like the CNRS, with full-time researchers, and on the other are university laboratories uniting faculty members whose time is split between teaching, research, and university administration. Both spheres intertwine because the professional researchers are usually employed in university laboratories and follow

---

1. Until now, this particular *agrégation* had only sessions in 1990, 1998, and 2000.

a career in the civil service close to (although distinct from) that of the academics. However, their number is small in economics (as in the social sciences generally, by contrast with "hard" sciences). The priority in recruitment, therefore, does not go to HET, which is not better represented in other economic research centers, whether public (like the statistical agency Institut National de la Statistique et des Études Économiques [INSEE], the planning agency Commissariat Général du Plan [CGP], or the forecasting division of the ministry of economy, Direction de la Prévision [DP]) or private (like the research departments of the banking and insurance sectors). This means that there are not many opportunities to practice high-level research in HET full-time.

A third institutional factor is the recruitment procedure for full professors in economics. The *agrégation externe*, which takes place every other year, contained until 1997 a lecture in "History of Economic Thought and of Economic Facts from 1750 to 1980," which was prepared (with the assistance of a team) in twenty-four hours, presented by the candidate in forty-five minutes, and followed by a fifteen-minute discussion with the jury. The underlying assumption was that every professor of economics should have enough knowledge in HET to defend (if not to write him- or herself) a lecture in this field. This lecture was canceled in 1999, but HET was reintroduced in 2001 as one of two lectures whose subjects are selected randomly and prepared by each candidate in eight hours: the first one on "economic theories" may bear on "the history of theories," and the second one deals with a specialized field chosen from nine, including "history of economic thought." The rationale of this formula is now that each candidate should be familiar enough with HET to trace the historical origin of a theory, and that any candidate could specialize in HET as well as, for example, in econometrics or in money and finance.

On the whole, are these institutional factors favorable or not to HET? A consequence of the first two is that for both teaching and research HET is mostly practiced in universities. This may look trivial and not peculiar to France, but one must keep in mind that, in France, the economic elite of business managers and high-ranking civil servants are *not* trained in the universities (this is the task of the *grandes écoles*). Then while most of the university students in economics become middle (sometimes senior) executives or civil servants, the best of them end up in the higher education and research system, not in corporations or state bodies. This endogamous element is a positive factor for HET, which is still considered a useful component of the formation for teaching in economics, as testified by its place in the *agrégation*. From various points of view, there are certainly good reasons to dispute the divisions of both higher education and research, or the endogamous bias of the teaching programs in economics, or the clan character of the *agrégation*. Nevertheless, one should recognize that these factors have probably helped to prevent HET from becoming a marginalized subdiscipline in France.

The Evolution of French Economic Thinking

The institutional division of French higher education has always put its mark on the development of the economic discipline. Until the 1960s, the teaching of economics at the university did not emancipate from the law faculties, and an absence of communication with the economists of the *grandes écoles* lingered from the nineteenth century. On the one hand, economics in the universities was dominated since World War II by "the economists with a realistic and sociological conception" (Marchal 1953, 33). This school was characterized by two aspects (Arena 2000): (1) what the marginalist approach usually considers as given (preferences, resources, techniques) is here supposed variable, and even becomes the main subject of inquiry, which calls for history and sociology to understand long-term changes in "structures" and institutions; (2) the inductive method is preferred to the deductive one, and a real talent for typological observation is combined with a distrust of mathematization. These two aspects explain the scope but also the limits of this approach: "The systematic use of effective or supposed inputs from neighboring social sciences has been the often disappointing substitute for a specific economic analysis" (988). On the other hand, economic analysis developed after World War II outside the universities in two directions: the neomarginalist approach implemented in the *grandes écoles* and the CNRS by René Roy, François Divisia, Maurice Allais, and the latter's pupils Gérard Debreu and Edmond Malinvaud, and the Keynesian approach promoted in state administration and enterprises by senior civil servants like Pierre Massé, Robert Marjolin, or Claude Gruson.

This situation changed dramatically in the second half of the 1960s on the university side. Some general reasons obviously played a role: the opening of French society to outside influences and the rejection (illustrated by May 1968) of conventional schemes. But an extraordinary coincidence in our discipline should also be stressed. At a time when the emancipation from the law faculties encouraged young academics in France to look outside the traditional "realistic and sociological conception," new "years of high theory" were flourishing in Great Britain and the United States, with raging debates such as the capital controversy, the case for Sraffian economics, the critique of the Keynesian "counterrevolution," or the monetarist attack on Keynesian monetary policy. This was a revelation more than a revolution: as often in France, the novelty was immediately wrapped in old clothes. For example, the agitation around foreign ideas led to the creation of two economic laboratories at the University of Paris, the Séminaire Aftalion, mainly oriented toward Cambridge (U.K.) and Marxian economics, and the more orthodox Séminaire Jean-Baptiste Say; these laboratories were at the same time teams to prepare the *agrégation*, which had survived May 1968.

This drastic change narrowed the previous gap between economics in and out of the universities: ideas were exchanged (with, for example, the above-mentioned INSEE, CGP, DP, or the CNRS laboratory Centre d'Études Prospectives d'Économie Mathématique Appliquées à la Planification [CEPREMAP]), whether adapting or criticizing mainstream concepts. This change was also reflected in the evolution of the generalist review *Revue économique*, which had been created in 1950 with a "realistic and sociological" program and moved between the mid-1960s and 1980 toward mainstream economics (Lapidus 2000; Steiner 2000). Since the 1980s, economic thinking in France has more and more reflected the general evolution of economic analysis in the Anglo-American world, but without the brutal changes seen elsewhere. For example, it has never been shameful to be a Keynesian in France, and macroeconomics in the universities never ceased to be dominated by Keynesians, although of various types. Such an atmosphere has been favorable to HET: by contrast with the attitude common to new classicals and new Keynesians, which consists to bury Keynes in HET and separate him from modern theory, French economists never were reluctant to consider the links between the past and the present of their discipline. This has been important in shaping the type of HET practiced in France.

Which HET in France?

Two Conceptions

For the convenience of the exposition, let me distinguish two kinds of attitude toward HET, which seem to me representative of how it is practiced in France and, probably, elsewhere. The common ground of these attitudes is: (1) an endogenous view of HET, considered as part of the economic discipline and practiced by economists (as opposed to HET as part of the history of sciences or literary genres and practiced by whoever is interested in it); (2) a retrospective view of HET, which takes for granted that HET cannot help but involve the current state of the economic discipline—and agrees that it should do so, because of the endogenous view already mentioned. Now on this common ground one may have a "cultural" approach to HET. Whether economics is considered a social science or an applied art, it needs to be put in a general perspective, which requires a sufficient knowledge of the way economic problems have been represented and treated in past history. HET may contribute (with other branches of economics such as economic history) to fulfill that function by *complementing* modern economic theory, in the classrooms (for example, as one of the introductory courses or part of them) and the scientific debate (with articles in generalist economic reviews, not only HET ones).

A second attitude may be called analytical. Whether modern mainstream theory is viewed as satisfactory or flawed, its achievements or deficiencies can be ascertained not by empirical tests alone but also by its capacity or failure to overcome analytical difficulties faced by former theories. HET may then be considered a specific approach to economic theory, based on the study of the texts that have marked the history of the discipline. Not only can it provide a rational understanding of how we got (for better or worse) where we are, but it is also a sort of library in which shelves correspond to fundamental issues and books or articles are ranked according to their importance, whatever their date of publication. "Analytical" HET does not complement modern economic theory: it is an *integral part* of it, in the classrooms (with advanced compulsory courses) and the scientific debate (with articles in all types of economic reviews, including those specialized in the various fields of the discipline). This "analytical" approach to HET is exemplified by the editorial policy of the main French review in the field, *Cahiers d'économie politique* (Messori 1997).

The legacy of the old bias toward economics as a "realistic and sociological" discipline was a "cultural" conception of HET: it was typical for a French professor in the 1950s to sum up his views on the discipline in an HET textbook, in the great tradition of Gide and Rist (1909), or to devote a significant part of his book on any subject to its treatment by earlier authors. With the revelation of foreign debates around 1970, HET was used to put them in perspective and facilitate their understanding, so that "cultural" HET evolved to adapt its role of complementing a more and more formalized economic teaching. But, at the same time, "analytical" HET developed with a bias toward a critique of mainstream theory and an attempt to implement a heterodox research program.

Because the situation of HET *in* the discipline depends crucially on the state *of* the discipline itself, it has not more recently escaped the general tendency to greater specialization, particularly among younger generations. But this did not make the distinction between the two conceptions disappear, because they may both be practiced in a more or less specialized way.[2] The main consequences of this specialization process have been, on the "cultural" side, to concentrate on neglected authors, and, on the "analytical" one, either to aim at a neutral (neither apologetic nor critical) view of the relation between past and present theories, or to shift attention to new types of dissidents (such as Austrians or institutionalists). However, there still exists among senior scholars in HET a heterodox "analytical" current, marked by the convergence of two aspects: an internal critique of modern mainstream theory (adopting as a starting point the question, what goes wrong in it, rather than what goes right?), and an attempt to confront it with some "great authors" (Quesnay, Smith, Ricardo, Marx, Walras, Keynes, Debreu, Sraffa) investigated for the logical structure or the relevant results of their theories. Whether broad or specialized, the "analytical" conception of HET appears to be greatly responsible for having maintained a relatively strong position of HET in France.

2. Although a discussion about the relevance of the proposed distinction is beyond the scope of the present essay, it may be contrasted with the recent one put forward by Blaug (2001): the "historical reconstruction" approach may be viewed as belonging to the present "cultural" one, while the "rational reconstruction" is a part (albeit limited, because of its reduction to the use of modern analytical tools) of the "analytical" one.

An Active Link between HET and Modern Theory

The statistics above testify to this link in teaching. But there are also various illustrations of it in research. One is the significant proportion of articles published in France in the field of HET that exemplify the "analytical" approach: for example, fifty-five out of seventy-four papers (85.9 percent) published in the last eleven issues of *Cahiers d'économie politique* (from 1997 to fall 2001) were concerned with the analytical structure of economic theory (forty-three of them since *General Theory*); also, the 2001 conference of Association Charles Gide had this expressive title: "Value from Aristotle to Sraffa, Shapley, and Debreu." Furthermore, as already mentioned, the postgraduate winter school of the CNRS is devoted to the relation between HET and various fields in economics. Another illustration is the invitation made to mainstream economists to contribute to publications on the recent evolution of theory—and the positive response to this invitation. For example, the review *Cahiers d'économie politique* started in 1999 to publish special issues on "What's new in A since X?" (with until now A = the wage-employment relationship, imperfect competition; and X = Keynes, Cournot, respectively), mixing articles by specialists of A and of HET. Also, the third collective volume of Béraud and Faccarello 2000, devoted to twentieth-century theory, has been written mostly by specialists of the various fields. Conversely, historians of economic thought are invited and take part in conferences and publications implemented by mainstream economists: for example, a workshop in HET is regularly held at the annual conference of AFSE, and the annual conference of a CNRS structure on "money and finance" hosts a workshop on the history of theories and facts in this field. Also, a new collection of books, *Théories économiques*, which explicitly links modern economic theories and HET, appeared in 1999 in a respected publishing house (Dunod).

An Uncertain Future

Some concern about the future of HET in France may result from various elements on both the demand side and the supply side of economic education. Training in economics at the university is usually provided in the same departments as business administration, and the two curricula compete to attract a demographically diminishing number of students, whose demand is now oriented for the vast majority toward business.

This induces many departments to reduce the number of courses offered in economics and also questions the above-mentioned endogamous aspect of this curriculum. Both elements weaken the case for HET.

At the other end of the chain—the *agrégation externe* of full professors—the recent avatars of HET are a symptom of embarrassment. It was not the first time in 1999 that the compulsory lecture in HET was canceled: the "1968 Revolution" had already killed it, but it had been resurrected in 1979 by one of the last "economists with a realistic and sociological conception," Raymond Barre, when he became prime minister. Twenty years later, this new storm in a teacup reflects the conjunction of two elements. One concerns the *agrégation* itself: some sectors of the economic discipline have always opposed the specificity of this procedure (as compared to the standard one in other disciplines), either because it reinforces the clan character of the recruitment, or because it imposes some literary requirements that penalize mathematical research. The abolition of the *agrégation* would imply political risk because this competition is strongly supported by the sensitive fellow discipline, law; its simplification looked better, and HET bore the cost of it.

It is fair to say that this simplification was widely acclaimed by the younger generation of candidates, surely because the collective preparation of this lecture in twenty-four hours was heavy and unevenly shared, but also because their attitude toward HET is not the same as that held by their seniors. This generational effect has an objective basis: we have seen that the weight of HET in recruitment at the full-professor level has been for younger generations (through the *agrégation externe*) roughly one-third of what it is for older ones (through the *agrégation interne*). Thus the inducement to practice HET cannot be the same in both cases, and it is too early to know what the reintroduction of HET in 2001 (along the formula described above) will signal. There is also a subjective component in the generational effect: HET is viewed by young scholars— even by those who specialize in HET and, among them, by those who embrace the "analytical" approach—less and less as a way to make one's judgment about the present state of the economic discipline. This phenomenon is important because, in the decade to come, this new generation will completely replace the one that was recruited for the massive student influx of the early 1970s, and that has maintained a "cultural" interest in HET or promoted an "analytical" conception of it.

One has to look beyond France to explain this generational effect. We have seen that the present situation of HET in France has been influenced not only by institutional idiosyncrasies but also by the conditions in which French economic thinking opened itself around 1970 to outside (Anglo-American) influences. What about today? As witnessed by other articles in the present volume, it seems that the situation of HET in many countries during recent years has evolved in two directions, which are not encouraging for the future of HET in France: its place in university teaching programs and faculty recruitment has steadily declined (while it remained significant in France), and its orientation toward a "cultural" approach in research has been paramount (while an active "analytical" link with modern theory has been a key factor in the strength of HET in France). There is a risk for this tendency to be imported in France, not through trivial imitation but because, in my view, both aspects are linked.

The opening of French economic thinking to outside influences around 1970 boosted HET because it led to the importation of *controversies about fundamentals*. It can no longer be so today: a *consensus about tools* has been established in economics at the international level, and this may explain both above-mentioned aspects of the evolution of HET. The so-called Whiggish HET contributed to establish that consensus, by suggesting that the present state of economics was the inevitable outcome of the past, and this task being done, historians of economic thought are left to specialize in telling stories about how everything occurred. More profoundly, it is not only the existence of the consensus in economics that marginalizes HET, but also its content. It links the legitimacy of any research program in economics to the analysis of ever more sophisticated individual agents, in contrast with the deliberate attempt by many great authors of the past (from Quesnay and Ricardo to Debreu and Sraffa) to found their theories on minimal behavioral assumptions. As a consequence, the branch of economics that may bring some light about past theories is today rightly put aside by the view according to which everything written before 1980 is useless for the advancement of economic analysis because it lacks microeconomic sophistication.

Where then can we turn for some hope of a living future for HET? The recent revival of the debate about "what and how to teach economics" may be promising. This debate was launched in 2000 by a student petition complaining about the excessive use of mathematics in the teaching of economics and the lack of concern for actual issues and dissenting theories. Academics jumped into the debate with a petition and a counter-petition, one camp accusing the other of being removed from reality and of imposing a unique mainstream view, the other accusing the first of turning its back to science and of launching a political witch-hunt. This episode illustrates a need in France (and hopefully elsewhere) to clarify (including with the use of mathematics) the stakes and the short-comings of accepted analysis, and to put the practical issues of the public debate in theoretical and historical perspective. If it is not done at the university, there is little chance that it will be done elsewhere. This task requires more commentary than new results. Only rare geniuses produce new results a few times in a century; the rest of the economists just practice commentary. As Dennis Robertson once wrote: "It will not be easy for *anyone* for another twenty years to produce a positive and constructive work which is not in large measure a commentary on Keynes—that is the measure of his triumph" (quoted in Anyadike Danes 1987, 210). Now the historians of economic thought have a comparative advantage over the other economists: they are trained for commentary, practice it full-time, and know that they are doing so. They are happy (not ashamed) commentators. One may hope that this quality will still be recognized in teaching and research in the future.

References

Anyadike Danes, Michael. 1987. Robertson, Dennis. In vol. 4 of *The New Palgrave: A Dictionary of Economics*, edited by John Eatwell, Murray Milgate, and Peter Newman. London: Macmillan.

Arena, Richard. 2000. Les économistes français en 1950. *Revue économique* 51.5:969–1007.

Association Charles Gide pour l'Étude de la Pensée Économique. 1999. Enquête sur l'enseignement et la recherche en histoire de la pensée et méthodologie économiques. *La lettre Charles Gide* June: 5–6.

Béraud, Alain, and Gilbert Faccarello, eds. 2000. *Nouvelle histoire de la pensée économique*. Vols. 2 and 3. Paris: La Découverte.

Blaug, Mark. [1962] 1999. *La pensée économique*. Translated by Alain and Christiane Alcouffe. Paris: Economica.

———. 2001. No History of Ideas, Please, We're Economists. *Journal of Economic Perspectives* 15.1:145–64.

Combemale, Pierre. 1999. *Introduction à Keynes*. Paris: La Découverte.

Defalvard, Hervé. 2000. *La pensée économique néoclassique*. Paris: Dunod.

Deleplace, Ghislain. 1999. *Histoire de la pensée économique: "Du royaume agricole" de Quesnay au "monde à la Arrow-Debreu."* Paris: Dunod.

124   Ghislain Deleplace

Denis, Henri. [1966] 2000. *Histoire de la pensée économique*. Paris: PUF.

Duboeuf, Françoise. 1999. *Introduction aux théories économiques*. Paris: La Découverte.

Etner, François. 2000. *Histoire de la pensée économique*. Paris: Economica.

Gide, Charles, and Charles Rist. [1909] 2000. *Histoire des doctrines économiques depuis les physiocrates jusqu'à nos jours*. Paris: Dalloz.

Gnos, Claude. 2000. *Les grands auteurs en économie*. Caen: EMS.

Jeannin, Pierre. 1993. Auteurs et articles de la *Revue économique* (1980–1990): Une analyse comparative. *Revue économique* 44.1:117–41.

Lapidus, André. 2000. Introduction: 2000–1950 . . . et retour. *Revue économique* 51.5:955–67.

Marchal, André. 1953. *La pensée économique en France depuis 1945*. Paris: PUF.

Messori, Marcello. 1997. Histoire de l'analyse économique et économie politique: A propos des *Cahiers d'économie politique*. *Cahiers d'économie politique* 29:7–19.

Montoussé, Marc, ed. 2000. *Histoire de la pensée économique*. Rosny: Bréal.

Poulon, Frédéric. 2000. *La pensée économique de Keynes*. Paris: Dunod.

Ravix, Joël-Thomas. 1999. *La pensée économique classique, 1776–1870*. Paris: Dunod.

Steiner, Philippe. 2000. La *Revue économique* 1950–1980: La marche vers l'orthodoxie académique? *Revue économique* 51.5:1009–58.

Reflections on the Past and Current State of the History of Economic Thought in Germany

Bertram Schefold

Apart from the general history of economic thought—which is basically the same in every country, although modified by specific experiences and research interests—there are "national" histories of economic thought. National histories are concerned with the development of economic ideas in a particular nation as those ideas were affected by political history, the growth of institutions, and the general history of ideas. It is natural in the case of Germany to include Austria and the German-speaking part of Switzerland when discussing modern and early modern times, and the borders get less well defined if one goes further back to the Middle Ages. Language then is not a clear criterion either, since important early works were written not only in German, but also in Latin, French, and, relatively recently, English.

Cameralists already provided surveys of each other's writings in the eighteenth century. The first important German book on the history of economic thought was that by Julius Kautz ([1860] 1970). Theory, history, and the history of economic ideas were much more closely related during the era of the historical school in the nineteenth century than they are today. The advance of pure theory around the time of the first world war and the simultaneous emergence of a new historicism in Max Weber, Werner Sombart, and Arthur Spiethoff (See Schefold 1994a) resulted in a separation of the history of economic thought as history of economic analysis (Schumpeter 1924) and history of economic ideas (Salin 1923; see also Morgenstern and Schams 1933). The historical school had disappeared completely by about 1960. According to the recollections of older colleagues, the history of economic thought was not in high esteem at that time, since it was no longer regarded as indispensable for providing the economist with a general orientation in his or her subject. On the other hand, it had not yet become a discipline for special research. Investigations by Jürgen Backhaus (1983, 1997) show, however, that the form, volume, and intensity of teaching in the history of economic thought did not change much throughout the entire second half of the twentieth century. The history of economic thought is being taught in most departments of economics, primarily by colleagues who are employed for teaching and research in some other, special field but who like the subject and provide an overview in a one-semester course of two hours per week. Of course, there have also been some more extensive courses, special seminars, special lectures, and so on.

Specialization within the history of economic thought increased around 1980, when the *Dogmenhistorische Ausschuß* of the *Verein für Socialpolitik* was founded. This is a commission for the history of economic thought within the German economic association. Access is granted only to specifically elected members of the association. There are annual meetings that last for two days, and a distinguishing feature is that the papers presented are not limited in length; they are circulated in advance, and each usually is discussed at the meeting for two hours. Revised versions are published in the annual journal of the *Ausschuß*, with sometimes extensive footnotes referring to the discussions.

Chairs exclusively dedicated to the history of economic thought are exceptional, and most colleagues in Germany doubt whether a full professionalization of this subject would really be to its advantage. Increased concentration on the history of economic thought, however, has created a need for new associations, with open access for all scholars interested in the field, especially the young ones, and for new journals. This need is being fulfilled mainly by international institutions.

Research and Teaching in the History of Economic Thought in Germany: Some Special Aspects

I have already had the opportunity to describe the working of the *Dogmenhistorische Ausschuß* for this journal in 1994 (Schefold 1994b), and I wrote a sequel to this for the Gide Society in 1998 (Schefold 2001); only a few points shall be repeated. In particular, it should be stressed again that important work is being done also outside the *Dogmenhistorische Ausschuß*. The East should not be omitted. There were fewer interesting economists in the former German Democratic Republic than in some other East European countries, like Hungary and Poland, but history of economic thought was being taught in the Marxist tradition and there resulted some editions of classical texts that continue to be useful, in particular the Marx-Engels edition, editions of physiocratic writings and of Johann Heinrich von Thünen, and others. A number of textbooks and special studies in the history of economic thought appeared in Germany around the time of unification, such as the textbook by Gerhard Kolb (1997). The special studies followed different orientations. Without concealing the subjectivity of my choice, I mention A. Bürgin's (1993) remarkable treatise on the emergence of the concept of political economy. The analytical *History of Economic Theory: Classic Contributions, 1720–1980*, by Swiss economist Jürg Niehans (1990), was published in English. At the other extreme were contributions linking the history of economic thought with cultural history. Several studies were concerned with Goethe: Bernd Mahl (1982) earlier had demonstrated that Goethe's economic knowledge was quite extensive; Hans Christoph Binswanger (1985) provided a highly original and stimulating interpretation of the Faust drama in economic terms. Work in Ph.D. dissertations has ranged widely. For instance, J. X. Kraus (2000) wrote on the Stoa and its influence on physiocracy and Adam Smith, and C. Baloglou (1995) addressed early mathematical economics in Germany. There were also projects: a group around G. Bombach (1976, 1981) in Basel investigated the pre-Keynesians in Germany, H. Hagemann (1997) published on German emigration, and new attention has been given to national socialism (Janssen 1998). Jürgen Backhaus in Maastricht (now Erfurt) regularly has convened conferences on history of economic thought in Heilbronn, and conference volumes have appeared, such as those dedicated to Gustav Schmoller and to Sombart. The *Klassiker der Nationalökonomie*, a very large project that I took over from Horst Claus Recktenwald in 1991 and that is scheduled for completion in 2002, entails the reprinting of one hundred classical texts, each as a bibliophile facsimile of the first edition and accompanied by a separate volume of commentaries. Many of the best known economists of the world have contributed new essays (translated, if necessary, into German) on the classic text in question in the perspective of modern theoretical achievements. A complete edition of the comments on the classics, ranging from Xenophon to Paul Samuelson, is in preparation. An attempt was made to represent all the important past schools and national currents of economics in the series, including a small number of texts that do not pertain to the European and American tradition (e.g., Ibn Khaldun, a Chinese classic, and a Japanese classic), and it was natural, given the place of publication, that special emphasis was given to German texts.

The history of economic thought in Germany is, not surprisingly, influenced to a considerable extent by the wish to improve our understanding of German political history and to replace simplistic accounts of what led to the German catastrophe by a differentiated appraisal. A significant contribution to this effort has been made by an American, Heath Pearson (1997). Pearson argues that the German historical school was part of a European movement that was interesting not so much because history and economics were brought together, but because the foundations of modern institutional economics were laid. Erich Streißler (1990) has emphasized that the authors of the historical school, especially of the older historical school, were more theoretical than is commonly thought, and that they prepared the ground for the neoclassical revolution, with Carl Menger being indebted to Wilhelm Roscher. On the other hand, it seems clear to me that the *Verstehende Nationalökonomie* (intuitive economics) of Weber, Sombart, and Spiethoff, a later outgrowth of the historical school, represented an attempt to describe the specificity of economic forms prevailing in a given period and area in terms of economic styles in order to overcome the idea of linear progress and of an incessant evolution toward "higher" forms. Development was not denied, but the economic forms encountered in the past or on other continents were to be regarded not as primitive precursors of modern economy, backward in technique, rationality, and institutions, but as specific formations, to be characterized in positive terms, by showing how prevailing mentalities, economic organization, methods of production, and the social and cultural life fitted together. Thus, there has been a revival also in Weber as an economist (Nau 1997).

The embedment of the economy in society has been compared in the conceptions of the historical, the neohistoricist, and the Austrian schools (Peukert 1998), and the concept of the economic style has been reintroduced into economics in order to analyze actual problems, such as that of European unification (Klump 1996). The interdisciplinary character of the historical school has been taken seriously, and two conferences have been organized, attended by representatives of law, economics, sociology, and political sciences, in order to investigate how each of these disciplines changed internally and in relation to the others in consequence of the first and the second world wars, which are, with the associated political movements, regarded as intellectual turning points. If a simplifying account is permitted: it was demonstrated that the delusion associated with the defeat of the first world war helped the move toward neohistoricism on the part of a small but interesting group of German economists who promoted the idea of *Verstehende Nationalökonomie* (intuitive economics). The second world war, meanwhile, led to a break with specific German traditions and the installment of a new paradigm of progress around 1960, associated with the rise of Keynesianism, econometrics, and the program of controlling growth and the cycle by means of fiscal and monetary policy (Nörr, Schefold, and Tenbruck 1994; Acham, Nörr, and Schefold 1998; Schefold 1999).

Much more could be done, especially if one takes earlier periods into account. The cameralist literature in Germany is vast. Most of it may be unexciting from a modern theoretical point of view, but the texts should be reread nevertheless in the perspective of a new generation, asking new questions regarding trends in the development of ideas, international cross-connections, and so forth. Economics was established as an academic discipline in Germany relatively early, which adds to the weight of material to be considered. Roscher's *History of Economics in Germany* ([1874] 1992) is still unsurpassed as a guide to the rich literature on economics in Germany prior to the Thirty Years' War. In particular, the time of the Reformation should be reconsidered, when a period of prosperity led to remarkable reflections, such as those of Conrad Peutinger in Augsburg on monopoly and competition (around 1530) and Leonhard Fronsperger's praise of self-interest of 1565, printed in Frankfurt, 150 years prior to Bernard Mandeville and much in the same spirit (Schefold 2000).

The European Society for the History of Economic Thought

The history of economic thought at the European level will have to mediate between two opposed tendencies. On the one hand, English is becoming the international language of economists, and the knowledge of other foreign languages is diminishing so that even historians of economic thought concentrate more on research in English sources. On the other hand, it is becoming increasingly clear that economics had been more diverse at least until the First World War and that it would be misleading to speak of a dominance of English economics up to that period. National schools of economics developed almost everywhere between mercantilism and historicism, beginning in the sixteenth and seventeenth centuries. These continued to exert their influence even after the emergence of a more cosmopolitan political economy and of economics in the eighteenth and nineteenth centuries. The links that existed between those earlier schools, for instance between Spanish mercantilism and Austrian cameralism (in that case mediated by the Hapsburg administration), have begun to be uncovered only recently and thanks to specialized studies that require a high degree of dedication to the subject (see Lluch 1996). There was perhaps not more international communication among scholars in the nineteenth century than earlier, but it is more easily traced. New tasks for the historian of economic thought emerge in this perspective; they require a multilingual and interdisciplinary approach.

Meanwhile, a European Society for the History of Economic Thought (ESHET) was founded in December 1995 in Nice, the initiative having been taken by Richard Arena. It has since grown rapidly to more than five hundred members. Five annual conferences have been held in Marseilles, Bologna, Valencia, Graz, and Darmstadt. Three conference volumes have been edited by Luigi Pasinetti and Bertram Schefold (1999), by Pier Luigi Porta, Roberto Scazzieri, and Andrew Skinner (2001), and by Stephan Böhm, Christian Gehrke, Heinz Kurz, and Richard Sturn (2001). An annual newsletter is also being published.[1] The constitution states, among other things, that the society shall promote teaching and research in the history of economic thought in Europe, taking account of different traditions and languages. In fact, informal groups have arisen within the society that help to achieve that goal, and they get together at the conferences in special sessions, either because the conference organizers are aware of the links or because the groups organize special sessions themselves. There are, for example, those with a special interest in physiocracy, in Adam Smith, or in the economics of antiquity. A significant number of participants at each conference contribute to the

1. For details on these organizational points and to consult the newsletters, see http://www.eshet-web.org/.

conference theme from the point of view of their national traditions. In this way, I have learned that Keynesian ideas had been anticipated not only in Germany, but also in Italy and in countries to which I might not have looked, like Spain and Portugal. Only gradually, more communication grows between East and West Europeans on the history of economic thought. West Europeans know in principle that intense debates took place in Russia from the eighteenth century onward on all kinds of economic questions, with all the significant schools being represented there (classical and liberal economics, historical school, Marxists of different varieties, etc.), but very few details are known in the West. In one of the sessions at the 2001 Darmstadt conference we had a very lively discussion on whether it is legitimate to speak of a Russian school of economics, in spite of all the foreign influences, and if so, on what basis it was formed. Hypotheses ranged from the thesis that the Russian schools were all similar because of a certain tradition of state interventionism to the idea that they had certain traits of thinking in common because of the Orthodox religious tradition.

Complaints have arisen and been discussed at roundtables that the history of economic thought is becoming less important in some European countries, especially in Great Britain, that only relatively senior colleagues participate, and that younger ones are prevented from doing so because there is pressure on them to publish theoretical and empirical articles in refereed journals, but not to engage in history. While the complaints, no doubt, have a basis in reality, it is difficult to be pessimistic as long as the society continues in its spectacular growth. At any rate, there are many colleagues with a genuine interest to approach economic problems in a historical perspective, and there is the desire on the part of students to improve their orientation and general knowledge on the basis of a historical overview. Both sides feel that many ideas are best understood by tracing their historical origin.

Some Personal Observations and Conclusions

I have some messages to offer for a critical discussion. The first regards the history of analytical economics (which has here been neglected a little because the theme forced me to focus on national traditions): precisely the best-known modern theorists who participated in the work for the *Klassiker der Nationalökonomie* as commentators proved amazingly competent and knowledgeable in the history of the subdiscipline in which they are active themselves. This is known for Paul Samuelson, but I can testify that it is also true for Kenneth Arrow, Edmond Malinvaud, and others who have read authors like Ricardo, Walras, or Pareto carefully in order to promote their own ideas. The immediate prehistory to a problem is usually best known to the person who recently has done most to solve it. This is obvious, and the historian of economic thought therefore usually retreats to earlier periods. But good theorists extend the prehistory they feel they ought to know. Hence, the good modern monetary economist knows the great nineteenth century debates about monetary economics. It is important to convey this to those young colleagues who erroneously believe that it pays not to know history.

It is possible for the present-day economist to pursue economics without knowing any language other than English. It is impossible to study the broad past of economics without knowing other languages, and it may occasionally become necessary to learn a foreign language at least to the point of being able to read it only to approach one important specific problem in the history of economic thought. Both Karl Marx and Max Weber learned Russian at a relatively advanced age: Marx in order to study the Russian peasantry, Weber in order to study the Russian revolution. They did this although they had already spent considerable time learning other foreign languages in earlier phases of their lives. Many nineteenth-century economists were able to at least read texts in Latin, Greek, and three or four modern languages. The decline in language skills is possibly the worst threat to the general history of economic thought.[2] We shall have to do more to make texts of different national traditions accessible in other languages, in particular in English, but there are clearly limits to what one can do by way of translation, and serious research on any author will always presuppose that one learns the language in which that author expressed him- or herself. I am inclined to say this even in the case of Marx, although almost everything he ever wrote has been translated into English at the expense of Russian and East German workers. An easy way to impress the public with the importance of going back to the original formulations would be this: journals should make it their policy to encourage authors to publish quotations in the original language and to provide translations or summaries of translations in the language of the journal only in footnotes.

2. It is also deplorable from a cultural point of view, but this is not my concern here.

The national traditions that remain to be discovered for an international audience are many. Given the theme of this roundtable, I have mainly emphasized Eastern Europe. It is clear that we also know very little about India, China, Korea, Japan, and other countries whose traditions will continue to influence the course of world development. We should encourage students from distant countries to broaden our knowledge by writing theses on some subject taken from the history of economic thought of their countries.

I believe that it is good if the history of economic thought remains a hobby of many economists and a specialty only for a few. Every reader with a good general culture and the required special knowledge in the field can participate in the research aimed at providing better interpretations of given texts, but it is perhaps the main task of specialists to make texts accessible by providing critical editions, publishing manuscripts, and making translations available. I am sorry that German historians of economic thought have not done as much as might perhaps be expected, given older German traditions in philology. Editions are published but only as reprints, only selections of the correspondence of authors even of the rank of Joseph Schumpeter have been edited, and translations of key works by authors like Schmoller (whether one likes him or not, he was of historical importance) are available only in small selections.

I believe that courses in the history of economic thought should primarily address second- or third-year students, not beginners or Ph.D. students. Seminars on special topics in the history of economic thought can be profitable for Ph.D. students, however. We at J. W. Goethe-Universität have also had seminars in which Ph.D. students of any orientation within economics were encouraged to present research on the prehistory of the problem of the theses on which they were working. The level of historical knowledge and the ability to present historical materials turned out to be very modest in the case of the average student, without a special historical orientation—to that extent, they lacked a good general culture—but I believe the endeavor was worthwhile nevertheless. The European Society for the History of Economic Thought offers special Ph.D. seminars at the beginning of each conference, where the Ph.D. students are given more time to present their papers than in ordinary sessions and where several senior colleagues provide comments. These students (who write theses in the history of economic thought) were grateful for the opportunity provided.

The tasks in the history of economic thought are many, and interest in the subject is widespread among students; the difficulty, at least in Germany, concerns the colleagues who are under pressure to sacrifice chairs of economists that are to be transformed into posts for business administrators. Most faculties of economics are therefore reluctant to offer chairs to young scholars who, by writing their theses or books for the habilitation on a historical subject, became specialized in the history of economic thought.[3] In order to obtain a chair, the historian of economic thought in Germany must, with very few exceptions, be able to demonstrate that he or she is as competent as any rival in some other speciality (e.g., economic theory). This is a demanding requirement (although it is not formal, some have met it). Setting aside this worry (which is a serious one), the outlook is not bad.

References

Acham, K., K. W. Nörr, and B. Schefold, eds. 1998. *Erkenntnisgewinne, Erkenntnisverluste. Kontinuitäten und Diskontinuitäten in den Wirtschafts-, Rechts- und Sozialwissenschaften zwischen den 20er und 50er Jahren.* Stuttgart: Steiner.
Backhaus, J. 1983. Theoriegeschichte—wozu? Eine theoretische und empirische Untersuchung. In vol. 3 of *Studien zur Entwicklung der ökonomischen Theorie*, edited by H. Scherf. Berlin: Duncker & Humblot.
———. 1997. Der augenblickliche Stand der dogmenhistorischen Lehre an deutschsprachigen Universitäten (1976–1995): Fortführung einer Erhebung. In vol. 17 of *Studien zur Entwicklung der ökonomischen Theorie*, edited by E. W. Streißler. Berlin: Duncker & Humblot.
Baloglou, C. 1995. *Die Vertreter der mathematischen Nationalökonomie in Deutschland zwischen 1838 und 1871.* Marburg: Metropolis.
Binswanger, H. C. 1985. *Geld und Magie.* Stuttgart: Weitbrecht.
Böhm, S., et al., eds. 2001. *Is There Progress in Economics? Knowledge, Truth, and the History of Economic Thought.* Cheltenham, U.K.: Elgar.
Bombach, G., et al., eds. 1976. *Der Keynesianismus.* Vol. 2 of *Die beschäftigungspolitische Diskussion vor Keynes in Deutschland.* Berlin: Springer.
———, eds. 1981. *Der Keynesianismus.* Vol. 3 of *Die geld- und beschäftigungspolitische Diskussion in Deutschland zur Zeit von Keynes.* Berlin: Springer.
Bürgin, A. 1993. *Zur Soziogenese der Politischen Ökonomie. Wirtschaftsgeschichtliche und dogmenhistorische Betrachtungen.* Marburg: Metropolis.

3. German universities traditionally demand a second book (after the thesis for the Ph.D.) as a qualification for a permanent academic appointment. The process by which this book is accepted by the faculty is called *habilitation*; acceptance entails the right to lecture.

Hagemann, H., ed. 1997. *Zur deutschsprachigen wirtschaftswissenschaftlichen Emigration nach 1933*. Marburg: Metropolis.

Janssen, H. 1998. *Nationalökonomie und Nationalsozialismus. Die deutsche Volkswirtschaftslehre in den dreißiger Jahren*. Vol. 10 of *Beiträge zur Geschichte der deutschsprachigen Ökonomie*. Marburg: Metropolis.

Kautz, J. [1860] 1970. *Die geschichtliche Entwicklung der National-Ökonomik und ihrer Literatur*. Glashütten: Auvermann.

Klump, R. 1996. *Wirtschaftskultur, Wirtschaftsstil und Wirtschaftsordnung. Methoden und Ergebnisse der Wirtschaftskulturforschung*. Marburg: Metropolis.

Kolb, G. 1997. *Geschichte der Volkswirtschaftslehre*. Munich: Vahlen.

Kraus, J. X. 2000. *Die Stoa und ihr Einfluß auf die Nationalökonomie*. Marburg: Metropolis.

Lluch, E. 1996. L'Espanya vençuda del segle XVIII. Cameralisme, Corona d'Aragó i "Partit aragonès" o "Militar." In *La Catalunya vençuda del segle XVIII*. Barcelona: Editions 62.

Mahl, B. 1982. *Goethes ökonomisches Wissen*. Bern: Lang.

Morgenstern, O., and E. Schams. 1933. Eine Bibliographie der allgemeinen Lehrgeschichte der Nationalökonomie. *Zeitschrift für Nationalökonomie* 4:389–97.

Nau, H. H. 1997. *Eine Wissenschaft vom Menschen*. Berlin: Duncker & Humblot.

Niehans, J. 1990. *A History of Economic Theory: Classic Contributions, 1720–1980*. Baltimore, Md.: John Hopkins University Press.

Nörr, K. W., B. Schefold, and F. Tenbruck, eds. 1994. *Deutsche Geisteswissenschaften zwischen Kaiserreich und Republik. Zur Entwicklung von Nationalökonomie, Rechtswissenschaft und Sozialwissenschaft im 20. Jahrhundert*. Stuttgart: Steiner.

Pasinetti, L. L., and B. Schefold, eds. 1999. *The Impact of Keynes on Economics in the Twentieth Century*. Cheltenham, U.K.: Elgar.

Pearson, H. 1997. *Origins of Law and Economics: The Economists' New Science of Law 1830–1930*. Cambridge: Cambridge University Press.

Peukert, H. 1998. *Das Handlungsparadigma in der Nationalökonomie*. Marburg: Metropolis.

Porta, P. L., R. Scazzieri, and A. Skinner, eds. 2001. *Knowledge, Social Institutions, and the Division of Labour*. Cheltenham, U.K.: Elgar.

Roscher, W. [1874] 1992. *Geschichte der National-Oekonomik in Deutschland*. Düsseldorf: Verlag Wirtschaft und Finanzen.

Salin, E. 1923. *Geschichte der Volkswirtschaftslehre*. Berlin: J. Springer.

Schefold, B. 1994a. Nationalökonomie und Kulturwissenschaften: Das Konzept des Wirtschaftsstils. In *Deutsche Geisteswissenschaften zwischen Kaiserreich und Republik. Zur Entwicklung von Nationalökonomie, Rechtswissenschaft und Sozialwissenschaft im 20. Jahrhundert*, edited by K. W. Nörr, B. Schefold, and F. Tenbruck. Stuttgart: Steiner.

————. 1994b. The Revival of Economic Thought in Germany: The Dogmenhi-storischer Ausschuss. *HOPE* 26.2:327–35.

————. 1999. The Afterglow of the German Historical School, 1945–1960. In *Economics, Welfare Policy, and the History of Economic Thought: Essays in Honour of Arnold Heertje*, edited by M. Fase, W. Kanning, and D. Walker. Cheltenham, U.K.: Elgar.

————. 2000. Wirtschaft und Geld im Zeitalter der Reformation. In *Vademecum zu drei klassischen Schriften frühneuzeitlicher Münzpolitik*. [Kommentarband zum Reprint: Die drei Flugschriften über den Münzstreit der sächsischen Albertiner und Ernestiner: a) Gemeyne stimmen von der Muntz (Dresden 1530); b) Die Müntz Belangende. Antwort und Bericht (o.O. 1530); c) Gemeine Stymmen Von der Müntze: Apologia . . . und Vorantwortung (Leipzig 1548).] Düsseldorf: Verlag Wirtschaft und Finanzen.

————. 2001. L'histoire de la pensée économique en Allemagne. History of Economic Thought in Germany: Some Recent Activities. *La lettre Charles Gide* 5 (April): 4–8.

Schumpeter, J. 1924. Epochen der Dogmen- und Methodengeschichte. In *Grundriß der Sozialökonomik*. 1st division, 2d enlarged edition. Tübingen: Mohr.

Streißler, E. 1990. The Influence of German Economics on the Work of Menger and Marshall. In *Carl Menger and His Legacy in Economics*, edited by Bruce J. Caldwell. *HOPE* 22 (supplement): 31–68.

The History of Economic Thought in Spain and Portugal: A Brief Survey

José Luís Cardoso

In December 1999, the Iberian Association of the History of Economic Thought was created in Barcelona. The basic objective of its founding members (thirty Spanish and ten Portuguese) was to promote the organization of academic conferences every two years, so that, by means of this regularly held forum, greater visibility and projection might be afforded to the results of the research being undertaken in both countries.

The creation of this association was the culmination of a series of bilateral contacts that have intensified over the last ten years and that, in a certain way, also correspond to a particular process for the renewal of the scientific study of the history of economic thought being followed in both Spain and Portugal. The aim of this short text is therefore to provide an overview of this activity and summarize the current situation of the discipline in the two countries.[1] Although the central focus is inevitably directed toward more recent developments, it is worth remembering how it all began.

In Spain, the first histories of economic thought, or, to be more precise, the first reports and guides seeking to record the legacy of past economists, date from the end of the eighteenth century. In their writings, Gaspar M. de Jovellanos and, above all, Pedro de Campomanes (1775) have left us with valuable testimonies about the work of those authors who wrote about economic and financial matters throughout the

---

1. For a more detailed guide to the historiography of economic thought in Portugal, see Cardoso 1998; for Spain, see Braun and González 1991, Almenar 1989, and Perdices 1999.

sixteenth and seventeenth centuries. Both Juan Sempere y Guarinos (1801–21) and José Canga Arguelles ([1826] 1968) undertook a similar effort of providing a written record of past authors.

In Portugal, it was not until the end of the 1810s that the first systematic report appeared about the contents and significance of the economic doctrines and ideas of the past, seeking to integrate Portuguese authors into the context of the European production of economic literature (Lisboa [1819] 1994).

These pioneering historians of Iberian economic thought share at least one particularly interesting facet with their counterparts in other countries: namely, that they were simultaneously protagonists in and creators of their own object of study. In fact, all those who helped to keep alive the memory of their predecessors also later enjoyed unanimous recognition for the importance of their own works. In other words, acting as historians of economic thought represented for them both a starting point and a useful tool for making a general assessment of the significance of the discursive practices that they themselves continued by following either similar or distinct methodological, doctrinal, or theoretical paths.

In Spain, the compilation of such summaries continued into the second half of the nineteenth century, having reached a particularly important moment with the work of Manuel Colmeiro ([1861] 1978). Similar attempts at summarizing economic ideas were also made in Portugal during the same period, namely through the inclusion of brief histories of the discipline in university textbooks for the teaching of political economy, which were themselves given a certain systematization in the work of Moses B. Amzalak (1928).

In both countries, we are faced with a historiographic tradition that is important, above all, for its collection of biobibliographical information and the identification of sources to which a less specialized public would normally have difficulty gaining access. Or, in other words, it represents a type of approach that has eminently heuristic concerns and avoids any attempt to deliver a critical interpretation or detailed assessment of the significance of the works recorded and consulted. It would not be too outrageous to consider that such a historiographic tradition imposed its own authority and extended its influence over several decades, albeit with one or two honorable exceptions that were, nonetheless, not sufficient to break a hegemony that was maintained until the end of the 1970s. For the specific case of the history of Spanish economic thought, it is important to highlight among these exceptions the contributions made by foreign historians (such as Joseph A. Schumpeter, Marjorie Grice-Hutchison, Earl J. Hamilton, and Robert S. Smith) who, in the 1950s and 1960s, were interested in, and produced innovative works about, certain specific periods or authors, such as the Salamanca school, the *arbitristas*, and the reformers of the Enlightenment (cf. Quintana 1999, 15–27).

From what has just been said, it can be understood that over the last twenty years, in both Spain and Portugal, there has been a profound renewal in the way in which the history of economic thought is produced.[2] I shall now attempt to show the main characteristics of the change and renewal that have taken place, highlighting some of the aspects that are common to both countries.

One of the first points that should be highlighted is the critical reedition of classical works and, in some cases, the critical edition of unpublished works. In keeping with the elementary principle that it is impossible to study and write the history of economics without a full knowledge of the primary sources, there has been a notable amount of publishing activity designed to afford greater access to the works and authors that are considered to be among the most fundamental. Academic institutions from both countries have managed to obtain generous partnerships for the publication of works of this type, which it would be difficult to justify through market rules alone. In Spain, the Institute of Fiscal Studies began, in 1974, to publish the series *Clásicos del Pensamiento Económico Español*, which so far has produced twenty-three titles. In Portugal, it was the Bank of Portugal that began in 1980 to publish the *Colecção de Obras Clássicas do Pensamento Económico Português*, with twenty works published so far in a total of thirty volumes. All the books published include introductory studies written by the respective editors, as well as explanatory notes and, in the case of the Portuguese works, indexes organized according to both name and subject. In this way, the publication of new editions of classical texts also became a pretext for a critical review of the interpretations provided by the historiographic tradition, while, at the same time, making it possible to provide new readings and fresh suggestions for their interpretation.

2. Some signs of a certain growing maturity, which proved to be a decisive stimulus for this movement of renewal, were provided in Portugal through the syntheses written by Castro (1978, 1979, and 1980), and in Spain through the contributions of Beltrán (1976), Estapé (1971), and Velarde (1974).

It should also be said that, in the case of Spain, in addition to the works of the Institute of Fiscal Studies series, there are other series either published or supported by organizations belonging to the autonomous governments, such as the collection of *Clàssics del Pensament Econòmic Català*, the collection of *Clásicos del Pensamiento Económico Vasco*, and the *Biblioteca de Economistas Aragoneses*. If we add to all these series and collections the separate publication of classical texts by the better known authors, we may conclude that anyone wishing to research the economic works of Iberian authors will have easy access not only to the main primary sources, but also to a wide range of interpretative essays and exhaustive bibliographical records about original works and the secondary literature.

The editorial work undertaken has made it possible to amass information and knowledge and, moreover, make it accessible to a less erudite, but much vaster, public through works designed to register and disseminate the most important data available about authors and works from the past. The preparation of historical dictionaries and small books included in widely circulated collections is the clearest sign of this desire to jump the university walls and ensure that a new form of knowledge can actually reach the wider public, both in Spain (Perdices and Reeder 2000) and Portugal (Cardoso 2001). In the Spanish case, attention should also be drawn to the preparation of the monumental and encyclopedic eight-volume work *Economía y Economistas Españoles*, which establishes a pattern that would be hard to achieve in other countries, especially in view of the diversity of themes that it covers, its extensive time span, and the rich interpretation provided by the numerous contributions.

The historians of economic thought in Spain and Portugal are mainly to be found working in the economics departments or faculties of the most important state universities in these countries. In the case of Portugal, the main centers with regularly organized teaching and research activities are based at the Universidade Técnica de Lisboa and the Universidade do Porto. There is also a very active group organized under the auspices of the department of the history of ideas at Universidade Nova de Lisboa. As far as Spain is concerned, not only are there many more researchers undertaking regular work in this area, but they are also more dispersed. However, the main centers of production are the economics faculties at the Universities of Barcelona, Complutense in Madrid, Valencia, and Zaragoza.

These universities compel undergraduate students to spend at least one semester studying the history of economic thought. The typical program of these disciplines covers the customary sequence of authors and schools from mercantilism to the new classical economics. The same program is followed in other Spanish universities that have not been named here, although in many cases these disciplines are optional. At the Faculdade de Economia da Universidade do Porto, it is also compulsory for students taking a Ph.D. in economics to study the history of economic thought, a unique requirement among Iberian universities. Although there are no specific master's degree or Ph.D. programs available in the history of economic thought, dissertations are frequently written (both in economics and history courses) on themes that can be classified within this area.

One of the most evident features in the activity of Iberian historians of economic thought is the close contact and permanent dialogue that they maintain with researchers working in other disciplinary areas, namely philosophy, the history of ideas, sociology, political science, cultural studies, and economic history. Consequently, there is an interesting ambivalence to be noted in terms of their home institutions, since they are mostly based in economics departments but maintain close links with other social sciences. This would seem to be one of the most promising signs of the vitality of a field of knowledge that claims to be open to, and shared by, different but complementary perspectives of analysis. In the specific case of economic history, attention is drawn to the pioneering role played by some of its more prominent contemporary representatives in making widespread use of sources from the history of economic doctrines and theories. Similarly important are the annual meetings of the Spanish and Portuguese economic history associations, which have organized thematic sessions at which historians of economic thought have also been made welcome.

In view of the prevailing cult of interdisciplinarity and the difficulties in engaging in—and resistance to—excessive specialization, there are no Spanish or Portuguese journals on the history of economic thought. Publication strategies are geared, above all, toward the production of national journals devoted to economics, history, and the social sciences. This results in the production of only a few works for the market of international journals published in English, which means that the most significant part of the original research work undertaken by Iberian historians of economic thought remains largely unknown. This situation is a cause for particular concern in Spain, in view of its larger number of researchers and the significant number of studies produced each year.

As for the subjects and themes that have been the main focus of study in both countries, there is a serious imbalance that works to the detriment of universal authors and problems and tends to favor national topics and personalities. Clearly, because of the simple fact that economics professors in Spain and Portugal teach courses in the history of economic thought that extend far beyond the frontiers of their own countries, there is a certain amount of research work being conducted on subjects and authors that have carved a particular niche for themselves in the universal history of economic science. However, much of this work is motivated by the usefulness that it has for improving understanding of national situations or problems. This is a subject requiring most careful justification, since it is here that one finds the specificity of the Iberian historiography that is being examined in this survey.

One of the main factors linking historians of economic thought in the two Iberian countries is the experience that they share in relation to the formation and development of economic science. In fact, we are dealing here with two countries that have never reached, or only very episodically drawn close to, the front line of theoretical production in the field of economics.

Such a circumstance explains an essential feature of Iberian historiography, namely, the special attention that has been paid to the study of the processes involved in the transmission, assimilation, and original adaptation of economic ideas, theories, and policies produced in other international spheres. And this gives rise to the particular concern, to be noted at the level of methodology, with defining the basic foundations that explain and justify the construction of a national history of economic thought.

Attempts have been made both autonomously (Lluch 1980, Cardoso 1997) and jointly (Cardoso and Lluch 1999) to define a general framework for the study of national cases, accepting as an essential methodological premise that the analysis should be centered on a comparative study of the experiences of different countries. For those who are committed to this type of research, such a strategy also represents a justification of the benefits that this may provide for the further development of the universal history of economic science. The main guidelines that have aroused the interest of Iberian researchers, within the scope of their analysis, are as follows:

1. Assessing the awareness of the abstract theoretical principles that define mainstream economics, so that the levels of perception, familiarization, and distortion of source ideas or conceptual relations may be tested.
2. Analyzing the processes involved in the reception, assimilation, adaptation, and social appropriation of economic discourse produced abroad, while bearing in mind the particular features of the receiver countries' social and economic reality.
3. Studying the institutional and technical mechanisms for the spread of, and access to, economic discourse, as in the case of the translations made and their quality, the circulation and reading rates of foreign and national books, linguistic adaptations, images associated with the territory of political economy, standardized forms of academic and journalistic rhetoric, and professional jargon.
4. Analyzing the conditions underlying the production and spread of economic knowledge and practices, involving the participation of informal social groups; institutions of an academic, scientific, or professional nature; and the organs of political power.
5. Studying the formation and gradual enrichment of a tradition (or various traditions) of economic thought, while also explaining how, in an adaptive or innovative manner, such a tradition has had repercussions on continuous or discontinuous phases of evolution.

The main conclusion that can be drawn from the importance given to these guidelines, and applied to different authors, schools, and periods, is that over the last few years the Iberian historiographic agenda has been centered on the construction of national histories. It is a focus that has affected the very choice of the most recurrent research themes. Thus, the importance that, ever since the pioneering work of Marjorie Grice-Hutchison (1978), has been given to the study of the renewal of scholastic thought and the School of Salamanca is fully justified by the emergence in Spain (and their repercussions in Portugal) of these innovative forms of economic thought. In fact, their origins and developments within the Iberian Peninsula cannot be contested in any way.

The same thing can be said in relation to both the mercantilist economic literature, which is particularly given to the discussion of monetary matters, and the rich and diversified set of opinions, suggestions, memoirs, proposals, and projects normally considered together under the Spanish title of *arbitrismo* and the Portuguese title of *alvitrismo*. In fact, the attention given to these movements, which together express the particular Iberian originality in regard to the discussion of matters of interest to princes and merchants, has been one of the main themes to which Spanish and Portuguese historians have devoted their attention.[3]

Another case in which Iberian economic thought has shown some capacity for original adaptation and which has consequently aroused the attention of scholars is that relating to the economic thought of the Enlightenment and the simultaneous use of physiocratic, Smithian, and cameralist influences in the construction of a reforming economic discourse. The desire to overcome the obstacles raised by the social, economic, and financial structure of the ancien régime, without the need for recourse to violent political revolutions, led to the creation of various institutions (societies, associations, academies) geared toward the production and dissemination of useful knowledge, with a view to achieving a better identification and improved allocation of available resources. Besides the practical know-how that had direct implications for the organization of the structures of production and trade, a great deal of importance was also given to the knowledge provided by the studies of political economy; that is, by the science that supposedly had the prerogative of explaining the nature and causes of the wealth of nations.

The Iberian historiographic production about this period between 1780 and 1810 has also stressed the role played by the knowledge of political economy in forming a different attitude toward the economic role of the Iberian colonies in South America. Despite the inevitable processes tending toward independence, it was interesting to note the attempts made to renew the empires, only this time no longer through recourse to the colonial pact based essentially on the principles of mercantilism, but through an appeal to the advantages of the principles of free trade.

In this and other matters—and in the light of the guidelines referred to above, which provide the framework for the study of national cases of the history of economic thought—the works produced by Iberian historiography point to the need to pay even closer attention to the connection between, on the one hand, doctrinal and ideological presuppositions and

3. A complete bibliography of books and articles produced on these and other research themes would exhaust the word limit fixed for this text. Those readers interested in further explanations and bibliographical references for the various subjects mentioned here will find up-to-date information for Spain in Quintana 1999, and for Portugal in Almodovar and Cardoso 1998 and Cardoso 2001.

positive and preferably universal laws and, on the other, the pragmatic actions and measures of economic policy that were in fact implemented. It is also through this type of careful methodological attention that we may understand that, after all, the theoretical fragility of the followers and disseminators of classical economics represents a renunciation of the political implications of classical economics. However, the importance that has been assumed by critical and heterodox currents of thought, almost completely left out of the traditional textbooks of the history of economic thought, shows how much better suited such currents were to the aim of providing the sort of doctrinal guidelines and instruments of economic policy that brought the Iberian economies closer to the patterns of greater development enjoyed by the main European countries.

Just as Ricardian classical economics had only a very scanty influence, marginalist and neoclassical economics also fell on fairly stony and unfertile ground in the Iberian Peninsula. This aspect has been fairly well highlighted by the historians of economic thought in the two countries. It does not mean that there were no isolated voices seeking to disseminate the fundamental principles and methodological guidelines of Marshallian and Walrasian economics. Nonetheless, in global terms, what generally prevailed until the 1940s was an eclectic economic way of thinking that was fairly insensitive to the process of disciplinary normalization and conceptual standardization lying at the origin of modern economic science.

At the beginning of the 1940s in Spain, and at the end of the same decade in Portugal, there occurred a number of significant changes in the structure of university economics teaching. Besides the particular Iberian adaptation of the language and toolbox of neoclassical economics, there was also the introduction of Keynesian economics. In this way, it was possible to begin to gradually eliminate the lags between the economic languages used in the Iberian Peninsula and those used in the main countries of the Western world. The process involved in the assimilation, diffusion, and adaptation of Keynesianism has in fact been one of the themes that have most attracted the attention of researchers in both countries. One of the reasons for such interest is certainly to be found in the fact that, in this way, it has been possible to achieve a renewed understanding of the doctrines of economic corporatism and the economic policy experiments associated with the authoritarian regimes of Franco and Salazar. Keynes's work should not be confused with the founding principles of such regimes. However, Keynes's lack of belief in the market's self-correcting capacities and the importance that he attaches to state intervention to stimulate demand and guarantee full employment represent an important intellectual mainstay for those who make these arguments an integral part of their political action.

For the various themes and problems that have been briefly mentioned here, I have tried to highlight those that have aroused the simultaneous interest of researchers from the two countries, without seeking to provide an exhaustive inventory of what have in fact been their specific subjects of study.

I have also tried to leave to one side the methodological and ideological divergences or antagonisms that inevitably come to the fore whenever one observes and assesses the work that has been produced by different people, working in different institutions, in relation to either the same period, the same author, or the same theme. Under the present circumstances, the concealment of such divergences or antagonisms serves the purpose of arguing that they are of lesser importance when compared with the efforts of convergence and complementarity that have made possible much progress and a greater institutional consolidation of the discipline of the history of economic thought in the two Iberian countries over the last twenty years.

In December 2001, a total of forty-five participants convened at the University of Porto for the second conference of the Iberian Association of the History of Economic Thought. This is the best indicator of the enduring readiness to continue to make fresh efforts for the renewal and development of the discipline in Spain and Portugal.

References

Almenar, Salvador. 1989. Notas sobre la historiografía del pensamiento económico en España. Siglos XVIII e XIX. *Revista de historia económica* 7.2:127–38.

Almodovar, António, and José Luís Cardoso. 1998. *A History of Portuguese Economic Thought*. London: Routledge.

Amzalak, Moses B. 1928. *Do estudo e da evolução das doutrinas económicas em Portugal*. Lisbon: Museu Comercial.

Arguelles, José Canga. [1826] 1968. *Diccionario de hacienda*. Madrid: Instituto de Estudios Fiscales.

Beltrán, Licas. 1976. *Historia de las doctrinas económicas*. 3d ed. Barcelona: Editorial Teide.

Braun, Carlos Rodríguez, and Manuel Jesús González. 1991. La historiografía del pensamiento económico en España. In *Due storiografie economiche a confronto: Italia e Spagna*, edited by Alberto Grohmann. Milan: EGEA.

Campomanes, Pedro Rodríguez. 1775. *Apêndice al discurso sobre la educación popular de los artesanos*. Madrid: Imprenta A. de Sancha.

Cardoso, José Luís. 1997. *Pensar a economia em Portugal: Digressões históricas*. Lisbon: Difel.

———, ed. 1998. *Pensamento económico português, 1750–1960: Fontes documentais e roteiro bibliográfico*. Lisbon: CISEP.

———, ed. 2001. *Dicionário histórico de economistas portugueses*. Lisbon: Temas & Debates.

Cardoso, José Luís, and Ernest Lluch. 1999. Las teorías económicas contempladas a través de una óptica nacional. In vol. 1 of *Economía y economistas españoles*, edited by Enrique Fuentes Quintana. Barcelona: Galaxia Gutemberg.

Castro, Armando. 1978. *As ideias económicas no Portugal medievo (séculos XIII a XV)*. Lisbon: Instituto de Cultura Portuguesa.

———. 1979. *As doutrinas económicas em Portugal na expansão e na decadência (séculos XVI a XVIII)*. Lisbon: Instituto de Cultura Portuguesa.

———. 1980. *O pensamento económico no Portugal moderno (de fins do século XVIII a começos do século XX)*. Lisbon: Instituto de Cultura Portuguesa.

Colmeiro, Manuel. [1861] 1978. *Biblioteca de los economistas españoles de los siglos XVI, XVII e XVIII*. Madrid: Real Academia de Ciencias Morales y Políticas.

Estapé, Fabián. 1971. *Ensayos sobre historia del pensamiento económico*. Barcelona: Ariel.

Grice-Hutchison, Marjorie. 1978. *Early Economic Thought in Spain, 1177–1740*. London: George Allen & Unwin.

Guarinos, Juan Sempere. 1801–21. *Biblioteca española de economía política*. Madrid: Imprenta A. de Sancha.

Lisboa, José da Silva. [1819] 1994. *Estudos do bem comum e economia política*. In vol. 2 of *Escritos económicos escolhidos (1804–1820)*, edited by António Almodovar. Colecção de obras clássicas do pensamento económico português. Lisbon: Banco de Portugal.

Lluch, Ernest. 1980. Sobre la historia nacional del pensamiento económico. Introduction to *Curso de economía política (1828)*, by A. Florez Estrada. Madrid: Instituto de Estudios Fiscales.

Perdices, Luis. 1999. Los historiadores y sus aproximaciones a la historia del pensamiento económico. In vol. 1 of *Economía y economistas españoles*, edited by Enrique Fuentes Quintana. Barcelona: Galaxia Gutemberg.

Perdices, Luis, and John Reeder. 2000. *Diccionario de pensamiento económico en España, 1500–1812*. Madrid: Editorial Síntesis.

Quintana, Enrique Fuentes. 1999. Ensayo introductorio. In vol. 1 of *Economía y economistas españoles*, edited by Quintana. Barcelona: Galaxia Gutemberg.

Velarde, Juan. 1974. *Introducción a la historia del pensamiento económico Español en el siglo XX*. Madrid: Editora Nacional.

A Brief History of History of Economic Thought Teaching in the Netherlands

Albert Jolink and Mark Blaug

The history of the history of economic thought teaching in the Netherlands is an unwritten story. It consists of scattered, local, individual stories and of particular events that have remained unnoticed in Dutch histories of higher education. Yet, in retrospect, the individual stories and
events build up an impressively consistent picture of a history of history
of economic thought teaching in Dutch economics curricula.

The information that has shaped this brief history comes from those
who were involved in the teaching of the history of economic thought at
Dutch universities during the period 1945–2001. These (oral) histories
were gathered by interviewing several generations of lecturers at different universities in the Netherlands. Due to the relatively low mobility
of Dutch lecturers during a large part of the period under investigation,
most individual stories related to the specific circumstances of one university town and could often be confirmed by predecessors or successors. The sheer size of the country, with at most nine faculties offering
(elements of) an economics curriculum, offers the opportunity to distill
some general traits that may compose a brief history of the history of
economic thought teachings in the Netherlands.

The oral history mainly covers the post–World War II era, although
most stories also referred to the pre–World War II period, in part as an
explanation, in part as a (self-) justification of the present situation. Although the pre–World War II history of history of economic thought

Albert Jolink thanks Mark Blaug for being so insistent.

teaching is mainly a history of hearsay, it seems to be in conformity with the overall picture of the history of economics in the Netherlands. As such, a brief sketch of the pre–World War II period will be presented first.

The Pre–World War II Period

The economics teaching at Dutch universities during the interbellum is characterized by a charming simplicity: a handful of professors would cater to a dozen students, mostly at law faculties. The exceptions, here, were the Rotterdam School of Economics and the Economics Department of Tilburg University, which started in the 1910s and 1920s as business schools but later developed an economics curriculum. The main actors in the 1930s were the economics faculty of the University of Amsterdam and the business school at Rotterdam, who considered each other as direct rivals from the start. Although there were (minor) differences among the approaches at different universities and schools, in general the economics teaching was characterized by (1) an orientation toward the so-called Austrian school of economics, (2) a strong emphasis on applied economics and practical affairs, and (3) a historical approach toward teaching economics.

Most of the economics teaching in the 1930s was inspired by the marginal utility approach represented by the Austrian school of economics, in particular Eugen von Böhm-Bawerk's work. The Dutch economists, inclined as they were toward German economics, had experienced the *Methodenstreit* from a distance but wholeheartedly adopted the move away from the German historical school. Yet the theoretical amalgam that emerged in economics teaching at Dutch universities combined elements that may have illustrated a Dutch preference for consensus but otherwise seemed incompatible as an outcome of the *Methodenstreit*. One of the elements of the theory that dominated the economics teaching was the emphasis on the specific conditions of time and place that determined the potential applications in practical affairs. One possible exception was a theory of money. In retrospect, the liberal interpretation of the Austrian school's contributions to economics does not always qualify Dutch economics teaching as "Austrian." Nowadays one may classify it even as "institutionalist."

The teaching of economics found its justification in the practices of trade or political applications. Although some philosophical insights may have sneaked into the curriculum, the expectation of the students was a practical study with direct relevance for their future working environment. As most professors were somehow involved in politics or industry, their academic interests were slightly curtailed by practical interests.

Instruction in economics itself was presented in a chronological order, suggesting a sequence or progress. Lectures were presented commonly as a culmination of economic thought with the professor's contribution as the grand finale. The lectures were presented against a background of the history of economic thought, although mainly through the lens of the topic at hand. The verbal, literal style dominated, and the modernisms of statistics and economic modeling were regarded with suspicion and contempt. Although Jan Tinbergen's statistics classes in Rotterdam attracted a few students, the majority of the students felt that the choice would be between Austrian economics and Keynesian economics.

The Post–World War II Period

After the Second World War the general economics classes were divorced from the historical line of presentation. Lesser gods, often young assistant professors, were requested to sketch the background of newly emerging theoretical insights. As the west wind blew into the Netherlands and Dutch economists turned their backs on German economics, the economics curriculum lost most of its "Austrian" gloss and was reshaped according to new international standards.

The new history of economic thought courses were often reformed to include elements of institutional economics (e.g., Jan Zuidema in Rotterdam) or elements of methodology or philosophy (such as Pieter Hennipman in Amsterdam on economic motives). The early historians of economic thought were aware of a *Dogmengeschichte* but hardly convinced of its relevance for economics if it were not related to some other issue (e.g., welfare) and in support of the full professors' lectures.

Only in the late 1960s, when history of economic thought was picking up speed in the international arena with specialist journals and conferences emerging out of the blue (from the Dutch perspective), the economics departments rediscovered the history of economic thought. By this time, the zeitgeist allowed for more ideological input in the curriculum and found the history of economic thought course a compliant victim. New chairs of history of economic thought were founded, satisfying the greedy forces of democratization, on the one hand, and indicating the awareness of international changes, on the other.

By the late 1970s, history of economic thought courses had been passed on to the second generation of historians of economic thought, often as a successful attempt to derail the careers of atheoretical economists, but university administrations had kept the chairs for more promising new fields. By the late 1980s, it had become obvious to nearly all academics at Dutch universities that despite a continuing student interest, the history of economic thought courses would have to be minimized, and for the wrong reason: money. By this time, Dutch higher education had to undergo serious corrective measures to compensate for the unbridled expansions of staff during the 1970s. As competition among subfields within the economics curriculum intensified, the second generation of historians of economic thought lacked the time-honored instruments of defense, such as a publication record or international prestige. To some extent, Dutch historians of economic thought defended a self-elected image of "scientificity" comparable to their own perception of the eighteenth century but in no sense related to the reality of Dutch universities in the 1980s. History of economic thought courses had become caricatures of themselves with little or no innovation for decades. The economic trinity (Adam Smith, Alfred Marshall, John Maynard Keynes) had become a repetitive tune of yesteryear, representing the wrong ideas of dead men.

The Present Situation

As the second generation of historians of economics had sung their swan song, lamenting the new achievements in economics, today most history of economic thought courses have lost their foundational character in the curriculum, often replaced by philosophy, and have become an elective for the die-hards. At some Dutch universities (e.g., Groningen, Wageningen), history of economic thought has gone down with the people teaching it. At the Universities of Tilburg and Maastricht, history of economic thought has disappeared completely from the curriculum. At other institutions history of economic thought courses have been supported by student evaluations (Amsterdam) and have temporarily survived the storms. The University of Amsterdam is exceptional as it has also been blessed with a remarkably good choice for J. Klant's successors (Neil De Marchi, Mary Morgan, Mark Blaug, John Davis), who have given

Amsterdam a strong comparative advantage over its main competitors. Moreover, it is unique in the Netherlands, and indeed in Europe, in combining economic methodology and the history of economics in a single professorial chair.

The University of Rotterdam has downgraded the history of economic thought courses to the absolute minimum but seems to recognize that its strategy is backfiring. It has now introduced a new course of a history of economic thought type, although carefully keeping *history* out, introducing students to the plurality of economics in the twentieth century. Also at Rotterdam, a new Erasmus Center for History in Management and Economics (CHIMES) has been founded to recover some of the remaining HET research and to explore new combinations of history of economic thought and history of management thought.

The University of Utrecht has surprisingly retained a course on the history of economic thought in its newly established economics curriculum, hence, ironically, trying to distinguish itself from other economics curricula in the Netherlands.

A Lesson to Be Learned

We may draw the following conclusions from a brief history of history of economic thought teaching in the Netherlands: History of economic thought in the Netherlands has always been related to something else. In the pre– and post–World War II periods it was related to a tradition of economics teaching that allowed for, and perhaps even required, a historical backing. When the economics teaching and history of economic thought were divorced, history of economic thought temporarily served the (ideological) zeitgeist. But when even that spell lost its glamour, history of economic thought became "useless" in the economics curriculum. The outside (from the perspective of the Netherlands) influence on the history of economic thought as a specialist discipline proved to be fata morgana for the Dutch situation. Only in those cases where the history of economic thought was able to adapt to a new host could it continue its parasitical existence: in Amsterdam it was able to contribute to the history of econometrics; in Rotterdam it could contribute to the history of management thought.

If the history of economic thought is to survive in the Netherlands it will be because it is a "history of economic thought of something" rather than *Dogmengeschichte*, because it is an approach rather than a discipline, because it is extrovert rather than introvert.

The History of Economic Thought in Australia and New Zealand

John Lodewijks

The History of Economic Thought Society of Australia (HETSA) was formed in 1981 at a conference at the University of New England (UNE), Armidale. John Pullen, Ray Petridis, and John Wood were the main initiators of the formation of the society, the objectives of which included a regular newsletter or bulletin, as well as a biennial (and now annual) conference. John Wood edited the first five issues of the newsletter, and Peter Groenewegen the sixth. John Pullen took over in 1987 and produced eight issues of the *HETSA Bulletin* in four years. The *Bulletin* was filled with book reviews, news and notes, conference reports, and a small number of generally short articles. I took over the editorship in 1991 with issue 15 of what was now called the *History of Economics Review* (*HER*). Under my editorship sixteen issues appeared (two of which were double issues) containing 184 articles or substantive review articles. Acknowledging the double issues, this averages out at about ten articles per issue. John King took over the editorship with issue 31 in 2000. The success of the journal helps explain the growth of the HETSA from 70 members in 1991 to 154 in 1995. Membership has now stabilized at about 170

I would like to thank the following for providing information and valuable comments: Jim Alvey, Tony Aspromourgos, Tony Endres, Moira Gordon, Peter Groenewegen, Geoff Harcourt, Warren Hogan, Murray Kemp, John King, Peter Kriesler, Chris Nyland, Allen Oakley, Phil O'Hara, John Pullen, Ken Rivett, Michael Schneider, Anthony Waterman, and Mike White. The comments of participants at the 2001 *HOPE* conference in Durham, North Carolina, were also helpful.

members, of whom 40 percent are overseas-based (overseas subscribers also doubled in the first half of the last decade).

An examination of the 184 articles published during my editorship gives us some useful information about the state of HET in Australasia. Of these articles, 62.5 percent were provided by authors affiliated with Australian institutions. The remaining sixty-nine articles (37.5 percent) came from ten other countries. More than half (55 percent) came from North America (United States, thirty; Canada, eight). The Australian contributions came from twenty-two universities. This is a welcome result in terms of coverage and includes representation from all of the "Group of Eight," Australia's leading research-intensive universities. Contributions from these eight universities account for 24 percent of all articles. The universities omitted are generally very small institutions or inactive in a research sense. There are only about six universities where one might have expected some HET research, but none has surfaced in *HER*. Surprisingly, the South Australian HET contribution is meager—one article from the three universities combined. Eight Australian universities account for 66 percent of the Australian *HER* articles. These are the University of Sydney (fifteen), University of New South Wales (UNSW) (twelve), Murdoch (ten), Newcastle and La Trobe (nine), Macquarie, Charles Sturt, and the Australian National University (seven). One could reasonably say that three out of every four Australian universities that are research-active have scholars who publish in the history of economic thought in *HER*.

Sixty-eight Australian authors accounted for the 115 domestic contributions. This figure illustrates that at least 15 percent of academic economists in Australia write on the history of economics, presumably a higher figure than a comparable North American survey would find. It is quite a pleasing result that so many economists devote at least part of their research effort to the history of the discipline. In Australia few academics have the luxury of specializing exclusively in the history of economics, and most have one or two other areas of research. This "multi-skilling" enhances their employability and means that they can keep up with latest developments in the discipline.

Despite the pleasing overall percentage of academics interested in historical inquiry, it should be noted that only in a few institutions is there a viable core or team of researchers in HET. At most places it is a single researcher with perhaps one or two other sympathetic colleagues. The leading Australian researchers were Robert Leeson (seven articles),

Peter Groenewegen (six), Allen Oakley and Alex Millmow (five), Mike White and Steve Kates (four), and John Pullen, John King, Rod O'Donnell, Tony Aspromourgos, and Evan Jones (three). Of these eleven authors, most are well known to *HOPE* readers, and combined they account for 40 percent of Australian contributions to *HER*.

Only at the University of Sydney, UNSW, Macquarie, and La Trobe do you have a sufficient cohort of historians of thought to prevent one scholar's output from dominating the total for that institution. For example, Peter Groenewegen's six articles stand in comparison to fifteen for the University of Sydney as a whole. Peter Kriesler and I account for only two each of the twelve contributions from UNSW. Rod O'Donnell has three of the seven Macquarie articles, and John King three of the nine from La Trobe. In contrast, Mike White accounts for all of Monash's contributions, and John Creedy all of the University of Melbourne offerings. Alex Millmow contributes five of the seven from Charles Sturt, John Pullen three of the five from UNE, Allen Oakley five of the nine from the University of Newcastle, and Robert Leeson has seven of the ten articles emanating from Murdoch. Tony Endres accounts for four of the University of Auckland's six essays.

Using only the *HER* articles obviously understates those historians of thought who publish books or publish in more prestigious HET journals; although the figures would be highly correlated. For comparison purposes, eighteen Australians have graced the pages of *HOPE* over the 1984–98 period. Our premier performer on this measure was John Pullen, who managed to place nine articles in the journal during this time. Including our New Zealand colleagues, such as Tony Endres, who published five articles in *HOPE*, means that Australasians represent about 5 percent of the authors who have published articles in this journal.

Nevertheless, it does illustrate the fragility of the history of thought community in Australia. Casual empiricism suggests that a small number of Ph.D. supervisors account for a disproportionate number of Ph.D. theses in the history of economics (Peter Groenewegen, Geoff Harcourt, John King, Allen Oakley). Should a number of these key researchers retire, and not be replaced by others with an interest in our craft, it may spell the end of this community. Only in the Sydney region are there sufficient numbers of staff to sustain interest in the subject, although even in some of those places the research interest is active but the teaching situation is not. Research productivity is enhanced in a team environment with a critical mass of researchers who encourage each other. These peer group effects appear very important and create desirable spillover consequences for Ph.D. students working in this area. Considering the small number of Australian universities with these features, the HET situation is even less promising.

The Research Dimension

The last two decades have been a productive period for historians of economics in Australia and New Zealand. There are just under a hundred Australian and New Zealand members of HETSA. The New Zealanders account for about 10 percent of this total. If we classify active researchers as those publishing in the subdiscipline's journals or writing books on the history of economics, then the antipodean research community of historians of economics is composed of about forty-five scholars. Most of these attend the annual HETSA conferences fairly regularly, and all have contributed to *HER*. Perhaps half of this group has had at least one book published on the history of economics over the last decade. A subset of ten or so of this antipodean group would be classified as exceedingly productive researchers with formidable international reputations.

The antipodeans have aggressively seized the opportunities provided by academic publishers keen on expanding their history of economics titles. Indeed, a case can be made that an Australian really started off this particular sort of publishing activity in the history of economics in a major way. Since 1982, John Cunningham Wood has edited ninety-two volumes on various great economists. Starting in 1982–83 with *Critical Assessments* of Alfred Marshall and John Maynard Keynes, and including the recently published volumes on Jean-Baptiste Say and Wassily Leontief, this series is planned to continue for at least the next decade. The first twenty-eight volumes were published by Croom Helm and the rest by Routledge. Despite the small print runs, there is clearly a market for this sort of work, even if it sometimes arouses the hostility of academic reviewers. Recently Tony Aspromourgos (2000) has written that "the plethora of cheap and easy facsimile editions of extant scholarship actually serves to *undermine* new scholarship . . . [and] is part of a wider and dangerous set of developments . . . the increasingly risky relationship between commercial publishers and academic scholarship."

Undoubtedly the major resident figure in Australian history of economic thought has been Peter Groenewegen, who has described the major milestones in his career in Groenewegen 1997. Groenewegen established the Centre for the Study of the History of Economic Thought at the University of Sydney in 1989. Groenewegen's links with European historians of economics and journals have been quite important for Australian researchers. Groenewegen has moved in tandem with another strong influence on Australian history of economics, Geoffrey Harcourt. While based at the University of Cambridge, Harcourt's influence through Ph.D. supervision—and hospitality to visiting Australasian historians of thought during sabbaticals at Cambridge—cannot be overestimated.

History of Thought in Australian Universities

There are two histories of Australian economics (Goodwin 1966 and Groenewegen and McFarlane 1990). What we focus on here is the teaching of the history of economics in a subset of Australian universities.

Groenewegen (1982) has outlined the strong HET tradition at the University of Sydney. Teaching of HET had been a striking feature of its syllabus for well over seventy years. By the early 1980s HET was an option in third year that attracted thirty to forty students annually, while during the previous decade the majority of honors students undertook a study of the classics (Adam Smith, David Ricardo, Marx, Marshall, or Knut Wicksell). Since then there has been a steady decline in both the quality and quantity of students studying the classics.

John Pullen (1990) recounts the experiences of a smaller regional university that originally was a branch of the University of Sydney. At that institution, HET was gradually weeded out of the honors program. First the HET course was reduced from two terms to one semester, and then students were permitted to substitute other options for HET. Frantic attempts were made to resurrect HET via time-tabling and a change of name and focus, to encourage the application of history to current issues. As a result, the fortunes of HET revived somewhat in the 1990s with the introduction of a postgraduate course in addition to the undergraduate one. But with recent financial cutbacks and falling enrollments in economics courses, HET reverted to just one course and is in danger of disappearing from the curriculum altogether.

In contrast, Curtin University in Western Australia is one of the few places where HET has been introduced and has prospered since the early 1990s. A third-year HET course is a strongly recommended prerequisite for the honors year, and HET is also taught at the honors and master's levels.

Generally, increasing formalism in economics has meant that there is less room in the curriculum for more literary and historical studies like HET. The teaching situation is quite desperate. In 1995 there were only three (out of six) states in Australia where history of thought was being taught, with twenty courses in total being offered. Since then there has been further attrition. The situation in New Zealand is equally tenuous. While they have no formal HET organizational structure, New Zealanders have always played a role in HETSA and attended its conferences, but there is not enough interest in HET to warrant a session at the annual New Zealand Economics Association Conference. New Zealanders present their HET work elsewhere. HET is offered at perhaps half the New Zealand universities. James Alvey and Alfred Oehlers teach HET at Massey, but the subject has been under threat for four years, and now it is not even taught internally but only in correspondence mode. The picture is brighter at Auckland. Tony Endres teaches the subject there, but he devotes more than half the course to post-1950 developments and includes surveys of evolutionary economics, psychological economics, new institutional economics, feminist economics, new Austrian economics, and other heterodox doctrines.

The Nature and Character of Australasian History of Thought

There has been a strong connection between work in post-Keynesian economics and the study of the history of economics in Australia (King 1997). Here I am using *post-Keynesian* as an umbrella term to cover a number of groups, even if later they proved incompatible with each other and uncomfortable with the label itself. John King's *History of Post-Keynesian Macroeconomics* (2002) examines these issues in detail. Harcourt (2001, chap. 19) has distinguished three streams of post-Keynesianism: fundamentalist Keynesian, Kaleckian, and Sraffian. My contention is that HET work related to these three streams, and the associated links with English Cambridge, has been far more prevalent in Australia than in North America or even the United Kingdom.

Not surprisingly, Keynes features most prominently in articles published by the *History of Economics Review*. More than one in five articles in that journal are on a Keynesian topic. Indeed, if we combined Keynes with Kalecki, Marx, and other articles in the post-Keynesian tradition, we would cover almost a third of the published articles in the journal. It is no coincidence then that Australasia has leading authorities on Cambridge economists such as Keynes (Rod O'Donnell, Athol Fitzgibbons, and Bruce Littleboy) and Marshall (Groenewegen and Ray Petridis). The expertise on Kalecki is also abundant: Peter Kriesler, Bruce McFarlane, Joseph Halevi, and Simon Chapple.

Groenewegen credits the efforts of G. C. Harcourt for spreading post-Keynesianism in Australia. Doctoral supervision gives some insight into the chains of influence at work. Harcourt has been an exceedingly popular Ph.D. supervisor, and even when he was not the formal supervisor, his support and encouragement were often crucial. He played a role in the research of O'Donnell, Kriesler, and Roy Green at Cambridge. Some of his other Australian postgraduate students who wrote on HET include Mike White, Prue Kerr, and Allen Oakley. Peter Groenewegen also has a long list of students who went on to achieve considerable reputations in the history of economics: Tony Aspromourgos and Murray Milgate come to mind immediately.

During the first decade of HETSA there was a distinct and influential subgroup within the society that carried the neo-Ricardian and post-Keynesian banners. It featured characters with very strong personalities like David Clark and Bruce McFarlane, and the group as a whole was well known for its heated debates, strong critiques of orthodoxy, and boisterous extracurricular antics. The interest in Cambridge economics and what has been termed "the Cambridge version of the history of economics" can be explained partly by historical circumstances and the influence of key figures. Its longevity in Australian history of thought also reflects the subdiscipline's receptivity to intellectual traditions outside the mainstream.

While post-Keynesians were influential, Australian HET was always more heterogenous, and the interest in post-Keynesianism must be set in the context of the 1970s, when there appeared to be a promising research program emerging to challenge mainstream thinking, and critiques of orthodoxy were common. However, it is fair to say that interest in neo-Ricardian and post-Keynesian ideas has waned even in Australian history of thought.[1] There are a number of possible explanations for this

1. For a recent and strongly worded statement in support of Piero Sraffa's conception of classicism, see Aspromourgos 1999.

decline. One is that the research programs failed to achieve the initial high expectations. Groenewegen (1995, 137) notes, "Post-Keynesian economics survives as a minority interest in a number of economics departments while its intellectual elite is an aging set of professors whose writings are falling on deaf ears in an increasingly homogenised profession built on the North American model."

Australian history of thought seems to have flowered, particularly over the last decade, in all sorts of different directions. While the interest in Cambridge is still there, researchers are active in many other areas, too. Perhaps some of this increased diversity reflects the role of international scholars who have taken up residence here, such as John Creedy and King. John King supervised the Ph.D. of one of Australia's most promising young historians of thought, Gregory Moore, who works on the historical school. Steven Kates is another student whom King has supervised, and his work on Say's law has created quite a storm. Another very promising young historian of thought is Mark Donoghue. Donoghue is a New Zealander who completed his Ph.D. at the University of Sydney under Groenewegen's supervision. He has written on Henry Thornton, Marx, John Stuart Mill, John Elliott Cairnes, and Marshall and over the last four years has had articles in *Manchester School*, *Scottish Journal of Political Economy*, *History of Economic Ideas*, and three in the *European Journal of the History of Economic Thought*. Chris Nyland's numerous publications on women in the history of economics should also be mentioned. Visitors have also left their mark. A. W. Coats first came in 1980 and has been a frequent visitor since, attending HETSA conferences and spending long periods of time at Australian Universities. Sam Hollander visited in mid-1985 and also attended the HETSA conference. More recently, we have had visits by Philip Mirowski, Roy Weintraub, Heinz D. Kurz, and Craufurd Goodwin.

The best-known modern New Zealand historian of thought is Tony Endres,[2] who has had a lot to do with Sam Hollander over the years. Hollander wrote a good part of his book *The Economics of T. R. Malthus* on two long visits to Auckland, funded by the University of Auckland. Endres has supervised, among others, Simon Chapple and Grant Fleming.

Western Australia also has a solid HET pedigree with the early work of R. N. Ghosh and Douglas Vickers, followed by Ray Petridis, John C.

2. Ronald Meek was also a New Zealander, and Peter Earl is well known for his work on economic psychology.

Wood, Ian Kerr, and Phil O'Hara. Michael McLure's book *Pareto, Economics, and Society* (2000) continues this tradition. At Curtin, O'Hara has published much on Thorstein Veblen and Marx, nationally and internationally, and edited the two-volume *Encyclopedia of Political Economy* (1999). Another well-known West Australian historian of thought is Robert Leeson. Leeson has broadened his research on modern economics, following his Ph.D. work on Bill Phillips, to look at the evolution of macroeconomics more generally. He is a highly prolific publisher of history of thought material, frequently gracing the pages of *HOPE* and *HER*. William Coleman's research, at the University of Tasmania, is also gaining greater exposure, and he won the 1997 History of Economics Society Award for the best article in the history of economics.

A Forward Glance

The research output in Australasia stands out in sharp contrast to the general teaching situation. The publication opportunities presented to those that practice our craft has resulted in tenure and promotion for existing staff, even if new staff find it difficult to be appointed in the area due largely to declining student numbers. A few scholars, such as Oakley, Nyland, O'Donnell, and Groenewegen, have also been successful in obtaining Australian Research Council funding to support their research. How long these publication options will continue is hard to say. Is it just a "bubble"? The high prices and low production volumes (around three hundred) were initially designed for the unique circumstances of the Japanese market. Whether this demand will continue is doubtful. Edward Elgar has stated that his company's earlier rapid growth has now reached a steady state and that HET will have a declining share of that output level. The Japanese market has fallen from over 70 percent to less than one-third of Elgar's sales.

One can certainly be gloomy looking at the teaching situation with respect to history of thought in Australia and the impending or recent retirement of some of our leading researchers (Groenewegen, Petridis, Harcourt). A number of individuals who might have been expected to lend support have retreated to the management sciences, where the grass is greener, or changed their research focus in other ways more conducive to the academic incentive structures. Others have developed comfortable niches of research in HET, yet have no broader concerns about strengthening the local community of historians of thought. The burden of

continuing the momentum of the last decade will fall on a very few practitioners in the major universities, under less than ideal circumstances.

It is also noticeable that a number of promising contributors do not
seem to have been able to broaden their work in the history of economics
beyond their Ph.D. research. Regrettably, those young researchers that
have expanded their scope are often in academic positions on the pe-
riphery and not ensconced in the major research universities. While the
future looks acceptable for perhaps the greater part of this decade, one
has to be vigilant that HET does not share the same fate as the economic
historians in Australia. The implications for *HER* are that it needs to find
further avenues to appeal to other (perhaps discontented) segments of
the economics community. It has done this successfully with the post-
Keynesian community and to some extent with the evolutionists-cum-
Schumpeterians. Perhaps further symposiums on the history of Australian economics, and reflective pieces on the state of the profession and
the history of contemporary developments, may be in order. Alternatively, greater links with the other social sciences might be forged.

One has a clear sense that historians of thought are most vulnerable to
cuts in staff positions in economics departments, and survival will dictate that those interested in the craft need to have strong skills in other
areas in economics, too—which may not be an undesirable development.
Despite the ominous clouds circling our craft, while the publishing avenues are abundant, the antipodeans will continue to aggressively seize
the opportunities available.

References

Aspromourgos, Tony. 1999. What Is Classical Economics? *History of Economics
    Review* 30 (summer): 159–68.
————. 2000. Review of Hutchison. *Contributions to Political Economy* 19:91–97.
Goodwin, Craufurd D. W. 1966. *Economic Enquiry in Australia*. Durham, N.C.:
    Duke University Press.
Groenewegen, Peter. 1982. History of Economic Thought in the Faculty of Econom-
    ics at Sydney University. *HETSA Newsletter* 3 (summer): 2–11.
————. 1995. Post-Keynesian Economics: A Memorial? *History of Economics Re-
    view* 24 (summer): 137–39.
————. 1997. Economics Does Have a Useful Past and Yes, History Is Important.
    In vol. 3 of *The Makers of Modern Economics*, edited by Arnold Heertje. Chel-
    tenham, U.K.: Edward Elgar.

Groenewegen, Peter, and Bruce McFarlane. 1990. *A History of Australian Economic Thought*. London: Routledge.

Harcourt, G. 2001. *50 Years a Keynesian and Other Essays*. New York: Palgrave.

King, John. 1997. Notes on the History of Post-Keynesian Economics in Australia. In vol. 1 of *Capital Controversy, Post-Keynesian Economics, and the History of Economic Thought: Essays in Honour of Geoff Harcourt*, edited by Philip Arestis, Gabriel Palma, and Malcolm Sawyer. London: Routledge.

————. 2002. *A History of Post-Keynesian Macroeconomics 1936–2000*. Cheltenham, U.K.: Edward Elgar.

McLure, Michael. 2000. *Pareto, Economics, and Society*. London: Routledge.

O'Hara, Phil, ed. 1999. *Encyclopedia of Political Economy*. 2 vols. London: Routledge.

Pullen, John. 1990. The Teaching of the History of Economic Thought at the University of New England. *HETSA Bulletin* 13 (winter): 30–40.

History of Economics in Japan: A Turning Point

Aiko Ikeo

Japanese historians of economics stand at a crossroads. For many of them, the history of economics (hereafter HE) is a subtype of Western study that is discussed in Japanese. Faced with the internationalization of economics, they should look for new directions, such as the awakening of a keen interest in contemporary economic discussion and the publication of their studies in English.

Education

At the high school level, standard textbooks on politics and economy (*seiji keizai*) include at least an hour-long class on HE. It usually introduces three major economists and their main works, namely, Adam Smith and his *Wealth of Nations* (1776), Karl Marx and his *Das Kapital* (1867–94), and John Maynard Keynes and his *General Theory of Employment, Interest, and Money* (1936). These works are placed in a historical context and are recognized as results of specific economic stages after the capitalist production system began to evolve. Some discuss David Ricardo's comparative advantage theory of production cost. High school students naturally get the impression that economics was

I would like to thank the respondents of my questionnaire on HE in Japan, *HOPE* conference participants, and the anonymous referees for their comments, and Janusz Buda and Mayumi Masuko for their stylistic comments. This work was supported by the Waseda University Grant for Special Research Project (2000A-843).

born in Britain in the eighteenth century, was critically assessed by a German scholar in the nineteenth century, and was introduced into Japan in the mid-nineteenth century.

At the undergraduate level in Japan, HE is usually taught in departments of economics and sometimes in departments of commerce. HE is compulsory for economics students at some universities, and often is taught to first- or second-year students as a sort of introduction to economics. It is expected that students will learn economic ideas and economic history and will get a general idea of what economics is. In lectures, Western canonical authors are invariably included, whereas Japanese thinkers are not necessarily covered. Takashi Negishi (1997, 3) suggests that the main body of contemporary economic theories has been so formalized that students may feel very far removed from it. Therefore, it is important for students to experience what earlier economists have gone through by trial and error.

HE is also taught to third- or fourth-year students reflecting research conducted by the professor teaching the course. Some larger departments of economics, which have relatively sizable faculties, provide courses on the history of Japanese economic thought and the history of social thought as well as HE. Economic thought is regarded as something common to people from every cultural background and is usually differentiated from social thought, which is peculiar to a given culture. In lectures of HE at this level, the majority of professors aim to teach students multiple points of view on economic issues and make them understand that there is more than one solution for each economic problem. For example, there are theoretically four or more solutions to the problem of high unemployment:

1. Emigration should be recommended in the case of excess population (neo-Malthusian view).
2. Keynesian fiscal policy is needed in the case of demand deficiency.
3. The capitalist production system should be abolished if a reserved army is necessary for the system. There should be a better, different socialist system than those of the former U.S.S.R. and Eastern Europe.
4. Structural reforms, including those in financial and construction sectors, are needed if growth-oriented policies lose effectiveness.

Although this example is perhaps too formal, the majority of HE scholars are critical of mainstream economics because it is too rigid and theoretical, lacking regard for cultural or historical elements. HE is recommended to give students a pluralist point of view in the study of economics.

At the undergraduate level, some economists who do not belong to the Japanese Society for the History of Economic Thought (JSHET) occasionally teach HE. They usually do not think of themselves as historians of economic thought. At the same time, some scholars who are members of JSHET do not teach HE at their universities, but rather teach an introduction to, or outline of, economics at departments of education, law, science, and engineering. In some cases, HE is regarded not as a specialist field but as a general field that can be taught by those economists who are interested in theoretical works by earlier economists.

A few graduate schools of economics and commerce have professors of HE and graduate students who are eager to specialize in HE. To my knowledge, no graduate school in Japan has a formal training course for HE. As mentioned in Ikeo 1996, 137, considerable changes in economics education (involving HE) took place in the mid-1990s. Several universities decided to place more weight on graduate rather than undergraduate education. In 1994, graduate schools began to expand their student intakes, and this resulted in their sending an increasing number of young people into the job market in 1999. The Ministry of Education and Science has pressured universities to increase international competitiveness in research areas faced with accelerating globalization. Japanese universities are experiencing an additional pressure: the student population is expected to decline constantly, and some universities will be expected to "merge" for survival.

Young scholars of HE are advised to present their papers to seminars and conferences held outside their universities and to submit their revised papers to refereed journals. On the one hand, HE scholars of the older generation are extremely demanding, and some of their guidance is the opposite of that given to students of economics in general. They lament students' lack of bibliographical skill and their poor command of European languages other than English. They are disappointed that young scholars tend to choose easy topics for journal articles. On the other hand, the young feel that choosing a minor topic or economist for their papers will make it harder to get a job, since it is difficult to demonstrate their teaching ability in job applications. As a result, many articles are published on famous economists such as John Maynard Keynes, Alfred Marshall, John Stuart Mill, and Adam Smith and topics related to their works. Those who study either a minor economist or a broader theme feel that it is hard to get relevant advice to improve their papers. Some occasionally come from remote areas to seminars held in large cities like Tokyo to get stimuli from presentations of recent papers by active historians of economics. Yet more systematic training is needed for HE students to compete with the students who are trained systematically in other areas of economics.

HE used to be compulsory at many departments of economics and was therefore one of the required areas in the public service entrance examination until 1990 (Yagi [1999] 2000, 200–201). Moreover, prior to World War II, the study of Léon Walras and Augustin Cournot was important for many Japanese students planning to become professional economists. After 1945, HE was critical because the promotion of HE alleviated Japanese parochialism in economic research and, until the 1980s, was key in enabling Japanese scholars to learn about the West. Later we will discuss the change that occurred in the situation of economics in the mid-1980s.

Japanese Society for the History
of Economic Thought

The Japanese Society for the History of Economic Thought (JSHET) had 819 members in June 2002 and is the largest of its kind in the world. It was the nineteenth largest among the fifty-seven member associations of the Union of National Economics Associations in Japan (UNEAJ) in March 2002. UNEAJ includes associations of economics, commerce, and administrative science (Ikeo [1999] 2000, chap. 1). JSHET was established in April 1950 with 123 initial members for the purposes of (1) promoting the study of the history of economics and social thought, and (2) fostering domestic and international exchange for its members. When it celebrated its fiftieth anniversary in 2000, JSHET held a number of commemorative events and made some changes in its regular societal activities (JSHET 2000a).

JSHET holds an annual two-day nationwide meeting. Its program committee organizes plenary symposium sessions or parallel forum sessions on specific themes. Since 1994 these sessions have been held biannually. Recent symposium session themes have been Malthus and modern times (1992), the history of Japanese economic thought (1993), the three-hundred-year anniversary of François Quesnay's birth (1994), the

German historical school (1996), John Stuart Mill and modern times (1998), and understanding and assessing the market economy from the viewpoint of the history of economics (2000). The number of contributed papers has paralleled the increase in numbers of graduate students.

A mailing list nicknamed "SHET" was officially approved in November 1996. It conveys official information, announcements of local meetings, calls for papers, discussions, and so on. The list is restricted to members and carries messages mostly in Japanese. In July 2002, 237 members were subscribed to the list. The JSHET Web site has been developing on the Ehime University Web server since 1997. The society is indebted to the personal efforts of Michio Akama for the maintenance of both electronic media.

JSHET has been annually issuing its journal *Keizaigakushigakkai Nenpo*, or in English *Annals of the Society for the History of Economic Thought*, since 1963. The *Annals* introduced a referee system in 1989 and carries refereed articles submitted by its members (in Japanese or English), as well as commissioned papers, surveys, book reviews, and communications (mostly in Japanese). Article submission was open exclusively to JSHET members until 2000, when it was decided that the *Annals* should accept submissions from nonmembers (together with a publication fee). The *Annals* began semiannual publication in 2001, although the name has not yet been changed. JSHET has issued its newsletter in Japanese since 1992.

The JSHET members who teach at universities have opportunities to get their papers published in their university journals (Ikeo 1996). Their academic articles are scattered in many unrefereed, closed journals. Therefore, JSHET sometimes organizes a book project and asks selected members to write chapters on specific topics. For many Japanese scholars in social sciences, it is a greater privilege to be asked to write a paper for a project than voluntarily to submit a paper to a journal. It is noteworthy that JSHET has published four books in Japanese (JSHET 1967, 1976, 1984, 1992), the first two of which, on Marx and Smith, had English summaries. JSHET has edited its history on commemorative occasions in 1961, 1980, and 2000 (for an example, see JSHET 2000a). It published *Dictionary of the History of Economic Thought* (2000b) as the result of intensive societal efforts during the celebration of its fiftieth anniversary.

JSHET has also helped publish two books in English. After years of discussion about publication in English, JSHET chose a book form rather than the establishment of a journal on HE and picked the history of Japanese economic thought as the theme for the first book. The editorial committee then decided to focus on economic thought and modernization in Japan, which became the title of the book. The committee believed that this subject was very important not only for Japanese but also for those in developing and developed countries who were interested in the relationship between the modernization process and the development of economic thought in Japan (Sugihara and Tanaka 1998, ix–x). It is noteworthy that *modernization* is the theme most discussed by Japanese historians of Japanese economic thought since 1945 (Ikeo 2001a).

The second book, *German Historical School* (2000), was edited by Yuichi Shionoya. The idea that prompted Shionoya to choose this theme was that notions and elements similar to those of the German historical school must be found in other countries as well, because this type of historical approach was very natural for any scholar beginning the study of a capitalist or market economy prior to the establishment of economics. This volume has been successful, so much so that the authors of the articles in the volume began to earn royalties in the very same year that it was published.

Issue 38 of the *Annals* (2000) featured special articles written by eminent Japanese historians of economics looking back over their own academic history, as requested by the editorial committee. Kanae Iida recalled his study of the history of Japanese economic thought; Noboru Kobayashi summarized the historical position of the *Wealth of Nations*; Yuichi Shionoya criticized HE without philosophical foundations; Shiro Sugihara discoursed on the present and the past of the history of Japanese economic thought; Shoji Tanaka traced his own path to Adam Smith; Toshihiro Tanaka addressed the history of American economic thought; Yoshio Nagai recollected his study of R. Owen and J. Bentham; Takashi Negishi summarized two problems in the history of international trade theory; Izumi Hishiyama covered his study of François Quesnay, Alfred Marshall, Piero Sraffa, and John Maynard Keynes; Kazuo Mazane reflected on his study of Ricardo; Mizuta Hiroshi looked back on his study of the history of social thought; and Saiichi Miyazaki reminisced on his study of Smith and Marx.

Issue 39 of the *Annals* (2001) carried thirteen commissioned articles on HE toward the twenty-first century, including a survey of the past ten to fifteen years. These articles as a whole proved the pluralist attitudes toward HE in Japan. The topics discussed were James Steuart, the Scottish Enlightenment, the French Enlightenment, Smith, Ricardo, Marx, institutional economics, Marshall, Keynes, modern (non-Marxian) economics, Austrian economics, and Japanese economic thought.

Connections with HE

There are many historians of social thought among JSHET members. After the collapse of East European socialism, a group of historians of social thought stepped into the field of HE. For example, Hiroshi Tanaka, who had been interested in social thought and the role of the state or the central government, organized a comparative study of national welfare systems covering Europe, the Americas, Russia, Africa, Asia, and Oceania as well as international organizations including the International Labor Organization. The results were published as *Contemporary World and Welfare State* (1997).

Several Japanese historians of science and economics are interested in both the historical development of academic institutions for promoting scientific activities—such as the role of universities and the establishment and allocation of grants for scientific research—and the activities of the Science Council of Japan (a governmental organization).

A group of Japanese economists are interested in the German historical school and ethics in economics. Yuichi Shionoya is eager to promote the study of things that are missing in current mainstream economics, such as ethics, value judgments, justice, and the theory of rights. However, Japanese philosophers do not appear to be interested in economics.

The Works Respected by Japanese
Historians of Economics

HE has a strong tradition in Japan. There seems to be a virtuous circle of flowery and elegant works on HE initiating other similar works on HE. The circle was transmitted from one generation to the next by monographs rather than journal articles. It can be said that HE in Japan was a part of Western studies discussed in Japanese.

Based on the answers to my questionnaire, I am in a position to list the six works most respected by Japanese scholars.[1]

1. I distributed a questionnaire on HE in Japan. In July 2000, I placed the questions on my Web site and posted to the JSHET mailing list the announcement of my research project for

1. Noboru Kobayashi's *Complete Works on the History of Economics* (1976–89) is respected by five scholars. Another three list one of his books, namely, *Study of the Ending of Mercantilism* (1955), *Establishment of the System of the "Wealth of Nations"* (1973), and *Productivity Theory of Friedrich List* (1948).
2. Yoshihiko Uchida's *Birth of Economics* (1953) is respected by five. Another two list his *World of "Das Kapital"* (1966) and *Steps of Social Recognition* (1971).
3. Marx's *Theories of Surplus-Value* (1905–10) is respected by five.
4. Joseph Schumpeter's *History of Economic Analysis* (1954) is respected by four. One lists his *Economic Doctrine and Method* (1914).
5. Eiichi Sugimoto's *New Lights upon Economics* (1950) is respected by three scholars, and his *History of Modern Economics* (1953), by three.
6. Kiyoaki Hirata's *Creation of Economic Science* (1965) is respected by three.

These selections are all based on a wide reading of Western classical economics literature. The Japanese authors on this list read not only the original classical economics literature but also the secondary writings by both foreign and Japanese scholars, and their writings read smoothly like a historical novel full of intellectual insight.

As mentioned, N. Kobayashi (1916–) contributed his retrospective essay on the relativization of Smith's *Wealth of Nations* (1776) in HE to the *Annals* in 2000. From Kobayashi (2000), we can learn that in Japan there was a vibrant controversy on the position of Smith in HE. On the one hand, Marxian economists such as Y. Uchida (1913–89) tend to regard the *Wealth of Nations* as the first book in political economy, and Uchida symbolized it as giving birth to political economy. On the other hand, Kobayashi made a special study of British mercantilism, Smith, and Friedrich List from around 1940 on and came to recognize James Steuart as another creator of political economy. This controversy promoted the study in Japan of Smith and his contemporaries, as well as of the Scottish Enlightenment. K. Hirata (1922–95) made a special study

---

the *HOPE* conference and the URL of my questionnaire. Then by e-mail I sent the questions to people I knew and asked them to respond to my questions and send me their syllabi. With reference to the answers I had received by E-mail, I mailed my questions to those scholars who might not use the Internet. I sent the questionnaire to more than two hundred JSHET members and about twenty nonmembers. I received answers from fifty-five scholars.

of French economic thought and various versions of Quesnay's *tableau économique*. E. Sugimoto (1901–52) started as a non-Marxian economist but later accepted the labor theory of value as true.

It is noteworthy that Kobayashi, Uchida, and Hirata are all known as talented writers. They impressed readers deeply, especially at the time of original publication. Their readers were subsequently drawn into the world of Western classical economics literature; they started to read the originals themselves and made the first steps toward becoming historians of economics. Their Japanese works attracted the scholars of the next generation, who are now leading JSHET members.

However, the works published by scholars of the previous generation, such as Zenya Takashima (1904–90) and Seiichiro Takahashi (1884–1982), were never mentioned by respondents to the questionnaire, although those historians of economics respected by active scholars openly acknowledged their debt to their predecessors. It may be said that works respected by Japanese scholars change from one generation to the next. There has been a virtuous circle in HE in Japan.

Turn for the Future

In the discussion of policy issues, a number of Japanese economists in the areas of international and applied economics began to take economic ideas and institutional arrangements in policy making into consideration in the mid-1980s. They realized that the theoretical analysis of government policies, such as comparative statics in macroeconomics, was not enough to rebut the critical remarks on Japan's economic policies made by foreign economists. American economists especially, including Paul R. Krugman, blamed Japan's large trade surplus on economic and industrial policies that were implemented to increase Japan's savings rates and the international competitiveness of targeted industries such as iron and steel and oil refinery. Some Japanese realized that applied economists should get out of the ivory tower, arm themselves with relevant facts and ideas, and face American professional economists in policy debate (Ikeo 2001b).

In the late 1990s, Japanese economists began to be involved in the process of policy making more deeply than just attending government deliberation committees. In 1999, two economists were appointed to positions at the Bank of Japan and the Ministry of Finance. In January

2001, when the central Japanese ministries and agencies were institutionally reformed, three economists were appointed to new cabinet office positions, and two joined the Council on Economic and Fiscal Policy. Finally in April 2001, Heizo Takenaka was nominated as minister of state (economic and fiscal policy) by Prime Minister Junichiro Koizumi and became the first economist-minister in Japan. These economists at the cabinet office are promoting the policies and reform plans in accord with neoclassical, market-oriented economics (Ikeo 2001b).

Japanese economists have kept pace with economic globalization and the internationalization of economics. They pay attention to economic ideas, cultural underpinnings, and the institutional arrangements in policy making. Japanese historians of economics need to start regarding their subject as something other than a subtype of Western studies. They should pay more attention to contemporary economics to join the discussion relating to economic ideas. Or they should publish their research results in English and communicate with international historians of economics, who have various cultural backgrounds but are interested in topics similar to their own.

References

Hirata, Kiyoaki. 1965. *Keizai Kagaku no Sozo* (Creation of economic science: *Tableau économique* and the French Revolution). Tokyo: Iwanami Shoten.
Ikeo, Aiko. 1996. Internationalization of Economics in Japan. In *Post-1945 Internationalization of Economics*, edited by A. W. Coats. Durham, N.C.: Duke University Press.
———, ed. [1999] 2000. *Japanese Economics and Economists since 1945*. London: Routledge.
———. 2001a. History of Japanese Economic Thought. *Keizaigakushigakkai Nenpo* 38:94–102.
———. 2001b. Keizaigakusha ga zenmen ni tatsu jidai (Time for economists to come to the front). *Ronza* 77 (October): 50–59.
JSHET (Japanese Society for the History of Economic Thought). 1967. *"Shihonron" no Seiritsu* (Formation of *Das Kapital*). Tokyo: Iwanami Shoten.
———. 1976. *"Kokufuron" no Seiritsu* (Formation of the *Wealth of Nations*). Tokyo: Iwanami Shoten.
———. 1984. *Nihon no Keizaigaku* (Economics in Japan: Tracking the economic thinking of Japanese). Tokyo: Toyo Keizai Shinposha.
———. 1992. *Keizaigakushi* (History of economic thought: Surveys and problems). Fukuoka: Kyushu Daigaku Shuppankai.

———. 2000a. *Keizaigakushigakkai 50nenshi* (A fifty-year history of JSHET). Unpublished document.

———. 2000b. *Keizaishisoshi Jiten* (Dictionary of the history of economic thought). Tokyo: Maruzen.

Keynes, John Maynard. 1936. *General Theory of Employment, Interest, and Money*. London: Macmillan.

Kobayashi, Noboru. 1948. *Furidorihhi Risuto no Seisanryokuron* (Productivity theory of Friedrich List). Tokyo: Toyo Keizai Shinposha.

———. 1955. *Jushoshugi Kaitaiki no Kenkyu* (Study of the ending of mercantilism). Tokyo: Miraisha.

———. 1973. *Kokufuron Taikei no Seiritsu* (Establishment of the system of the *Wealth of Nations*). Tokyo: Miraisha.

———. 1976–89. *Kobayashi Noboru Chosakushu* (Complete works of Noboru Kobayashi on the history of economics). 11 vols. Tokyo: Miraisha.

———. 2000. "Kokufuron" no gakushiteki ichi no sotaika (My study of the early modern systems of economics, and resulting relativization of the historical position of the *Wealth of Nations*). *Keizaigakushigakkai Nenpo* 38:13–20.

Marx, Karl. 1867–94. *Das Kapital*. 3 vols. Hamburg: Meissner.

———. 1905–10. *Theorien uber den Mehrwert* (Theories of surplus-value). Edited by K. Kautsky. Stuttgart: Dietz.

Negishi, Takashi. 1997. *Keizaigakushi Nyumon* (Introduction to the history of economics). Tokyo: Hoso Daigaku Kyoiku Shinkokai.

Schumpeter, Joseph Alois. 1914. Epochen der Dogmen- und Methodengeschichte (Economic doctrine and method: A historical sketch). In vol. 1 of *Grundriss der Sozialökonomik*. Tubingen: J. C. B. Mohr.

———. 1954. *History of Economic Analysis*. New York: Oxford University Press.

Shionoya, Yuichi, ed. 2000. *German Historical School*. London: Routledge.

Smith, Adam. 1776. *An Inquiry into the Nature and Causes of the Wealth of Nations*. London: Strahan and Cadell.

Sugihara, Shiro, and Toshihiro Tanaka, eds. 1998. *Economic Thought and Modernization in Japan*. Cheltenham, U.K.: Edward Elgar.

Sugimoto, Eiichi. 1950. *Kindai Keizaigaku no Kaimei* (New lights upon economics). 2 vols. Tokyo: Rironsha.

———. 1953. *Kindai Keizaigakushi* (History of modern economics). Tokyo: Iwanami Shoten.

Tanaka, Hiroshi, ed. 1997. *Gendai Sekai to Fukushi Kokka* (Contemporary world and welfare state). Tokyo: Ochanomizu Shobo.

Uchida, Yoshihiko. 1953. *Keizaigaku no Seitan* (Birth of economics). Tokyo: Miraisha.

———. 1966. *Shihonron no Sekai* (World of *Das Kapital*). Tokyo: Iwanami Shoten.

———. 1971. *Shakai Ninshiki no Ayumi* (Steps of social recognition). Tokyo: Iwanami Shoten.

Yagi, Kiichiro. [1999] 2000. Bureaucrats and Economists. In Ikeo [1999] 2000.

Part 3

Publication and Research

The Future of Publication in the History of Economic Thought: The View from *HOPE*

Craufurd D. Goodwin

When we look ahead to the future of publication in the history of economic thought (HET) we are undertaking a market forecast, a task at which economists are notoriously inept. But we must give it a try. For at least two reasons this particular forecast is unusually complex: first, the market for publication in HET is extremely fragmented, and second, there is considerable uncertainty about behavior—on both the demand and the supply sides of the market—among those who write for and those who read our books and journals. It seems to me that the best way to grapple with this challenge is to look at the pieces of the market one at a time. I can see at least a dozen component parts, and probably there are more.

1. HET for the People

John Kenneth Galbraith is the prime example of a twentieth-century author who has successfully served a larger public beyond academe with HET. In *The Affluent Society* (1958) and then in his television documentary *The Age of Uncertainty* (1977), he used the history of economics to advance his theses about the condition of our economy and changes he thinks should be made in it. In this way, however, quite incidentally, he made known to hundreds of thousands, and perhaps millions, of people the names of Adam Smith, David Ricardo, John Maynard Keynes, Thorstein Veblen, and lesser lights in our discipline. Kenneth Boulding (see, e.g., 1966, 1976) had some of the same skills, but he did not use them with as wide an audience. I can think of no one in our subdiscipline who today follows in their footsteps. The closest parallel is the reporting on contemporary economic theory by sophisticated journalists such as Louis Uchitelle, Robert Samuelson, and David Warsh, who often illuminate the present through discussion of the past. The late Leonard Silk and Herbert Stein did this for an earlier age. Unfortunately, Paul Krugman, probably the most widely read economist-turned-journalist of our time, seldom laces his columns with HET.

2. HET in the Liberal Arts

A landmark of publication in the history of economics in the twentieth century by any criterion is Robert Heilbroner's *Worldly Philosophers* (1953). This brilliant short volume has introduced countless college students to HET who either never went further in the economics discipline or were persuaded to do so by this exposure. For those who did go on in the field, this book often led them into specialized historical courses. The book takes the position, implicitly, that the history of economics, as of other major disciplines, is an important part of a liberal arts education. It does this not through exhortation but through charm and effective writing. Heilbroner's literary gifts are not given to many, and they have been bestowed on few others among us in our time. This is a pity, because the opportunities for extension of this genre seem endless, and the externalities for the broad field of HET abundant.

3. HET for All the Disciplines

Several of the great works in the history of economics were written, it would seem, for a wide scholarly audience, extending certainly beyond specialists in HET and even beyond the economics discipline. In this category Joseph A. Schumpeter's *History of Economic Analysis* (1954), Donald Winch's (1978) works on the politics of the classical economists, and Joseph Dorfman's *Economic Mind in American Civilization* (1946–59) stand out. Certainly, when I tell colleagues in another department my specialty, after their eyes cast off their glaze they may say, "Oh, Schumpeter" or "Oh, Winch" or "Oh, Dorfman." Do we have works of more recent vintage that reach out across the disciplinary divides in the way these do? I have trouble coming up with candidates. In the more recent adventures of historians of economics with the history, sociology, and philosophy of science, I think we are perceived less as important contributors than as playing catch-up. Another piece of evidence for the growing disinterest of other disciplines in HET is the decline in the number of reviews of our research in their journals. It used to be that historians of economics would routinely look for reviews of their latest work in the *American Historical Review*, the *American Political Science Review*, the *American Journal of Sociology*, and other such flagship periodicals. Now they look in vain.

4. HET for Economics Majors and Graduate Students

Occasionally we in HET have set out to demonstrate that history is valuable to the training of professional economists and that indeed we can frame our questions and answers in the same arcana as contemporary theorists. From this perspective modern theory becomes part of a seamless web emerging from earlier great works, and HET is relevant to practical concerns and deserving even of a place within the sacred "core." Mark Blaug's pioneering textbook *Economic Theory in Retrospect* (1962) is the signal work in this category. But this book is now approaching its golden anniversary, has not been widely adopted, and still has few successful imitators; recently Blaug (2001) himself has disavowed the genre of the book that he calls "rational reconstruction" in a statement reminiscent of John Stuart Mill's recantation of the wages fund. Meanwhile HET continues to disappear from undergraduate and graduate core curricula (see Gayer, this volume).

5. HET in the Subdisciplines

Throughout the twentieth century, leaders of many of the subdisciplines in economics sought to understand their specialized fields by exploring them historically in depth, and the works they produced sometimes became classics of HET. Many examples come quickly to mind: Jacob Viner (1937) in international economics, George Stigler (1941) in micro theory, Gottfried Haberler (1939) in macroeconomics, Joseph Spengler (1942) in economic demography, Martin Bronfenbrenner (1971) in distribution theory, Lionel Robbins (1952) in policy formation, and John R. Commons (1934) in institutional change. But when have we last seen a major endeavor of this kind? We have in the discipline an abundance of "surveys of the literature," but these typically place an emphasis on modernity, not history, and are quite a different thing from HET. A few contemporary scholars still do set their historical agendas from their theoretical interests—for example, Perry Mehrling (1997) in monetary theory and Philip Mirowski (1989) in price theory—but the welcome their work receives outside the community of historians is certainly more muted than that received by the subdisciplinary historical texts of yore.

6. HET and the View from Mount Olympus

It was customary throughout much of the twentieth century for the giants in economics to look back upon their special fields at moments of triumph, such as the receipt of honors or awards or when delivering presidential addresses. Historians were often sniffy on these occasions, proclaiming this to be bad history. But at least it was history! And I suspect these moments did cause others to reflect historically if for no other reason than to correct the record. We still do occasionally see history of this kind in the literature, but now it comes mainly from octogenarians. One fears that most of the younger Olympians do not know enough history even to start such reflections.

7. HET as a Guide to Policymakers and
to the World of Affairs

During the nineteenth century, politicians, public servants, and private-sector leaders often would self-consciously use HET in their day-to-day affairs. Gladstone or Peel might refer to Adam Smith or John Stuart Mill to make the case for a favorite policy or project (Fetter 1980; Gordon 1977). It didn't hurt that Ricardo or Mill or Robert Torrens might be in their parliamentary audience. This practice could be seen still in the twentieth century, but rather less often. Keynes ([1933] 1972) directed his biographical essays partly at his political audience, and Arthur Burns (1978) regularly used historical references as chairman of the Council of Economic Advisers and of the Federal Reserve Board. (He was one of the earliest subscribers to *HOPE*.) But these were conspicuous exceptions. Kermit Gordon and Joseph Pechman experimented at the Brookings Institution in the 1970s with the history of economics as a kind of postaudit of economic policy formation (Goodwin 1975, 1981). But the experiment did not survive their departures from Brookings. One of the

few protagonists of this use for HET today is Thomas Humphrey, vice
president of the Richmond Federal Reserve Bank, who uses essays on
the history of economics to illuminate contemporary issues for his board
and readers of the bank review.

8. HET as a Refuge from Technique and Ideology

During the second half of the twentieth century, as the economics discipline became increasingly abstract and technical, and as free market ideology came to dominate the profession, HET was perceived by some dissidents as a place of succor where they could pass their declining years.
They came from virtually all of the subdisciplines but especially from
those that experienced the most sudden and rigorous doctrinal cleansing,
such as economic history, economic development, and labor economics.
The work produced by these refugees has sometimes been remarkably
fresh and insightful and has reflected an intimate understanding of institutional detail. But often it has also been problematic, presented by
the authors with anger against the discipline they believe has expelled
them, and with the questionable historical standards and quality control
familiar in an autodidact. It remains to be seen whether this component
of the market for HET will endure. As the generations move through the
pipeline, it seems doubtful that many of the to-be-unselected from the
current generation of applied mathematicians entering graduate school
will see history as an agreeable safe harbor. Who knows where they will
go—perhaps into business education. Moreover, the very visible presence of the older refugees in HET may discourage the new ones from
moving in. It is hardly inspiring to those perhaps contemplating a career
in HET to be told by their economist colleagues that this is where you
will find all the "troublemakers" and "dead wood."

9. HET as a Haven for Heresy

For reasons that are not entirely clear—perhaps because there are few alternative locations—HET has become a home for numerous embattled
sects within the larger mother church of economics, most of them only
remnants of their former selves: institutionalists, Marxians, Austrians,
post-Keynesians, Sraffians, all are conspicuously present in HET today.
It may be that this different, and often more assertive, brand of refugee finds that they may speak under the guise of history what otherwise

could be labeled treason. In most cases, these refugees also have been accustomed to using historical evidence in their argument, and in HET at least this is still respectable. Or the heretics may be puzzled by their marginalized status within the economics discipline and think that they can discover where things went wrong from a study of the past. Heresy may be a continuing source of demand for and supply of HET into the future, but with the increasing homogenization of the economics discipline, less heresy will be able to take root. We have not seen the rise of a strong new heresy in several decades, and it is striking to watch with the passage of time the decline of the old heresies, such as the old institutionalists who were so prominent in HET for so many years but are a mere shadow today.

10. Catering to the Cults through HET

A feature of economic thought through much of the nineteenth and twentieth centuries has been a tendency to generate cults of personality around certain individual economists who sometimes take on an almost mythical status and become larger than life. The cults often give strength to HET because they generate a continuing demand for and supply of historical studies of their persons. Sometimes their enthusiasm leads even to specialized societies, journals, newsgroups, Web sites, institutes, and other academic paraphernalia. Jeremy Bentham, Friedrich Hayek, Keynes, Alfred Marshall, Marx, Schumpeter, Piero Sraffa, Veblen, and Léon Walras have all sustained some cult followings in recent years. But the cults also present certain problems for HET: at times the cult figures are simply codes for modern ideologies that may be only loosely associated with the honoree; HET comes then to be perceived by outside observers as deeply politicized. The cults are also sometimes intolerant; they often insist on doctrinal purity and that their sacred persons can do no wrong. Two of the most bitter attacks on *HOPE* over its three decades have come after publishing articles that suggested, in one case, that there might be differences between the old and the young Marx and, in the other, that Friedrich Hayek, together with Schumpeter and Keynes, might have harbored some feelings of "ambivalent anti-Semitism."

It takes a heroic figure to become the object of a cult, and as modern economists come to look less like visionaries and more like engineers or, as Keynes speculated, dentists, it becomes harder to foresee many new cults appearing any time soon. My colleague Roy Weintraub argues otherwise, however, and suggests Milton Friedman, Herbert Simon, and Amartya Sen as examples of possible future cult figures.

11. Return to Roots through HET

An informal survey of manuscripts submitted to *HOPE* since the 1960s shows a marked decline in papers received from prominent mainstream economists making a one-time excursion into the history of topics on which they were then engaged. The interests of these authors were contemporary, but they discovered in their reading of an earlier literature data or insights that informed their inquiries. Why have these submissions declined? I suspect that it is because of the change in the graduate training of economists. In the 1960s, when *HOPE* began publication, virtually every professional economist had taken a course in the history of economics as a standard part of his or her training, and these economists were not intimidated by history. Indeed, they might even follow it casually by picking up a copy of *HOPE* from the departmental magazine rack and exclaiming, "This article reminds me of what I am working on now! Why don't I send them one myself?" That reaction seldom happens today. Most professional economists trained since the 1960s have not had a course in HET and have little conception of the field. They think it is a branch of genealogy. They seldom look at *HOPE*, and even less often consider sending in a manuscript. They presume their roots are largely irrelevant to their current concerns and are in the hands of obscure specialists with whom they contemplate no meaningful interaction.

12. Pursuit of HET for Its Own Sake

Clearly this is a category of HET about which we need to be especially concerned. Its practitioners provide many of the best books and articles in our journals, and they are probably our most committed readers overall. This is HET by scholars trained for the subject and committed to a career within it. Although the data do not exist to make the claim conclusively, my strong sense is that this category is on the decline. The net reproduction rate of well-trained and truly committed historians of economic thought must be less than one. As the old-timers go over the horizon, I do not see their replacements emerging in equal numbers. Partly this is because the graduate training programs have all but disappeared. And the powerful figures who led promising juniors into

the subject—Spengler, Robbins, Stigler, Frank Knight, Viner, Wesley
Mitchell, Schumpeter, and so forth—are long gone. But it is also because
at most graduate schools the incentives are strongly against this specialization. Almost anywhere in North America, certainly, a graduate student
must have strong moral fiber (and something like a self-destructive urge)
to look a director of graduate studies in the eye and declare exuberantly,
"HET's for me!" In the pages of *HOPE* we do, of course, still have some
wonderful contributions from young voices who are in the field by design rather than by accident. But they are not as abundant as when the
likes of the young Donald Winch, Bob Black, Denis O'Brien, Sam Hollander, Mark Blaug, Warren Samuels, and Bob Coats walked the boards.

The Bottom Line

As we reflect on these dozen categories of the demand for and the supply of published work in HET at the moment, we find, I think, that what
characterizes the field of HET the most today is its proclivity to look in-
ward. Historians of economics now are writing mainly for themselves.
Any scholarly field requires a critical, inward-looking component of this
kind. But if existing alone, it is probably not self-sustaining. Recently
Mark Blaug (2001) has noted the paradox that while the reputation of
HET has sunk steadily in recent years in the economics profession, the
number of self-identified historians of thought, the number of scholarly
journals, activity within the burgeoning professional associations in the
subdiscipline, and other measures of academic vigor have all risen dramatically. Are these signs of good health and promise for the future? I
think not necessarily. My explanation of this paradox is that HET currently and for a few decades back has depended heavily on the refugee
population described in categories 8, 9, and 10. The apparent good signs
are lagged and are not likely to be good predictors of the future. We see
a bubble, a temporary phenomenon associated with rapid change in the
economics mother discipline. When it passes, which is likely to be soon,
HET may settle down to a steady state that will look more like one of
the subdisciplines of philosophy or classics than the populous community we now enjoy. That is not to say the future could not be different.
But if that is to happen it will require us to reinvigorate several of the
categories of published work that have recently been neglected and have
become attenuated.

Let us now, in conclusion, briefly review the troops. The revival of categories 1 and 2 will depend on good luck and the rebirth of a Galbraith or a Heilbroner. Category 3 may be reinvigorated, I think, if we redevelop our connections, long atrophied, to other disciplines. Science studies may be the most promising route, but I would urge attention also to bridge-building with the humanities and the arts. Category 4, the rational reconstruction of the history of economics, as even Blaug agrees, has not served to revive HET broadly. Indeed, it has been found usually to serve only a committed coterie. By seeming to discredit historical reconstruction it may even perform a disservice and, overall, contrary to expectations in the 1960s, turn people away. Probably we cannot expect much from this direction. There should be real opportunities for reconnecting HET with the subdisciplines of economics, category 5, and for regenerating this aspect of HET that was so strong throughout much of the twentieth century. Success in category 5 could lead ultimately to a revival in category 6, historical reflections from leaders of the discipline. Category 7, the use of HET as a guide for policy, offers real opportunities for creative advances. The journalists have shown imagination in this regard and should be brought more directly into academic activity in HET to guide our way. I find it embarrassing that the most stimulating recent discussion of the vicissitudes of behavioral economics, and its use in policy formation, appears in the pages of the *New York Times* and not of *HOPE*.

As discussed above, I expect that categories 8 and 9, which now loom so large on our horizon, the work of refugees from technology, ideology, and accusations of doctrinal or methodological heresy, will soon be on the wane. The same may be said for category 10, too, unless new charismatic cult figures appear, and they are not now visible. Category 11, occasional forays into HET by generalists in economics, seems bound to decrease unless somehow HET is reintegrated into the graduate training of economists. This brings us back to category 12, the demand for and supply of HET from persons specifically trained for and seriously committed to the field, and upon which to some substantial degree the other categories depend. How to nourish and reinvigorate this category of HET remains a critical puzzle.

It is not unreasonable to prophesy the proximate, even if not necessarily imminent, demise of serious publication in HET. So many of the signs are ominously negative. But there may be some reason for optimism. The future of HET looked even more bleak than it does now in the 1960s, and look what has been accomplished since then! Historians of economics, perhaps hardened by adversity, have proven themselves to be resourceful, and they may once again respond to opportunity and prove the Cassandras wrong.

References

Blaug, Mark. 1962. *Economic Theory in Retrospect*. Homewood, Ill.: Irwin.
————. 2001. No History of Ideas Please, We're Economists. *Journal of Economic Perspectives* 15 (winter): 145–64.
Boulding, Kenneth E. 1966. *The Impact of the Social Sciences*. New Brunswick, N.J.: Rutgers University Press.
————. 1976. *Adam Smith as an Institutional Economist*. Memphis, Tenn.: P. K. Seidman Foundation.
Bronfenbrenner, Martin. 1971. *Income Distribution Theory*. Chicago: Aldine Atherton.
Burns, Arthur F. 1978. *Reflections of an Economic Policy Maker*. Washington, D.C.: American Enterprise Institute.
Commons, John Rogers. 1934. *Institutional Economics*. New York: Macmillan.
Dorfman, Joseph. 1946–59. *The Economic Mind in American Civilization*. New York: Viking Press.
Fetter, Frank Whitson. 1980. *The Economist in Parliament, 1780–1868*. Durham, N.C.: Duke University Press.
Galbraith, John Kenneth. 1958. *The Affluent Society*. Boston: Houghton Mifflin.
————. 1977. *The Age of Uncertainty*. Boston: Houghton Mifflin.
Goodwin, Craufurd D. 1975. *Exhortation and Controls*. Washington, D.C.: Brookings Institution.
————. 1981. *Energy Policy in Perspective*. Washington: Brookings Institution.
Gordon, Barry. 1977. *Political Economy in Parliament*. New York: Barnes and Noble.
Haberler, Gottfried. 1939. *Prosperity and Depression*. Geneva: League of Nations.
Heilbroner, Robert L. 1953. *The Worldly Philosophers*. New York: Simon and Schuster.
Keynes, John Maynard. [1933] 1972. *Essays in Biography*. London: Macmillan.
Mehrling, Perry. 1997. *The Money Interest and the Public Interest*. Cambridge: Harvard University Press.
Mirowski, Philip. 1989. *More Heat Than Light*. Cambridge: Cambridge University Press.
Robbins, Lionel. 1952. *The Theory of Economic Policy in English Classical Political Economy*. London: Macmillan.
Schumpeter, Joseph Alois. 1954. *History of Economic Analysis*. New York: Oxford University Press.
Spengler, Joseph John. 1942. *French Predecessors of Malthus*. Durham, N.C.: Duke University Press.

Stigler, George. 1941. *Production and Distribution Theories, 1870 to 1895.* New York: Macmillan.

Viner, Jacob. 1937. *Studies in the Theory of International Trade.* New York: Harper.

Winch, Donald. 1978. *Adam Smith's Politics.* Cambridge: Cambridge University Press.

Heaven Can Wait: Gatekeeping in an Age of Uncertainty, Innovation, and Commercialization

Steven G. Medema, José Luís Cardoso, and John Lodewijks

The position of journal editor provides a unique vantage point from which to view the status of and future prospects for the history of economic thought. Obviously, much of the scholarly work being done in the field flows across our desks. Moreover, because of the increasing resistance to publishing work in the history of economic thought among prominent mainstream economics journals, the role of specialist journals in the subject has taken on added importance.

In what follows, we will attempt to provide our assessment of the state of and issues facing our subject. We do not necessarily place the same weight on each of these issues, but then we do not necessarily face identical situations, either. While the history of economic thought is a worldwide field of study, our differing geographical locations and associated academic cultural milieus—in part reflecting different historiographic traditions in our respective cultures—belie attempts at homogenization. Nevertheless, we hope that our discussion here provides some useful insights into the challenges facing our subject.

A Bit of History

The first specialized journal in the field, *History of Political Economy* (*HOPE*), was founded in 1969. The history of economic thought remained a one-journal field for some fifteen years until the research annual *Research in the History of Economic Thought and Methodology*

(*RHET&M*), edited by Warren J. Samuels, was established in 1983. In the late 1980s, the *History of Economics Society Bulletin* evolved into a refereed journal, and the name was changed to the *Journal of the History of Economic Thought* (*JHET*) in 1990. The History of Economic Thought Society of Australia's *Bulletin* became a refereed journal, *History of Economics Review* (*HER*), in 1991, and the *European Journal of the History of Economic Thought* (*EJHET*) and *History of Economic Ideas* (*HEI*) were established in 1993.[1]

At least some of the rationale for the establishment of all of these new journals in the field in the latter part of the century parallels that for the proliferation of specialist journals in the economics profession at large and no doubt relates to the spread of the enormous pressures toward refereed publication throughout the profession. But for a field that often perceives itself and is perceived by others as under attack, on the run, and in decline, there may well be more to the story—particularly given that the close of the millennium witnessed, simultaneously, a heightened sense of insecurity within the field and a mood of innovation on multiple fronts, including journals publication.

The creation and launch of the *European Journal of the History of Economic Thought* in 1993 sought to achieve two main objectives. The first was to underline the need for historians of economic thought to maintain an unequivocally assertive attitude in relation to the importance of their discipline. Such an attitude was justified by disturbing evidence of the removal of the history of economic thought as a compulsory, or even optional, subject in both graduate and undergraduate courses in economics. Further evidence of this marginalization of the subject emerged from the growing reluctance of general economics journals to publish articles on historical themes. The creation of a new journal thus represented an attempt to present the inevitable specialization between the various subfields of economics as an accomplished fact, opening up a new space for publication that would be available to a significant number of authors committed to demonstrating the importance of the history of economic thought. This objective continues to justify our readiness to find the most suitable solutions for preserving the future of the discipline.

1. *HOPE* was semiannual until 1974, when it became a quarterly. *HER* has published two issues per year since its inception as a refereed journal, while *JHET* and *EJHET* were established as semiannual journals but both evolved to quarterly status in the latter part of the 1990s.

A second objective that the *EJHET* has attempted to pursue since its inception is that of affording greater visibility to the research activities undertaken in the field of the history of economic thought in various European countries that were (and continue to be) unknown largely as a result of the language barrier. The solution that was found for increasing the visibility of these works was precisely that of encouraging scholars from these countries to publish in the lingua franca of today's academic community, making it immediately clear that the journal's European scope, as stated in the title, should not impose any restrictions on the acceptance of articles submitted from any geographical quarter.

When John Lodewijks took over the editorship of *History of Economics Review* in 1991 with issue 15, he had a number of objectives for the journal (no ranking is implied):

1. To make *HER* into a respected journal, rather than a bulletin, with an international audience. To that end, high-quality articles were to be published and contributions sought from leading historians of thought.
2. To encourage submissions from economists with an interest in the history of economics but who would not normally submit to a history of economic thought journal.
3. To target graduate students and those very early in their careers.
4. To publish articles that might otherwise fall between the cracks of the established history of economic thought journals—to create a niche for nontraditional history of economic thought.
5. To promote Australasian contributions to history of economic thought.
6. To give authors an opportunity to write extensive review essays, rather than the conventional one- or one-and-a-half-page effort.
7. To publish pieces quickly so that when an issue goes to the printer there is no backlog. When an article is accepted, it goes in the next issue. There is no lag. This has meant that the page size of issues varies considerably.
8. To publish interesting and provocative pieces, not just antiquarianism.

The State of the Art

To examine the future of the history of economic thought at the turn of the millennium from the perspective of a journal editor in the field, it is useful to refer to the types of articles that we publish, as well as the much larger body of work that crosses our desks.

Doing so reveals, among other things, why it is (in some ways, at least) exciting to be the editor of a history of economic thought journal at the dawn of the new millennium—the incredible diversity of work going on in the field, both in terms of topics covered and, perhaps especially, in terms of historiographic methods employed. Works informed by the perspectives of rational reconstruction, historical reconstruction, science studies, intellectual history, and biography are submitted with regularity. Some works evidence a purely antiquarian interest, others explore larger intellectual currents, and still others attempt to inform the practice of contemporary economics by reference to the ideas of the past. Some of this work appears to be fruitful, whatever its purpose; some seems to constitute a waste of time for editor, referees, and author alike. But the simple fact of the matter is that all of it—regardless of subject and quality—serves to define what the history of economic thought is today.

To some extent—perhaps to a great extent—the editor of a history of economic thought journal sets the tone and direction for the field, ultimately determining the success or failure of work in a profession dominated by the need to publish successfully. It was not so many decades ago when this job was relatively "easy"—there was an accepted paradigm for working within the field (in essence, the study of the texts), and what needed to be assessed was simply whether the work in question demonstrated some novel point about the great thinkers of the past and their works. The modern editor, however, is besieged by works of multiple genres—genres often unacceptable or at least frowned upon by many in the field. And there are as many resistant to the new ways of doing things as there are to the old. The use of pejoratives—for example, "thick" versus "thin" histories—abounds, and the field seems at times at war with itself over the proper manner—as if there were such a thing—of doing its business. Some would have us "break away," fleeing the unwelcome environs of the economics community and departments to join forces with science studies, history of science, philosophy, or whatever group. Others recoil at those "who want to turn us into the literature department" and "emasculate us as economists." It is mildly ironic that it is those groups that feel themselves disenfranchised that often attempt to disenfranchise many within their own numbers and also seem to have the highest propensity toward imploding from within.

Because of this, the "gatekeeper" function of the editor is perhaps more important than ever before. We know immediately upon glancing at a paper what referees we can and cannot send the paper to if it is to have a chance at survival, simply based on historiographic perspective. When one adds this factor to the standard "so-and-so will hate this piece because it is directly contrary to their interpretation of the subject," one can run into real issues in terms of getting a moderately objective assessment of certain papers from multiple referees.

So, how does an editor deal with all of this? For starters, each of us, as editors, strives for catholicity and balance. There can be no doubt that there is plenty of bad work being done in the field, as in all areas of economics. But there is also much more good work being done than ever before (in absolute terms if not percentages), and not simply because of the plethora of new ways of doing the history of economics. A referee, in sending to one of us his report on a paper on which he had been asked to comment, said, "Bad history and bad economics never add up to good history of thought." What we need to guard against is an overly rigid definition of what constitutes good history, a definition that rules out-of-bounds certain types of history not currently fashionable. We have much to learn from the Mirowskis and Weintraubs of the world but also from the Blaugs, Stiglers, and Samuelsons. The wider is the currency of this notion, the easier the editor's job will be, and the benefits will redound to the field as a whole.

What does the history of economic thought look like today? And what does that portend for the future? At *JHET* several trends are discernible. Work on preclassical economics has waned significantly. William Petty and the Physiocrats retain some interest, but beyond that there is not much on offer. Adam Smith remains a popular subject for analysis, but Malthus, Ricardo, Senior, and Mill are seldom heard from. Once we get to the 1870s, however, the situation changes. William Stanley Jevons, the early Austrians, and Alfred Marshall remain, it seems, fruitful subjects for new discoveries. Institutionalism, various facets of Keynesianism, and turn-of-the-century monetary economics attract more than a bit of interest, although work on Keynes per se seems to be subsiding substantially since the deluge of the 1980s and 1990s. Post–World War II economic thought is clearly on the rise as a subject of study, particularly among young scholars in the field, as well as the larger body of scholars who advocate for and practice a science-studies approach to the subject.

In terms of the topics that are featured in the *HER*, Keynes is far and away the most popular. More than one in five articles (22 percent) are on a Keynesian topic. Admittedly there was a voluminous special issue on Keynes in 1996 edited by Athol Fitzgibbons and Bruce Littleboy, yet this may simply demonstrate that demand creates its own supply. This issue was our most popular one in terms of sales. Even without the special issue, the Keynesian concentration, and the interest in post-Keynesian economics, is clear. Following Keynes in popularity are the marginalists (11 percent), the classical political economists (10 percent), and the Austrians (6.5 percent). The Austrian contribution comes primarily from the special issue devoted to them in 1997 and edited by Tony Endres. There are twelve articles devoted to the history of Australian economics (6.5 percent), and, while *HER* has attempted to promote such work, the incentive structures may not encourage this type of research. There were only four articles on the pre-Smithian period, and of those only one on the ancients. If we were to combine several groups under the heterodox banner—Michal Kalecki (five articles), Marx (three), post-Keynesians (three) and the institutionalists (four)—then this category would account for 8 percent of articles. These classifications cover more than two-thirds of the published articles. Almost 15 percent of articles deal with the history of postwar economics, which has healthy implications for the future of the subdiscipline.

Where articles had a predominate focus on contributions by specific economists we can ascertain the nationality of the writers examined. We have already mentioned that Australian subjects constitute 6.5 percent of *HER* articles. Fourteen percent of articles deal with British subjects (other than Keynes). Including Keynes raises the British quota to more than one-third of all articles. Ten percent of articles discuss American contributions, and 18 percent cover European contributions (for example, the Austrians, Marx, Knut Wicksell, and Kalecki). The last finding indicates that the English-language bias may be declining, although the availability of English translations may be important here.

It is interesting to compare this subject category breakdown with a similar exercise undertaken for *HOPE* articles. The most glaring comparisons are that the Australian journal devotes three times the attention that *HOPE* submissions pay to Keynes and the Keynesians and double that rate for *HOPE* acceptances. The American journal also devotes far more attention to methodological and philosophical questions relating to the growth of science. Only 6.5 percent of *HER* articles deal with these issues. Comparative exercises such as this between each of the journals in our subject would undoubtedly reinforce this evidence that there is a great deal of geographic heterogeneity in the study of the history of economic thought.

And perhaps the earlier point regarding the increase in work from a science studies perspective provides a degree of insight into the waning interest in the early history of our discipline and the meteoric rise of interest in the study of the history of modern economics. For much of the early work in the discipline, the materials necessary to weave a science-studies-oriented story are lacking—not completely so, of course, as witnessed by the subject of the 2002 *HOPE* conference, "Economics in the Age of Newton." But we believe that a reasonable case can be made that the stuff of science studies—including information about scholarly communities, the paper trail of correspondence, and so on that illuminate so much of this work—is much more readily available (and perhaps more amply present) for modern subjects. Of course, the notion that these older soils have already been heavily tilled almost certainly plays a role here as well, some evidence for which can be seen from the amount of work being done on "nongiants" in the field.

Issues and Challenges for the Future

In light of all of this, what challenges can we say face the history of economic thought in the future? In the debate about the future of journals in the field of the history of economic thought, it would be advantageous if the three fundamental types of problems were to be analyzed separately (regardless of their functional connections). These challenges have to do with the relationships that journals have with authors, readers, and publishers.

Authors

As journals represent an ideal space for the development of individual curricula, it is both obvious and natural that authors should be interested in publishing their articles in some of the most highly regarded journals in their respective area of specialization. This is particularly true in the case of authors who are either at the beginning or in the middle of their careers. This means that the rate at which articles are submitted depends above all else on the prestige and vitality of the history of economics as an area of research and teaching that is duly recognized and nurtured by university institutions. Attracting students who are undertaking M.Phil. and Ph.D. courses and theses in the history of economics will be one of the surest ways of guaranteeing a regular flow of articles.

If the trend is toward a sharp decline in academic interest in the history of economics—as would seem to be proved by the available diagnoses made in regard to this matter—then journals publishing in this area will be faced in either the short or medium term with the serious risk of having to survive from the (not eternally renewable) stock of articles written by those authors who are still active in this profession. Or else, in the event of what may prove to be a no less unpleasant scenario, journals in the history of economic thought will be coveted by authors linked to currents of thought that have been marginalized or ostracized by the dominant currents and interests in the academic community, with the result that the journals will become trapped in the ghetto that they themselves have unwittingly and involuntarily created.

This latter scenario presupposes that the quintessential source for the recruitment of the authors publishing in our journals is university economics departments. In this way, should the persuasive efforts made to demonstrate the importance of the history of economics not immediately have their expected effect on the university establishment, it will be necessary to broaden the scope of journals in the history of economic thought to include other areas of academic output. This is a challenge that will make it possible to renew the discipline itself, without necessarily any desire to substantially alter its status. Through the incorporation of new insights provided by authors with greater experience in such fields as history of science, economic history, history of ideas, economic sociology, sociology of knowledge, economic methodology, philosophy, and political science (to mention only the most relevant), the boundaries of the framework for research that have so far tended to predominate will be opened up quite significantly.

Besides this strengthening of the traditional source of recruitment and its expansion to include other sources, a crucial aspect that needs to be taken into account has to do with the consolidation of a relationship of greater trust between authors and the journals that may accept their contributions. If we look at the annual volume of activities (conferences, workshops, seminars, summer schools, etc.) promoted by university

departments or by the many different associations and societies existing not only in the United States, but also in Europe, Japan, and Australia, we are led to conclude that the total supply of potential articles
is more than enough to satisfy demand and keep in balance the various
segmented markets for publication. However, many of the results of this
activity do not succeed in getting beyond an intermediate stage of preparation, never even reaching the submission stage for publication in the
established journals that are most respected by the community of historians of economic thought. It also happens that some of these works end
up being published in volumes of conference proceedings, contributing
to the general satisfaction of the respective editors, or simply because
this is an imposition inherent in the actual organization of the events in
which they take part.

We have already argued that there is much good work going on in
our field. But is there enough to continue to support five journals? We
now find historians of economic thought publishing their work in history of science and related journals. The fact that much scholarly activity
is devoted to writing for edited volumes turns out to be a mixed bless-
ing. The publication opportunities in the history of economic thought
afforded by publishers such as Routledge and Edward Elgar have been
an important stimulus to work in the field. These publishers recognize
the import of our subject (or at least the ability to make money on it)
and have been steadfast in providing publishing opportunities, both for
established figures in the field and for young scholars attempting to carve
out a professional identity. But at the same time, the avalanche of edited
volumes has meant a substantial decrease in the per capita effort devoted
to publication in scholarly journals. This presents potential difficulties
both for the journals themselves and for the quality of scholarship in the
field. The former, of course, is self-evident: journals see a smaller flow
of manuscripts than they would otherwise, and since the heavy hitters
in the field are constantly in demand to contribute to these volumes, the
pinch would seem to be felt on the higher end of the quality spectrum.
The latter problem arises from the lack of scholarly checks and balances
in edited volumes. We would not wish to disparage these works (particularly as each of us has edited or contributed to a number of them!),
but the rigorous refereeing by subject-specific experts that one finds in
the journals in the field is all but absent for the edited volumes. We believe that it is unambiguously true that the surest route to enhancing the

strength of scholarship in the field is for more of the work to flow through scholarly journals.

And without wishing to declare war on these conference volumes (which have given so many headaches to book reviewers desperately seeking some coherence and unity in these collections of sundry texts), we believe that the authors, too, will greatly benefit from a closer relationship of trust with journals. This is the requirement made by the university hierarchy, which has the power to decide upon applications for posts and career promotions. It is also a requirement that authors must begin to impose on themselves, in the certain knowledge that the greater difficulty and longer wait necessary for publication in a journal are suitably rewarded by the greater visibility and academic projection that their articles will then enjoy.

Another way of encouraging submissions from authors is to seek to satisfy their specific research interests through the organization of issues devoted to particular themes, regardless of whether or not these are the result of conferences previously held on this same subject. *HOPE*'s experience in this field, whether in symposia published in the journal or in the annual supplements incorporating material presented at *HOPE* conferences, is an excellent example of how it is possible to maintain and stimulate research into themes that are considered important for the development of the discipline, without compromising the sacred rules of the peer review system. Likewise, *HER* has run a number of excellent symposia, and *JHET* currently has several in the pipeline.

A further potential problem for the history of economic thought journals, as unrealistic as it may seem at present, is that things may come full circle, and those of us who study the history of economic thought may again find ourselves welcomed as full members of the larger scholarly community of economists, with concomitant publishing opportunities in the major journals of the profession. Indeed, the study of modern history of economic thought may endear us to the profession at large and open up new publishing opportunities in these journals. This may not be good for business at the history of economic thought journals—although it may stimulate the supply side—but it certainly will be welcome for the field as a whole.

Readers

The number of individual and institutional subscriptions to a journal is one of the indicators of its receptivity and impact among its intended audience. In the case of both *JHET* and *EJHET*, the complete separation between editorial responsibility and the production and commercial administration of the journal has been an important factor in easing the tension that inevitably affects editors who are scrupulously concerned with the extension of the market for their journal. In view of what has just been said about the growing specialization of the various subfields of economics, with its inevitable repercussions on the fragmented universe of increasingly specialized journals, the number of active readers has tended to remain confined to the more or less restricted groups of people interested in each of the subfields.

The term *active readers* applies to those who regularly read a significant number of the articles published in each issue of a certain journal, seeking to update their knowledge and enrich their intellectual understanding of the subject area. In the case of journals in the history of economics, the number of such readers does not seem particularly large, nor is there any notable trend toward this increasing in the near future. In fact, year upon year, there has been no great change in the names and faces that we have grown used to seeing at the various conferences we attend. This means that a great effort needs to be made to increase the number of potential readers (i.e., those who do not regularly read the journal but may find their interest aroused by a more frequent contact with it). Such a move presupposes that we must concentrate our efforts at two different levels: on the one hand, at the level of editorial policy, by promoting a wider range of contents, in keeping with what was said earlier about expanding the thematic boundaries of the discipline; on the other hand, at the level of commercial administration, by further marketing the contents of already published issues and creating the conditions for easier on-line access by those using the libraries of the different institutions that subscribe to the journals.

As far as the first aspect is concerned, an improved performance depends essentially on the editorial strategy that is followed, with all that this implies in relation to the spirit of initiative and the risk of innovation. In the case of the second aspect, more complex factors are brought into play, which go far beyond the mere goodwill and professionalism of those responsible for the commercial promotion of a journal. The case of *EJHET* is instructive here.

On entering its third year of publication, the *EJHET* succeeded in gaining the first sign of external recognition of its editorial maturity, with a reference to the journal's title in the printed publication of the *JEL* and the contents of each issue being indexed in the on-line records of *EconLit*. In view of the importance of these classification and indexing systems for the analysis made by university libraries to justify their decisions regarding annual journal subscriptions (such decisions are almost always made within the context of very strict budget constraints), the next step taken by the editors and publishers of the *EJHET* was to submit the journal to the appreciation of the Institute of Scientific Information (ISI), with a view to its inclusion in the *Social Sciences Citation Index* (*SSCI*). Their efforts have yet to produce any positive results, and a reply was received saying that the limited number of citations made to articles published in journals in the history of economic thought would not justify taking the *EJHET* into consideration.

This is neither the time nor the place to question the validity of the criteria and methods followed by those in charge of the ISI. However, as the journal's failure to be included in the *SSCI* may significantly affect the decisions of university libraries, the conclusion must be drawn that the possibilities of launching new journals in very specialized areas are limited by the confines of a vicious circle. Institutional subscribers need the guarantees provided by the referencing systems; these systems require citation levels that can only be reached if the journal maintains an outstanding quality guaranteed by top-level authors; these authors, in turn, prefer to publish in journals that are already indexed by the *SSCI*, since this is one of the criteria that university institutions increasingly require for the curricular assessment of their members. In short, it is a catch-22: journals are not known or sought after by authors because they are not indexed; journals are not indexed because they are not known or sought after by authors.

The consequences of this vicious circle go far beyond the legitimate concerns that the editors of journals necessarily have with regard to the expansion of their audience and the number of their potential readers. In fact, the crucial question resulting from this approach is, once more, the weakening of the relationship of trust that exists between the authors and the journals that organize the territory for publication in a certain academic field. The logic of "publish or perish" may persuade certain authors to define individual research strategies that lead them to abandon a preferred field they had pursued as a result of a specific vocation (the history of economics) and choose less-appetizing research areas that are nonetheless more profitable from the point of view of the management of a university career. Consequently, the strong assertion of the importance of the history of economics is an urgent and fundamental task not only for the creation of conditions of greater stability and continuity for academic journals, but above all for helping young researchers become established in this area of study

Publishers

The question raised at the end of the previous section may also be discussed under the following terms: in view of the difficulties encountered in getting journals on the history of economic thought admitted to the *SSCI*, why should we not attempt to find alternative processes for the recognition of journals, thereby bypassing the formal obstacles that librarians like to evoke when deciding to which journals they wish to subscribe? And this question may be taken further: in view of the exorbitant price of institutional subscriptions, why not create alternative models for publication that free authors, editors, and referees from the straitjacket that is frequently associated with the commercial strategies of the major publishing companies?

These questions have been increasingly discussed by the academic community, primarily in the scientific, technical, and medical fields, giving rise to the formation of associations and partnerships that challenge the traditional order of the academic journals marketplace.[2] In the field of the social sciences, identical initiatives have enjoyed an ever greater impact on academic public opinion,[3] and their effects have been

2. One of the best-known cases is that of SPARC—the Scholarly Publishing and Academic Resource Coalition—which began as an initiative of the U.S. Association of Research Libraries and defines itself as "a worldwide alliance of research institutions, libraries and organisations that encourages competition in the scholarly communications market. SPARC introduces new solutions to scientific journal publishing, facilitates the use of technology to expand access, and partners with publishers that bring top-quality, low cost research to a greater audience. SPARC strives to return science to scientists."

3. See the case of the ELSSS (Electronic Society for Social Scientists), which began as a reaction aimed mainly at the exorbitant pricing policy pursued by the journals of the Elsevier group, and which defines itself as "a new, non-profit-making society, whose mission is to improve scientific communication in the social sciences, especially by the provision of electronic publications of high quality, wide diffusion and low cost for the direct benefit of the academic

particularly noticeable in the field of economics.[4] As far as the specific field of the history of economics is concerned, this subject has also given rise to a certain amount of debate and resulted in the public demonstration of points of view questioning the hegemony of the almighty publishers[5] or proposing the creation of a new electronic journal in the history of economic thought.[6]

This brief outline (which has by no means sought to discuss the subject in the sort of depth that it deserves) would seem to demonstrate sufficiently that reactions against the traditional supports for the publication of academic journals are not designed simply to challenge the policy of high prices pursued by the main publishing companies. What is in fact under discussion here is the creation of alternative means for disseminating the knowledge produced within a certain field of study. The opinion most frequently heard is that electronic journals may represent more effective vehicles for the production and circulation of this new knowledge by exclusively serving the academic community and eliminating the excessive transaction costs imposed by the insatiable publishers.

In regard to this same subject, it is worth remembering the lessons of experience. It is immediately important to stress that relations between the editors and the publisher of *JHET* and *EJHET* (both now published under the Routledge imprint by the Taylor and Francis Group) have always been marked by great frankness and a high level of mutual understanding.[7] This has not, however, prevented situations in which the publisher's commercial strategy has had direct repercussions on the activity of editorial management. This was the case when, as early as its second year of existence, the *EJHET* began to publish three issues per year (instead of the two issues that had initially been established as the journal's norm), and, in particular, when it began to publish four annual issues as from volume 6 onward in 1999.

---

community (and indirectly to the taxpayer and the general public)." For further information about reactions to high-priced journals, see Bergstrom 2001.

4. The most significant example is that of the bepress.com journals, founded by a team of academics whose stated aim is to construct "a radical new approach to academic publishing" and to combat "the inefficiencies of the traditional peer review model."

5. See Aspromourgos 2000.

6. This was suggested last December by H. Plasmeijer, Glenn Hueckel, Mike Robinson, and others through the HES list. This debate informed us that the host to this conference will be the associate editor for the history of economic thought in a new, forthcoming e-journal on general economics.

7. *HER* is not associated with a commercial publisher.

In this latter case, the change in the rhythm of publication was clearly dictated by reasons arising from the relationship between the publisher and the institutions subscribing to the journal. As evidence that this new phase was embarked upon for reasons of commercial strategy, it should be noted that when the change was made to four issues, the number of pages per volume remained more or less the same. The adjustments programmed by the publishers dictated a much higher increase in the price of institutional subscriptions than in the price of individual subscriptions, which also highlights the main motivations of this change. So far, it does not appear that the commercial behavior adopted by the publisher of *EJHET* and *JHET* has had any negative effect on the journals' academic activity or on their aim of providing a useful service to the scholarly and intellectual community of the historians of economic thought. Needless to say, we shall remain particularly attentive to signs that may suggest any alteration to our present diagnosis.

In view of these experiences, and bearing in mind the markedly non-commercial nature of the main journals published in this area, it is important to know the extent to which our own particular case is affected by the alarming news about the unfathomable intentions of the commercial publishers. If such a threat were to be confirmed, it would mean that the sharp fall in institutional subscriptions might give rise to a gradual exodus of those authors who would lose interest in publishing their articles in journals with increasingly lower circulations that consequently offer them far fewer citations. It does not seem that this threat is likely to materialize.

This response naturally gives rise to an attitude of some reservation and prudence with regard to initiatives for the creation of new journals, particularly those with an electronic format. The mirage of enjoying rapid publication without the inevitable disturbances caused by the workings of the editorial machine of printed journals must not allow us to overlook the need for the certification of quality that is guaranteed by the methods normally used by existing journals. Does this represent a defensive attitude on the part of those who wish to see their market share safeguarded and protected?

We think not. Once again, the fundamental question is the relationship of trust existing between authors and journals, insofar as there is a firm belief that these will continue to follow the rules and principles of the peer review system that is universally accepted by the academic community. Journals need to see their quality recognized through the referencing and indexing processes that are promoted by outside bodies and established independent organizations, or through other suitable procedures agreed between university institutions. In either case, the important thing is always to ensure recognition of the history of economic thought as a field of fundamental knowledge, to which a contribution is to be made by specialists from the various social sciences (and not only those that rub shoulders with each other in university economics departments).

Disciplinary Identity

Moving farther away from editorial self-interest, a further challenge facing the field, and perhaps its largest one from an "internalist" perspective, is that of developing a disciplinary identity. This has multiple aspects. One facet of our current identity involves the fighting of rearguard battles to justify our existence. Apart from being unproductive (no one is listening anyway), those who constantly feel compelled to justify their existence inherently seem to arouse suspicion as to the very justifiability of their existence. But more importantly, the history of economic thought community needs to face up squarely to the question, "What are we, and what are we to be?" Are we to be historians of science? intellectual historians? economists? Are we to be all of these (and others), coexisting harmoniously (or not!)? Members of the history of economic thought community have expressed to us the following sentiments: "I am *not* an economist, I am a historian"; "I am not a historian of science; I prefer to be called a cultural historian"; "I am an economist" (followed by disparaging comments about those who would take us in the direction of the current historical trends in the field).

Further to this same point regarding professional identity, do we wish to celebrate diversity or to impose on the work in our field the sort of homogeneity that so many among our numbers decry within the economics profession at large? Hiding under the cover of "good history" will only take us so far. All too often that is a mere fig leaf intended to cover a statement that translates as "history as *I* would do it." Historians of economic thought are now as slave to the fashions of their intellectual culture as are their standard economist brethren and colleagues in other disciplines. Many of those who rebel against the very notion of progress in economics are quick to point to the supposed progress introduced in the history of economic thought by certain currently fashionable ways of doing history. We clearly have come some considerable distance since the Spiegels, Samuelses, and Winches began to lead us away from the realm of rational reconstruction and toward that of intellectual history. Times change, and with every new era come fads, fashions, and fancies. The course of events separates wheat from chaff, fruitful endeavor from passing fancy—always imperfectly and often cyclically. Through all of this, we attempt to learn, build, and improve how we go about our business. But just as the rise of science studies within our community has led to the attempt in some quarters to stamp out the menace of rational reconstruction, the tide will turn one day, and those currently gaining ascendancy will find themselves on the run.

How does this relate to the issue of professional identity? The way we see ourselves profoundly affects what we will become. While we cannot escape the fact that we are perpetually "becoming," we can, if we wish, choose to be overtly self-conscious about this process and in doing so chart for ourselves one of the several professional identities available to us. It should be clear by now that if we are to argue normatively here, it will be for openness and inclusion—not for bad work, but for good work of whatever genre. The question that we face is whether we are going to draw the boundaries of good work broadly or narrowly, whether we are going to attempt to impose from within a rigid, "like me" definition or take the more difficult road of opening ourselves to the notion that important contributions to our subject can flow from perspectives very different from our own. In his wonderful brief book on methodology published some twenty years ago, Bruce Caldwell called his fellow economists to pluralism; historians of economics would do well to heed this advice.

Yet another issue confronting the future of our subject is that of narrowness. The younger generation, although perhaps reasonably healthy in numbers, is abjectly devoid of generalists in the field. The same sort of niche-building that pervades the rest of the profession seems to have become epidemic in our own field as well. We will leave the question of why unanswered, instead examining briefly the implications. From an editor's perspective, the trend toward narrowness of study makes referee selection increasingly difficult. It has become progressively harder to find classicists, to say nothing of suitable referees for papers invoking scholars as diverse as, say, Cantillon, Smith, and Wicksell. But more importantly, the history of economic thought scholar whose depth of knowledge falls within a relatively narrow band is only marginally above the "economist" who is generally ignorant of the discipline's history. Mastery of the details of various facets of post–World War II economic thought without an accompanying mastery of what came before is as dangerous as being a contemporary theorist with no knowledge of history. Indeed, one of the benefits of editing a history of economic thought journal is that it forces us to expand the depth of our knowledge beyond the narrow areas that we are mining in our own research. Teaching a survey course in the history of economic thought does not accomplish this. It requires active reading and writing across our discipline, just as being a good specialist in public finance, labor, or econometrics requires an in-depth knowledge across those specialities.

Perhaps all of this will leave the reader with the impression that we are rather pessimistic about our field. On the whole, this is not the case. We see reasons for hope for the future but also a number of challenges ahead of us. We cannot control those larger professional attitudes that determine the degree of acceptance of our work within the profession as a whole, but we can chart our own course, for better or for worse.

References

Aspromourgos, Tony. 2000. Historical Scholarship and Publication, or Why Do Commercial Publishers Exist? *History of Economics Review* 32 (summer): 1–9.

Bergstrom, Ted. 2001. Free Labor for Costly Journals. *Journal of Economic Perspectives* 15.3:183–98.

Coming Together: History of Economics as History of Science

Margaret Schabas

> At the other extreme is the antihistorical school, which is now common in the United States, where the history of thought is regarded as a slightly depraved entertainment, fit only for people who really like medieval Latin, so that one can become a full-fledged chartered Ph.D. economist without ever reading anything that was published more than ten years ago.
> —Kenneth Boulding, "After Samuelson, Who Needs Adam Smith?"
> (1971)

If one revisits the early years of *History of Political Economy*, one cannot help but be struck with the impression that the field was already very much on the retreat. Kenneth Boulding (1971, 232–33) deplores the lack of historical thinking in the education of American economists; A. W. Coats (1969, 9) observes that the pressures of government and business have rendered the history of economics into "an unnecessary luxury or, more frequently, . . . a wasteful diversion of time and energy." Their complaints have withstood the tests of time. While the history of economics, at least in American universities, is often recommended if not required for undergraduate students of economics, most graduate students never take a course in the subject. The history of economics is more deeply woven into the curriculum in France, the Netherlands, and

I would like to thank Simon Schaffer for some important feedback. Others have helped with factual information: Steve Medema, Bernard Cohen, Esther-Mirjam Sent, Noretta Koertge, Margaret Rossiter, Margaret Osler, Jay Malone, Tim Alborn, Tom Broman, and Paul Dudenhefer. I owe special thanks to Sheila Dow and Roy Weintraub, who helped me with retrieval difficulties in the midst of relocating.

Japan, for example, but the situation in the United States is unlikely to improve anytime soon. Research in the field, however, has grown, in that there are more journals, more books, and more active scholars than ever before. But the economics profession has grown as well, such that our constituency in the profession is at best 1 percent.[1]

Adaptation is often the key to survival. It will come as no surprise for those who are already familiar with my work that I am a keen advocate of treating the history of economics as a branch of the history of science. Some articles in *History of Political Economy*, for example those by Paul Christensen (1989), Salim Rashid (1981), and Richard Romano (1982), had already begun to steer the subject in that direction. These were followed by some books that linked the two fields, notably Ingrao and Israel 1987, Mirowski 1989, and Schabas 1990. And since I published my "Breaking Away" manifesto in 1992, many more works have appeared that draw firm connections between the history of economics and the history of science.[2] The most notable contribution in this respect is Philip Mirowski's edited volume, *Natural Images in Economic Thought* (1994), which included articles by such prominent historians of science as I. Bernard Cohen, Ivor Grattan-Guinness, Sharon Kingsland, Camille Limoges, and Theodore Porter. Other monographs in this vein are those by Robert B. Ekelund Jr. and Robert F. Hébert (1999), James Henderson (1996), Judy Klein (1997), and Deborah Redman (1997). Historians of economics have also published numerous articles in mainstream history of science journals such as *Isis*, *Science in Context*, and *Studies in the History and Philosophy of Science*. See, for example, the articles by Sergio Cremaschi and Marcelo Dascal (1998), Robert Dimand (1993), Francesco Guala (2001), Bruna Ingrao (1994), Gérard Jorland (1996), Robert Leonard (1998), Harro Maas (1999), Uskali Mäki (1997), Philip Mirowski (1992b, 1999), Bert Mosselmans (1998), Mary Morgan (1997), Esther-Mirjam Sent (2001), and Yuval Yonay (1994).[3]

1. My estimate is based on the following statistics. There are about three hundred active scholars in the history of economics in North America, and about thirty thousand members of the American Economic Association and Canadian Economic Association combined. Of course there are many more economists in America, easily one hundred thousand who adopt the title, but a more limited number are academic economists and thus form the relevant comparison group. In 1983, De Marchi and Lodewijks (334) observed that the publication rate of articles in history of economics had grown linearly, but the economics literature over the past twenty years had grown exponentially.

2. A provocative follow-up can be found in Emmett 1997.

3. There are also some examples that precede 1992. See, for instance, Gordon 1989, Hollander 1983, and Schabas 1989.

As a frequent attendee at history of science gatherings, I have formed the impression that the history of economics is no longer viewed as a deviant pursuit. A cluster of collected volumes appeared circa 1990 that included one or more articles on the history of economics, notably Patrick Brantlinger's *Energy and Entropy* (1989) (with an article by the present author), I. Bernard Cohen's *The Natural Sciences and the Social Sciences* (1994) (Camille Limoges, Giuliano Pancaldi, Margaret Schabas, and S. S. Schweber), Tore Frängsmyr's *Science in Sweden* (1989) (Sven-Eric Liedman), Tore Frängsmyr, John Heilbron, and Robin Rider's *Quantifying Spirit in the Eighteenth Century* (1990) (Karin Johannisson, Svante Lindqvist, and Henry E. Lowood), and Lorenz Krüger, Gerd Gigerenzer, and Mary S. Morgan's *Probabilistic Revolution* (1987) (Gérard Jorland, Claude Ménard, and Mary Morgan). The tide changed most explicitly, however, with the work of three prominent historians of science: Theodore Porter (1986), Norton Wise (1989–90), and Simon Schaffer (1989, 1994). This was in part due to the shift by historians of science toward what has come to be known as cultural history. The abandonment of a strict "internalist" history of science in the 1970s of the sort exemplified by Alexandre Koyré (1965) led to a strong emphasis on institutional factors in the development of science as, say, in the work of Jack Morrell and Arnold Thackray (1981). But this tended to neglect the actual content of scientific theories, and in dialectical fashion, there was an effort to restore the play of ideas while also drawing links to the broader social setting of science. Some leading exponents of this are Lorraine Daston, Ian Hacking, and Bruno Latour. But perhaps what most consolidated the presence of economics was the appreciation of standardization in the history of science literature, spearheaded by Porter, Wise, and Schaffer. That commercial interests spawned the motifs of precision and objectivity in science is music to the ears of those who believe that science is deeply political. This is most exemplified by Theodore Porter's *Trust in Numbers* (1995), Norton Wise's collection *Values of Precision* (1995), and Michael Power's *Accounting and Science* (1996). Other examples of this appreciation for applied economics and its implications for standardization are, for example, Judith Grabiner 1998, Svante Lindqvist 1990, and James Sumner 2001.

By the mid-1990s, history of economics had become part of mainstream history of science. Indeed, prizes from the History of Science Society for the best book and *Isis* article, respectively, went to works that explicitly link economics to other sciences, Pamela Smith's *Business of*

Alchemy (1994) and William Ashworth's (1996) essay on Charles Babbage and John Herschel. Other noteworthy monographs of the past ten years that feature economic ideas in their treatment of the history of the natural sciences are Joel Kaye 1997, Lisbet Koerner 1999, and Jean-Pierre Poirier 1993. Recent articles on the history of economics that are in either edited volumes or journals in the history of science are Timothy Alborn 1996, Myles Jackson 1994, Gérard Jorland 2000, Norriss Hetherington 1993, Jessica Riskin 1998, Andrea Rusnock 1999, Margaret Schabas 1997, Emma Spary 1996, Sylvana Tomaselli 1995, and Norton Wise 1993. And the recent volume on models, edited by Mary S. Morgan and Margaret Morrison (1999), has highlighted yet another point of intersection between the natural sciences and economics.

A more minor objective on my part has been to promote the name *history of economics* in lieu of *the history of economic thought*, as a way to both mimic other branches of the history of science and help steer our field away from its internalist orientation. So if one can extrapolate even from the title of the 2001 *HOPE* conference, there is cause for optimism. Not only has the simplified name for our pursuit gained greater currency, but it is evident from the list of citations just given that the history of economics has drawn considerably more ties with the history of science since 1992, and vice versa. If one looks to leading textbooks in the history of economics—for example, Mark Blaug (1997) and Henry Spiegel (1991)—one finds a longstanding recognition of the ideas of Thomas Kuhn and Imre Lakatos. For what it is worth, Joseph Schumpeter's great tome (1954) drew extensive connections to the history of science. More significantly, one can now find readings on the history of economics in a number of history of science graduate courses, such as those offered at Princeton (with readings from Michael Mahoney), University of Toronto (Sungook Hong), University of Wisconsin (Tom Broman), University of California, Los Angeles (Ted Porter and Norton Wise), and Cambridge (Simon Schaffer), to note only a few. Philip Mirowski's *More Heat Than Light* (1989) is widely read among historians of science, as is the collection of articles edited by Neil De Marchi (1993) that attempt to make sense of it.

The links between the history of economics and the history of science, at least in the Anglo-American world, are longstanding. Economics has had a constant though relatively minor presence in the discourse of the history of science since its earliest professional days (*Isis* was founded in 1912; the History of Science Society was founded in 1924), and a marked increase in recognition has transpired in the past two or so decades. Given the relatively secure status of the history of science profession in the academic world, I will argue that historians of economics could only benefit from closer ties to this larger group of scholars. Moreover, one of the factors that brought about the success of the history of science as a discipline was its emancipation from the science professions. By developing their own disciplinary methods and standards, historians of science are able to speak to themselves and thus cultivate stronger disciplinary boundaries.

Interestingly, some of the leading contributors to economics of the distant past also wrote on history of science. One might make that case even for Aristotle, who, relative to his contemporaries, provided historical overviews on various sciences. But that would be stretching matters more than is warranted. Certainly, however, the case can be made for Adam Smith (1980), whose essays on the history of astronomy and the history of ancient physics are some of the very best accounts of the time. During the nineteenth century we find several eminent economists writing on the history of science, namely William Whewell, John Stuart Mill, A. A. Cournot, and William Stanley Jevons. Jevons even attempted to chronicle the development of mathematical economics, resulting in the unprecedented effort to do both history of science and history of economics. But these were done more or less in separation from one another. It is only in the twentieth century that historians of science began to include economics in a systematic manner.

Historians of economics have undoubtedly been the poorer cousins among professional historians of science, the ones, as Thomas Robert Malthus would have put it, who were left out at nature's feast. In the formative years of the history of science, say, from 1915 to 1960, the thing to do was the history of the exact sciences, namely, mathematics, physics, and astronomy. Even the history of chemistry suffered from the aspersions of "sooty empiricism" once cast by Descartes. Until about 1960, as Thomas Kuhn (1977, 111) recognized, the number of American academics appointed explicitly as historians of science was scarcely more than half a dozen. Only then did the subject begin to grow professionally and make its way into the core curriculum of many universities. The histories of the life sciences and of psychology had received relatively short shrift up until that time but began to gain a full-fledged identity with the introduction of the *Journal of the History of the Behavioral Sciences* (1965) and the *Journal of the History of Biology* (1968). These publications commenced in tandem with the formation of our cherished and beloved *HOPE* (1969). Nevertheless, it is possible, within this Comtean hierarchy, to discern the presence of the history of economics right from the very start. In other words, it had a toehold in the history of science world, even if it did not have the level of general acceptance that has come about in the past two decades.

To provide some evidential support to these impressions, I perused the *Dictionary of Scientific Biography* (Gillispie 1970) to see if the science of economics had made any entries.[4] To my surprise, my recent survey yielded several entries that acknowledged contributions to economics, including William Petty, Anne-Robert-Jacques Turgot, David Hume, Jevons, and John Maynard Keynes (Karl Marx and Friedrich Engels appear in the supplementary volume of 1978). Moreover, economics was explicitly recognized in the subheadings that listed scientific contributions. Some, such as John Locke, Étienne Bonnot de Condillac, and the Marquis de Condorcet, had entries, but no mention was made of their interests in economics. Others, such as Adam Smith, Léon Walras, and Irving Fisher, were omitted altogether. A couple of prominent chemists, Antoine Lavoisier and Frederick Soddy, had their writings on economics acknowledged in their articles, but not in the front set of scientific specialties.

The fact that the first list could have economics featured in the description of scientific pursuits after those names shows that economics was not entirely neglected even if it did not figure prominently at the time. As the general editor, Charles C. Gillispie, made clear in the preface, those in the behavioral and social sciences were included only in the instances of persons whose work was intrinsically related to the sciences of nature or to mathematics. Turgot was listed as a contributor to economics and philosophy, Hume to philosophy, economy, political theory, and history. Turgot was included, however, for his work on the theory of vapors, which was of seminal importance in the so-called chemical revolution. No doubt Hume made an appearance because of his later influence on logical positivism and on Albert Einstein.

It is worth noting that Gillispie, the dictionary's editor-in-chief, is himself one of the first historians of science to write about the work of economists. His *Genesis and Geology* (1951), drawing heavily on the

4. As graduate students in the history of science at the University of Toronto, we were encouraged to commit the entire dictionary (fifteen volumes) to memory, but of course I failed on that score.

work of Élie Halévy, made numerous references to Victorian economists such as Thomas Chalmers. His 1957 *Isis* article, "The Natural History of Industry," referred to the role of the physiocrats, and his celebrated *Edge of Objectivity* (1960) drew connections to classical political economy, notably the ideas of Adam Smith and Malthus. One of the best examinations of the economic work of Lavoisier and Turgot can be found in his more recent study, *Science and Polity in France at the End of the Old Regime* (1980). Not by accident, one of Gillispie's most famous students, Theodore Porter, has championed the presence of economics in mainstream history of science since he began to publish in the early 1980s.

To gain a better understanding of the presence (or absence) of the history of economics within the history of science world I decided to look closely at the contents of *Isis*, from its formation in 1912 up to the time of Thomas Kuhn's landmark work, *The Structure of Scientific Revolutions* (1962). Not only has *Isis* retained its standing as the journal of choice for historians of science right up to the present (its subscription level is close to four thousand), but it also provides an annual critical bibliography, which scans hundreds of books and journals that might pertain to the history of science (*HOPE*, alas, was only entered into its charts in 1979). Each issue also provides commentaries, news about the profession, and *éloges*.

Isis was founded by George Sarton, a Belgian scholar, in 1912, shortly before the Great War. It originally published articles in numerous languages, not only French, English, and German, but also Greek and Arabic. Volume 1 actually appeared in 1913 and explicitly recognized "les sciences sociologiques." There were also articles on the history of art, music, ethnology, and geography. The first issue of volume 2 appeared in 1914, but no more appeared until the war had ended. The remaining part of volume 2 appeared in 1919, and volume 3 spanned the years 1920–21, delayed by Sarton's move to Harvard. In 1920, Sarton announced in a preface that the journal would henceforth publish exclusively in English. With a passionate plea for universal humanism, Sarton deemed English the language of hope and democracy, because it belonged to the many countries that had brought peace and freedom back to the world. Interestingly, Émile Durkheim was on the original "comité de patronage" of thirty-two men, along with other eminences such as Jacques Loeb and Henri Poincaré. But in fact Sarton alone put the journal together for many years. He never issued another patronage committee, and not until his student I. Bernard Cohen took over in 1953 did the journal appear to be run by more than one person. Cohen worked together with a four-man advisory board.[5] An editorial committee of seven scholars was listed for the first time in 1969! That is a considerable period of time for a journal to be run so autocratically.

Sarton's approach to the history of science was anything but narrow. In volume 3, his opening article was on Herbert Spencer, who was best known for his work on philosophy, psychology, and social Darwinism (Sarton 1921, iii). In volume 5 of *Isis*, Sarton's (1923, 2) opening remarks construed the field of history of science as broadly as possible: "The history of science is essentially a story of human achievement. . . . The task of the historian should not be restricted to the more technical aspect of scientific discovery." In volume 23, he featured Adolphe Quetelet on the centenary of his *Sur l'homme* (1835), which Sarton (1935, 6) deemed "one of the greatest books of the nineteenth century." He traced Quetelet's work back to the political arithmetic of William Graunt, William Petty, and Edmund Halley. These are just some indications that Sarton, at least, did not confine the field to mathematics, physics, and astronomy, even though these were the areas of his most celebrated research.

Sarton included a critical bibliography (*bibliographie analytique*) at the end of each issue from the very start. Indeed, *Isis* appears to have grown out of his efforts to catalog scholarship in the history of science. There were entries for the subjects of *psychologie* (section 18), *sociologie et politique positive* (section 19), and *anthropologie*. But these sections, grouped under the broader rubric of *sciences sociologiques*, only occupied about one-half of a page, much less than the other four categories of mathematics, physical sciences, biological sciences, and medical sciences. Under section 19 in volume 1 (issue 3) are two entries, one of which reads, "Charles Gide et Charles Rist, *Histoire des doctrines économiques depuis les physiocrates jusqu'à nos jours*, 2e ed." By volume 3 (1920–21), there is a separate heading for economics (number 11), with seven entries in the first issue, including the English translation of Gide and Rist and the new and enlarged edition of John Kells Ingram, *A History of Political Economy*. At this point, Sarton arranged the subheadings alphabetically, so *economics* came between

5. Robert Multhauf (1975, 461) calls this group an "editorial board," with Cohen as the "chief editor."

chemistry and *education*. But the entries for economics mostly pertained to economic history, presumably because of its relevance for the history of technology.

There are three entries on economics in the critical bibliography of volume 5, including a short pamphlet by the distinguished chemist Frederick Soddy entitled "Cartesian Economics." In subsequent volumes, there are a number of additional entries to the category of economics (number 11 of part 3, following number 9 for botany and number 10 for chemistry), although in most years the entries average two or three listings. For volume 8, the number of subsections had greatly expanded, such that economics became number twenty-eight, immediately after superstition (number 27)! "Superstition and the Occult" had been a separate heading from the start, but Sarton appears to have imposed a Comtean hierarchy in place of the earlier alphabetical format. Both belonged to the broader category of anthropological and historical sciences ("Knowledge of Man, Past and Present") for several volumes thereafter, and economics came to reside fairly permanently as number 42, sandwiched between "Superstition and Occultism" (number 41) and "Sociology, Jurisprudence, and Positive Politics" (number 43). No wonder economists had little truck with *Isis*!

Other entries in the critical bibliography that are worth noting are works by William Ashley (1928), Florian Cajori (1929) (Cajori was a regular contributor to the journal, mostly on the history of mathematics), and Alexander Gray (1932). The founding of *Econometrica* is given a detailed entry in volume 20 (1933–34). In 1953, the year after Cohen took over from Sarton, Joseph Schumpeter's *Essays* (Clemence 1951) are listed in the critical bibliography, but it is the only entry in an otherwise veritable desert for economics. This may be partly due to Henry Guerlac's (1953) suggestions for a new classification scheme for the bibliography. Oddly, Schumpeter's major tome of 1954 did not make it into the journal, either as a book review or as an entry in the critical bibliography, even though it makes an exemplary effort to address developments in the history of science and intellectual history more generally. In 1955, the broader category was renamed the "Sciences of Man (psychology, cultural anthropology, sociology)," and "Economics" bit the dust as far as *Isis* was concerned. There are only a few entries on economics over the next two decades, hardly representative of the extant scholarship. Yet this transpired precisely when the critical bibliography was much expanded by its new editor, Harry Woolf, who devoted some ninety pages to it. John Neu of the University of Wisconsin was thereafter brought in as the editor of the critical bibliography (he is a trained librarian, not a scholar in the history of science), and things stayed much the same until 1979, when *HOPE* became part of its database. Only in 1988 was "Economics" once again listed as a distinct subheading in the table of contents for the bibliography.

The histories of psychology and of anthropology most certainly fared better treatment throughout these years, partly, I believe, because they did not have as developed an alternative as the history of economics and partly because, as I noted in my "Breaking Away" (Schabas 1992), there were more obvious points of entry via the history of medicine and biology. It took time before more than a handful of historians of economics fully grasped the depth of intersection between economics and the other sciences, both natural and social. The books by Vernard Foley (1976) and Claude Ménard (1978) are notable exceptions. There were, however, several efforts at cross-fertilization by historians of science, namely, William Coleman (1982), Martin Rudwick (1974), S. S. Schweber (1977), and Robert Young (1985). Scott Gordon's (1973) entry in a well-known collection also served to make economics part of the status quo, as did his appointment in 1985 to the History and Philosophy of Science Department at Indiana University.

The first full-fledged article in *Isis* that counts unambiguously as the history of economics is Joseph J. Spengler's "On the Progress of Quantification in Economics" (1961). Others that could qualify are the 1957 article by Conway Zirkle and the 1958 article by none other than John Maynard Keynes. To this list could also be added Howard Gruber's (1961) and Stillman Drake's (1967).

Another indication that economics had a toehold in the history of science world in its formative stage can be seen in the work of Theodor Merz and John Desmond Bernal. Merz issued a monumental four-volume *History of European Thought in the Nineteenth Century* (1904–12), in which economics received a very respectable treatment. In the opening preface to volume 1, Adam Smith, François Quesnay, and the physiocrats are briefly mentioned, and they are given a more lengthy examination in volume 4 along with the classical economists of the nineteenth century (429, 452–59, 540–44). While Merz's work was not exclusively on the history of science, it has long remained compulsory reading for historians of science. So it is fair to say that most historians of science have had some brush with the field.

J. D. Bernal's sweeping *Science in History* (1954) assigned volume 4 to the social sciences, with lengthy accounts on the history of economics. As a pronounced Marxist, this might have seemed like an obvious step to Bernal. It might also explain why, as Mirowski (1992a) noted in his comments to my 1992 *HOPE* piece, mainstream historians of science steered clear of economics during the height of the Cold War. The *Isis* eclipse of economics as a reference heading in its critical bibliography ran almost exactly in step with the war, from 1955 to 1988. A set of "Critiques and Contention" on "Marxism and the History of Science," based on lectures given at the Bucharest meeting of the International Congress of the History of Science (1981), were not jingoistic but, in the case of R. S. Westfall (1981, 402–5), were nevertheless firmly against Marxist accounts.

There are two distinct but clearly related ways in which the history of economics and the history of science can merge. One is institutional, the other is intellectual. I have all along been more interested in the latter issue, though many of my critics took me to task on the former. The reason the first is of lesser importance to me is that the history of science, while clearly established in the university curriculum, is not housed in any typical pattern. As several critics pointed out, for all of the separate departments at major universities (and some, such as Yale and Michigan, lack even that), there are numerous other practitioners housed in departments of history, philosophy, and even, occasionally, science, although this is the least likely configuration. So it seems foolhardy to offer prescriptions given all of the institutional idiosyncrasies. Ideally, every university of some size would have a history of science or science studies department, and there would be at least one historian of economics. But that is not a world we are likely to see anytime soon, if ever. I suggest, for the near future, we set more modest goals.

One proposal is to begin cross-listing history of economics courses with history of science, history, or philosophy courses. I tested this for two semesters at the University of Wisconsin at Madison, where I taught the course cross-listed with my department of the history of science. This attracted a number of students from both groups, including graduate students in the history of science. I will do something similar at my new post at the University of British Columbia, where the course will be given as the "History and Philosophy of Economics," cross-listed with economics and philosophy. Some of my critics, notably Samuel Hollander (1992) and Donald Walker (1992), expressed worries that economics majors would cease to take history of economic thought were it housed elsewhere. If the course carried humanities credit, however, it might well find an increased enrollment by economics majors in search of a kindred subject that would fill distributional requirements.

The potential for greater intellectual mergers is unbounded, particularly as we move away from the history of separate disciplines and embrace cultural history more fully. We see this already in the cited works of Porter, Schaffer, Pamela Smith, and Wise, to name only a few historians of science. Analogously, several prominent historians of economics, for example, Neil De Marchi, Judy Klein, Robert Leonard, Philip Mirowski, Mary Morgan, Esther-Mirjam Sent, and Roy Weintraub, are weaving economic strands into a cloth that would more properly be recognized as cultural history.

The other point on which I was misunderstood was our intended audience. I believe that the history and philosophy of science is read and appreciated by practitioners in the natural sciences, and this has been more the case in recent decades as the field matures (I view the Sokal affair as an aberration).[6] The American Association for the Advancement of Science (AAAS), for example, normally has a distinguished historian of science give an address at its annual meetings. Indeed, the first meeting of the History of Science Society (in 1924) was with the AAAS, and for many years thereafter the society met in alternate years with the scientists. The magazine *American Scientist*, which is aimed at readers with at least one degree in the sciences, usually features some historical articles. It is my belief, though this can only remain a conjecture, that we historians of economics would actually garner more respect from the economics profession if we distanced ourselves from mainstream economists and acquired a more independent voice. As George Basalla (1975) observed, the history of the natural sciences accomplished this circa 1970–75.[7] Maturation is always about autonomy. My depiction (Schabas 1992) of the typical historian of economics as a prodigal son was fully intended. We need to become more independent and self-confident in order to speak more forcefully to, and be better heard by,

6. Alan Sokal, a physicist, published an article in *Social Text* that was intended to expose the superficial rhetoric of postmodern studies of science. It was a hoax that sparked the so-called science wars between mainstream scientists and those in science studies (history, sociology, and philosophy of science).

7. Basalla (1975, 469) in a retrospective address implored historians of science to stop just writing for their own group and to make more ties with historians of technology (his area) and the educated public at large.

contemporary economists. They will become our most valuable recipients if and when we start to write the history of economics on its own terms.

Giovanni Caravale (1992) and Donald Walker (1992), in critiques of my "Breaking Away," suggest that history serve current analysis. This I think it can never do satisfactorily, as it would result in half-baked attempts to render Ricardo into the calculus. What purpose does this serve other than an intellectual exercise? One might as well play a game of chess. To understand Ricardo is to put him in a historical context, to link his ideas to the intellectual milieu in which he lived. The more the past economic ideas are treated in their own right, rather than as precursors to present theory, the better. The reason for this strikes me as obvious. We no longer believe in objective knowledge or a determinate history. All ideas are contingent, and hence no past idea necessitates a present one. To impose present concepts and terminology on the past is thus to distort the historical record. History is at best an indirect tool for understanding the present, in that it exposes us to alternative worlds and thus informs us about the diversity of the human condition. Economists might learn something by understanding the different approaches to their subject matter, rather than by simply mining past theories for what they consider significant verities. As Ted Porter (1992, 235) woefully pointed out, "history as legitimation is still very strong in history of economics." Nevertheless, there are signs that the balance has tipped in the other direction. Humility is difficult to earn, but the wisdom gleaned from the past strikes me as the preferable way to proceed.

References

Alborn, Timothy. 1996. The Business of Induction: Industry and Genius in the Language of British Scientific Reform, 1820–1840. History of Science 34:91–121.
Ashley, William. 1928. The Bread of Our Forefathers. Vol. 11. Oxford: Oxford University Press.
Ashworth, William J. 1996. Memory, Efficiency, and Symbolic Analysis: Charles Babbage, John Herschel, and the Industrial Mind. Isis 87:629–53.
Basalla, George. 1975. Observations on the Present Status of History of Science in the United States. Isis 66:467–70.
Bernal, James Desmond. 1954. Science in History. 4 vols. New York: Cameron Associates.
Blaug, Mark. 1997. Economic Theory in Retrospect. 5th ed. New York: Cambridge University Press.

Boulding, Kenneth. 1971. After Samuelson, Who Needs Adam Smith? *HOPE* 3:225–37.

Brantlinger, Patrick, ed. 1989. *Energy and Entropy: Science and Culture in Victorian Britain.* Bloomington: Indiana University Press.

Cajori, Florian. 1929. New Data on the Origin and Spread of the Dollar Mark. *Scientific Monthly* 22:212–16.

Caravale, Giovanni. 1992. Comment. *HOPE* 24:204–7.

Christensen, Paul. 1989. Hobbes and the Physiological Origins of Economic Science. *HOPE* 21:689–709.

Clemence, R. V, ed. 1951. *Essays: On Entrepreneurs, Innovations, Business Cycles, and the Evolution of Capitalism,* by Joseph Schumpeter. Cambridge, Mass.: Addison-Wesley.

Coats, A. W. 1969. Research Priorities in the History of Economics. *HOPE* 1:9–18.

Cohen, I. Bernard, ed. 1994. *The Natural Sciences and the Social Sciences.* Dordrecht: Kluwer.

Coleman, William. 1982. *Death Is a Social Disease: Public Health and Political Economy in Early Industrial France.* Madison: University of Wisconsin Press.

Cremaschi, Sergio, and Marcelo Dascal. 1998. Malthus and Ricardo: Two Styles for Economic Theory. *Science in Context* 11:229–54.

De Marchi, Neil, ed. 1993. *Non-Natural Social Science: Reflecting on the Enterprise of "More Heat Than Light."* Supplement to volume 25 of *HOPE.* Durham, N.C.: Duke University Press.

De Marchi, Neil, and John Lodewijks. 1983. *HOPE* and the Journal Literature in the History of Economic Thought. *HOPE* 15:321–43.

Dimand, Robert. 1993. The Case of Brownian Motion: The Contribution of Bachelier. *British Journal for the History of Science.* 26:233–34.

Drake, Stillman. 1967. A Seventeenth-Century Malthusian. *Isis* 58:401–2.

Ekelund Jr., Robert B., and Robert F. Hébert. 1999. *Secret Origins of Modern Microeconomics: Dupuit and the Engineers.* Chicago: University of Chicago Press.

Emmett, Ross B. 1997. Reflections on "Breaking Away": Economics as Science and the History of Economics as History of Science. *Research in the History of Economic Thought and Methodology* 15: 221–36.

Foley, Vernard. 1976. *The Social Physics of Adam Smith.* Lafayette, Ind.: Purdue University Press.

Frängsmyr, Tore, ed. 1989. *Science in Sweden: The Royal Swedish Academy of Science, 1739–1989.* Canton, Mass.: Science History Publications.

Frängsmyr, Tore, J. L. Heilbron, and Robin E. Rider, eds. 1990. *The Quantifying Spirit in the Eighteenth Century.* Berkeley.: University of California Press.

Gillispie, Charles Coulston. 1951. *Genesis and Geology.* Cambridge: Harvard University Press.

———. 1957. The Natural History of Industry. *Isis* 48:398–407.

———. 1960. *The Edge of Objectivity.* Princeton, N.J.: Princeton University Press.

————. 1980. *Science and Polity in France at the End of the Old Regime*. Princeton, N.J.: Princeton University Press.

————, ed. 1970. *Dictionary of Scientific Biography*. 15 vols. New York: Scribner.

Gordon, H. Scott. 1973. Alfred Marshall and the Development of Economics as a Science. In *Foundations of Scientific Method: The Nineteenth Century*, edited by R. N. Giere and R. S. Westfall. Bloomington: Indiana University Press.

————. 1989. Darwin and Political Economy: The Connection Reconsidered. *Journal of the History of Biology* 22:437–59.

Grabiner, Judith V. 1998. Some Disputes of Consequence: Maclaurin among the Molasses Barrels. *Social Studies of Science* 28:139–68.

Gray, Alexander. 1932. *The Development of Economic Doctrine*. Vol. 17. London: Longmans, Green.

Gruber, Howard. 1961. Darwin and *Das Kapital*. *Isis* 52:582–83.

Guala, Francesco. 2001. Building Economic Machines: The FCC Auctions. *Studies in History and Philosophy of Science* 32:453–77.

Guerlac, Henry. 1953. A Proposed Revision of the *Isis* Critical Bibliography. *Isis* 44:226–28.

Henderson, James P. 1996. Early Mathematical Economics: William Whewell and the British Case. Lanham, Md.: Rowman and Littlefield.

Hetherington, Norriss S. 1993. Isaac Newton and Adam Smith: Intellectual Links between Natural Science and Economics. In *Action and Reaction*, edited by Paul Theerman and Adele F. Seeff. Newark, N.J.: University of Delaware Press.

Hollander, Samuel. 1983. William Whewell and John Stuart Mill on the Methodology of Political Economy. *Studies in the History and Philosophy of Science* 14:127–68.

————. 1992. Comment. *HOPE* 24:212–14.

Ingrao, Bruna. 1994. Physical Metaphors and Models in Pareto's Thought. *Archives internationale d'histoire des sciences* 44:63–91.

Ingrao, Bruna, and Giorgio Israel. 1987. *La Mano Invisibile*. Roma-Bari: Laterza and Figli Spa.

Jackson, Myles. 1994. Natural and Artificial Budgets: Accounting for Goethe's Economy of Nature. *Science in Context* 7:409–31.

Jorland, Gérard. 1996. Le rejet du programme de Condorcet à l'époque romantique. *Sciences et techniques en perspective* 35:31–38.

————. 2000. The Coming into Being and Passing Away of Value Theories in Economics (1776–1976). In *Biographies of Scientific Objects*, edited by Lorraine Daston. Chicago: University of Chicago Press.

Kaye, Joel. 1997. *Economy and Nature in the Fourteenth Century: Money, Market Exchange, and the Emergence of Scientific Thought*. Cambridge: Cambridge University Press.

Keynes, John Maynard. 1958. A Mathematical Analysis by Newton of a Problem in College Administration. *Isis* 49:174–76.

Klein, Judy L. 1997. *Statistical Visions in Time*. Cambridge: Cambridge University Press.

Koerner, Lisbet. 1999. *Linnaeus, Nature, and Nation*. Cambridge: Harvard University Press.

Koyré, Alexandre. 1965. *Newtonian Studies*. Chicago: University of Chicago Press.

Krüger, Lorenz, Gerd Gigerenzer, and Mary S. Morgan, eds. 1987. *The Probabilistic Revolution*. Vol. 2. Cambridge: MIT Press.

Kuhn, Thomas S. 1962. *The Structure of Scientific Revolutions*. Chicago: University of Chicago Press.

———. 1977. The History of Science. In *The Essential Tension*. Chicago: University of Chicago Press.

Leonard, Robert J. 1998. Ethics and the Excluded Middle: Karl Menger and Social Science in Interwar Vienna. *Isis* 89:1–26.

Lindqvist, Svante. 1990. Labs in the Woods: The Quantification of Technology during the Enlightenment. In Frängsmyr, Heilbron, and Rider 1990.

Maas, Harro. 1999. Mechanical Rationality: Jevons and the Making of Economic Man. *Studies in the History and Philosophy of Science* 30:587–620.

Mäki, Uskali. 1997. Universals and the Methodenstreit: An Examination of Carl Menger's Conception of Economics as an Exact Science. *Studies in the History and Philosophy of Science* 28:475–95.

Ménard, Claude. 1978. *La formation d'une rationalité économique: A. A. Cournot*. Paris: Flammarion.

Merz, Theodor. 1904–12. *A History of European Thought in the Nineteenth Century*. 4 vols. New York: Dover.

Mirowski, Philip. 1989. *More Heat Than Light*. Cambridge: Cambridge University Press.

———. 1992a. Comment. *HOPE* 24:221–23.

———. 1992b. Looking for Those Natural Numbers: Dimensionless Constants and the Idea of Natural Measurement. *Science in Context* 5:165–88.

———, ed. 1994. *Natural Images in Economic Thought*. Cambridge: Cambridge University Press.

———. 1999. Cyborg Agonists: Economics Meets Operations Research in Mid-Century. *Social Studies of Science* 29:685–718.

Morgan, Mary S. 1997. The Technology of Analogical Model Building: Irving Fisher's Monetary Worlds. *Philosophy of Science* 64:304–14.

Morgan, Mary S., and Margaret Morrison, eds. 1999. *Models as Mediators: Perspectives on Natural and Social Sciences*. Cambridge: Cambridge University Press.

Morrell, Jack, and Arnold Thackray. 1981. *Gentlemen of Science*. Oxford: Clarendon Press.

Mosselmans, Bert. 1998. William Stanley Jevons and the Extent of Meaning in Logic and Economics. *History and Philosophy of Logic* 19:83–99.

Multhauf, Robert P. 1975. Reflections on Half a Century of the History of Science. *Isis* 66:454–67.

Poirier, Jean-Pierre. 1993. *Lavoisier: Chemist, Biologist, Economist.* Translated by Rebecca Balinski. Philadelphia: University of Pennsylvania Press.

Porter, Theodore. 1986. *The Rise of Statistical Thinking, 1820–1900.* Princeton, N.J.: Princeton University Press.

———. 1992. Comment. *HOPE* 24:234–36.

———. 1995. *Trust in Numbers.* Princeton, N.J.: Princeton University Press.

Power, Michael, ed. 1996. *Accounting and Science: Natural Inquiry and Commercial Reason.* New York: Cambridge University Press.

Rashid, Salim. 1981. Political Economy and Geology in the Early Nineteenth Century: Similarities and Contrasts. *HOPE* 13:726–44

Redman, Deborah A. 1997. *The Rise of Political Economy as a Science.* Cambridge: MIT Press.

Riskin, Jessica. 1998. Poor Richard's Leyden Jar: Electricity and Economy in Franklinist France. *Historical Studies in the Physical and Biological Sciences* 28:301–36.

Romano, Richard M. 1982. The Economic Ideas of Charles Babbage. *HOPE* 14:385–405.

Rudwick, Martin. 1974. Poulett Scrope on the Volcanoes of Auvergne: Lyellian Time and Political Economy. *British Journal for the History of Science* 7:205–42.

Rusnock, Andrea. 1999. Biopolitics: Political Arithmetic in the Enlightenment. In *The Sciences in Enlightened Europe*, edited by William Clark, Jan Golinski, and Simon Schaffer. Chicago: University of Chicago Press.

Sarton, George. 1921. Herbert Spencer. *Isis* 3:375–90.

———. 1923. Knowledge and Charity. *Isis* 5:5–19.

———. 1935. Lusitanian Memories. *Isis* 22:440–55.

Schabas, Margaret. 1989. Alfred Marshall, W. Stanley Jevons, and the Mathematization of Economics. *Isis* 80:60–73.

———. 1990. *A World Ruled by Number.* Princeton, N.J.: Princeton University Press.

———. 1992. Breaking Away: History of Economics as History of Science. *HOPE* 24:187–203.

———. 1997. Victorian Economics and the Science of the Mind. In *Victorian Science in Context*, edited by Bernard Lightman. Chicago: University of Chicago Press.

Schaffer, Simon. 1989. Defoe's Natural Philosophy and the Worlds of Credit. In *Nature Transfigured: Science and Literature, 1700–1900*, edited by John R. R. Christie and Sally Shuttleworth. Manchester: Manchester University Press.

———. 1994. Babbage's Intelligence: Calculating Engines and the Factory System. *Critical Inquiry* 20:203–27.

Schumpeter, Joseph A. 1954. *History of Economic Analysis.* New York: Oxford University Press.

Schweber, S. S. 1977. Darwin and the Political Economists: Divergence of Character. *Journal of the History of Biology* 10:195–289.

Sent, Esther-Mirjam. 2001. Sent Simulating Simon Simulating Scientists. *Studies in the History and Philosophy of Science* 32:479–500.

Smith, Adam. 1980. *Essays on Philosophical Subjects*, edited by W. P. D. Wightman and J. C. Bryce. Oxford: Oxford University Press.

Smith, Pamela. 1994. *The Business of Alchemy*. Princeton, N.J.: Princeton University Press.

Spary, Emma. 1996. Political, Natural, and Bodily Economies. In *Cultures of Natural History*, edited by N. Jardine, J. A. Secord, and E. C. Spary. Cambridge: Cambridge University Press.

Spengler, Joseph J. 1961. On the Progress of Quantification in Economics. *Isis* 52:258–76.

Spiegel, Henry. 1991. *The Growth of Economic Thought*. 3d ed. Durham, N.C.: Duke University Press.

Sumner, James. 2001. John Richardson, Saccharometry, and the Pounds-Per-Barrel Extract: The Construction of Quantity. *British Journal for the History of Science* 34:255–73.

Tomaselli, Sylvana. 1995. Political Economy: The Desire and Needs of Present and Future Generations. In *Inventing Human Science*, edited by Christopher Fox, Roy Porter, and Robert Wokler. Berkeley, Calif.: University of California Press.

Walker, Donald. 1992. Comment. *HOPE* 24:243–45.

Westfall, Richard S. 1981. Reflections on Ravetz's Essay: Bernal's Marxist Vision of History. *Isis* 72:402–5.

Wise, M. Norton. 1989–90. Work and Waste: Political Economy and Natural Philosophy in Nineteenth-Century Britain. *History of Science* 27:263–301, 391–449; 28:221–61.

———. 1993. Mediations: Enlightenment Balancing Acts, or the Technologies of Rationalism. In *World Changes: Thomas Kuhn and the Nature of Science*, edited by Paul Horwich. Cambridge: MIT Press.

———, ed. 1995. *The Values of Precision*. Princeton, N.J.: Princeton University Press.

Yonay, Yuval P. 1994. When Black Boxes Clash: Competing Ideas of What Science Is in Economics. *Social Studies of Science* 24:39–80.

Young, Robert. 1985. *Darwin's Metaphor: Nature's Place in Victorian Culture*. Cambridge: Cambridge University Press.

Zirkle, Conway. 1957. Benjamin Franklin, Thomas Malthus, and the United States Census. *Isis* 48:58–62.

A Hunger for Narrative: Writing Lives in the History of Economic Thought

Evelyn L. Forget

Historians of economic thought have always made use of life writing.[1] We draw on memoirs, correspondence, interviews, diaries, minutes of committee meetings, notebooks, and autobiographies as source material in our histories. But not since the multivolume biographical tomes of the Victorian age, skewered so definitively by Lytton Strachey (1918), has there been such an outpouring of biography and autobiography in all fields of inquiry as in recent decades. The history of economic thought has not been exempt. We have seen, over the past twenty years, full-length biographies of some of the major figures of our past supplemented by collections of biographies of less well known figures, and volumes of autobiography, interviews, and oral histories. This resurgence parallels developments in the history of science. Only very recently has there been any study of the development of the genre of science biography (see Shortland and Yeo 1996). Neither the status nor influence of life writing, nor the methodological challenges of the genre, has attracted much comment in the history of economic thought.

The most astonishing aspect of the recent revival of biography is that it exists at all. Since the end of the eighteenth century, the role of the merely personal in historical study has been an uneasy one. During the

I would like to thank two anonymous referees and the participants in the 2001 *HOPE* conference for helpful suggestions.

1. I use *life writing* the way it is used in sociology, to include formal biographies and autobiographies, but also less self-conscious memoirs, interviews, correspondence (whether intended for publication or not), journals, diaries, and so on.

twentieth century, biographical writing in the history of economic thought weathered at least three significant challenges. The personality of the individual economist was attenuated in histories that made use of rational reconstruction. The sociology of knowledge literature undermined the role of the individual economist, who became a pawn in thrall to forces much greater than any individual. And the most devastating attack, from a philosophical perspective, emerged from postmodern literary criticism. If the subject itself is neither stable nor recoverable, the biographer's task becomes impossible. And yet biographies, autobiographies, and memoirs proliferate.

This essay reviews some of the literature related to life writing in intellectual history and attempts to account for its recent revival in the history of economic thought. The first section examines the intellectual challenges to life writing that have emerged over the past two centuries, from the scientific sensibilities of the Enlightenment to the "contested self" of postmodern discourse. The second considers two forms of life writing in the history of economics. Literary biography serves many of the same purposes as fiction and owes at least as much to the biographer as to the subject. Except possibly for John Maynard Keynes's *Essays in Biography* ([1933] 1972), historians of economics have made few attempts to exploit the genre's potential. By contrast, biographies written from the perspective of social history and relevant to examinations of the sociology of knowledge have played an important role in our discipline. They could be improved by adopting tools of qualitative analysis developed in sociology and other social sciences. Both literary biographies and social histories, however, are narratives, the similarities of which matter more than their putative differences in objectives. Recognizing the pervasiveness of narrative in the history of economics frees us to consider the potential of life writing, in terms of new ways of writing history, new audiences for our writing, and new ways of teaching. The final section does just that.

The Challenge of Life Writing

Thirty years ago, the first voices began to call for a resurgence of biography in the history of science. Thomas Hankins (1979) implored historians of science to consider biography as the test of broader theories of the development of ideas in science, but he had to title his plea "In Defence of Biography." S. Shapin and A. Thackray (1974) made a similar case for "prosopography as a research tool in history of science," a focus echoed in some recent interest in collective science biographies (Pyenson 1977; Elliott 1982, 1990; Sturges 1983; Abir-Am 1991; Abir-Am and Outram 1987). Larry Holmes (1981) argued that biography is crucial for any study of scientific creativity.

These calls heralded a flood of new science biographies that captured the attention of both the public and working scientists. They include Richard Westfall's *Never at Rest: A Biography of Isaac Newton* (1980), Walter Moore's *Schrödinger* (1989), Crosbie Smith and Norton Wise's *Energy and Empire: A Biographical Study of Lord Kelvin* (1989), Adrian Desmond and James Moore's *Darwin* (1991), Geoffrey Cantor's *Michael Faraday* (1991), Arthur Donovon's *Lavoisier* (1993), and James Gleick's *Genius: The Life and Science of Richard Feynman* (1992), among many others. This outpouring seems to support Susan Sheets-Pyenson's (1990, 399) conclusion that "historians of science today . . . have scarcely rejected the biographical approach." But Michael Shortland and Richard Yeo (1996, 5) argue that she can make such a claim only by redefining biography as a sort of social history and that "since the 1940s a concern with the 'merely personal' has been seen as peripheral to the aim of understanding the scientific enterprise as a collection of institutionally based cognitive disciplines. From the 1970s, scholarly developments in the social history of science and the sociology of scientific knowledge, and inquiries indebted to either Thomas Kuhn or Michel Foucault, have confirmed this situation." Consequently, the recent intellectual energy devoted to science biography has, generally, begun with a defense of biography.

The use of biography in the history of economic thought has been similarly fraught. As in the case of the history of science, there has been a recent resurgence. Peter Groenewegen's *Soaring Eagle: Alfred Marshall* (1995), Robert Skidelsky's *John Maynard Keynes* (1983–2000), Ian Simpson Ross's *Life of Adam Smith* (1996), Don Moggridge's *Maynard Keynes: An Economist's Biography* (1992), and Sylvia Nasar's *Beautiful Mind: A Biography of John Forbes Nash* (1998) have added to our knowledge about significant figures of our past. These full-length works have been supplemented by collections of biographies of lesser-known figures, such as Philip Arestis and Malcolm Sawyer's *Biographical Dictionary of Dissenting Economists* (1992) and *A Biographical Dictionary of Women Economists* (Dimand, Dimand, and Forget 2000). Autobiographical sketches of contemporary economists have been collected by

Mark Blaug and P. Sturges (1983), Roger Backhouse and Roger Middleton (2000), Arnold Heertje (1993–99), J. Kregel (1988–89), W. Breit and R. Spencer (1995), and M. Szenberg (1992, 1998). Keith Tribe (1997), B. Snowdon and H. Vane (1999), and C. U. Ibanez (1999) have published collections of interviews.

Yet as in the case of science biography, twentieth-century history of economics has largely marginalized biographical writing. But it would be wrong to see our uneasiness with the genre of biography as of recent origin. There are two basic ways of telling the story of intellectual innovation. One narrative portrays intellectual history as owing much to the achievements of individual genius. A naïve form of this story wrenches the individual from the historical context and speaks of innovation in a peculiarly timeless way. A more sophisticated version of the same story recognizes that an individual always operates in a particular time and place and seeks to portray historical events through the lens of an individual life. A competing narrative tells of intellectual innovation as the result of large transpersonal forces, either embodied within the methods of the discipline itself or linked to broader social or historical changes. This story, in its starkest form, operates almost independently of individual writers and thinkers and speaks instead of ideologies and modes of production, or scientific research programs. The tension between these two narratives finds its roots in the seventeenth and eighteenth centuries.

The notion that intellectual history can be other than a series of great thinkers is very largely a creation of the eighteenth century. Francis Bacon's *New Atlantis* ([1627] 1974) anticipated the idea, which portrayed learning, and especially science, as a corporate undertaking, the progress of which is ensured by the marginal contributions of many unremarkable individuals following a specific method of inquiry. And yet his *Advancement of Learning* ([1605] 1974) classified biography as a form of history and argued that biography allowed an accumulation of detail not possible in larger histories.

However, it was at the end of the eighteenth century that the battle for a narrative of scientific progress was played out. The great encyclopedias of the eighteenth century, including the *Encyclopédie* (Diderot and d'Alembert 1751–80) and Ephraim Chambers's *Cyclopaedia* (1728), did not include biographical entries, instead presenting the development of ideas as the result of abstract laws (see Yeo 1996). This differs from the earlier historical dictionaries, such as Pierre Bayle's *Historical and Critical Dictionary* (1710), that presented scientific progress as the result of individual efforts of genius. David Hume (1993, 56–76) argued that progress in science is the result of social and political factors. Joseph Priestley's *History and Present State of Electricity* (1775) downplayed the role of individual discovery. It would seem that individual genius had been undermined and replaced by Bacon's story of progress depending on the contributions of many lesser individuals, all of whom are subject to the determining influence of historical forces and the scientific method.

Yet even in this period, life writing flourished in *éloges*, obituaries, and biographical dictionaries. And Priestley, notwithstanding his dismissal of the role of individual genius, published a *Description of a Chart of Biography* (1765) that suggested that scientific progress could be visualized through the contributions of individual thinkers. In his *Course of Positive Philosophy* ([1830] 1892–94), Auguste Comte similarly downplayed the role of individual genius and wrote of abstract laws that moved society through its various stages. But Frederic Harrison, one of his English followers, published *The New Calendar of Great Men: Biographies of the 558 Worthies of All Ages and Nations in the Positivist Calendar of Auguste Comte* (1892).

These tensions continued into the nineteenth century. John Playfair's "Preliminary Dissertation" to the *Supplement to the Encyclopaedia Britannica* (1815–24) attempted to trace both the role of individual genius and the influence of circumstances. William Whewell's *History of the Inductive Sciences* ([1837] 1857) similarly tried to present scientific progress as subject to laws of progress that were dependent on historical conditions, although he still told the story through the discoveries of masters such as Newton, Kepler, and Faraday.

The eighteenth century, then, questioned the well-established notion that intellectual history *is* biography. But it did not eliminate individual genius from the story. And it remained for the nineteenth century to invent the multivolume biographical tome that would do so much to create distaste for biographical writing in twentieth-century history. The great biographical undertakings of the nineteenth century began with several generations of family history, heralded the birth of the infant genius of great character somewhere around the second volume, and then followed the subject uncritically but very closely for the rest of his or her life.[2] An

2. See, for example, Hanna 1850–52 for a four-volume biography of Thomas Chalmers. This style is the motivation for Strachey—and Keynes.

afterword often contained the will and the subject's personal and intellectual legacy. Often, the "life" was accompanied by the "letters"—all carefully edited and expurgated by an attentive widow or son. Little wonder, then, that Lytton Strachey's *Eminent Victorians* (1918, 2) castigated Victorian biographies as "ill-digested masses of material" and criticized their "slipshod style, tone of tedious panegyric, lamentable lack of selection, of detachment, of design."

As in the case of the eighteenth century, though, this picture is too simple. The same period that generated these tedious "lives and letters" also produced such gems as John Stuart Mill's *Autobiography*. And even the unselective biographies represent an important source of evidence for other kinds of historical reconstructions. Nevertheless, the massive outpouring of uncritical life writing during this period created the backdrop against which twentieth-century historical writing tried to come to terms with life writing.

Twentieth-century challenges to the genre of biography in the history of economics take three forms. The first came from attempts to reconstruct the history "rationally"—that is, to focus on the inherent logic of the ideas themselves. The individual economist never disappeared from the picture; his or her ideas served as source material for the reconstruction. The historian may well make use of private correspondence, memoirs, notebooks, or anything else that might help uncover the true structure of the ideas, but it was the ideas that were paramount. Anything uniquely personal about the author of the ideas—passions, idiosyncrasies, and even "vision"—was considered irrelevant. This may have reflected a "scientific" distaste for the personal invasion of Victorian biographies, which encouraged prurience and gossip in their readers partly because their high-minded authors prissily skirted anything controversial. It may have reflected a fundamental agreement with Walter Bagehot (1965–86, 1:397–98), who had argued that intellectuals are inherently and irremediably boring: "An aloofness and abstractedness cleave to their greatness. There is a coldness in their fame" contrary to "the taste of most persons." It certainly reinforced the self-image of economists in a rapidly professionalizing discipline. The "merely personal" had little role in the gradual accumulation of "truth."

This position is well illustrated by Joseph Schumpeter. Schumpeter (1954, 39) wrote a history of economic analysis, which he thought displayed scientific progress in the same way "in which we may say that there has been technological progress in the extraction of teeth between the times of John Stuart Mill and our own." But he also recognized that scientific analysis "is an incessant struggle with creations of our own and our predecessors' minds and it 'progresses,' if at all, in a criss-cross fashion, not as logic, but as the impact of new ideas or observations or needs, and also as the bents and temperaments of new men, dictate" (4). The individual economist did not disappear; the story was told, after all, through the disembodied ideas of the great masters. But all of the unique passions and the personality of the individual vanished in the telling. All that was considered relevant was pure, stylized thought. By focusing on economic analysis, Schumpeter necessarily downplayed the importance of individual discovery, notwithstanding his recognition that "the highest claim that can be made for the history of any science . . . is that it teaches us much about the ways of the human mind" (5).

It is not difficult to challenge the philosophical dismissal of the person inherent in "rational reconstructions." Recent scholarship amply demonstrates the impossibility of brutally separating reason from passion and imagination as historians of economics begin to focus more on the social and political context of economic ideas. One might have imagined that this would open a door for more sophisticated biographies, and ultimately it did. But the initial effect raised a second challenge to life writing, in that it further weakened interest in the individual author. Instead of being simply "cleaned up" by historians intent on demonstrating what Adam Smith would have written if only Smith had read Paul Samuelson, the individual became largely irrelevant from a sociological point of view. We seemed to fear that looking too closely at the author would lead us to neglect important questions about the social circumstances, or the institutional environment, which were primarily responsible for the discovery in the first place.

Ultimately, though, it is social history and the sociology of knowledge that led to the recent spate of biographical writing. Almost all recent biographies have redefined themselves as a form of social history. The individual is portrayed within a social, political, and institutional context. The biographer tries to go beyond the personal quirks of the author and portray events and ideas through the life story of an individual embedded in a network of overlapping communities. Only someone with an understanding of the intellectual environment can write these kinds of biographies. Therefore, the recent efflorescence of biographical writing in the history of economic thought should not be seen as a revival of the notion that individual genius is primary. Indeed, it is recognition of just the reverse. Forces well beyond his or her control and, probably, comprehension buffet the individual. Biography, from this perspective, is no longer about writing lives of individuals with distinct personalities and passions; it is a subordinate form of social history.

The third challenge to biographical writing in the twentieth century concerns the problematic nature of the subject. The "death of the author" has had interesting implications for the interpretation of autobiographical writing (Eakin 1985, 1992). Literary critics have denounced biographies based on "the myth of personal coherence" (Clifford 1978, 44–45). The poststructuralist challenge claims that human subjects are "merely an effect of language" (Barthes 1977, 56)—"incarnated vocabularies" (Rorty 1989, 88). Vivienne Brown (1993) argues that such a position privileges the reader rather than the writer, resists closure of texts, and encourages an appreciation of the richness of open textual meaning rather than a search for authorial intention.

This is a considerable challenge to the genre of biography. Perhaps it is not surprising that it has not made significant inroads among those who write biographies. Ian Simpson Ross (1996, xxviii) is typical when he writes in his *Life of Adam Smith* that "the a priori assumptions of the criticism of our times which rejects the concept of authorship, and stresses the indeterminacy of meaning of texts . . . may well divert rather than instruct, by dancing on the grave of Adam Smith. The stand of this book is that interpretation linked to the biographical record is a verifiable guide to a significant body of thought." Lest this be taken as a plea for a naïve "life" that depicts clues to authorial intent in family background, Ross explicitly recognizes as quixotic any attempt to "foreclose meaning by strictly delimiting an author's intentions." He seeks rather to portray "a remarkable personality . . . in identifiable settings, at work as a writer" (xvii).

A more troubling picture emerges when a biographer attempts to take seriously the position of the postmodern critics. David Nye (1983, 17–18), in his fascinating attempt to create an autobiography of Thomas Edison, claims that "the fundamental error of biography lies in the attempt to construct a definitive figure at all." As Nye explains, "If [the subject] can be expressed as sixteen different figures, [the biographer] will do so rather than perform a reduction" (19). This brings to mind the old "anatomy" books where a series of transparencies showing bone structure, musculature, the circulatory system, and so on build up the "visible man." But, in contrast to the multilayered but ultimately coherent textbook character, Nye proposes a multilayered and incoherent subject where the creator of the portrait does not trouble him- or herself to search very hard for unity.

I have argued elsewhere that the history of economics owes a great deal to the history of medicine, borrowing techniques of analysis and favorite metaphors (Forget 1999). I suggest that a pragmatic response to the poststructuralist challenge can also be borrowed from medicine. An innovation of recent years is "narrative-based medicine," recognized by a series of articles in the *British Medical Journal.* It is founded on the premise that patients' narratives "provide us with far more than factual information of the kind that might be more efficiently obtained when they . . . carry electronic smart cards encoded with their entire 'medical history'" (Greenhalgh and Hurwitz 1998, 6). Perhaps ironically, the movement rests on the notion that *illness* and *wellness* are, like individuals, rhetorical constructs and that the narrative interplay between patient and physician is important. That recognition, however, is used to argue for, rather than against, narrative unity. "Healing" involves substituting a coherent narrative of wellness for one of ill health. And patients who do not have a coherent narrative at all are recognized to have a real problem.[3]

This treatment paradigm is offered as a response to too great a reliance in contemporary practice on "evidence-based medicine," typified by population-cohort studies or randomized clinical trials. This "scientific" approach, it is claimed, finds its roots in the late eighteenth century, when physicians, emboldened by new developments in physiology, stopped listening to the unique histories of their patients and instead searched for commonalities between patients (Greenhalgh and Hurwitz 1998, 142). Narrative-based medicine seeks to restore the individual patient and her or his story, created interactively with the physician, to the center of treatment. The relationship between the physician and the patient parallels that between the biographer and the subject. The "story" need not disintegrate simply because we recognize the importance of language or notice that neither the physician/biographer nor the patient/subject tells an objective story independently of the efforts of the other.

3. See Hacking 1995 for a fascinating account of the impact of narrative disunity on mental health in contemporary society.

Forms of Life Writing

We are economists. All of the philosophical discourse imaginable cannot compete with a simple market fact: life writing in the history of economic thought continues to exist and grows in importance. Bookstore shelves devote more space to *The Worldly Philosophers*, the biographies of economists of the past, and the life philosophies of the laureates than they do to other forms of the history of economic thought. Working economists are more likely to have read Nasar's *Beautiful Mind* than they are to pick up other historical writing. Life writing is here. How can we exploit its potential?

Most recent biographies in science and in economics justify their existence, at least in part, by the light they cast on institutional arrangements and the historical context. It is no surprise, then, that most of the calls for a renewed commitment to life writing focus on its potential from this perspective. Shapin and Thackray (1974), for example, justify prosopography (or group biography) as the source of data useful to historians investigating the sociology of science. When we recognize that sociology is the social science that currently makes the greatest use of life writing, it is reasonable to ask whether there are techniques that we could borrow.

Some of the most interesting life writing in economics exists in the form of transcribed interviews. Interviewing is a skill, the method of which has been much studied. It is no mean feat to encourage subjects to move beyond their own preoccupations so that they address your concerns, while simultaneously recognizing that their stories have an integrity that must be respected and acknowledged.[4] This is a form of the "narrative interplay" between physician and patient recognized by narrative-based medicine. It is similarly a skill to extract from subjects something that they are not aware that they know. But there are best-practice techniques developed by a discipline whose practitioners have more experience in their use than do most economists.[5]

Autobiographies may unwittingly betray information that the author is either blind to or deliberately hiding, but for the most part, autobiographical writing is limited by the author's awareness of the intellectual and historical context in the same way that biography is limited by

4. For an illustration of the power of well-done interviewing, see Shea 1998.

5. The Oral History Association has developed a set of guidelines used to evaluate oral history projects. These are available at http://www.dickinson.edu/organizations/oha/EvaluationGuidelines.html.

the knowledge of the biographer. Can collections of autobiographies, or collections of biographies for that matter, transcend the limitations of their authors' perspectives? One of the most useful tools in clinical science is the notion of the structured abstract or structured review. It has its parallel in the structured case study in medicine or psychotherapy. The problem that the technique attempts to address is the particularity of evidence—exactly the problem of biography. Each life, like each case study, is unique. Even a clinical trial might have a sample size of only fifteen subjects. And yet these are regularly made generalizable through the imposition of a structure that allows connections to be drawn and similarities charted. This requires that you have a theory from which to infer what aspects of experience ought to be emphasized.

My work with my colleagues Robert Dimand and Mary Ann Dimand, *A Biographical Dictionary of Women Economists* (2000), for example, gathers together short biographical sketches of women and includes many of the Progressive Era. The similarities between their personal lives, their careers, and the linkages they forged with one another and with others are striking. Systematically mining these sketches, which are in very disparate styles and by economists of quite different sensibilities, yields insights into institutional structures. Until I read the biographies, I had no idea how frequently these women changed their institutional affiliations and how common it was to move from academia to the Office of the Budget, to the Labor Office, to the Department of Agriculture, and then back to academia. Nor did I know how many of these trained economists made their intellectual homes in academic departments other than economics. I had no conception of the very rich networks that existed between these women, who mentored one another, coauthored books, took over each other's students, and worked side-by-side on the same projects. Until I read *Lives of the Laureates* (Breit and Spencer 1995), *Recollections of Eminent Economists* (Kregel 1988–89), and *Exemplary Economists* (Backhouse and Middleton 2000), I had no idea just how dense, and just how closed at its pinnacle, economic theory is today.

These observations lead to another suggestion, and the "visible man" will again come to my aid. Sociologists have documented just how dense and varied are the networks and communities to which most of us belong. Mapping the connections between economists of a particular period is difficult but would be historically rewarding. But it is essential to recognize that these networks are neither exclusive nor unchanging. Some care spent in defining the boundaries of a particular network, mapping its contours and the connections between its members, and then layering the networks one over another would, ultimately, see the emergence of a more multidimensional intellectual context than traditional literary biography has been able to capture. If we can avoid the temptation of reductionism, the potential is dramatic.

All of these sociological techniques, however, favor one particular justification for life writing in the history of economic thought. They accept that life writing can be used as a source for historical work in the sociology of knowledge tradition. Is there no room left for a biography that celebrates the eccentricities of the individual?

Schumpeter claimed that the most important reason to study history is because it helps us to understand the human mind. This is an old idea and like so much finds its best expression in the eighteenth century. Benjamin Franklin and the other commissioners who investigated Antoin Mesmer included this statement in the preface to their report to the King of France:

> Perhaps the history of the errors of mankind, all things considered, is more valuable and interesting than that of their discoveries. Truth is uniform and narrow; it constantly exists, and does not seem to require so much an active energy, as a passive aptitude of soul in order to encounter it. But error is endlessly diversified; it has no reality, but is the pure and simple creation of the mind that invents it. In this field the soul has room enough to expand herself, to display all her beautiful and interesting extravagances and absurdities. (Franklin et al. 1785, xvii)

This poetic introduction touches on one of the reasons that people read biography. They are intrigued by eccentricity. The process of creativity fascinates them. Robert Young (1988), a psychoanalyst and historian of science, has gone so far as to argue that biography is the basic discipline for the human sciences.

The operation of the human mind may not be well understood, but psychologists and psychoanalysts have worked the field—sometimes with results that are more entertaining than helpful (Runyan 1984 surveys the territory). But there are interesting techniques that could be adapted and used. Ira Progoff's *Life-Study: Experiencing Creative Lives* (1998) offers an experiential approach to life writing based on Jungian analysis and on emphasizing the creative personality. All such analytical systems, while distinct and sometimes inconsistent, are similar in that they impose a grid over an individual life, directing us toward certain experiences and away from others.

An alternative is to undertake a meta-analysis of the psychology literature to determine the correlates of creativity. Then, the "life" of the subject becomes a case study in which to uncover the operation of the correlates that theory tells us ought to appear. We can use the data to address interesting psychological questions. Is creativity in economics the same as creativity in science, medicine, art, or literature? How does productivity change over a lifetime, and in response to personal and historical challenges and institutional changes? Michael Sokal (1990) advocates this kind of undertaking in the history of science.

We are, however, economists and historians rather than psychoanalysts or psychologists. Is there no room left for an old-fashioned life that is more a work of art than a case study in psychology or sociology? Thomas Söderqvist (1996) makes an eloquent plea for the old-fashioned life in the history of science, suggesting that working scientists have need of such biographies. They need, he argues, models of ethical lives lived in science and cautionary tales of flawed heroes. He suggests that only the creation of biographies that recognize and take seriously the subject's "existential project" can achieve this almost nineteenth-century goal.

Keynes's classic *Essays in Biography* is the best example of literary biography in the history of economics. The work is far from naïve. Keynes ([1933] 1972, xix) mirrors Strachey's style in order, he tells us, "to bring out the solidarity and historical continuity of the High Intelligentsia of England, who have built up the foundations of our thought in the two and a half centuries since John Locke, in his *Essay Concerning Human Understanding*, wrote the first modern English book." His attempt to achieve that end is not artless, although he dismisses it as "some touches of detail." Like his *Essays in Persuasion*, his biographical writing is a thoughtful attempt to create a historical narrative.

Literary biographies are, and ought to be, read in the same way that novels are read. It is a short step to argue, as does Söderqvist (1996, 78), that such biographers ought to be encouraged to adopt the tools forged by creators of fiction. They should play, he argues, with "collage, narrative discontinuity, multigenre narratives, unsuspected time-shifts, with stream of consciousness, symbolism, poetical reconstructions, and polyvocal texts." The result might be as charming as *Night Thoughts of a Classical Physicist* (McCormmach 1982), a fictionalized account of the history of physics in the first decades of the twentieth century, or as controversial as Simon Schama (1989), who has been criticized for not respecting traditional norms of historical accuracy and objectivity.

To suggest that literary biographies have a role to play in the history of economics alongside sociological life writing may challenge some of our notions of objectivity. But in fact, these claims have been made explicitly in other fields. Hayden White (1999, 4) argues that all historical writing is essentially narrative, and "narration requires that historical agents, events, institutions and processes be . . . enfigured . . . as the kind of characters, events, scenes, and processes met with in stories—fables, myths, rituals, epics, romances, novels, and plays. And secondly they must be troped as bearing relationships to one another of the kind met with in the plot-structures of generic story types." Ethnography has similarly begun to become self-conscious of narrative and of the ways in which "objective," "scientific," anthropological writing mirrors fiction (Clifford and Marcus 1986). Neither history nor ethnography loses value by embracing narrative; rather, they become richer. New projects become legitimate for practitioners, and new audiences are reached.

Prospects for Life Writing in the History of Economic Thought

This essay has emphasized the potential of life writing from the perspective of historians of economics, examining new research tools and different narrative forms. I have made two suggestions. First, we ought to recognize that life writing is a genre in its own right and begin to think about its peculiar challenges. Second, we ought to adapt methods of qualitative analysis developed by other disciplines, such as interviewing techniques and the idea of the structured review or case study.

This volume contains autobiographical writing by some of the newer adepts of our field—Esther-Mirjam Sent, Derek Brown and Shauna Saunders, Matthias Klaes, and Stephen Meardon. These authors have constructed "training tales"—narratives that focus on a brief period of their education and subsequent employment. The role of these narratives in constructing a portrait of our field contrasts with a more common genre of autobiographical writing in which senior scholars reflect back over years of work and history, creating narratives with a depth of experience. The training tale, by contrast, is a relatively raw report of an experience that the author has not yet had time to digest. The lack of perspective makes them less rather than more compelling mirrors of the world. And yet these stories are valuable. They take a critical position and ask disturbing questions. Sent's essay goes a step further and raises issues of morality and ethics. Life writing is not a simple reflection of experience that can be judged in terms of its truth-value for either the reader or the writer.

There are more direct ways in which life writing might address some of our current challenges. Craufurd Goodwin (this volume) has asked us to think about the future of our field in terms of potential new audiences. Heilbroner and Nasar have both shown us that life writing can reach general readers and working economists. Goodwin has asked us whether historians of economics have a role to play in communicating across the disciplines or in informing policy analysis. Life writing is inherently multidisciplinary and can engage readers in ways that are not standard in economics. Brad Bateman (this volume) has asked us to consider how history of economics fits into the education of undergraduates. Keynes has shown us that life writing can educate painlessly, teaching important points of economics, politics, and history to readers intent on the "plot" of his biographical essays. Students, however, can learn at least as much from creating as from reading biographies. Ira Progoff's *Life-Study*, for example, has been seized upon by, among others, Roman Catholic religious communities in which current members examine their own spiritual development while reconstructing the lives of mentors and models.[6] Life writing holds equal potential for students of economics and its history, particularly those who persist in seeing the social dimensions of economics.

Life writing is a seductive form of narrative that emerges naturally from our work. It would be self-destructive not to use all of the tools available to create good, rich tales that cast light on particular times and places and teach well the most fundamental ideas of economics. If we do not satisfy the demand that exists for captivating writing about the lives of economists, we will hardly be in a position to complain that the journalists who take our place write something other than what we would have liked.

---

6. The approach is intellectually sophisticated enough that we might reexamine our reflexive contempt for hagiography.

References

Abir-Am, P. 1991. Noblesse Oblige: Biographical Writings on Nobelists. *Isis* 82:326–43.

Abir-Am, P., and D. Outram, eds. 1987. *Uneasy Careers and Intimate Lives: Women in Science, 1789–1979*. New Brunswick, N.J.: Rutgers University Press.

Arestis, P., and M. Sawyer, eds. 1992. *A Biographical Dictionary of Dissenting Economists*. Aldershot: Edward Elgar.

Backhouse, R., and R. Middleton, eds. 2000. *Exemplary Economists*. Vols. 1 and 2. Cheltenham: Edward Elgar.

Bacon, F. [1605] 1974. *Advancement of Learning*. In Johnston 1974.

———. [1627] 1974. *New Atlantis*. In Johnston 1974.

Bagehot, W. 1965–86. *The Collected Works of Walter Bagehot*. Edited by N. St. John-Stevas. 15 vols. London: Economist.

Barthes, R. 1977. *Roland Barthes by Roland Barthes*. New York: Farrar.

Bayle, P. 1710. *An Historical and Critical Dictionary, by Monsieur Bayle. Translated into English with Many Additions and Corrections, Made by the Author Himself, That Are Not in the French Editions*. 4 vols. London: Harper.

Blaug, M., and P. Sturges, eds. 1983. *Who's Who in Economics*. London: Wheatsheaf.

Breit, W., and R. Spencer, eds. 1995. *Lives of the Laureates: Thirteen Nobel Economists*. Cambridge: MIT Press.

Brown, V. 1993. Decanonizing Discourses: Textual Analysis and the History of Economic Thought. In *Economics and Language*, edited by W. Henderson, T. Dudley-Evans, and R. Backhouse. London: Routledge.

Cantor, G. 1991. *Michael Faraday: Sandemanian and Scientist*. London: Macmillan.

Chambers, E. 1728. *Cyclopaedia, or An Universal Dictionary of Arts and Sciences*. 2 vols. London: J. Knapton.

Clifford, J. 1978. "Hanging up Looking Glasses at Odd Corners": Ethnobiographical Prospects. In *Studies in Biography*, edited by D. Aaron. Cambridge: Harvard University Press.

Clifford, J., and G. E. Marcus, eds. 1986. *Writing Culture: The Poetics and Politics of Ethnography*. Berkeley: University of California Press.

Comte, A. [1830] 1892–94. *Cours de philosophie positive*. 5th ed. 6 vols. Paris: Société Positiviste.

Desmond, A., and J. Moore. 1991. *Darwin*. London: Michael Joseph.

Diderot, D., and J. d'Alembert. 1751–80. *Encyclopédie, ou Dictionnaire Raisonné des Sciences des Arts et des Métiers*. 35 vols. Stuttgart: Bad Cannstatt.

Dimand, R., M. A. Dimand, and E. L. Forget, eds. 2000. *A Biographical Dictionary of Women Economists*. Cheltenham, U.K.: Edward Elgar.

Donovon, A. 1993. *Lavoisier*. London: Blackwell Science Biographies.

Eakin, P. J. 1985. *Fictions in Autobiography: Studies in the Art of Self-Invention*. Princeton, N.J.: Princeton University Press.

———. 1992. *Touching the World: Reference in Autobiography*. Princeton, N.J.: Princeton University Press.

Elliott, C. A. 1982. Models of the American Scientist: A Look at Collective Biography. *Isis* 73:77–93.

———. 1990. Collective Lives of American Scientists: An Introductory Essay and a Bibliography. In *Beyond History of Science: Essays in Honor of Robert E. Schofield*, edited by E. Garber. Bethlehem, Pa.: Lehigh University Press.

Forget, E. 1999. *The Social Economics of Jean-Baptiste Say: Markets and Virtue*. London: Routledge.

Franklin, B., et al. 1785. *Report of Dr. Benjamin Franklin and Other Commissioners, Charged by the King of France, with the Examination of the Animal Magnetism, as Now Practised at Paris*. Translated from the French with a historical introduction [by William Godwin]. London: J. Johnson.

Gleick, J. 1992. *Genius: The Life and Science of Richard Feynman*. New York: Little, Brown.

Greenhalgh, T., and B. Hurwitz, eds. 1998. *Narrative Based Medicine*. London: BMJ Books.

Groenewegen, P. 1995. *Soaring Eagle: Alfred Marshall*. Aldershot, U.K.: Edward Elgar.

Hacking, I. 1995. *Rewriting the Soul: Multiple Personality and the Sciences of Memory*. Princeton, N.J.: Princeton University Press.

Hankins, T. 1979. In Defence of Biography: The Use of Biography in the History of Science. *History of Science* 17:1–16.

Hanna, William. 1850–52. *Memoirs of the Life and Writings of Thomas Chalmers*. New York: Harper and Bros.

Harrison, F. 1892. *The New Calendar of Great Men: Biographies of the 558 Worthies of All Ages and Nations in the Positivist Calendar of Auguste Comte*. London: Macmillan.

Heertje, A., ed. 1993–99. *Makers of Modern Economics*. Vols. 1–4. Aldershot, U.K.: Edward Elgar.

Holmes, L. 1981. The Fine Structure of Scientific Creativity. *History of Science* 19:60–70.

Hume, D. 1993. *Selected Essays*. Edited by S. Copley and A. Edgar. New York: Oxford University Press.

Ibanez, C. U., ed. 1999. *The Current State of Macroeconomics: Leading Thinkers in Conversation*. London: Macmillan.

Johnston, A., ed. 1974. *The Advancement of Learning and New Atlantis*, by Francis Bacon. Oxford: Clarendon Press.

Keynes, J. M. [1933] 1972. *Essays in Biography*. Vol. 10 of *Collected Writings of John Maynard Keynes*. London: Macmillan.

Kregel, J. A., ed. 1988–89. *Recollections of Eminent Economists*. Vols. 1 and 2. London: Macmillan.

McCormmach, R. 1982. *Night Thoughts of a Classical Physicist*. Cambridge: Harvard University Press.

Mill, J. S. 1981. *Autobiography*. Vol. 1 of *Collected Works of John Stuart Mill*. Toronto: University of Toronto Press.

Moggridge, D. 1992. *Maynard Keynes: An Economist's Biography*. London: Routledge.

Moore, W. 1989. *Schrödinger*. Cambridge: Cambridge University Press.

Nasar, S. 1998. *Beautiful Mind: A Biography of John Forbes Nash*. New York: Touchstone.

Nye, D. 1983. *The Invented Self: An Autobiography from Documents of Thomas A. Edison*. Odense: Odense University Press.

Playfair, J. 1815–24. Dissertation Second: Exhibiting a General View of the Progress of Mathematical and Physical Science, since the Revival of Letters in Europe. In *Supplement to the Encyclopaedia Britannica*, edited by M. Napier. 6 vols. Edinburgh: Constable.

Priestley, J. 1765. *A Description of a Chart of Biography, with a Catalogue of Names Inserted in it, and the Dates Annexed to Them*. Warrington: Printed for the author.

———. 1775. *The History and Present State of Electricity, with Original Experiments*. 2 vols. 3d ed. London: C. Bathurst and T. Lowndes.

Progoff, I. 1998. *Life-Study: Experiencing Creative Lives*. New York: Dialogue House.

Pyenson, L. 1977. "Who the Guys Were": Prosopography in the History of Science. *History of Science* 15:155–88.

Rorty, R. 1989. *Contingency, Irony, Solidarity*. Cambridge: Cambridge University Press.

Ross, I. S. 1996. *Life of Adam Smith*. New York: Oxford University Press.

Runyan, W. M. 1984. *Life Histories and Psychobiography: Explorations in Theory and Method*. New York: Oxford University Press.

Schama, Simon. 1989. *Citizens: A Chronicle of the French Revolution*. New York: Knopf.

Schumpeter, J. 1954. *A History of Economic Analysis*. New York: Oxford University Press.

Shapin, S., and A. Thackray. 1974. Prosopography as a Research Tool in History of Science: The British Scientific Community 1700–1900. *History of Science* 12:1–28.

Shea, S. C. 1998. *Psychiatric Interviewing*. 2d ed. Philadelphia: W. B. Saunders.

Sheets-Pyenson, S. 1990. New Directions for Scientific Biography: The Case of Sir William Dawson. *History of Science* 28:399–410.

Shortland, M., and R. Yeo, eds. 1996. *Telling Lives in Science*. Cambridge: Cambridge University Press.

Skidelsky, R. 1983–2000. *John Maynard Keynes*. 3 vols. London: Macmillan.

Smith, C., and N. Wise. 1989. *Energy and Empire: A Biographical Study of Lord Kelvin*. Cambridge: Cambridge University Press.

Snowdon, B., and H. Vane, eds. 1999. *Conversations with Leading Economists: Interpreting Modern Macroeconomics*. Cheltenham, U.K.: Edward Elgar.

Söderqvist, T. 1996. Existential Projects and Existential Choice in Science: Science Biography as an Edifying Genre. In Shortland and Yeo 1996.

Sokal, M. 1990. Life-span Developmental Psychology and the History of Science. In *Beyond History of Science: Essays in Honor of Robert E. Schofield*, edited by Elizabeth Garber. Bethlehem, Pa.: Lehigh University Press.

Strachey, L. 1918. *Eminent Victorians*. London: Chatto and Windus.

Sturges, P. 1983. Collective Biography in the 1980s. *Biography* 6:316–32.

Szenberg, M., ed. 1992. *Eminent Economists: Their Life Philosophies*. Cambridge: Cambridge University Press.

———., ed. 1998. *Passion and Craft: Economists at Work*. Ann Arbor.: University of Michigan Press.

Tribe, K., ed. 1997. *Economic Careers: Economics and Economists in Great Britain*. London: Routledge.

Westfall, R. 1980. *Never at Rest: A Biography of Isaac Newton*. Cambridge: Cambridge University Press.

Whewell, W. [1837] 1857. *History of the Inductive Sciences*. 3d ed. 3 vols. London: J. Parker.

White, Hayden V. 1999. History as Fulfillment. Keynote address given to the Interdisciplinary Scholars Network meeting, 12 November, Tulane University, New Orleans. Available at www.tulane.edu/~isn/hwkeynote.htm.

Yeo, R. 1996. Historical Dictionaries and Encyclopaedias. In Shortland and Yeo 1996.

Young, R. M. 1988. Biography: The Basic Discipline for Human Science. *Free Associations* 11:108–30.

Surfing the Past: The Role of the Internet in the Future of the History of Economics

Ross Emmett

I have no intention of arguing that the Internet will save the history of economics as a discipline, that the teaching of the history of economics will be radically reformed by on-line resources, that print journals in the history of economic thought will disappear, or that Web connectivity will transform the interpretative work of the historian. Rather, the purpose of this essay is to explore realistically what opportunities and challenges the information technologies available through the Internet pose for scholarship in the history of economics in the near future.

Despite the fact that historians of economics have recently followed historians of science into the exploration of how scientific tools and technologies shape the history of the science, little attention has been given to the technologies used by historians of economics. I am sometimes told that it is fortunate I am a historian of economic thought: given my position in a liberal arts college, I would otherwise feel the lack of access to large libraries and databases, or to colleagues who can help me with new econometric techniques, or to research assistants, or to a constant stream of visiting speakers allowing me to keep abreast of the latest developments in my subfield. The underlying assumption is that, as a historian of economics, all I have to do is read and write.

A preliminary version of this essay was presented at the Seminar for the Preservation of the History of Economic Thought, Center for the Study of Public Choice, George Mason University, July 2000. I wish to thank Bill Goffe, David Levy, Roy Weintraub, and an anonymous reviewer for helpful comments.

Well, I do read, and I write. But the range of technologies available to assist me in the historian's craft has changed significantly in the last two decades. The new technologies have not only provided opportunities, but they are also restructuring and resituating my activity, changing the infrastructure that supports my scholarly activity, and reshaping my identity as an academic (see Golinski 1998). As almost every academic knows, these changes also come with a set of institutional, social, and political tensions that the academy is still working out.

This essay will be organized around the technologies available: e-mail lists; on-line text archives; archival resources on-line; on-line archives of abstracts and current research; the potential for on-line journals; and digital projects. At the end, the essay will consider some of the possibilities for the teaching of the history of economic thought. Throughout our consideration of the opportunities and challenges enabled by Internet technologies, the essay will include a look at the institutional issues around the provision of Internet technologies to historians of economics. Particular attention will be paid to the role of scholarly societies and independent journals and to the potential for collaborative efforts among historians of economics and other colleagues.

E-mail Lists

The infrastructure of academic life was transformed during the mid-1990s by the simplest form of Internet interactivity—e-mail. E-mail technology lowered the cost of communication among individuals, making near-constant communication possible. Scholars today routinely use e-mail to share preliminary drafts for critical commentary, and the process of editorial review by journal referees has been facilitated (somewhat) by the ability to send comments and files electronically.

Historians of economics have also benefited from the interactivity provided by the History of Economics Society (HES) e-mail list (see appendix for this and the other addresses of the Web sites mentioned in this essay). Regardless of what its creators or initial subscribers thought it would become, the list's primary function today is an extension of the individual historian's own research activity. Need to know the source of a quotation, the existence of an archive, or whether Keynes's predecessors said anything about liquidity preference? Rather than spending hours searching for the answers yourself, an inquiry on the list can often produce an answer within a few days and sometimes come up with a few surprises as well. The list's emphasis is apparent from the fact that 65 percent of the postings to the list during 2000 were either inquiries or responses to inquiries. To date, the HES list has more than 600 subscribers from around the world and averages more than 450 messages per year.

The limitations of list interactivity are also clear from an examination of the HES list. Detractors have sometimes said that list interaction is nothing more than talk around the water cooler (Lodewijks 1997). Certainly Frank Knight's (1991) "first law of talk" also seems to operate in the realm of virtual talk: "Bad talk drives out good." Overzealous participants come to dominate discussions, and sustained discussion of a theme usually moves off-list as it becomes less general, in terms of both interest to list members and the number of contributors. Of course, the very expectation that an e-mail list could provide a forum for significant discussion may be misguided.

On-line Text Archives

The primary focus of the historian's craft remains the text. Researchers will adopt Internet technologies that provide greater access to texts and expand the range of available texts. Copyright laws complicate the issue, but one can reasonably expect that any text the historian of economics is interested in will eventually be available on-line (although perhaps for a fee or through a subscription service). On-line access to historical texts also enhances the teaching of the history of economic thought, by making a wider range of material available to students than that usually provided by textbooks and course reading packets.

The McMaster University Archive in the History of Economic Thought is the primary on-line archive of public domain texts in the history of economic thought. Rod Hay, the McMaster Archive's creator, has done the field a service by providing a large and expanding number of texts on-line. The prominence of the archive is enhanced by the links created to it within several other text sites, in Japan (Akama 2000), Australia (Dixon n.d.), and England (Brewer n.d.).

Yet the McMaster Archive has several drawbacks. Most important, there is no long-term institutional support for site development. Hay is no longer in an academic position, McMaster University has no institutional commitment to the site, and no one has a plan for long-term site development. This last problem with the McMaster Archive leads to still more drawbacks. For example, the archive lacks a site-specific search engine for use within and across texts. Advanced users may know how to restrict the domain in a search on some of the major Internet search engines (Google and Altavista are two that contain this feature) in a way that enables a search across the McMaster Archive, but to date these search capabilities have not been included in the site design. Also, there are enough mistakes in the scanned versions of the texts provided in the McMaster Archive to make their use difficult for research purposes. One always has to check the text against the published version before using it. Finally, the current on-line format is unattractive and, more important, does not allow the researcher to know the pagination of the material in its print original. The on-line texts provided by Paulette Taieb (www.taieb.net) and the Pôle d'Histoire de l'Analyse et des Représentations Économiques are better in this latter regard.

The problems with the McMaster Archive could be solved if an agreement between Rod Hay and a scholarly organization (or another scholar with institutional backing) were reached. The establishment of a long-term site development plan is essential to the archive's ongoing service to the scholarly community. In the absence of an arrangement for the McMaster Archive, scholarly organizations in the history of economic thought may wish to collaborate in the creation of a more comprehensive and better-serviced historical text archive.

Several other text archives relevant to the history of economic thought can be mentioned in passing. The Making of America digital project includes material related to economics in nineteenth-century North America. The collection currently holds approximately eight thousand books and fifty thousand articles from journals and magazines of the period. In its depths, David Levy (2001) discovered the original version of Thomas Carlyle's dismissal of the "dismal science" (missed by even the *Oxford English Dictionary*), overturning the long-standing belief that Carlyle's focus was on the Malthusianism of classical economics rather than their advocacy of radical egalitarianism. Many of the problems with the McMaster Archive do not exist in the Making of America site because the funding base (provided by the Andrew W. Mellon Foundation) is larger and an excellent search engine is incorporated into the site. Yale Law School's Avalon Project provides on-line access to documents related to law, history, and diplomacy, including a number of texts of interest to some historians of economics. Scholars interested in the intersection of economics and the humanities will find the University of Virginia's

Electronic Text Center, the University of Michigan's Humanities Text Initiative, and Project Gutenberg helpful.

Copyright issues have prevented the inclusion of most twentieth-century economics work in freely accessible on-line archives. However, researchers in larger academic centers do have access to several other on-line archives that expand the range of texts available to them. The most important of these is JSTOR, the archive of journal "back files" originated by William G. Bowen, president of the Andrew W. Mellow Foundation. The JSTOR journal agreement uses a "moving wall" of three to five years, which allows the journal to provide current issues on-line as a commercial service through outlets such as EBSCO Information Services or SilverPlatter's WebSPIRS. JSTOR provides users with an image of each journal page, which is searchable via a hidden full-text version. Thirteen of the most prominent journals in economics are included, as are another eleven journals in each of mathematics and statistics. JSTOR provides a full-text search engine with advanced search features.

There are two limitations to JSTOR. First, although the archive provides access to the entire run of the most important journals in economics, it does not include all journals in the field. Researchers cannot access many key articles published in less prominent journals. Second, the cost of a JSTOR subscription is prohibitive for some smaller libraries, and a number of historians of economics work in smaller liberal arts colleges.

While the combination of the McMaster Archive, JSTOR, and other text collections provide on-line access to a large number of texts that historians of economics use in research and teaching, the one major set of texts that have not been provided on-line are books that remain in copyright. Because the vast majority of economics books are in this category, historians of economics today, like their predecessors, remain dependent on the quality of the libraries to which they have access.

Archival Resources On-line

Archives recognized fairly quickly the expanded access the Internet provided for their collections. While privacy and consent issues have prevented rapid expansion of the on-line provision of archival material, archives have been quick to make catalogs of their collections available. Today an increasing amount of archival resources is now available on-line, with more material being added daily.

There is a positive correlation between the on-line provision of archival resources and the use of archival materials by historians of economics. Correspondence, unpublished materials like drafts and reports, oral histories, and lecture notes have become increasingly important to the historiography of economics as the discipline moves from doctrinal history to a study of the various processes by which research programs develop (Weintraub et al. 1998). As archives move on-line, they perform two services for historians of economics: they enable the historian to search more easily for relevant material that may be available, and they make some of that material directly available on-line.

The largest listing of archives and manuscript repositories in the world is the University of Idaho's "Repositories of Primary Sources," although the Society of American Archivists and Tulane University's library have combined for another excellent site, "Ready, 'Net, Go! Archival Internet Resources." Unfortunately, there is no search engine specifically devoted to archival materials, and few of the generic search engines provide trustworthy searches of archives and manuscript repositories. Where an archive's resources are incorporated into the on-line catalog of its university library, site-specific searches are possible, and there are a number of search engines dedicated to searches across library catalogs. The California Digital Library's American Heritage Virtual Archive, which provides access to the archival resources of Duke (including the Economists' Papers Project), Stanford (including the Hoover Institution's archives), the University of Virginia, and the various University of California libraries, is also worth noting.

On-line Archives of Current Research

JSTOR, mentioned in an earlier section, provides on-line access to the back files of major journals in the fields of economics, mathematics, statistics, and others. And most journals today provide on-line access to their current issues through services such as EBSCO Information Services or SilverPlatter's WebSPIRS. However, the length of the publication process in print journals remains,[1] and researchers who want access to the most current research must search elsewhere. What interactive services allow researchers access to unpublished current research?

---

1. See Ellison 2000 for a discussion of why the publication process in economics has slowed down over the past thirty years.

The foremost model of academic interactivity is the arXiv.org e-Print Archive of the Los Alamos National Laboratory, which serves the high-energy physics community. In a very short period, the common practice among physicists of circulating preprints was replaced by an on-line depository of unpublished articles and research reports. The e-Print Archive has decreased the cost of communication among physicists dramatically (departments used to spend thousands of dollars circulating preprints) and increased the number of researchers who have access to current material—the archive includes more than 150,000 papers and averages 13,000 connections per hour during weekdays. The archive has recently been expanded to include mathematics, nonlinear science, computational linguistics, and computing science. Central to e-Print's success has been its financial ability to maintain a free service.

The economics discipline was quick to catch on to the benefits of using the Internet to provide fast and relatively inexpensive access to the latest research. While other disciplines have not been able to match the e-Print Archive's success, economics has three services that have been more successful than those in other disciplines. "Research Papers in Economics" (RePEc) provides on-line working paper archives for economics as a free service. The Social Science Research Network (www.ssrn. com/) is a commercial service, run by economists, which has succeeded by establishing site licenses for most major university libraries and research institutes. Scholars in those institutions enjoy the benefits of the Social Science Research Network in a manner similar to their access to JSTOR; others pay a fee for individual access to the service. Finally, EH.Net runs a free abstract service for both economic history and the history of economic thought where scholars can provide abstracts of working papers and recent publications. To date, however, we have seen almost no effort by historians of economics to use this service as a regular means of communicating their current work. Like their colleagues in the humanities and history, historians of economics probably find that near-instantaneous communication regarding current research has little additional benefit over more traditional means of scholarly communication. Whether the possibility of peer-to-peer file sharing (the technology first developed by Napster) will nudge historians of economics in the direction of on-line research interactivity remains to be seen.

On-line Journals

Despite the widely shared assumption that on-line journals would replace print journals in academia, this has not happened yet, and is not
likely to happen in the near future (see Odlyzko 1997; Tenopir and King
1998). For a variety of institutional reasons, not least of which is the
peer-review process, which keeps control of journal content within the
hands of disciplinary practitioners, the standard journals of economics
are likely to continue to dominate the field. These journals have responded to the call for electronic access, however, and today almost all journals
in economics have some form of on-line access to their content (although
access is usually restricted to those with individual or institutional subscriptions).

Among journals in the history of economics, however, the story is
somewhat different. The publishers of the *Journal of the History of Economic Thought* and the *European Journal of the History of Economic
Thought* provide on-line access to individual and institutional subscribers of the journals. Subscribing libraries, for example, can provide users
direct on-line access from the campus library system without paying
an additional fee. The leading journal in the field—*History of Political
Economy*, published by Duke University Press—is available on-line via
the press's association with Project Muse, an enterprise of Johns Hopkins University Press. However, Project Muse is only available to institutional subscribers and only as a package deal including a wide variety
of journals published by university presses. Libraries that carry many of
the journals included in Project Muse find it cost-effective to become
members, but libraries with few Project Muse journal holdings would
find the subscription cost-prohibitive. Project Muse currently provides
167 journals on-line. Two smaller journals—*History of Economics Review* and *History of Economic Ideas*—do not provide on-line access,
which is likely explained by the fact that these journals are published
independently.

What are the prospects for an exclusively on-line journal in the history
of economics? A recent discussion of this topic on the HES list confused
two issues: (1) the exclusive provision of a journal on-line, and (2) free
access to an on-line journal (whether or not there is a print version available as well). We can treat each of these issues in turn.

The creation of an exclusively on-line journal devoted to the history of
economics is quite possible and will probably happen in the near future.

Economics is a field that several publishers of on-line journals have targeted for development, with the Berkeley Electronic Press being among the leaders. These publishers have moved the entire publication process, from submission to peer-review to publication, on-line. If a group could assemble a qualified editorial team, any of these publishers would probably add a history of economics journal to their collection.

The bigger issue is whether a freely accessible on-line journal in the history of economics is possible. There has been a lot of discussion of this arrangement among academic societies and journals (see Goffe 2000), with perhaps only the big commercial publishers opposing it. Two journals in economics that provide free on-line access to their contents can serve as models. The *Journal of Economics and Finance* moved on-line in 1994 and provides free access to its contents. The *Journal of Economic Education* made its on-line version freely accessible in 1998. Both journals have a print version, for which there is a subscription fee. Neither journal has seen a decline in its print subscribers, but their on-line readership far exceeds their subscription base. Of course, more readers means more citations for the articles' authors, and hence more submissions to the journal.

Could any of the existing journals in the history of economics provide their content on-line for free? The majority of the journals' costs are fixed and are presumably already covered by the subscription base. The central issue, then, would be funding the marginal costs of on-line access. Those journals supported by a society could use organizational revenues to fund a free on-line version of their journal, in the same manner as some of them already provide their newsletters on-line—for example, the British *History of Economic Thought Newsletter* and the European Society's *Newsletter*. However, the most likely organization to undertake such a venture, the HES, is already in a contractual agreement with a publisher that includes on-line provision, but only for subscribers. Thus, despite the apparent advantages for an expanded readership via free on-line access, my conclusion is that the prospect of a freely accessible on-line journal in the history of economics seems at best a remote possibility. Bill Goffe (2000) has recently encouraged the American Economic Association to study the prospect of making several journals in economics freely available on-line, and the journals in the history of economic thought might want to participate in that study.

Digital Projects

One of the ironies for historians of economics is that, just when they wrestled textuality away from a focus on doctrinal interpretation, the Internet provided the possibility of hypertextuality. The basic ability of the hypertext medium is to collect and display multiple media within a single format, what we usually call a Web page. Hypertext is not a particularly attractive medium for narrative, and historians have typically used it only to complement a linear story with diagrams or pictures. Yet the hypertext medium poses significant alternatives for academic presentation, and scholars in other fields have begun to explore the possibilities (McAdams and Berger 2001). The possibility we will consider here is the digital project.

Digital projects are virtual creations that use hypertext and other Internet protocols to bring together a variety of media around a common theme. A couple of simple examples from existing digital history of economics projects can illustrate the possibilities. In the process of writing an editorial for the HES list, Steve Meardon (1998) and the staff of the Duke Special Collections Library created a Web site devoted to a sample from the correspondence between John Hicks and Don Patinkin (Rare Book, Manuscript, and Special Collections Library 1998). The site is a relatively simple digital project, including an interpretive essay, images of the letters (in both handwritten and typed form), and photographs of the two economists. Daniele Besomi (n.d.) has created a more extensive Web site for a selection of correspondence between Roy Harrod and John Maynard Keynes.

Further projects like Meardon's and Besomi's would be welcome additions for historians of economics, both in expanding the range of research materials available on-line and, equally important, in providing primary sources for teaching purposes. But what are the prospects for more extensive digital projects to appear in the history of economics, with a greater use of the advantages of hypertextuality?

Here are a variety of feasible suggestions. Each of them requires organizational and financial support beyond that currently available within the history of economics community, but each is possible without a great deal of additional support. First, a series of on-line lectures on leading topics in the history of economics could be created, similar to the lectures currently available in psychology, philosophy, and the sciences on Boxmind.com and other similar services. The Boxmind.com lectures provide a video of the lecturer (usually a leading scholar in the field), accompanied by slides the lecturer wants to include (pictures, diagrams, etc.) and an extensive set of notes. A similar on-line series of lectures in the history of economics could promote recent research, provide assistance to those teaching the subject, and attract general interest as well.

Second, a group of scholars could cooperate to create a Web site devoted to a specific person, school of thought, or topic in the history of economics. To a certain extent, this has already been done with Marx, Hayek, and, on a larger scale, the New School University History of Economic Thought site. But could a group of historians of economics create a site on the scale of "The Victorian Web," or even the "Making of America" site?

Mention of sites like the New School History of Economic Thought site leads us to the next option, an on-line encyclopedia of the history of economics. The New School site is quite valuable for its coverage but also idiosyncratic, reflecting its origins as the work of a graduate student in Robert Heilbroner's classes. The site's permanence is also questionable: it has moved several times, was off-line for extended periods twice in the year 2000, and its creator has a professional career planned in economic research rather than the history of economic thought.

One of the central issues in creating an on-line encyclopedia is the intended audience. The New School site and, on a more limited scale, many others provide general knowledge about leading economists and economic schools of thought. These sites are appropriate for general audiences, including lower-level undergraduate students. Advanced researchers in the field, however, do not have access to an encyclopedia that summarizes current research. The *Stanford Encyclopedia of Philosophy*, which provides peer-reviewed entries updated by their authors as the current literature on the topic evolves, is a model that could serve historians of economics well in this regard. The *Stanford Encyclopedia* assembled an editorial board of leading scholars in the field, who review every entry and revision before it is put on-line. The site is funded by a variety of federal agencies and scholarly organizations; its institutional affiliation also adds to its credibility. EH.Net has recently launched an on-line, edited *Encyclopedia of Economic and Business History* with articles written by experts in the field, which could also serve as a model.

Fourth, historians of economics could cooperate with archivists and other scholars to create virtual exhibitions on particular themes. For

example, the recent interest in the visual representations used by economists could form the basis of a virtual exhibition sponsored by a university archive or museum. The project might well bring together historians of economics, economists, economic historians, archivists, Web
designers, financial historians, historians of science and technology, and
others in the process of creating the exhibit. Other suggestions for ex-
hibits would include: the mercantilists; the work of several economists
associated with a particular university (like the University of Chicago or
the New School) whose papers are housed in the university's archives;
policy-related activities of economists during the New Deal or the Cold
War; the South Sea Bubble and Mississippi Scheme; the activities of
economists involved in economic development in Africa, Asia, or Latin
America; and the history of the American Economic Association or similar scholarly organizations in other countries. The list, of course, is only
limited by the imagination of historians of economics.

There are two key obstacles to the creation of any of these digital
projects. The first is the willingness of historians of economics to consider Internet exhibition a legitimate part of their academic activity. Of
course, their willingness to consider this activity is directly related to the
academic rewards that emerge from the activity, and the present structure of academic decisions regarding tenure and promotion in economics departments across North America is not likely to reward this activity highly. Second, digital projects cost money, and unless institutional
support for a project is available, outside funding is necessary. Some
foundations are willing to support digital projects, and there may be government funding available in certain cases. But the primary financial responsibility will probably fall on scholarly organizations. For example,
the HES could approach the American Economic Association (AEA)
about jointly sponsoring a virtual exhibition on the history of the AEA.
Are scholarly organizations willing to accept this responsibility?

Prospects for Teaching the History
of Economic Thought

The majority of this essay has dealt with Internet technologies that facilitate the process and dissemination of academic research. But historians
of economics also have the responsibility of teaching their students and
should play a role in informing the public about economics' past. I will

therefore conclude the essay with some observations on the Internet's role in the teaching of the discipline.

Several of the possibilities already discussed in this article contribute to enhancing the teaching of the history of economic thought. For example, the McMaster Archive has expanded the number of texts accessible to undergraduate students in history of economic thought courses. Digital projects like the New School site provide basic information about many economists and schools of economic thought, amplifying the discussion available in the students' textbook. And, for advanced students, the availability of primary sources on the Internet opens up research topics that were previously impossible to pursue until one began thesis work.

Two other projects that are specifically aimed at enhancing the historian's teaching role are the EH.Net's on-line archive of syllabi in the history of economic thought and "Ask the Professor" service. Because many instructors of the history of economic thought are not specialists in the field, and those who are specialists are always interested in improving their courses, the on-line archive of syllabi provides the opportunity to sample a large number of current history of economic thought courses. The "Ask the Professor" service allows students to pose research or general interest questions regarding the history of economic thought and receive answers from specialists in the field. Several years of experience with the service has enabled EH.Net to screen questions that are unacceptable, such as class assignments.

Given the number of economics programs that no longer have adequate staffing for history of economic thought courses, there could be demand for a virtual master class, offered on-line by one of the leading programs in the history of economic thought but drawing on the expertise of scholars across the world. The on-line lecture series suggested earlier could become the core of such an on-line course. To date, the only on-line course in the history of economic thought is offered by the New School Online University.

Conclusion

Historians of economics have a wide variety of Internet resources at their disposal. This essay has surveyed these activities and discussed the opportunities and challenges they present. But to what extent have these technologies changed the way historians of economics operate as scholars? Have historians of economics made "surfing the past" an integral part of their scholarly work or simply a diversion with some benefits for easing their correspondence burden?

The Internet has significantly changed the way historians of economics operate in two areas: scholarly correspondence and bibliographic research. E-mail correspondence is common among all scholars today, and historians of economics regularly use it to exchange papers, manage the business of their scholarly societies, keep up with other scholars through the HES e-mail list, and submit to, or referee for, journals. The modern scholar also cannot help but use Internet technologies to search for books, articles, and archival resources, as Internet technologies make the search process both less costly and more readily accessible. But which of the services surveyed above has enabled historians of economics to make Internet technologies other than e-mail and on-line bibliographic searches a normal part of their scholarly activity?

The most likely candidates are the on-line text archives and on-line access to archival resources. Because search engines make it possible to use on-line text archives as a substitute for the indexing feature of a book, one can use the text archive to search for a particular quotation, a theme, or a commentary on the work of other economists. Despite their drawbacks, the on-line text archives are helping historians of economics conduct their research faster and with greater accuracy. In a similar manner, the recent increase in interest in archival research has also been enhanced by the use of the Internet.

These are significant steps in the process of integrating Internet technologies into the common working practices of historians of economics. Other forms of Internet activity will become standard parts of the work of historians of economics if they enable the latter to accomplish their objectives as researchers, scholars, and teachers, and if they can be delivered in cost-effective ways. Scholarly organizations such as the History of Economics Society and the American Economic Association can play a significant role in making these activities available to scholars.

Appendix 1 Web Sites and Their Addresses

McMaster University Archive in the History of Economic Thought. socserv2.socsci.mcmaster.ca/~econ/ugcm/3ll3.

Pôle d'Histoire de l'Analyse et des Représentations Économiques.
phare.univ-paris1.fr.
Avalon Project (Yale University). www.yale.edu/lawweb/avalon/
avalon.htm.
Electronic Text Center (University of Virginia Library).
etext.lib.virginia.edu.
Humanities Text Initiative (University of Michigan). www.hti.umich.edu.
Project Gutenberg. www.gutenberg.net.
Making of America. moa.umdl.umich.edu.
JSTOR (Journal Storage). www.jstor.org.
EBSCO Information Services. www.ebsco.com.
SilverPlatter. www.silverplatter.com.
Repositories of Primary Sources (University of Idaho). www.uidaho.edu/
special-collections/Other.Repositories.html.
Ready, 'Net, Go! Archival Internet Resources. www.tulane.edu/~lmiller/
ArchivesResources.html.
American Heritage Virtual Archive Project. sunsite.berkeley.edu/amher.
e-Print Archive (Los Alamos National Laboratory). xxx.lanl.gov.
RePEc (Research Papers in Economics). repec.org.
Social Science Research Network. www.ssrn.com.
EH.Net. www.eh.net/HE.
Project Muse (Johns Hopkins University Press). muse.jhu.edu.
Berkeley Electronic Press. bepress.com.
Journal of Economics and Finance. www.mtsu.edu/~jeandf.
Journal of Economic Education. www.indiana.edu/~econed.
History of Economic Thought Newsletter. www.ecn.bris.ac.uk/het1/
index.htm.
Newsletter, European Society for the History of Economic Thought.
www.ecn.bris.ac.uk/het1/eshet/index.htm.
Marxists.org Internet Archive. www.marxists.org/archive/marx.
The Friedrich Hayek Scholars' Page. www.hayekcenter.org/
friedrichhayek/hayek.html.
History of Economic Thought (New School University).
homepage.newschool.edu/het.
The Victorian Web. www.victorianweb.org.
Stanford Encyclopedia of Philosophy. plato.stanford.edu.
Encyclopedia of Economic and Business History. www.eh.net/
encyclopedia.
History of Economics Society e-mail list. eh.net/HE/hes_list.

References

Akama, Michio. 2000. Akamac E-Text Links. www.cpm.ehime-u.ac.jp/Akamac HomePage/Akamac_E-text_Links/Akamac_E-text_Links.html.

Besomi, Daniele. n.d. J. M. Keynes/R. Harrod: Letters and Memoranda. www.e.u-tokyo.ac.jp/Exhibition/keynes/index.htm.

Brewer, Tony. n.d. Documents for the History of Economics. www.ecn.bris.ac.uk/het/index.htm.

Dixon, Robert. n.d. Archive for the History of Economic Thought. melbecon.unimelb.edu.au/het.

Ellison, G. 2000. The Slowdown of the Economics Publishing Process. papers.nber.org/papers/W7804.

Goffe, W. L. 2000. The Internet and the American Economic Association. wuecon.wustl.edu/~goffe/fut.pdf.

Golinski, J. 1998. *Making Natural Knowledge: Constructivism and the History of Science*. Cambridge: Cambridge University Press.

Knight, F. H. 1991. The Case for Communism: From the Standpoint of an Ex-liberal. *Research in the History of Economic Thought and Methodology* (archival supplement) 2:57–108.

Levy, D. 2001. *How the Dismal Science Got Its Name: Classical Economics and the Ur-Text of Racial Politics*. Ann Arbor: University of Michigan Press.

Lodewijks, J. 1997. Societies, Journals, and Research in the History of Economics. www.eh.net/HE/hes_list/Editorials/lodewijks.php.

McAdams, M., and S. Berger. 2001. Hypertext. *Journal of Electronic Publishing* 6 (March). www.press.umich.edu/jep/06-03/McAdams/pages.

Meardon, S. 1998. The Economists' Papers Project at Duke University—A Sample from the Don Patinkin Papers. www.eh.net/HE/hes_list/Editorials/meardon.php.

Odlyzko, A. M. 1997. The Slow Evolution of Electronic Publishing. In *Electronic Publishing '97: New Models and Opportunities*, edited by F. Rowland and A. J. Meadows, 4–18. Washington, D.C.: ICCC Press.

Rare Book, Manuscript, and Special Collections Library. 1998. The Patinkin-Hicks Correspondence, 1957–58, Duke University. scriptorium.lib.duke.edu/economists/patinkin.

Tenopir, C., and D. W. King. 1998. Designing Electronic Journals with Thirty Years of Lessons from Print. *Journal of Electronic Publishing* 4 (December). www.press.umich.edu/jep/04–02/king.html.

Weintraub, E. R., Stephen J. Meardon, Ted Gayer, and H. Spencer Banzhaf. 1998. Archiving the History of Economics. *Journal of Economic Literature* 36 (September): 1496.

Part 4

The Next Generation

Confusion and "Interstanding": A Figured Account of Hope

Matthias Klaes

Confusion is properly a mixture of such liquid things as are fluid, and of one and the same nature.
—John Woodall, *The Surgions Mate* (1617)

The history of economics is an embattled field of academic research. Its subject matter and basic approach have become embroiled in emotionally charged debates (see Klaes 2001), while its institutional and disciplinary loci are opaque. Not infrequently, practitioners give in to historicist temptations to look back to a golden age predating the schism between economics and (its) history. At the coming of age of the field at the turn of the millennium, it is worth bearing in mind, however, that its institutional emergence and a certain self-aware sense of crisis are difficult to disentangle (see Winch 1962 and Coats 1969).[1] When reflecting on the position of young entrants to the history of economics, there is thus a certain danger of being seduced by the current state of affairs in reporting on the particular difficulties they are faced with. Whether

The original version of this essay was presented at the *HOPE* 2001 conference as part of a session titled "The Next Generation," which focused on the perspectives of new entrants to the field. This revised version responds to stimulating comments received from participants at the conference, an anonymous referee, the editor, and my colleagues at the Centre for Social Theory and Technology, in particular Robert Cooper, Mihaela Kelemen, Rolland Munro, and Martin Parker.

1. One should not overlook that historiographical discourse in general has turned to describing our time in terms of a crisis in historical consciousness and method (see Burke [1991] 2001, 1–2).

young historians of economics have a harder time establishing themselves than other graduates in economics or history is a fascinating sociological question that cannot be further pursued here. Instead, as a participant-observer, I seek to explore the situation of a young entrant to a field that, apart from its sense of crisis, is characterized by a constant search for its identity, disciplinary allegiance, and institutional affiliation.

The present essay is thus an attempt to reflect, through my own situation and experiences, on the current state of history of economics. I intend to submit to the reader a collection of encounters that, as fragments of discourse, may allow a glimpse on the history of economics vis-à-vis economics and other disciplines. Each of these encounters should be read as a snapshot of the currently negotiated boundaries of the history of economics. Young entrants to the field are in a good position to report on these encounters, as they will find themselves crossing a number of boundaries while seeking admission to the guild of historians of economics. Nevertheless, simply reading what follows as an autobiographical account would risk missing the point. I will present not a coherent narrative but a collage of "figures" (Barthes [1977] 1990), followed by a metanarrative that interprets this collage as a representation of the current state of the history of economics in terms of Mark Taylor's (1995) metaphor of "interstanding."

A further word of caution: *figure* in the sense employed here refers neither to persons nor to a stereotype. Instead, the ambition is to follow ethnomethodologists in their attempts to capture the choreography of discursive encounters. While based on actual encounters, figures both go beyond these encounters and fall short of them. They fall short because they do not intend to accurately reproduce the encounters, and they go beyond because they reach out further than the particularity of the moment. In the present context, the figures presented below would speak not just as idiosyncratic experiences but as expressions of the complex boundary dynamics of the history of economics. In Roland Barthes's ([1977] 1990, 4) words, successfully crafted figures would tempt us to say, "That's so true!"

A Figured Account of History of Economics

The Agnostic:[2] "Surely you are not suggesting that Coase and his 1960 paper had nothing to do with the Coase theorem!?"[3] Some practicing economists seem to have a peculiar relationship with past literature. They may not have read the sources themselves but will vehemently defend any questioning of the canonized readings of these sources, right down to calling your economic expertise into question. From my own experience, sometimes it does not even help going through the original sources with them as they tend to lack the taste for detailed exegesis.

The Bystander: "To be honest, your chances will be slim, but I have done some historical research myself in the past so I can sympathize with your situation."[4] I have encountered a number of economists who were very open to my research interests. At the same time, they readily admitted that I was unlikely to get a job in their departments. If much of what is happening in a discipline is driven not by genuine research interests but by external research and internal promotion incentives, the result seems inevitable: frustrated academics and less interesting and original research output due to lack of intrinsic motivation.

Economics Divided: "Some of the papers at this conference have even been straightforwardly neoclassical!" "Which ones?" "Well, for example, *his* paper."[5] Somebody educated within an orthodox curriculum might actually find some aspects of that learning interesting and useful while regarding other aspects clearly limited and unsatisfactory. As a result she might decide to concentrate on some of the perceived shortcomings, or develop a powerful immanent critique. The downside of

2. I have followed Barthes by opening each figure with a partial sentence similar to what Barthes calls the figure's "heading": its unique theme or underlying motive (in the musical sense). Furthermore, to emphasize that the collection of figures as a whole does not aggregate into a "story," I have adopted his practice of presenting figures in the alphabetical order of their headings.

3. The exasperated outcry of one of my supervisors in economics after a lengthy meeting in which I tried to convince him that the Coase theorem was due to George Stigler and that Coase had actually argued the opposite in that essay.

4. The response from the head of an economics department whom I approached to explore whether I should bother to apply for a lectureship.

5. The comments of an agitated conference delegate complaining in the crowded annual meeting at a major heterodox conference about the exclusion of his paper from a conference volume, challenging the organizers' implicit definition of what counts as heterodox and, more to my bemusement than horror, publicly pointing in my direction. He was referring to an essay that had been consistently rejected by orthodox conference selection committees.

pursuing this strategy is the risk of losing simultaneously large parts of both orthodox and heterodox audiences.

Incommunicado: "You have managed to completely mystify us yet again."[6] Presentations of methodological research in economics departments, or historical research that is not straightforwardly "Whig," can turn into severe trials of patience on both sides. Given that economists are frequently unfamiliar with even basic issues in social scientific and historical research, misunderstandings are very likely to occur. I found that the most *unsuccessful* strategy for overturning these communication barriers was trying to speak to those colleagues in their own language. Provided with a graph or formula to better illustrate a particular point, they would invariably home in on the familiar and completely disregard the actual argument put to them.

Hedging: "I think you would be well advised to keep in touch with technology studies."[7] Looking back, this was very wise advice that I heeded, at least initially, without grasping the underlying rationale. Were it not for my interest and research in technology studies, it is unlikely that I would be employed in academia right now. Technology studies, unlike science studies or historical and methodological research, has found a comfortable institutional home in many management schools, which greatly expands one's range of choice in seeking permanent employment.

Hostility: "I can barely keep a history of thought course going because of my colleagues' attitudes."[8] It has become commonplace to deplore the ongoing decline of history of economics courses in the economics curriculum. What is less often acknowledged is the systematic marginalization of colleagues. Open-minded economists who would tolerate my historical and methodological research interests were frequently uncompromising when this affected institutional practices like curriculum design, departmental seminars, or conference programs. Incidentally, I observed similarly assertive attitudes toward the preservation of the perceived disciplinary core in philosophy and sometimes even in sociology.

Impartial Umpires versus Reformers: "I think what you are trying to do is actually something like *Begriffsgeschichte*."[9] Some historians

6. A remark by a member of an economics department in which I used to present the results of my historical and methodological research at regular intervals.

7. Advice offered by the supervisor of my M.Sc. thesis when she found out that I was pursuing a Ph.D. at the boundaries of economics and sociology.

8. A prominent scholar reporting on the adverse climate in a leading economics department.

9. One of my supervisors made this remark toward the end of a long meeting in which I tried to convince him that I did not want to do to an SSK study of the emergence of transaction costs.

regard history of economic theories and related historiographies as the main pursuit of the historian of economics (see Klaes 2001). They are concerned that shifting the focus to social history or approaches inspired by the sociology of scientific knowledge (SSK) would entail sacrificing a potentially fruitful conceptual dialogue between them and practicing economists. In fact, frequently they regard themselves, or are seen, as belonging to that group. Some of these historians are convinced that history of economics forms an important component of economic research and teaching, and they include it in their efforts to reform the prevailing orthodoxy. In contrast, SSK seems to offer little basis for direct conceptual debate between economists and historians. The principle of impartiality defended by the Edinburgh School (Bloor [1976] 1991) explicitly rules out any such engagement. Somebody who understands herself first and foremost as an economist, who at times is also engaged in history of economics, will be reluctant to embrace SSK-type historiographies.

The Myth of Origin: "I learned something from your paper as I was not aware that the concept goes back to Marschak."[10] Practicing economists will listen to historical research if it helps establish that the concepts they use actually reach further back into the past than had been commonly thought. Increasing the historical base of a body of literature in this way seems to add respectability. As a result, there were occasions when I felt tolerated as a historian of economics with an orthodox audience, but more as a quaint curiosity than a peer. This translates into a credibility problem if one engages exclusively in historical research without entertaining a "proper" subspecialty as a primary interest.

The Opening: "I have no clue what you are doing, but I like it."[11] Not every economist in a "mainstream" department is narrow-minded and rejects history and methodology of economics. In fact, I was surprised by how many economists are quite the opposite, and I feel sorry for the narrow contemporary definition of what kind of research is appropriate for an economics department. I encountered two types of this species: those who have accommodated to a niche in which they can pursue their true interests on a limited basis, and those who have achieved prominence and are thus in a position to deplore openly the current state of economics. One colleague in an orthodox economics department once

10. Comment from a prominent (orthodox) economist acting as a discussant of a paper in which I tried to make a point against the quest for origins.

11. I heard this from one of my supervisors in economics, only months before I submitted my dissertation.

told me that she did not know a single economist who took the present model-driven approaches seriously. In private they would admit openly that they engaged in this type of research only for career motivations. In public, however, they would strongly defend economics against its critics.

The Pharmakon:[12] "History of economics? Well, during my undergraduate studies, I actually came across a course in the history of economics. I did not take it. But I bought a history of economics textbook. Do not read it very often, though   it is dangerous, if you know what I mean."[13] Might it be that we are marginalized because we seduce the young and lead them astray? If I am honest I have to admit that I was very close to taking up a conventional Ph.D. in an economics department with a solidly formalist bias. When I was deciding where to do my thesis, I felt strongly that I wanted to become an economist. If any of my economics teachers had actively discouraged me from pursuing my historical interests, by saying that this was the most likely strategy for *not* becoming an economist, it is unlikely that I would have persisted.

Rational Reconstruction: "I focused on these three articles because I felt this was perfectly appropriate. I refuse to apologize for having done so, because Joan Robinson has done the same."[14] It still surprises me how many historians of economics find delight in tracing predecessors of key concepts and models, but when I witnessed the above reply during my first attendance at a history of economics conference I was simply baffled. It is unlikely that this lack of historiographical finesse would have been tolerated by a science studies or history of science audience.

Safe Play: "I admire your doing what you are interested in, but where will you find a job with it?"[15] While some "orthodox" friends managed to find attractive positions, others, to their surprise, encountered an unexpectedly narrow academic labor market after finishing their thesis, although they had concentrated on what seemed to be up-and-coming

12. As Derrida ([1968] 1972) has reminded us, in Plato's *Phaedrus* books are likened to a "pharmakon," which in the original Greek carries the meaning of both poison and remedy.

13. A mainstream econometrician sitting next to me on a flight packed with (almost exclusively male) Chicago economists heading for the annual AEA/ASSA meetings.

14. Prominent economist and historian of economics responding to a question from the floor about why he had focused on what appeared to be an arbitrary selection of historical sources.

15. I heard this from a fellow Ph.D. student who at the time was convinced that with a doctorate from a very respected economics department and a hot microeconomic topic there would be little difficulty in making an academic career.

mainstream topics. While I had been aware of my precarious situation from early on, they found out late that getting this first job might require careful preparation. In the end, I doubt that our situations were fundamentally different.

The Specter of Internalism: "It seems to me that what you are doing is completely legitimate from the perspective of intellectual history."[16] Presenting papers with an exclusive focus on the conceptual level to an audience with science studies sympathies or legacies has never been an easy undertaking, no matter how well I thought I had prepared them with my historiographical arguments. As soon as they realized that I would not finally turn to bringing in "social" explanatory factors in my studies of the development of concepts as social institutions, they would dismiss the research as interesting but "internalist" (although, conceptually, they were aware of the effective collapse of the internal-external dualism in recent SSK discussions). This is equivalent to being labeled "neoclassical" by heterodox economists and some other social scientists.

Folding Up

Historians of economics tend to wear many different hats.[17] Depending on their institutional and departmental affiliation, they might call themselves economists; economic, intellectual, or social historians; or sociologists, historians of science, or science or cultural studies scholars, not just historians of economics or of economic thought. Conversely, more tightly integrated disciplinary groups feel inclined to identify us as belonging to "the other" tribe. For them we are *not* economists, or *not* sociologists, science studies scholars, or historians of science, respectively. It is this "interstanding" (Taylor 1995), the standing in-between disciplines, both intellectually and institutionally, that the preceding section sought to draw out in sketching a microcosmos of figured encounters of a young historian of economics.

It would be tempting to interpret this situation of flux, of fuzzy boundaries, and of unclear affiliations sociologically as the typical state of a discipline that is either emerging or redefining itself, in particular as one

16. This was the well-meant comment of a prominent science studies scholar after I delivered a paper in which I tried to establish my approach to conceptual history as a complement to established forms of SSK, keeping it distinct from and opposed to intellectual history. I went away with the fear that my whole project had failed.

17. "Folding up" rather than "concluding" follows Cooper 1993, 306.

would expect new entrants to the field to feel these processes of rene-
gotiating boundaries in an amplified way. Alternatively, one could resort
to the commonplace observation that the current state of affairs simply
reflects the interdisciplinary nature of the history of economics. Neither account is satisfactory. The existence of stable and clearly defined
disciplinary boundaries is questionable both conceptually and empirically and is at best an exception, not the rule (Barnes, Bloor, and Henry
1996). Furthermore, to define interdisciplinarity in terms of such boundaries relegates interdisciplinary pursuits, while potentially innovative, to
a secondary activity.

For the historian, interdisciplinarity cannot be a merely secondary
pursuit. It is worth recalling at this point Hans-Georg Gadamer's ([1975]
1993) characterization of the locus of hermeneutics as the "in-between."
Historians are intimately familiar with the hermeneutical process of un-
locking records of the past. Gadamer is adamant to stress the ontological
nature of this hermeneutical "circle." Similar to this vertical process of
transmission, interdisciplinarity can be regarded as a horizontal form of
interstanding. Moving in interdisciplinary space may be regarded as ful-
filling the role of a messenger, albeit one whose home is neither here
nor there. Does this mean that the messenger is necessarily confused?
The Latin *confundere* is less pessimistic than our *confusion*. Apart from
"throwing into disarray" it also denotes "mixing" in the sense of "fus-
ing together." Gadamer ([1975] 1993, 306) describes understanding as
a fusion of horizons. It is thus precisely the task of the interstanding
messenger to con-fuse. This exposes the linear account of the interdisciplinary crossing of boundaries as simplistic. I find myself circulating.
Instead of crossing boundaries, I find myself negotiating them in a constant balancing act of interstanding.

The home of the interstanding messenger is the fold (Taylor 1995;
Deleuze [1988] 2001).[18] "The place or nonplace of the middle is the
fold. . . . Neither here nor there but always in-between—entre deux—
the fold is neither one nor two but is the pleat that deploys unity and
multiplicity" (Taylor 1995). One does not have to be a committed post-

18. Deleuze's fold goes beyond assuming "fuzzy" disciplinary boundaries. Fuzziness describes a boundary property, while the fold locates the in-between in its own right.

modernist to find this expression attractive. Simply folding a straight line into Koch's curve, for example, can result in a fractal that is neither one- nor two-dimensional (see Mandelbrot 1983, 35–37) but, to use the present terminology, assumes interstanding dimensionality. B. B. Mandelbrot's contribution was to show that Euclidean geometry, not interstanding dimensionality, represents the special case rarely born out by nature. Above, I have tried to argue in figures that one can identify a similar interstanding position for the history of economics. History of economics is located in the fold between economics, economic history, methodology of economics, and the field of science studies. This should be a situation not of despair, but of potential and hope. Rather than continuing on their quest of recovering an identity deemed lost, historians and aspiring historians of economics should assertively ride the fold. Their interstanding can only add to the ongoing process of fruitful confusion.

References

Barnes, B., D. Bloor, and J. Henry. 1996. *Scientific Knowledge: A Sociological Analysis*. London: Athlone.

Barthes, R. [1977] 1990. *A Lover's Discourse*. Translated by R. Howard. London: Penguin.

Bloor, D. [1976] 1991. *Knowledge and Social Imagery*. 2d ed. Chicago: University of Chicago Press.

Burke, P. [1991] 2001. Overture. The New History: Its Past and Its Future. In *New Perspectives on Historical Writing*, edited by P. Burke. 2d ed. Cambridge, U.K.: Polity.

Coats, A. W. 1969. Research Priorities in the History of Economics. *HOPE* 1:9–18.

Cooper, R. 1993. Technologies of Representation. In *Tracing the Semiotic Boundaries of Politics*, edited by P. Ahonen. Berlin: Mouton de Gruyter.

Deleuze, G. [1988] 2001. *The Fold*. Translated by T. Conley. London: Athlone.

Derrida, J. [1968] 1972. La pharmacie de Platon. In *La dissemination*, edited by J. Derrida. Paris: Editions du Seuil.

Gadamer, H.-G. [1975] 1993. *Truth and Method*. Translated by J. Weinsheimer and D. G. Marshall. Rev. ed. London: Sheed and Ward.

Klaes, M. 2001. *Begriffsgeschichte*: Between the Scylla of Conceptual and the Charybdis of Institutional History of Economics. *Journal of the History of Economic Thought* 23:153–79.

Mandelbrot, B. B. 1983. *The Fractal Geometry of Nature*. New York: Freeman.

Taylor, M. C. 1995. Rhizomic Folds of Interstanding. tekhnema.free.fr/2Taylor.htm.

Winch, D. 1962. What Price the History of Economic Thought? *Scottish Journal of Political Economy* 9:193–204.

The Interesting Narrative of a Duke-Trained Historian of Economics, from Prospectus to Ph.D. to Profession; or, How I Learned to Love Weintraub and Start Worrying

Stephen Meardon

The first part of my title may seem presumptuous, but I intend it to help make a modest point. The "interesting narrative" is an allusion to an autobiography I've never read, *The Interesting Narrative of the Life of Olaudah Equiano or Gustavus Vassa, the African, Written by Himself* (1789), brought to my attention by a friend and scholar of African American literature whose conversation has helped me think about the historiography of economics. She tells me that Equiano's text is considered by her colleagues to be the first black slave narrative—but it shouldn't be, and wouldn't be if Equiano were read in the context of his time. His text stands out because he was a product of the Enlightenment, the unconscious progeny of Adam Smith, and it shows. The victim of what could be called market behavior, Equiano nevertheless did not, indeed could not, condemn markets, only the malicious behavior of particular people acting within them.

My friend's idea sounds fascinating to me, and I would like to look into it. But I don't know why, really. When I wrote the first draft of this essay in the spring of 2001 I thought I might do so, but at my peril: it is one of many projects in the history of economics that would be a hard sell to economists even at a liberal arts college like Williams, where the idea was born and where such endeavors are viewed more or less benignly. At best the project would rouse their idle curiosity; it would

I thank Tess Chakkalakal, Roy Weintraub, Gene Bell-Villada, and an anonymous referee for comments and suggestions.

not affect the way they do economics. What's more, while listening to me in our internal seminar or reading my paper they would be conscious of the distraction from their economics. The opportunity cost would be even greater for the author, of course.

Since the spring of 2001 my circumstances have changed, but I will save that for last. Still, as before, Equiano's narrative raises problems for me as an economist and historian of economics; my own narrative is about my coming to grips with them.

The problems I have wrestled with in the couple of years since I finished my Ph.D. at Duke and took up my profession are two. The first—the one that is merely hard—has been reconciling expectations of my research in economics with my longstanding historical interests. The second—the one that is irresolvable on its own terms—is reconciling both with the present consensus that histories of economics are suspect unless they are thick and contextual, unless they are constructed "historically" rather than "rationally." Because Roy Weintraub has been so central to the emergence of the consensus, and because I hold him responsible for almost convincing me that it is right, in what follows I will pick on him.

Training

My short career has few other similarities to Olaudah Equiano's except the obvious: my language and thoughts have been influenced by Smith. Apart from Smith, from the beginning of my academic training and like every apprentice economist I also learned something of Paul Samuelson, metaphorically and literally. As one might expect, then, I learned to read Smith like Samuelson (1987) argued one should. I began doing so as an undergraduate. With my college mentor I wrote two papers that sought to show how Smith thought of topics as apparently disparate as the provision of streetlights (in the *Wealth of Nations*) and the acquisition of self-command (in *The Theory of Moral Sentiments*) in terms of noncooperative game theory and two-by-two game matrices. As a result I became fairly well acquainted with game theory and enthusiastic about Smith. But when I arrived at Duke in 1993, and for about five years afterward, I had a terrible time fathoming what Roy Weintraub was talking about.

I completed my requirements for the Ph.D. field in history of political economy by taking the oral exam administered by Neil De Marchi,

Craufurd Goodwin, and Weintraub. For the exam I was told to hand over three papers I had written on historical topics so they could quiz me on them, which they didn't. Instead they asked me to talk about the history of economics as a subdiscipline: how it had served me in my graduate studies, why and how I practiced it, and where it appeared from my perspective to be going.

The first part of my answer was in the manner of a confession. Sure, I admitted, I had some purely antiquarian interest—mixed, I should have added, with another proclivity that still afflicts me. In my worn copy of *The Theory of Moral Sentiments*, where Smith ([1759] 1976, 185) wrote,

> We take pleasure in beholding the perfection of so beautiful and grand a system, and we are uneasy till we remove any obstruction that can in the least disturb or encumber the regularity of its motions. . . . From a certain spirit of system, however, from a certain love of art and contrivance, we sometimes seem to value the means more than the end,

I highlighted the lines in bright orange for two reasons. The pleasure of finding them in a book written beautifully by an author long dead was one. The other was that I found in them a reflection of the way my brain works. Although Smith meant the term critically, my own "certain spirit of system" endowed me with a natural affinity for him (particularly as read through the lenses of game theory). It endowed me likewise with an affinity for international trade theory, beginning with the "art and contrivance" of Heckscher-Ohlin-Samuelson. Trade theory thus became my second interest, equal to the history of economics.

But I mumbled only the first half of that confession, and only briefly. For most of the exam I explained that I studied the history of economics because it helped me do better economics. It improved my work by deepening my understanding of the work's meaning, like learning the etymology of a word helps me use language with more precision and satisfaction. I may have had a penchant to "value the means more than the ends" as the corollary of my spirit of system, but not where it came to historiography. Historiography, I thought, had to be grounded in more than that. It seemed terribly important that history should serve a purpose, and the purpose would justify the history. If the purpose was to inform current theory—say, trade theory—naturally the historiography had to be suited for the task. I read with approval Samuelson's "Program for the Whig History of Economic Science" and fancied myself a budding reactionary. At the end of my field exam I enumerated for my examiners my list of heroes: Samuelson, Mark Blaug, Don Patinkin . . . and the "old" Roy Weintraub (author of *Microfoundations* and *General Equilibrium Analysis: Studies in Appraisal*, not the "new" Roy of *Stabilizing Dynamics*). Weintraub cheerfully resisted *das Roy Problem*, but I still could not fathom him.

I began work on a thesis, supervised by Craufurd Goodwin, that combined my interests in international trade theory and the history of economics. I planned to extend the recent models of geography and trade, of which Paul Krugman is the most prominent exponent, to allow multiple regions in each of multiple countries. The set-up would correspond roughly to the United States and Mexico, so I could use the model to think generally about the effects of trade liberalization on the geographic distribution of industry in North America. I went to Mexico for a year to work on the model and then returned to Durham in the summer of 1998 to finish my job paper and enter the market. I planned to get a job first and afterward write the final part of my thesis, a history of location and trade theory up to Krugman and me.

Getting a Job

My conviction that history should be directed toward improving current theory was opportune. It was well known, or at least believed unquestioningly, that it would be impossible to get an academic job in the economics department of any respectable college or university by writing a thesis on the history of economics alone. The trick was to do both the history of economics and economics: the model Goodwin upheld of a Duke Ph.D. who did it right was Jeff Biddle. As he was a labor economist with historical interests, I would be a trade economist with historical interests. My strategy was to use the history of economics as a means of differentiating my product from the legions of other new Ph.D.s riding the elevators at the AEA meetings. In the half-hour interviews I talked about the history of economics only briefly and only when asked. In fly-outs I presented my modeling work in the seminar room and saved the history for one-on-one meetings, where I argued that it broadened my teaching portfolio and made me a more competent theorist.

The strategy got me an offer at Williams College. I pretended to mull over their offer for a week, then signed the contract without reading the middle part, forgot all about the job market, and started writing the history chapter of my thesis.

Worrying

The trouble with writing a history of location and trade theory up to Krugman and me was that somebody had already done it well, namely Krugman (1993, 1995). What would my history have to add? Its value, I thought, would stem from my training. As a historian I could see nuances Krugman missed; I would clarify matters he elided.

The history chapter eventually comprised more than half of my thesis. Because in the fall of 1999 it was freshest in my mind, and because I was more familiar with its potential audience than I was with that of my modeling work, as soon as I settled into Williams I put myself to work cutting and extending the chapter into three articles. During the activity my thoughts about the entire project changed. I am not sure how exactly, but I can describe the "before" and the "after" as follows: Before writing the papers I had a vague unease about the historical chapter of my thesis, an uncertain suspicion of Krugman even as I appreciated his work, and a decided appreciation of Weintraub even as I was suspicious of his work. After writing them I was left with a certain unease about my historical chapter, a decided suspicion of Krugman, and no longer any suspicion of Weintraub's work but unease about its implications. The turning point might have come while I was writing the second of the three papers, a contribution to the 2000 ESHET conference on the question "Is There Progress in Economics?" At that time I reread Weintraub's (1989) article "Methodology Doesn't Matter, but the History of Thought Might."

The essay gave voice to my suspicion of Krugman. I have written elsewhere that Krugman wears three hats, but the more apt metaphor may be that he wears a single and completely coordinated getup: the thinking cap of a theorist, the mantle of a prescriptive methodologist, and the accessories of a historian. His history is an extended account of the ideas he produces, and it might be paraphrased in a few paragraphs as follows:

The insights of geography and trade models like Krugman's (1991) issue from increasing returns to scale. Foremost among the insights is the logic of circular and cumulative causation. The logic is not entirely new: it was employed in one form or another by several earlier theorists, for instance, Gunnar Myrdal.

But Myrdal and the rest did not model the way Krugman does, in a way compatible with the general trend of communication in economics. That is, Myrdal and the rest did not model "formally," using a system of equations solvable simultaneously for the relevant variables, which represent decisions made by individuals and individual firms. They did not do so because they knew such models subverted the logic of circular and cumulative causation: the models were incompatible with increasing returns to scale. But because they did not do so, economists did not take their ideas seriously.

In the mid- to late 1970s some economists developed formal models compatible with increasing returns to scale. Krugman has adapted one such model to study problems of geography and trade, and he is thereby able to demonstrate formally the logic that earlier theorists could only employ discursively. The insights of Krugman's models are consequently sharper, easier to communicate, and easier to challenge and perhaps to falsify and fix. They are more likely to be taken seriously by the economics profession and to promote its progress. They redeem the "good ideas" of Myrdal and others that were "left to gather dust in the economics attic for more than a generation" before Krugman (1995, 85).[1]

Note how Krugman's theoretical work, his implicit methodological prescription, and his history all match.[2] In telling the story he appears either stunning or shabby, depending on whether your getup and his come from the same store. If you cross town to shop from colleagues in history, philosophy, or English—or stroll down the boardwalk to Weintraub's, which stocks similar goods—you might describe what you see as follows: Krugman's history is proffered as evidence that formal modeling is necessary to make progress. But "modeling formally" really amounts to modeling as Krugman was trained to do, and "making progress" really amounts to doing what Krugman does. Krugman's methodological prescription is hopelessly self-referential; his claim of progress, which supports the prescription, is unpersuasive; his history, which supports

1. This is how I read Krugman's views of history and methodology in several of his articles and books, among them Krugman 1991, 1993, 1995, and 1998.
2. The methodological prescription is made explicit in Krugman 1998.

both, lies under the shadow of Krugman's professional interests, obscuring our view of the past.

Weintraub's assertion that "Methodology doesn't matter" is misleading. It could be stated more accurately, "There is no position totally apart from the doing of economics which can inform the consideration of the doing of economics" (Weintraub 1989, 484)—which I am sure he stated repeatedly at Duke while I was not fathoming him. If I could not understand him for lack of an immediate application, understanding the implications for historiography was out of the question. As I catch on, the nice thing I find about Weintraub is that his ideas cohere (as a "beautiful and grand system," one could say). If there is no "God's eye" view of how to do good economics, then economists who read history as if there *were* such a view are likely to write histories as suspect as their methodologies. To be unconscious of, or to deny, the contingency of one's perspective would very likely lead an economist to write a history that tells the reader less about the past than about the present. One could ask of such a history, What should we call it: a history of economics, or economics? Krugman's history would appear to be more economics than history.

While Krugman owns a single matching getup that he wears all the time, Weintraub by contrast owns three markedly different hats, two of which he wears rarely: he keeps his theorist hat and prescriptive methodologist hat stored in the closet. He knows what good history means to *him*: historical rather than rational reconstruction as far as possible; lots of context, be it doctrinal, social, professional, psychological, educational, or other; emphasis on contingency, revealing that the given state of the world is not the only possible one. When the audience begins to apprehend that Weintraub's discussion of good history skirts the line of historiographic prescription, they see him back away: "I do not believe that any philosophical position *compels* any particular way of doing historical work, nor does any such position provide a warrant for believing that one kind of history is always, and for all purposes, better than another" (1992, 273). He keeps the closet locked.

For my purposes, I draw from Weintraub the maxim that I would do well to read Myrdal bearing in mind two things: he viewed problems through different eyes, and my view of him is inevitably clouded by contingent precepts that he did not share. But I wonder: *why* would I undertake such a reading? Surely not to improve myself as an economist; reading with current theory as my end would entangle me in exactly the trap I am trying to escape. Weintraub's (2002, 11) answer here, too, is consistent: "If the story enchants, delights, and raises the reader's empathetic understanding of the past, it will have done its job."

His position, in Ian Hacking's (1999, 19) language, is that of a "historical constructionist"—the species of constructionist that, like all others, emphasizes the contingency of X; but that, unlike the "reformist," the "rebellious," or the "revolutionary" constructionist, does not care to argue that X is bad or that X should be transformed or done away with. For that reason Hacking attributes to Weintraub's species the "lowest gradation of constructionist commitment." Rather the highest! Others who emphasize contingency in the history of economics, but do so by way of rebelling or revolting, as it were, may have found that their methodological prescriptions place them in opposition to economics. They may have learned from Wittgenstein and Foucault that to voice their opposition on the terrain and in the language of economics proper is futile: the language of economic theory already stacks the argumentative deck in favor of those who (1) find relevant the problems created by the language, (2) find necessary the solution techniques suggested by the problems, and (3) find persuasive the solutions yielded by the techniques. The way to argue is to snipe from outside, using history to "unmask" some hidden value premise or extratheoretical purpose of the theory. To do so, however, is to write a history whose end lies in current theory. Such history is the mirror image of the Whig history of the theory it wants to supplant. Weintraub's insistence that his preferred history proposes only to "enchant," "delight," and so forth is corollary to his insistence that he has no quarrel with the theories or thinkers whose history he is writing:

> I am not sympathetic to using history in order to criticize the discipline of economics. It is not that I have no beliefs about the strengths or weaknesses of particular lines of economic analysis. It is rather that, as a historian, both my interests and my task are different from those of an economist who wishes to argue with other economists about current economic analysis and policy. (2002, 7)

He has no quarrel with them, that is to say, *in his history.* He couldn't, because if he did it would hardly qualify as history. So here again Weintraub is consistent—and arguably the most committed of all. The system, it is pleasing to find, appears closed.

For that I am persuaded, resolved to abandon Samuelson's (and Krugman's) historiographic standard and stand under Weintraub's, although it will probably require admitting that over half my thesis was no good at all.

And my resolve dissipates almost immediately when, since he will not enjoin, Weintraub leads by example to the territory emblazoned on the standard. I have in mind one of his shorter but most visible articles (Weintraub 1998), written for a wide audience, the readers of the controversy on "Formalism in Economics" in the *Economic Journal* (*EJ*). The controversy pits Weintraub against Paul Krugman, Roger Backhouse, and Victoria Chick—and ultimately finds him neither here nor there.

In a forum where the other participants try to tell economists about the consequences of their "formal" methods, Weintraub writes an essay drawing on expansive knowledge of the twentieth-century history of mathematics, and archival materials including correspondence between the protagonists of his story, to show that economists have not pinned down what they mean by formalism in the first place. The article is written with wit and glittering detail—but *why*? The purpose of the forum is clear, and the reason why economists would be interested is pretty clear, too. Where Weintraub fits in is not so. There are two clues in his article: "Were the history better understood, this set of papers might never have been solicited" (1837), and "My main assertion in this essay is that . . . an argument [that to formalize means to axiomatize, and *thereby* to make rigorous] is ahistorical, and therefore probably wrong on most interpretations" (1840). The clues lead me to a dead end.

If the history were better understood why might the papers never have been solicited? Suppose that I, like most others, am reading the controversy in the *EJ* because I want to understand better the consequences of my methods. Suppose I thought, before picking up the journal, that "to formalize means to axiomatize." Suppose now I read Weintraub's article and thereby come to understand that to formalize has not always meant to axiomatize, that the meaning of *formal* has not been stable throughout the twentieth century. Why at last should I have transcended my desire to understand better the consequences of my methods?

If the notion that to "formalize" means to axiomatize, and thereby to make rigorous, is ahistorical and even wrong—so what? I will find a less objectionable word to describe the same methods and get on with my business of trying to understand the consequences of those methods. Will the end result be substantially different?

The formalism article demonstrates why, having been mostly persuaded by Weintraub's historiography, I worry. The historiography may bear histories that are less problematic than others in most respects, but they are more problematic in this respect: economists have no compelling reason to read them. "Delight" alone does not move an article to the top of an economist's "to read" list, and other reasons seem either inconsistent with the historiography or contrived. One could advise, "Then don't write your histories for economists." That could be helpful, but it would still leave a problem unresolved. My job market experience suggests that candidates who molded themselves by the advice would not sell. My intuition is that the Equiano and Smith project, if done well, would not go far in getting me promoted. That may not be a good reason to cease an activity that delights, but it is something to worry about.

Two assuaging thoughts occur to me. Both involve the possibility that Weintraub has led me astray at least a bit.

First, my gut tells me that something as hubristic as the following must contain error. Regarding the commonly incompatible purposes of historians of science and scientists, the latter of whom could be said (most likely by the former) to prefer a Whiggish "romantic narrative," Jan Golinski (1998, 194) comments,

> This should not be taken to mean, however, that historians of science can never hope to address scientists themselves or that contemporary historical writing must inevitably lose its readers. On the contrary, there is no reason why many [scientists] may not come to appreciate the satisfactions of alternatives to the romantic narrative mode.

Why do we take it for granted that the scientists are the ones who must change their ways?

Second, a statement by Hayden White (1973, xii) strikes a chord: "We are indentured to a *choice* among contending interpretative strategies in any effort to reflect history in general; . . . as a corollary of this, the best grounds for choosing one perspective on history rather than another are ultimately aesthetic or moral rather than epistemological." His use of *moral* brings to mind Myrdal's *Political Element in the Development of Economic Theory* (1953)—the most persuasive exercise in unmasking extratheoretical purposes of economic theory that I have read. Myrdal's lesson is that we all carry value premises, and there is nothing wrong with that. Only, we must be careful to locate them and state them explicitly and be aware of where analysis stops and value judgments begin. Ultimately, though, value judgments have to be made. As Myrdal (1970,

301) wrote elsewhere about aid to underdeveloped countries, "*this is, at bottom, a moral issue.*"

Maybe Krugman's theoretician's cap and prescriptive methodologist's mantle and historian's accessories appear altogether gauche, but not irredeemably so. Maybe if he would just follow Myrdal's directive and pin on an additional accessory, a ribbon for self-awareness, evincing concern about the premises of his entire getup and their consequences to his history, he would appear perfectly swank. Then the choice between Whig history à la Krugman and thick history à la Weintraub (or some variant of both) would not be a choice between naïveté and complexity. It would be no more, but also no less, than an aesthetic and moral choice that everyone must make—and will make with more awareness of the purposes of one's history and the ethics of one's historiography for having struggled with the choice.

If that is right, then I still have reason to worry, but less. At least I can settle on a purpose for my histories, additional to enchantment and delight, without embarrassment. Doing so allows more possibilities and new audiences for the history of economics—which brings me back, finally, to my change of circumstances that I mentioned earlier. I left Williams while this essay was under review; the audience I am experimenting with now is a regional development bank. I have convinced my new employers that intellectual history will help them to think about where they stand, and where they *should* stand, on regional integration.

The results so far appear promising. Weintraub could be either thrilled or worried to find how few are the differences between his histories and the ones I propose.

References

Golinski, Jan. 1998. *Making Natural Knowledge: Constructivism and the History of Science*. Cambridge: Cambridge University Press.

Hacking, Ian. 1999. *The Social Construction of What?* Cambridge: Harvard University Press.

Krugman, Paul. 1991. Increasing Returns and Economic Geography. *Journal of Political Economy* 99:483–99.

———. 1993. On the Relationship between Trade Theory and Location Theory. *Review of International Economics* 1:110–22.

———. 1995. *Development, Geography, and Economic Theory*. Cambridge: MIT Press.

———. 1998. Two Cheers for Formalism. *Economic Journal* 108:1829–36.

Myrdal, Gunnar. 1953. *The Political Element in the Development of Economic Theory*. London: Routledge & Paul.

———. 1970. *The Challenge of World Poverty: A World Anti-Poverty Program in Outline*. New York: Vintage Books.

Samuelson, Paul A. 1987. Out of the Closet: A Program for the Whig History of Economic Science. *History of Economics Society Bulletin* 9.1:51–60.

Smith, Adam. [1759] 1976. *The Theory of Moral Sentiments*. Edited by D. D. Raphael and A. L. Macfie. Oxford: Oxford University Press.

Weintraub, E. Roy. 1989. Methodology Doesn't Matter, but the History of Thought Might. *Scandinavian Journal of Economics* 91:477–93.

———. 1992. Comment: Thicker Is Better. *Journal of the History of Economic Thought* 14.2:271–77.

———. 1998. Controversy: Axiomatisches Mißverständnis. *Economic Journal* 108:1837–47.

———. 2002. *How Economics Became a Mathematical Science*. Durham, N.C.: Duke University Press.

White, Hayden. 1973. *Metahistory: The Historical Imagination in Nineteenth-Century Europe*. Baltimore, Md.: Johns Hopkins University Press.

So You Want to Be a Historian of Economics? Reflections of a Recent Recruit

Esther-Mirjam Sent

3 January 2001

Mirjam Sent
Department of Economics
University of Notre Dame
Notre Dame, IN 46556

Dear Mirjam:

This letter concerns an essay I have been asked to write about your experiences as a recent Ph.D. in history of economics entering the "profession." I am scheduled to present the essay during the 2001 *HOPE* conference on "The Future of the History of Economics."

When Roy Weintraub, who is organizing the conference, approached me with the request, I figured you would be pleased to be thought of as a "recent Ph.D." After all, you graduated more than six years ago. At the same time, I felt awkward about having to write an account of such a short career. After some careful consideration, I decided to tackle my assigned task by interviewing you. I would like to find out from you whether you agree to this and when we could meet.

I hope to hear back from you soon.

Sincerely,
Esther Sent

Date: Thu, 11 Jan 2001 16:58:49 -0500
To: sent.2@nd.edu (Esther Sent)
From: Mirjam Sent <Mirjam.Sent.2@nd.edu>
Subject: Interview

Dear Esther,

In response to your letter of 3 January, I agree that you're faced with a rather difficult task. I'll be more than happy to help you, of course. Why don't we conduct the interview before classes start again next week?

Best,
Mirjam

From the desk of Esther Sent

Attached is a transcript of our interview. Please let me know if you have any corrections.

Interview: Esther Sent with Mirjam Sent,
Conducted on Monday, 15 January at the
University of Notre Dame.

Esther Sent: For the record, can you give me a brief overview of your educational and professional background?
Mirjam Sent: Yes, I am currently employed as an assistant professor in the Department of Economics at the University of Notre Dame. And I am also a faculty fellow in the Reilly Center for Science, Technology, and Values. I started here in 1994. Before that, I did my Ph.D. at Stanford University from 1989 until 1994. And before that, from 1985 until 1989, I was an undergraduate student at the University of Amsterdam.

Esther: How did you become interested in economics?
Mirjam: Um . . . How did I become interested in economics? Well, mostly, I grew up in a socialist family, so to speak, and in the Netherlands

that is actually something that you can be proud of. I suppose, in the United States, you have to be kind of careful about expressing such backgrounds. My grandfather was chair of the society for sexual liberation [*laughs*], which, incidentally, is connected to the fact that my parents were only sixteen and eighteen when I was born, but that is a long story and I am moving away from the subject. So, my dad, then, was a member, an active member, or still is an active member, of the labor party, is very active in the union, in environmental movements. And that was the tradition that I grew up in. So, I have always been very active in radical youth movements and things like that. So, I had this desire to improve the world, and, little did I know, I felt that I could do that by studying economics and probably going into politics. That was my goal. One thing I should explain is that, in the Netherlands, when you start your undergraduate education at the age of eighteen, you just do your major. You do not do anything else. So you basically do your major for four years.

Esther: How did you become interested in the history of economics, then?

Mirjam: As I mentioned, the reason I started studying economics is because I had this idea to improve the world, and then I realized that economics was not going to help me much in improving the world, so maybe instead of improving the world, what I should do is improve economics. And that is how I became interested in history and also philosophy of economics.

Esther: Wait a minute. I thought you became interested in history of economics because during your first year as an undergraduate you had one elective in your studies, and you decided to choose a class that you would never ever ever . . . or the topic of which you would never ever ever encounter again in the rest of your studies and that is how you decided to take a class in history and philosophy of economics. Is that not how you became interested?

Mirjam: Oh, I do not know. Let me get back to my original narrative. Little did I know that the whole notion of improving something has come under attack in history and philosophy of economics, and, in addition, you know, this idea that economists would pay any attention to what is done in history of economics was very idealistic, I suppose, or overly, yeah, I suppose, idealistic is the common term, or the way to phrase it.

So, but I still, that really still is my inspiration, I would say, that I still have the hope that history of economics and philosophy of economics is going to be able to, um, sort of transform economics by pointing out avenues that were left behind, approaches that were left behind; by pointing out difficulties or peculiarities in economics. And this, incidentally, also explains why I am mostly focusing on the history of contemporary economics in my research. One example is some of the research I have done on bounded rationality. What is so fascinating about bounded rationality is that it was a very active research program, say, in the 1960s, but has since died. And now, apparently, there is a revival of interest in bounded rationality in game theory and rational expectations economics. But, upon close consideration, what you find is that the inspiration behind current research in bounded rationality is very different from the inspiration of the earlier researchers. And I think . . . that an important research avenue was closed off and that the confusion over the interpretation of bounded rationality and the lack of interest in the history is limiting the possibilities and that we as historians of economics have a role to point out those possibilities and alternative avenues. So I do think that, you know, economists should pay attention to the history of economics, and my hope is that this will transform the practice of economics, and I know that this may be, um, a silly hope, or I do not know how to express this properly, but I have to believe in that. Otherwise, I do not see the point of what I am doing [*laughs*].

Esther: How did you react to the shift from Amsterdam to Stanford?
Mirjam: Well, moving from the Netherlands to Stanford was a major shock. The reason I started studying in the United States is because one of my advisors at the University of Amsterdam, Neil De Marchi, was from America, or was teaching at an American university, I should say— Duke University. And he asked me at one point what I was going to do after I was graduated . . . after graduation. And I told him I was thinking of getting a job. So he recommended instead that I go to the United States to get my Ph.D. For the longest time I thought I would be going to Duke, and I was very excited about it, of course. Um, so, um, okay, so I applied to graduate schools and then I was accepted by Stanford, and I guess I was just lured by the reputation and the location and knew very little about the perspective of economics . . . perspective on economics at Stanford. So it was a major shock when I arrived. The first

year, the only thing we had as far as classes were concerned was micro, macro, and econometrics. And I would have been much better prepared for my classes if I had had an undergraduate degree in mathematics. See, I thought I would have an advantage over the other students because I had studied economics for four years, whereas most of the Americans that came in had just done economics as a major. But I found that this advantage clearly did not exist because a lot of my fellow students came in with undergraduate degrees in mathematics, which prepared them much better for the classes at Stanford than my philosophically inspired background, or historically inspired background, in economics. Um, so I felt very alienated from my fellow students, and from my instructors. I remember that one did give a little bit of an introduction on history and philosophy, but that was one class period and then that was the end of it. After that, we just had to solve equations and, um, that was very different from the experience that I had had at Stanford, eh, I am sorry, at Amsterdam.

Esther: Hang on. I thought you were having lots of fun at Stanford. You were playing volleyball, taking ballet classes, going on trips to, um, Lake Tahoe, to Yosemite, to Las Vegas, backpacking, downhill skiing. . . . You know, it sounds like you connected pretty well with the students at Stanford in some respects.

Mirjam: Well, it was rather difficult, because my fellow students had no interest in history and philosophy. And the only interest that I shared with my fellow students was sports. Part of the reason was that when I came to the United States, I decided that it was important to familiarize myself with the culture, and I quickly realized that sports was an important part of the culture. So, I learned all about football, bugging my fellow spectators with questions about the rules, about baseball, about basketball. In fact, my husband, who teaches English at the University of Notre Dame but is a former baseball player, was very impressed when on one of our first dates we walked by a baseball game and I casually said "can of corn" after one of the plays. And it was actually only after Stanford that I realized that sports were an important part of some cultures in the United States, but definitely not all cultures. And that is actually one of the strengths of the United States, its diversity. But let me go back to my experience at Stanford. It was a rather competitive environment, my teachers had no interest in history and philosophy, and, in the end, actually, this worked out to my advantage, because what I ended up doing was writing a dissertation on one of my teachers at Stanford, Thomas Sargent, because [*coughs*], excuse me, because he was the one that ruffled my feathers the most, so to speak, because he would always start his classes with a bunch of equations, saying, "This is our economy" and "These are our agents" and "This is what we are going to solve." And I tried to ask him questions about why he felt justified to use that kind of approach, and he was particularly unwilling to answer any questions that I had about it. Um . . . so that is how I ended up writing a dissertation about one of my teachers, and that sort of explains how it relates to my earlier background.

Esther: Does that also explain why your interview with Sargent, which is part of your dissertation and also your book, is so boring?
Mirjam: That is not a fair assessment, I do not think. Um, in fact, people seem to read the interview in the book more so than they read the rest of the book.

Esther: So are we supposed to feel sorry for you now because nobody is reading your book properly? That is just a really immature attitude, I think.
Mirjam: Well, let me get back to Stanford. And then I was lucky enough to find at least one faculty member at Stanford, Ken Arrow, open-minded enough to be willing to supervise a dissertation of this kind. I remember my fellow students thought my project was very bizarre and the only thing they knew about my project was the title, which at that point was "Resisting Sargent." I tried to have that as the title of my book, but the publisher convinced me to use a less controversial title. And I have to confess that I feel somewhat ambivalent concerning controversy. On the one hand, inspired by Phil Mirowski, about whom I have nothing but good things to say, I have tried to state my claims in a provocative manner and tried to make innovative contributions to the field. But, then, on the other hand, there is only so much innovation that the field can really handle. So it is a difficult negotiation, not only between different parts of the profession in history, but also with economists. I have actually gotten into some disagreements with Herbert Simon, and it actually makes me deeply miserable to have to confront that.

Esther: I am sure you do not like to hear this, but, to me, this strikes me as an illustration of your immature attitude, much like the way you respond to the reception that your book had. But I suppose you do not like controversy, so let us go on and figure out then how you ended up at Notre Dame.

Mirjam: Well, there is a major part that I actually left out of my graduate education or graduate experience so far, which is that after I finished my required classes, after two years, I felt very much at a loss, did not really know where to take the interest that I had in history and philosophy and how to connect it with the mainstream education that I had had at Stanford. So what I did in my third year at Stanford is I took lots of classes in the philosophy department. And, um, there was one person in the philosophy department who had some knowledge of economics, John Dupré, but most people there were unable to really guide me in my future research, or thesis supervision. So I mentioned this to a Dutch friend of mine who was at the University of Notre Dame, working with Phil Mirowski. And this friend of mine mentioned it to Phil Mirowski, just sort of as an illustration of the fact that he was quite lucky to be at the University of Notre Dame, and how odd it was that well-known universities such as Stanford have no interest in history and philosophy of economics. And then Phil Mirowski suggested that I would spend a year at Notre Dame. So I spent my fourth year of graduate studies at Notre Dame, and that was really the life-changer for me. I think if I had not gone to Notre Dame, and if I had not had the support and enthusiastic backing of Phil Mirowski, I would not have finished my Ph.D. He was absolutely wonderful in supporting me, reading my work, giving me very valuable feedback. So he ended up on my dissertation committee, along with Ken Arrow, John Dupré, and a rational expectations economist, Orazio Attanasio. And my dissertation defense was quite fun, actually, because most of the time the committee members seemed to be arguing amongst themselves, and, so, I was let off easy.

Esther: So controversy is OK, as long as it does not involve you. Is that it?

Mirjam: You should be able to understand by now why it is that I will not respond to that accusation or observation and instead move on to the next phase. The next step was looking for a job, and that was quite stressful, especially in the competitive environment of the Stanford students, where jobs at liberal arts colleges and policy-making bodies are looked down upon. When I applied for jobs, I decided to apply both for jobs that explicitly mentioned history and philosophy of economics and for jobs that listed macroeconomics, because my dissertation focused on Tom Sargent, a macroeconomist. Um, and, I think, especially the liberal arts colleges appreciated this kind of focus on macroeconomics, a more historical perspective, but some of the research institutions were quite surprised that this was research that would get one a Ph.D. at Stanford and had a hard time seeing me as a macroeconomist. I remember at one interview, one of the interviewers said to me that my job or my career seemed to be going in the reverse direction, um, meaning that usually people make contributions to economics first before they evaluate their contributions and those of others. So you can be a historian at the end of your career, but apparently not at the start of their, your career. At least, that was their perspective. And, incidentally, that was also why Arrow taught history at Stanford. The idea was that he was such an important part of history, so, you know, he should be able to teach it. Um, and then finally I had several job offers, and I got a job at Notre Dame for complicated personal reasons that I am sure you do not want to hear about. But at the same time, for professional reasons I was also very happy to be at Notre Dame, because of its support of history of economics and mostly because I was lucky enough, or I am lucky enough, to have Phil Mirowski as a colleague.

Esther: How do you feel about the history of economics community?
Mirjam: Um, generally, I have been very happy to be part of that community. But I have also had my difficult experiences in it. I think partly because some people are somewhat critical of some of Phil Mirowski's work, they decided to go after me, but I am a much easier target than he is. So I have had a few instances where I have had discussants at conferences who were, um, very critical, and seemed to come out of the blue. You know, that has been very difficult to deal with.

Esther: How do you respond to older people in the profession who argue that the younger generation is complaining too much, and that it has a pretty cushy situation?
Mirjam: Well, I think that the conditions of the profession have changed.

A big, big difference, and this is actually part of the research that I am working on right now, is the changing pressures, the changing, harder requirements for tenure and promotion. And I think that this does make it harder for the current generation to do this kind of research. But I do not want to whine, for I am really enjoying it. I feel so fortunate to get paid for what I love to do. I love teaching, connecting with the students, although I sometimes get a little depressed when teaching is eating up so much of my time and does not give me enough of an opportunity to work on my research. So, my favorite times of the year are the start of the summer, the start of a break, when I can just sit down and read, write, dig up new interesting things to work on, and that is just a very fortunate situation to be in. Going back to my earlier whining, I suppose I just need to grow up and quit bellyaching and also confess that my very first publication was a review of one of Roy Weintraub's books, and it was quite unnecessarily critical, so I suppose I am just as guilty as those that I am charging, so to speak. I think, I should probably tell you why I am somewhat down at the moment. It is because, after I worked on Sargent, who generally did not really care all that much about what I was doing, I became interested in Herbert Simon. And Simon is very different from Sargent, in the sense that he cares tremendously about what I am doing, so much so that he is making it difficult for me to publish some of my papers. What happened recently is that I had used material from Simon's archives in two of my papers that had been accepted for publication. I sent a permission to cite the material to Simon, you know, fully expecting him to sign these permissions. I just thought of them as a formality. And then, just before Christmas, I get this really angry E-mail saying that he is refusing to give me permission to cite the material and, moreover, he is telling the archivist at Carnegie Mellon that I do not have access to the archives anymore. What really got Simon angry, I think, is an earlier article, which does not use any archival material, um, that I, um, have forthcoming in another journal, and they sent it to Simon as one of the referees. And, fortunately, they did not take his criticism seriously, but instead, or, well, they did take it seriously, but they thought at the same time that the essay should be published. And, um, there is going to be a reply by Simon in that paper, or in that journal. And that article, I suppose, you know, could be read as somewhat playful, or I would say postmodern, if that were not such a terrible word after the Sokal affair,

um, and I think it was the style more so than the content that really an-
gered Simon, and ever since our connections have been very troubled.
Going back to the essay that used the archival material, the plot thick-
ens, because I was able to replace the archival material with published
material from interviews and books and articles by Simon. And then the
publisher, apparently, started worrying about a defamation of character
lawsuit. So now, despite the fact that the article had been accepted for
publication, the editor of the journal is making me rewrite it very extensively because of the publisher's concern about a lawsuit, and I suppose
the story will continue. So I am sure this is more of my personal history
than you care to know about, but I thought I should explain, you know,
where I am coming from.

*Esther: Well, thank you very much for this interview. I am sure it is going
to be very helpful in dealing with the unusual task that Roy Weintraub
gave to me.*

Date: Mon, 5 Feb 2001 11:39:21 -0500
To: sent.2@nd.edu (Esther Sent)
From: Mirjam Sent <Mirjam.Sent.2@nd.edu>
Subject: Transcript

Dear Esther,

Thank you for sharing the transcript with me. After having read many
interviews with Simon, who always gives the impression of being a very
amiable person, I was struck by how unlikable I appear in the interview.
It is interesting that Simon is a true believer in facts but manages to twist
and turn these during interviews. At the same time, I am much more
suspicious of facts but tried to be "truthful" in the interview. Interestingly, I recently read an interview with Thomas Kuhn in which he himself notes how hard he found it to interview others because they would
tell the story as they wished it had happened, but not as it had actually
happened. Sadly, Kuhn's interviewers did not pick up on the reflexive
repercussions of this for their own task.

Whereas Simon sought to construct certain stories in his interviews,
I was constructing stories about Simon in my essays. The question then

becomes whose story one accepts. If I am serving as Simon's spokesperson, as he may have been led to believe as a result of our communications, why should one take my word over Simon's? If I have a different perspective to add, as journal editors may have been led to believe as a result of my paper submissions, where does this supposed superiority come from? On the one hand, I needed Simon's trust to elicit information from him. On the other hand, I had to distance myself from Simon in an effort to develop my own voice.

And the interactions between you and me are troubled with these tensions as well. Therefore, I will not give you permission to quote from your interview with me. You can only publish it if you also include our correspondence. Though these kinds of self-referential exercises tend to irritate some people (read: Simon), they allow you to foreground the constructedness of history, breaking down distinctions between reader and writer, form and content, process and product, and so on. And they help you deal with the awkward task you have been given!

Inspired by the recent developments in my career and related to the observation of these tensions, I have started a new research project on litigation in economics. Should you be interested, I am attaching an outline for a paper on this topic.

Best,
Mirjam
Attachment converted:
Harddrive:econtrial.doc (WDBN/MSWD)(000824B9)

Economists on Trial: Commodification versus Freedom

Mirjam Sent

With the end of the Cold War, science has entered what can be called the globalized privatization regime. The military-university complex has been replaced by an industry-university one, the search for the truth has been superseded by an interest in making money, and the freedom of information has been threatened by attempts to commodify knowledge. At the same time, with the fall of the positivist program, more and more scientific disputes are being battled out in the courts rather than the halls of academe. And economics has not been shielded from these developments, as witnessed by the rise of litigation involving economists.

Consider Graciela Chichilnisky's lawsuit, filed in the summer of 1994, alleging that Myrna Wooders, of the University of Toronto, and Frank Page, of the University of Alabama, stole her ideas. In 1995, Wooders and Page countersued, charging Columbia University's Chichilnisky with slander. The plot subsequently thickened when, in the course of legal research, it was discovered that Chichilnisky had ordered the production office of the journal *Economics Letters*, on the advisory board of which she served, to substantially change one of her articles that had been accepted for publication. When the editor of the journal learned of these changes, after the journal had already appeared, he ordered that a new issue be printed, without the unrefereed paper. In response, the publisher of *Economics Letters* removed Chichilnisky from the journal's editorial board. Chichilnisky abanonded her complaint in the spring of 1996, upon which Wooders and Page dropped their countersuit.

Another example is the two lawsuits against Harvard economist Andrei Shleifer and his associates of the Harvard Institute for International Development, one filed by the U.S. Justice Department and one by the Forum Financial Group. Shleifer, who won the 1999 John Bates Clark medal for outstanding young economists, ran part of the U.S. aid program in Russia, advising Moscow on the privatization of Russian assets and the creation of capital market laws and institutions. The U.S. Justice Department charges Shleifer with using his position managing the U.S. aid program in Russia for personal gain. Forum, a large mutual-fund service company, alleges that Shleifer defrauded it of a business to help Russia build capital markets. As the *Economist* (McCarthy 2000) noted: "Mr Shleifer, like the other defendants, is adamant that he is innocent. But at times like this he must wish he had stayed in his ivory tower—or entered a less murky career, such as politics."

Finally, an economics professor at Wesleyan, who shall remain anonymous for privacy reasons, is now a defendant in a lawsuit brought by a disappointed author who submitted an essay to a journal for which he is a regular referee. There was a feeling among the referees who read the paper that it might have been submitted elsewhere at the same time, and this concern was expressed in communications among the referees and the journal's editor. When the article was ultimately rejected for publication, the author filed a lawsuit against the referees individually and the journal itself for defamation of character, alleging that they had falsely put the author's reputation at risk by "accusing" him of double-submitting.

And these are just a few examples of the increased litigation in economics. As the stakes are getting bigger, it is no surprise to see more and more economists trek to the courts. To be sure, economics has always been known for its culture of attack, partly because its efforts to be a hard social science have been translated into attempts to be tough on its practitioners. Incidentally, this macho culture also partly explains why women have found economics to be such a hostile environment. Yet the globalized privatization regime has raised these developments to a new level. Academic reputations are no longer desirable in and of themselves but serve as a pathway to large monetary gains.

Whereas many economists supplement their incomes by appearing as expert witnesses on economic matters in the courts, it is highly likely that historians of economics will increasingly be asked to serve as expert witnesses on matters concerning the profession of economics. How do Chichilnisky's contributions compare to those of Wooders and Page? What is the economic justification for the claims Shleifer made concerning the U.S. aid program in Russia? Did the suing author double-submit, and how would such an accusation influence his academic (and commercial) reputation? In fact, historians of economics have opened the door in this direction due to their increased interest in contemporary developments in economics. At the same time, this has left them vulnerable to court appearances in which they themselves appear as defendants, much like journalists.

Journalism is notorious for its libel lawsuits, the most famous of which involved the accused murderer Jeffrey MacDonald and the author of his biography, Joe McGinness. In 1984, MacDonald sued the writer of *Fatal Vision* for fraud and breach of contract. McGinness had set out to paint a sympathetic portrait of MacDonald but slowly became more and more convinced of his subject's guilt. In the course of writing the biography, McGinness successfully hid from MacDonald the fact that his book would portray the subject as a psychopathic killer, so as not to jeopardize MacDonald's participation in the project. The lawsuit ended in a mistrial, with five jurors considering McGinness to be guilty and one believing that he was not guilty. In November 1987, three months after the end of the trial, a settlement agreement was reached in which McGinness promised to give MacDonald $325,000 without conceding any wrong.

Much like the authors of journalistic biographies, historians of economics perform a role in the validation of the legitimacy of economics, especially since the fall of the positivist program. Yet as economists become the children of historians of economics, frequently regarding them as their sympathetic mothers, the people writing the articles and books are more often their unforgiving fathers. And if economists cannot find solace from historians of economics, they will seek the therapeutic support of trial lawyers. Yet "the law is adversarial in structure, and thus antithetical to scientific method" (Malcolm 1990, 77). And "the fatal attraction of a lawsuit . . . is the infinite scope it offers for escape from the real world" (148–49). Hence, the unfolding of litigation in economics must be observed with great concern.

References

Malcolm, Janet. 1990. *The Journalist and the Murderer*. New York: Alfred A. Knopf.
McCarthy, F. T. 2000. A Tale of Two Economists: Shleifer and Hay in the Dock. *Economist*, 30 September.

Once and Future Historians: Notes from Graduate Training in Economics

Derek S. Brown and Shauna Saunders

Based on a True Story

> Besides, if you are bothered by the idea of this [story] being real, you are invited to do what the author[s] should have done and what authors and readers have been doing since the beginning of time: Pretend it's fiction.
> —Dave Eggers, *A Heartbreaking Work of Staggering Genius* (2000)

The last time that we unself-consciously identified ourselves as students with research interests in the history of economics was in our graduate school application essays. In retrospect, we might be tempted to add, several schools let us in anyway. Today, our answer to the question, "What are your research interests?" varies depending on who is asking. How is it, then, that we should find ourselves on a panel presumptuously called "The Next Generation"?

Our experience with the history of economics (history of economic thought, or HET) is embedded within our larger experience as graduate students in economics.[1] We are concerned here with the relationship

Thanks are due to the Duke *HOPE* workshop participants, the 2001 *HOPE* conference participants, an anonymous referee, and our classmates, past and present, for their comments on some of the ideas expressed in this essay.

1. We acknowledge that this is both a unique and privileged perspective. As discussed elsewhere in this volume (see, in particular, Gayer), the economics department at Duke is one of the few American economics departments to offer training in the history of economic thought at the graduate level. More important and despite the field's relative marginalization from the mainstream, we enjoy opportunities as graduate students in the history of economic thought that

between becoming "good economists"—as represented by the implicit and explicit criteria imposed by faculty and other graduate students— and the subdiscipline of the history of economics. We wish to describe how our identity as economists and as historians of economics is rooted in ambivalence and equivocation and how this identity is shaped by the reactions of faculty and other graduate students to the statement: "I am (maybe) a historian of economics."

In spite of our presence on this panel, we must admit to an ambivalent relationship with our future in the history of economic thought. This ambivalence is expressed mainly by the subordination of our historical research interests to our other (mainstream economics) research fields. This essay will attempt to describe how this happened. We wish to describe the concealment of our history of economics research interests as a response to the characterizations of the history of economics as an extracurricular activity and possible job market liability. We wish to describe how these characterizations have rendered our historical studies less significant than we originally intended and to consider the consequences of our equivocation for the field.

Our uncertainty and insecurities with the history of economic thought can perhaps be understood in two ways. On one hand, it may reflect a "normal" groping for an intellectual identity among graduate students. This essay can be read, in conjunction with the essays by Matthias Klaes, Stephen Meardon, and Esther-Mirjam Sent (this volume), as a chapter in an intellectual coming-of-age story, with the expected elements of melodramatic gloom. On the other hand, this essay may also reveal some of the larger challenges (or opportunities) currently facing the discipline of the history of economics, as these are played out in the lives of graduate students. While our personal futures with the history of economic thought are surely not of general interest, we leave it for the reader to determine what this essay (read with the other contributions to this panel) may imply about the future of the discipline more generally.

are not available to similar graduate students at other institutions because of the stature of our history of economic thought professors. We benefit not only from our association through them with visiting historians, the *HOPE* journal, the archives in the Economists' Papers Project, and so forth but also from the intellectual stimulation provided by their conversation and company. We are grateful for these opportunities.

Don't Ask, Don't Tell:
The Field That Dare Not Speak Its Name

One might not expect to find people concealing a research interest in the history of economics in a department with a weekly workshop or field exams in the subject. And yet many aspects specific to the Duke department make concealment rather simple. It is possible to choose the history of economics as one of your three fields of specialization, in conjunction with two more "mainstream" choices. The history field requirements are, in large part, independent of your dissertation. It is completely possible and not uncommon to have a field in the history of economics (satisfied through coursework, workshop attendance, and an oral exam) without a history of economics dissertation. More common is the "one-chapter" approach—writing one chapter of your (usually three-chapter) dissertation as a historical perspective on your mainstream research interest. It is entirely possible, then, to characterize your dissertation or your research interests without any reference to the history of economics. To be clear, this is not a description of the actual content of the history of economics field but a description of how it can be represented. Indeed, we would like to emphasize this difference. Despite the substantive content of the history of economics field it is possible to pretend that there is no real content at all.

As a general rule, we do not volunteer information on our historical research projects to faculty or other graduate students until we have a sense of their sympathy to the field. That we characterize our research interests in the history of economics as less significant than we hold them to be comes as a surprise to us. It might even seem like a betrayal. Indeed, we like to think that our introduction to the history of economic thought as undergraduates was crucial in forming our interest in graduate economics and in guiding our choice of Duke over other graduate programs. For example, the most significant faculty-student relationships that we had as undergraduates were with historians of economics. We had not fully anticipated what it might mean to be asked as graduate students to choose between "the history of economics" and "economics."

Although the opposition between the history of economics and economics (and its consequences for the field) has been much discussed in the pages of this journal and elsewhere, it seemed to come as a surprise to many participants at this conference that as graduate students we might experience the opposition acutely in our choice of dissertation research and in our interactions with faculty and other students. We feel the effects of this opposition (and contribute to it) in the characterizations of the history of economics as an extracurricular activity and job market liability. Yet many participants wanted to believe that we could—that we should—defy these characterizations. It is our claim that these characterizations are entrenched in our experience as graduate students. Negotiating the boundaries between economics and the history of economics leaves the graduate student with few simple options. Most are revealed through experimentation with different approaches: subterfuge, revolution, acquiescence, equivocation. At this midpoint in our graduate careers, we have self-consciously chosen the latter.

Basketball and Other Extracurricular Activities

> Like many social groups that do not reproduce themselves biologically, the experimental particle physics community renews itself by training novices. Gradually, the young physicists learn the diverse criteria for a successful career. This transmission of meaning occurs not only in formal education, but also in the daily routines and in "the formal annotations of everyday experience called common sense." . . . It is by making progress on this journey that the pilgrim becomes a scientist. The journey itself is marked by the telling of moral tales.
> —Sharon Traweek, "Pilgrim's Progress: Male Tales Told during a Life in Physics" (1998)

One of the more frequently repeated cautionary tales, told to each new class of graduate students, warns against "outside interests." An outside interest is anything that distracts the graduate student, particularly a first-year student, from the study of econometrics, microeconomics, or macroeconomics. There are several versions of the story, but, in essence, they all involve a croquet game set up in the quad in front of the economics building by some graduate students following their first-year qualifying exams. The sight of the reckless use of time proved too much for the then director of graduate studies (DGS), who opened his office window to order the students to stop the game because graduate students do not have time to play. Another version of the story has the DGS leaving notes in the mailboxes of all the graduate students. We have no idea if this event actually happened. The point is, however, every graduate student acts as though it did.

Graduate students quickly learn that outside interests need to be carefully hidden. We quickly learned that the history of economic thought is considered by many to be an outside interest, like foreign language classes or Duke basketball. Never mind that basketball is not actually a field of specialization offered by the department and the history of economics is: both are slightly suspect as a use of time that could otherwise be spent on, say, econometrics.

It is our conjecture that the characterization of the history of economics as a frivolous use of time begins during the first year of graduate school. During that year, your studies are completely devoted to "the core" (micro, macro, and econometrics). No one expects anything of you except to pass the qualifying exams by September of your second year. This, it hardly bears pointing out, is no small requirement. No matter what preexisting interests in the history of economics you bring to your first year, these must wait for stolen moments. During your first year, then, it is possible to hope that as soon as you have the time, you will devote more attention to the history of economics. And while the student with a research interest in, say, labor economics must also wait until he or she has passed the first year to devote much attention to that field, the student with a research interest in the history of economics finds that long after the first year and qualifying exams, the history of economics is still subordinate to work in other areas of economics. The student with an interest in the history of economics, unlike the student with a research interest in labor economics, is under pressure (particularly from advisers) to conform to the norms of economics departments, which do not view the history of economics as a legitimate or worthwhile primary research activity.

One of the main consequences of the representation of the history of economics as an extracurricular activity is the distortion of the standards of historical scholarship. The claim made by other graduate students and faculty that it can be pursued in one's spare time suggests that the history of economics is a hobby to be taken up once a few tricks are mastered and a tolerance for dusty books is acquired. Thus, despite the insistence by our history of economic thought professors on the standards of historical research, these standards of scholarship as they are perceived by graduate students outside the field (and, it hardly bears mentioning, future professional economists) are not well understood or perhaps even acknowledged to exist. Not only does this present a "conceptual barrier" (Schabas 1992, 197) between historians of economics and economists, but it distorts our own understanding of the standards of historical scholarship.

In addition, there are significant historiographic implications to the extracurricular characterization. The difficulty of finding a historiographic home for your dissertation is nicely described by Stephen Meardon (this volume). If one wishes to argue (to one's adviser, to the DGS, etc.), "No, in fact, my historical research interests are not extracurricular," then it surely helps to also have the historiographic views to argue that one's main research and one's historical research are in some sense related, possibly even that the latter informs the former. But what if one is uncomfortable with a Whiggish approach to the history of economics? Suppose one does not agree that mastery of current techniques in economics makes for a better historian. Suppose one does not believe that an "understanding" of the history of a research question makes one a better economist. How might one justify historical research to the DGS or to anyone evaluating one's progress in the program? To answer "for its own sake" is simply out of the question if one wants to be taken seriously as an economist.

Getting an HET Job—
or, Getting a Job with HET

A possible reason why we are apparently so willing to accept and participate in the characterization of the history of economics as an outside interest is its representation as a job market liability. The most common response of faculty members to our admission of interest in the history of economics is that it will not be of much help on the job market. Sole pursuit of research in the history of economics, at the expense of training in other fields of economics, is universally acknowledged by faculty members, both sympathetic and not so sympathetic to the history of economics, as tantamount to placing a curse on your curriculum vitae (at least if one wants a tenure-track job in an American economics department). But even in combination with more mainstream research interests, we are sometimes told that the history of economic thought carries with it a job market hit. Labor economics and the history of economic thought is okay; labor economics and econometrics is better.

American liberal arts colleges are often represented to us by faculty sympathetic to the history of economic thought as likely places where, say, labor economics and the history of economic thought is, in fact, better. These claims are usually accompanied by lists of Duke graduates to imitate. The job market candidate at one of these schools, we are told, may appear to be a more diverse teacher, perhaps better trained to offer popular "interdisciplinary" courses. Bradley Bateman's essay (this volume) confirms that the history of economics continues to be widely taught in many of the best American liberal arts colleges, and although not without certain challenges, it appears likely to remain part of the curriculum at these schools. Discussion among conference participants suggested that much of this teaching is done by those without formal training or research interests in the field. Many departments may fill the demand for history of economics classes with existing faculty, previously hired to fill other needs and who have since, mysteriously it would seem, fallen into the history of economics.

As graduate students, we are obviously not well placed to understand the hiring practices of these or other schools. Our main source of information concerning the job market for historians has come from the anecdotal evidence of recent candidates. But we can also have impressions of the job market for new historians of economic thought that are perhaps more objective, with the rather large caveat that graduate students as a whole are obsessive and not objective about the job market. What follows is a discussion of the job market for academic historians of thought, as represented in the American Economic Association's (AEA) *Job Openings for Economists* (*JOE*).

Two qualifiers to this exercise are perhaps necessary. The first is that our aim is not to recreate an exhaustive job search in the history of economics. That the *JOE* listings do not always include possible jobs listed in the *Chronicle of Higher Education* or unlisted jobs "created" with a specific candidate in mind does not prevent us from asking how job opportunities for historians of economics are represented in this source. The *JOE* remains the most important source of job market information for graduate students. That jobs in the history of economics are largely invisible in the *JOE* relative to the number of postings for other fields shapes our expectations and those of our classmates about the marketability of a field in the history of economics.[2] Second, as we read the *JOE* and discuss it with other graduate students, we come to understand

2. For a recent study of the job market for new economics Ph.D.s, see Siegfried and Stock 1999, which does not even mention the history of economic thought as a field of specialization, although it neglects other smaller fields, such as health economics, as well.

our opportunity costs of studying the history of economics not in terms of what might be if we were at another institution or at Duke a decade ago but rather relative to what it might be if we were more like our current graduate student colleagues at Duke and did not devote any time to the history of economics. These are the criteria that we use to evaluate both the number and desirability of listed job opportunities. Admittedly, these criteria are immersed in their own "moral tales" of legends and fallen heroes.

Using the on-line version of *JOE*, we surveyed the job openings at American colleges and universities for the 2000–2001 academic year by looking at the August 2000 through February 2001 issues.[3] A search of the primary headings of all job postings with the *JEL* codes B0 and B1 yielded eleven history of economic thought–related academic jobs. Expanding the search to include the text of each job description turned up six additional jobs. A summary of the listings:

Listings with HET as desired, or may be needed to teach	17
Tenure-track	15
Nontenure-track	2

Institutions represented (with *U.S. News* 2001 top fifty liberal arts college rankings in parentheses where applicable) were: Albright College, Bucknell University[4] (27), Colby College (19), Depauw University (39), Dickinson College (47), Humboldt State University, Indiana State University, John Carroll University, Loyola University, Mt. St. Mary's College, SUNY-New Paltz, Trinity University, University of Utah,[5] U.S. Naval Academy, Washburn University, Wagner College, and Western Kentucky University.

Although we have classified these as history of thought–friendly jobs, most of the hiring institutions do not appear to consider qualifications in

3. *JOE* is published ten times each year, but most academic jobs are posted in the fall. The restriction to U.S. jobs is not as limited as it sounds. We found only a handful of Canadian and foreign jobs.

4. The job listing for Bucknell identifies the qualified applicant as one "broadly educated in the political economy that originates in Marx, Veblen and related schools of economic thought. In particular, we are interested in an individual who is able to teach intermediate political economy [and courses in] . . . unemployment and poverty, feminist economics, the economics of race and gender, and topical courses in one or more of these fields in the university's general education program."

5. While several universities on this list offer professional degrees or graduate degrees from other departments, Utah is the only one with a graduate program in economics. This is consistent with Gayer (this volume) on the limited scope of graduate HET courses.

the history of economic thought essential. Most seek someone who can teach core undergraduate micro and macro courses, with a few extras to round out the department, possibly including the history of economics but also any number of other subfields. A typical listing reads, "Commitment and qualifications to teach microeconomics, macroeconomics and courses in one or more of the listed areas are essential" (Depauw).

The criteria that are explicitly and implicitly used to evaluate the desirability of any of these jobs emerge from many of the same forces and interactions in graduate education that we have discussed above. Research is preferred to teaching; lighter teaching loads are preferred to heavier loads; more selective schools are preferred to less selective ones; graduate programs are preferred to undergraduate-only programs; economic departments are preferred to other social science departments, and so on. These categories are not mutually exclusive, nor do they necessarily represent our own preferences. They apply not just to jobs in the history of economics but to all jobs in economics. These preferences are so entrenched in graduate education that they define, with the intellectual content of the program, what it means to become an economist.[6] While we do not claim to be captive to or unquestioning of these disciplinary preferences, we do claim that they shape our job expectations and the expectations that others have of us.

For example, the liberal arts jobs held out us to us as desirable by many faculty in the history of economics underline just how differently *desirability* is defined in the field as compared to the economics profession at large. A revealing section in Klamer and Colander 1990 recounts a discussion by students at MIT on the ranking and prestige of academic jobs. One student noted that Williams College, despite being a prestigious institution, still carried a liberal arts stigma for most economists: "That's definitely not the thing to do—to walk into Stan Fischer's office and announce that you want to teach at Williams." Another student added, "Williams and Amherst are somewhere out of sight" (78). And although we might be thrilled with a job offer from the likes of Williams or Amherst, we cannot be too careful about to whom we reveal this preference, lest we be completely dismissed by some of our advisers as not really serious about economics or on par with our classmates also competing for the time and attention of advisers.

6. See Klamer and Colander 1990 for a detailed discussion of the socialization of economics graduate students.

An alternative strategy is to attempt to find jobs and earn tenure completely independent of any history of economic thought activity, taking up the history of economic thought only in our spare time. In this case we would pursue history of economics as a "hobby," fully subordinate to the research and teaching for which we were hired.[7] On the surface, this would seem to extend our ambivalence and equivocation past graduate school. And yet if the trend in the field is indeed toward people falling into teaching and researching in the history of economics after tenure or picking it up on the side, perhaps we will not be so different from our future colleagues, the "Next Generation."

Conclusion:
Yes, We Understand the Concept of Sunk Costs

Is the picture we describe here too gloomy? Many conference participants thought so. By far the most common reaction to this essay from faculty was that the essay was a lot of moaning and bellyaching, or, more mildly put, that it lacked perspective and sophistication and ignored many of the benefits of a field in the history of economics. Furthermore, some thought that through our gloom, we were making our situation far worse than it actually is.

It seems to us, however, that we are the least well situated to offer a more balanced perspective or to change any of the ways that the subdiscipline is viewed by the larger profession. It would be dishonest for us to pretend to be optimistic, because in a very personal sense we are a site of many of the tensions surrounding the future of the history of economics. This is in addition to whatever insecurities and angst graduate students might be expected to experience throughout the course of the graduate career. That said, however, we could have abandoned ship many times and left the history of economics for the seemingly calmer waters of another subdiscipline. Sunk costs are, after all, sunk. Yet we are still here, and that surely says more than anything that we have written above.

---

7. This was the strategy most frequently repeated by our graduate student colleagues. Most indicated that the history of economics came with such a high opportunity cost relative to research in another field that it would have to wait until after tenure.

References

American Economic Association. 2000–2001. *Job Openings for Economists*. August 2000–February 2001. Available at www.eco.utexas.edu/joe. Accessed 15 February 2001.

Klamer, Arjo, and David Colander. 1990. *The Making of an Economist*. Boulder, Colo.: Westview Press.

Schabas, Margaret. 1992. Breaking Away: History of Economics as History of Science. *HOPE* 24.1:187–203.

Siegfried, John J., and Wendy A. Stock. 1999. The Labor Market for New Ph.D. Economists. *Journal of Economic Perspectives* 13.3:115–34.

U.S. News and World Report. 2001. America's Best Liberal Arts Colleges. www.usnews.com/usnews/edu/college/rankings/libartco/tier1/t1libartco.htm.

Reflections on the Tales of the Next Generation

Evelyn L. Forget

It is a challenging time to be working in the history of economics, and it is difficult to comment on such personal essays in a useful way. But your experiences raise important issues for all of us. I wonder if your representation of "the reality" is as empirically sound as it might be?

Why Do I Find Your "Facts" Suspect?

I think that sometimes perceptions of reality are based on a set of myths that, because they are not articulated, have more power than they would if they were exposed to the light.

Myth One: "There are no jobs."

Almost everyone represented in this volume has had the experience of searching for job candidates in recent years. We know that the market has shifted. We know (although you might not) that there are more jobs in economics than there are strong candidates. We know that we list desired fields, with little hope of actually appointing a specialist in the fields advertised. And we also know that, even in the much poorer job market

I would like to thank the authors of the "next generation" pieces, and anyone else I may have libeled, for being good sports. And, for Roy Weintraub, I'd like to paraphrase the immortal Paul Simon: "I'm not old. The Bible's old. The Koran is old. God is old. I'm not old."

of the 1980s and 1990s, most of us were hired even though we applied for jobs that did not list history of economic thought as a desired field.

Among the "facts" presented was a list of seventeen jobs (fifteen tenure-track!) from *Job Opportunities for Economists* between August 2000 and February 2001 (Brown and Saunders, this volume). If we put that number into the context of the past ten or fifteen years, seventeen jobs begin to look like quite a lot. But there was no list of jobs for other subfields, nor any indication of the number of potential candidates in our own or any other field. I don't think that we can conclude that the candidate-to-job ratio in our field is higher than in other fields. I have seen no evidence to support the claim.

What if, instead of reading the job ads in *Job Opportunities for Economists*, you read the front sections of the *Chronicle* or the *Times Higher Education Supplement*? This won't help you find jobs, but it will give you a sense of the anxiety that is motivating administrators who recognize that they are now beginning to face a sellers' market. It is very difficult for most small universities to hire economists of any persuasion; most are not in a position to be too selective about fields.

Myth Two: "There are no good jobs."

This is a little harder. Only one of the listings in *Job Opportunities for Economists* had a graduate program in economics. Most of the small colleges, you claim, are less selective than they might be. You also mention the presumed onerous teaching load at small colleges.

I can't help but give you some career advice here. Ignore it at your peril. The worst of all possible worlds is to take a job in a weak graduate department. Most graduate students think all Ph.D. programs are pretty much alike, and they imagine employment at such a place as an ideal. They imagine joint publications with good graduate students, a lot of interaction, and mentoring. It comes as a great shock to find yourself in a department full of weak Ph.D. students. The graduate program is exceptionally expensive; it sucks resources out of the undergraduate program so that you do a good job of teaching no one. You are under constant pressure from your chair to raise the grades in your graduate classes and to "help" various students pass their exams and write their dissertations. Most of the students are not competitive for national awards, and so you are under pressure to win grants to keep them alive by hiring them as research assistants. There is little satisfaction in watching a student graduate with a very marginal dissertation and seek a job for which he or she is not competitive. And it is not as if there will be boatloads of students dying to write theses in history of economic thought. Even weak economics graduate students believe there are more opportunities in other fields.

A liberal arts college is not a terrible fate. The ones I know about have a three-plus-two teaching load. You would be surprised at the number of larger departments that demand as much or more. You say that many of these institutions are "less selective" than you would have liked. It is easy to teach bright students, but there is a satisfaction in teaching students who may be the first in their families to go to university. There is a satisfaction in teaching undergraduates. It is a mistake to think that your most challenging or memorable students will be the ones who have the highest high school entering grades. The best ones are the inherently bright students who have not yet bought the academic line. These students challenge you, and it feels good to have an impact on their lives.

But what if you get your heart's desire? What if an excellent school— Stanford or Yale or MIT—calls and invites you to apply? What if they offer you a job? Do you want to be at a place where you have to fight for tenure and promotions, where you must compete for salary increases (where you are in a merit pool with Nobel laureates!!?), and where your potential doctoral students turn up their noses at someone who doesn't do "real" economics? Can you imagine a more dispiriting environment? If you feel undervalued now, steer clear of these places.

There are no perfect jobs out there. Each one of us has to negotiate the costs and benefits of each offer independently. And our evaluation of their relative merits might well change over our lifetimes. But never take someone else's ranking as gospel.

Myth Three: "I will not get a job as good as
the one Craufurd has."

Actually, this one is not a myth. It is unfortunate and no doubt very unfair, but it is a fact. There was a very brief period in the late 1960s and early 1970s when good graduate departments allowed highly prized recruits to specialize in their own fields of interest and to develop unique and personal courses. These jobs were taken by members of the "blessed generation"—a very small cohort of people whose parents were reckless enough to breed during the Great Depression. This cohort was consequently too young for the Second World War but too old for Vietnam. They are the people who came of age after Sputnik, who hit the academic labor market during the great expansion, and who never had to compete for any job in their lives. Need I continue? There are no new jobs like that. And the existing ones are red-circled and labeled "present incumbent only" in some provost's office. Get over it. (I almost have.)

The relevant comparison, however, is not with Craufurd Goodwin, but with your contemporaries in other fields of economics. What has been their job market experience? My guess is that many of your colleagues have taken jobs at liberal arts colleges and at big state universities—just like you will. They must have done; that is, after all, where most of the jobs are. The few exceptions hired by the Stanfords and MITs are probably rare enough that they have gained legendary status among faculty and graduate students. And because their fields were inevitably in theory or econometrics—certainly not in history of economic thought—I would wager that everyone has erroneously concluded that theory or econometrics will get you a job at Harvard or MIT. It doesn't follow.

Myth Four: "I'm a pawn with no control over my future.
All I can do is look for job ads and apply for the ones that list my field."

This is the most pernicious tale of all. Jobs do not just appear. They are created, often with specific candidates in mind, to fill needs that those listing the jobs can be convinced they have. Consider the recent experiences of people represented in this volume. Stephen Meardon did not apply to the Inter-American Development Bank because it listed a pressing need for a historian. He had other qualifications and managed to convince them that they needed him and would benefit from his historical perspective.

Margaret Schabas (a full professor and therefore virtually unemployable)[1] took a job in a philosophy program that listed a need for someone in the social history of science. She managed to convince them that she was qualified in that field and also competent to teach economic thought. And so she will teach (part-time) for the economics department. I (another unemployable full professor) succeeded in convincing a medical

---

1. I write of the rank and not of the person. Full professors have been quite immobile in Canada for the past decade at least, so her job offer was a coup for which she should be congratulated.

faculty that they needed a professor of economics. They consider what I do quaint but no less respectable than any other kind of economics. These are three good jobs. They must be because each of us accepted the offer in preference to the very secure but more standard jobs we held before. None of us answered an ad for a historian of economic thought, but none of us imagines ourselves to be leaving the field. There are many ways to have a satisfying career in this field.

Passivity—less kind people call it "learned helplessness"—is a recipe for unhappiness. I've never seen anyone with a Ph.D. in economics panhandling on a street corner. To reiterate: there are more posted jobs than there are applicants. When you add the jobs that are created by potential candidates, opportunity abounds.

Myth Five: "My fields of specialization will determine what I do for the next forty years."

Things happen. Opportunities emerge. Interests change. Almost everyone I know is doing something substantially different than they might have imagined when they graduated. And most were tenured and promoted. The horror stories are really quite exaggerated.

As for being required to publish well in the field for which you were hired in order to qualify for tenure—I think this is a myth. It is undoubtedly true of the Dukes and Yales of the world. It is much less true of the places most of us end up teaching. Refereed publications in good field journals will get anyone tenure almost anywhere. And if that has been true in a tight job market, imagine how much truer it will be as universities start recognizing that hiring replacements is not quite so simple anymore.

Myth Six: "Doing other things is detrimental to my historical work. If I specialized, I'd be more productive."

There is some truth to this, but less than you think. You obviously need the time and the resources to do some serious research and writing. But history is not like other fields. Intellectual capital grows slowly. The older you are and the more experience you have—good and bad—the better your historical writing. The more you know about anything, the better a historian you can be. Sometimes we economists see trade-offs where none exist.

I do not think that it is a tragedy that graduate students doing history of economic thought are expected to master other fields of economics. I think it is essential. This is especially true for those working on recent history. Phil Mirowski has been very critical of "practitioner histories." But can you imagine how contemptuous practitioners will be of histories written by people who have not mastered the techniques that they criticize? This is the greatest limitation of the histories of science and medicine; how can you comment if you don't understand? You have to share the work in order to understand it and, I emphasize, in order to convince your potential audience that you are credible. Undergoing the first-year initiation in graduate school is part of being an economist. Remember that students interested in labor don't get to do that in first year, and students interested in public finance don't get to do that in first year. Everyone does theory and econometrics, and most do mathematics.

I even think the "one-chapter history" has some advantages (Brown and Saunders, this volume). Not only does it acknowledge the job market, it actually prepares candidates to do better history. (And it sets you up for a pretenure *Journal of Economic Literature* article. I wish I had thought of it.)

Myth Seven: "I don't get no respect."

This is true—another hard and undeniable fact. If you need the support of other economists and other graduate students, this is not the field for you. But I would go further. If you need the support of other economists and graduate students, academic life is not for you. You have to grow a thicker skin. Any good academic has to be prepared to do things that others simply don't understand or appreciate. That, after all, is why we seek tenure. There is no virtue in conformity.

Myth Eight: "What we see now will continue
into the future forever."

Things change, often in unpredictable ways. There are cycles and fashions. In my more sensitive moments, I think about the Irish monks who saved civilization by toiling in obscurity and without reward (but with a good sound track in the background). Most of the time, I just do what I want to do and trust that things will work out, one way or another.

Something always happens. But at the same time, I keep my eyes open for opportunities; entrepreneurship is worth cultivating.

What Are the Consequences of These Myths?

If you believe these myths, you collude—as you have recognized—in your own subjection. You have convinced yourselves that you have no power and no control. You believe, despite what you write, that our field deserves no respect. If you thought it a worthy undertaking, you would be far less dependent on the good opinions of other graduate students and economists.

You are historians. Deconstruct these myths. Practitioners of queer theory have recognized that they can't let others choose how they will be represented. Why should you? Disability rights activists have seized ownership of the phrase *crip culture*. (I'll let you guess who might belong to the Toronto organization "Crips and Quacks.") At the risk of sounding like a cultural icon I will not name, you are only as powerless as you choose to let others make you feel.

Perhaps some of your angst is due to your socialization as economists. The "powerlessness" of the representative agent that we talk so much about in microeconomic theory is not very realistic. Neither is the idea of "fixed tastes and preferences." Just as in most markets, tastes and preferences in the academic labor market are very fluid and influenced by all kinds of things, including the imagination and persistence of the seller. The idea of trade-offs is so fundamental to our worldview that we can't think without it. But "synergy" is a more useful concept than "trade-off" when we are talking about the creation of intellectual capital.

More important, why should you internalize the value system that we try so hard to inculcate in graduate students? Who says that a Ph.D.-granting institution is preferable to a liberal arts college or to a policy think tank? And why would you believe them? You, like everybody else, need to determine exactly what you need for a happy and productive life. For that part of our lives that is dedicated to our work, we historians have it very easy. All we need is a seven-hundred-dollar computer and someone to talk to. And we don't even need someone to talk to if we have Internet access. I can't help but compare that to colleagues in science, whose career is effectively over at the age of thirty-two if their funding is cut off. We don't need labs or teams of research assistants whose support will become our responsibility. Unlike our colleagues in econometrics, we don't face a built-in expiry date on our intellectual capital. And a Ph.D. in economics is very vendible.

Your perspective is valuable, and those of us who are a little longer in the tooth do need to think carefully about it. In particular, we need to lay the blame where it belongs—on ourselves—for creating an apocalyptic view of the world and the job market that awaits you. We are all potential mentors and models, and we let you down by colluding with you in creating a version of reality that represents all of us as victims. I would be equally at fault if I stopped at a rose-colored view of the world. There are challenges and hardships in front of you, some of your own making and some outside your control. Life is not fair. But challenges do sometimes carry unexpected opportunities. (There is that sound track again.)

Something that you have not recognized, and perhaps should, is that it is not just you (who will do well whatever you choose to do) but the field itself that will change as a consequence of its representation. If there is no doctoral training in history of economics, then the kind of work that will be done will be very different. If the only graduate training is the "one-chapter model," then the kind of writing that will exist will be quite different. I am not necessarily prepared to say that *different* is synonymous with *worse*, because I do accept the idea of unintended consequences. But different it certainly will be.

Question your willingness to believe what people tell you and what you think you see from the common room. It is a very constrained perspective. And—most challenging of all—ask yourselves honestly what role(s) you play in creating the environment of which you despair. Once you recognize your own power, you'll be in a better position to determine whether the constraints are really there or self-imposed.

(Easy for me to say. I have tenure. And, as we all know, that makes me omniscient.)

Part 5

Heterodox Traditions

History of Economic Thought in the Post-Keynesian Tradition

Sheila C. Dow

Casual inspection of the post-Keynesian literature, like other heterodox literatures, reveals an extent of reference to historical texts and analysis of these texts that is unusual in modern economics, although not in earlier economic literature. The purpose of this essay is to provide an account of the part that history of thought plays in post-Keynesian economics, and how history of thought is understood within the school. I will argue that this understanding does not allow for history of thought to be fitted into dualistic categories, or indeed to be separated off from economics itself. While some have raised issue with post-Keynesian history of thought by means of this attempt at posing distinctions, we will explore here how the post-Keynesian approach to history of thought takes issue with the distinctions themselves.

The discussion therefore begins with a general account of the background of historiographical discussion, bearing in mind the way in which the heterodox economists' use of history of thought is viewed by others. I then offer an account of the organic way in which history of thought is embedded in post-Keynesian economics, looking first at the founders and then at the developing school of post-Keynesians. This account will refer more to the type of use made of, and contribution to, the history of

I am grateful to Victoria Chick, John King, Anthony Waterman, and an anonymous referee for comments and suggestions.

thought than to the specific content of the relevant history of thought.[1]
The essay then considers post-Keynesian history of thought in terms
of current categories: how far post-Keynesians draw on history of economic analysis as something distinct from "pure history," and the relationship between history of thought and methodology/Methodology
in post-Keynesianism. Finally, I consider the future role of history of
thought from the point of view of developing and promoting a particular
approach to economics.

1. The Role and Nature of History of Thought
in Post-Keynesian Economics

We consider here two sets of categories in the historiography literature
that have been used to characterize post-Keynesian economics in relation
to the history of thought. The first refers to how far history of economic
thought conforms to "proper" history, and the second to the relationship
between history of thought and methodology.

Discussion of history of thought has at times focused on two categories: intellectual history (IH) and the history of economic analysis
(HEA) (see Waterman 1998 and Coats 2000). The former, according to
A. M. C. Waterman (1998, 304), represents "an attempt to discover some
features of the past as it really was," while the latter is designed to "trace
the lines of descent to leading analytical themes in economics and to
study intellectual connections between the different lines," or doctrinal
history. One way of putting the distinction is that IH offers a historical
reconstruction, while HEA offers a rational reconstruction (Blaug 1990;
Winch 1998, 355).[2] Waterman maintained that each form of history has
value for economists, and that each can inform the other.

It has been argued by some that history of thought within a heterodox
school of thought inevitably falls into the category of HEA. Further, it
has been argued that history of economic thought scholars should instead
aspire to construct their history as historians do, that is, IH (see the fuller
discussion of this argument in Boettke, this volume). The argument to

1. An excellent history of post-Keynesian (macroeconomic) thought is due to be published
shortly by Elgar (King 2002). Post-Keynesian reference to past thought is embedded in this
account.

2. In Lakatosian terms, rational reconstruction involves constructing an account of theory
development according to a set of methodological principles that may or may not have been
part of the intention of the authors concerned.

be developed here is rather that post-Keynesian history of thought does not fit readily into either category. While history of thought is pursued primarily to inform modern economics (and thus is not IH), this goal is seen as being best served by building up a historian's understanding of older texts (and thus not HEA). While it may be argued that some of this is done well and some badly, like anything else, the point to be made here is that post-Keynesian history of thought does not allow for a separation between history and economics in the manner entailed by the IH/HEA distinction.[3] It consists of a "looking backward in order to look forward."[4]

The approach to history taken by post-Keynesians has a long pedigree. It can be found, for example, in the Scottish education tradition (which formed the likes of David Hume, Adam Smith, and James Steuart). What we would nowadays call transferable analytical skills were conveyed to students by a historical method of teaching—teaching mathematics, for example, by teaching the different forms of mathematical thought as they emerged in different historical contexts. In the Roman/Stoic tradition, the goal was to generate the capacity to address future practical problems, where there was no assurance that the scientific theory suited to the current context would continue to apply. This in turn involved a particular, analytical form of history: "The distinctive nature of the theory of history . . . may be found in its scientific temper and emphasis on economic forces as fundamental to historical and sociological investigation. The particular feature of this contribution . . . [may be] . . . that of finding principles which reduce the apparent chaos of history to order and thus enable us to understand our *present* condition" (Skinner 1965, 22).Why this historical approach should have been adopted by post-Keynesians will be explained further in section 3 in terms of post-Keynesian methodology.

A post-Keynesian analysis of historical texts may well differ from other readings. This has also been a source of criticism, since this reading is seen to involve methodological judgment (while others, by implication, do not). The second set of categories we consider here, therefore,

---

3. This is not to say that the IH/HEA distinction is irrelevant, if not treated as an all-encompassing dualism. Indeed, Gerrard (1991) has argued that much of the confusion in the literature interpreting Keynes arises from a lack of clarity as to whether or not modern categories and preoccupations are being applied. I will therefore refer to the distinction in what follows.

4. I am indebted to Victoria Chick for this phrasing.

is Roy Weintraub's (1989) distinction between "Methodology" as a prescriptive exercise and "methodology" as an interpretative exercise. Weintraub associates various schools of thought, including post-Keynesianism, with employing Methodology in their reading of orthodox economics. The implication is that descriptive "methodology" is not only desirable, but also feasible. In particular, the argument implies not only that historians *can* make interpretations without methodological judgment, but also that it is heterodox economists like post-Keynesians as a group, as opposed to orthodox economists as a group, who fail to be neutral.

In fact, some of the clearest examples of imposing modern concepts on interpretation of historical texts can be found in orthodox economics. Kenneth Arrow and Frank Hahn (1971), for example, saw themselves as completing Adam Smith's project of formulating a system of market coordination, while Robert Lucas (1980) saw himself improving on Keynes's theory of expectations by applying modern techniques. Neither gives evidence of having based his efforts on a reading of the original texts or an attempt to understand them in terms of the context in which they were written.

But in any case a misleading dualism is being put forward, this time between description and prescription. It is itself a methodological judgment that history of thought can be divided into IH and HEA, where IH is concerned with historical "facts" and the maintenance of historical "standards," while HEA is concerned with imposing a prescriptive interpretation on the facts and thus departing from the standards of good history. Prescribing IH and proscribing anything else as HEA (as diluting "standards") would therefore involve historians of thought themselves in engaging in Methodology. Indeed, the advocacy of IH as an account of the facts independent of modern concerns, and the reference to standards, bear an uncomfortable relation to positivist Methodology. It is now conventional in the methodology literature to accept that any one set of standards is contestable. In particular, the post-Keynesian approach to history sets standards just like any other approach.

In fact, within history itself, as much as in the economic historiography literature, there is much discussion about interpretive issues (see, for example, Tully 1988). While a historian may strive for the best interpretation, taking on board an interpretation of the context and intentions of the author, it is now widely accepted that there are generally a range of defensible interpretations. Indeed, this is a core feature of the history of science, or science studies, literature (see, for example, Weintraub 1999). It would seem that a post-Keynesian's interpretation of history of thought could reasonably be understood in these terms, just like any other interpretation.

Of course, this is not to argue that post-Keynesians are closed to criticism in their history of thought, any more than anyone else is. It is indeed the case that many post-Keynesians do not engage in intellectual history in the form of archival research, although many do so engage. However, if it is argued that post-Keynesians fall on the "wrong" side of an IH/HEA divide, or that post-Keynesian efforts at IH suffer from bringing a particular perspective to bear, then that criticism is itself laden with a contestable methodology. Further, the idea of one "best" way of doing history of thought seems to entail a puzzling contradiction with the modern science studies approach, which allows for a range of focus and thus of interpretation.

We will return in section 3 to explore further the reasoning behind the post-Keynesian approach to history of thought. But first, in the next section, I will provide some evidence of how post-Keynesians actually use, and contribute to, history of thought.

2. History of Thought in Post-Keynesian Economics

History of Thought and the Founders of
Post-Keynesian Economics

The two primary founders of post-Keynesian economics are John Maynard Keynes and Michal Kalecki. There is some dispute as to whether or not neo-Ricardian economics, inspired by Piero Sraffa, forms part of post-Keynesianism.[5] This question is relevant for the current discussion, since I would argue that the appropriate means of delineating a school of thought are methodological, with direct implications for the treatment of history of thought. (These implications are addressed in section 3.) But the continuing influence from two or three originators whose approaches had significant differences reduces the canonical influence of any one of

5. See Harcourt and Hamouda 1988 for an inclusive approach, but see Minsky 1990 for an argument that Sraffa is incompatible with Keynes, and Halevi and Kriesler 1991 that he is incompatible with Kalecki. A. Roncaglia (1995), a neo-Ricardian, has in turn suggested that the Sraffian approach should not be considered part of post-Keynesianism.

the three; the relations between each approach are a matter for periodic debate, involving reference to contextual history.

It is important for considering the use made by the three figures of the history of thought in the development and presentation of their economics that they were actively engaged also in history of thought, often published separately from their theoretical contributions. Keynes's *Essays in Biography* (1933) is a clear attempt to focus explicitly on the context of the writing of such key figures as Thomas Malthus, William Stanley Jevons, Alfred Marshall, and F. Y. Edgeworth. Further, his interest in original texts and his concern to make sense of them are evidenced by his discovery with Sraffa of Hume's ([1740] 1938) *Abstract* and their new interpretation of its origins set out in the introduction to the reprinting, which they organized in 1938. Sraffa similarly has credentials in the history of thought from his editorship of the multivolume *Works and Correspondence of David Ricardo* (1951), with scholarly introduction. Kalecki also contributed to the history of thought, on Marx's reproduction schemas and on Mikhail Tugan-Baranovsky and Rosa Luxemburg (Kalecki 1990–97, vol. 2), and with a short piece on historical materialism and a number of biographical reminiscences (Kalecki 1990–97, vol. 7). It could be argued that each brought his own agenda to what otherwise seems to fit into the IH category (see, for example, Waterman's [1998] discussion of Keynes on Malthus). But even those who explicitly aspire to as much objectivity as possible in pursuing IH accept that it is impossible, and indeed not necessarily desirable, to avoid bringing additional knowledge to the exercise (see, for example, Winch 1998).[6]

In developing their theories, all three presented their work in awareness of the history of thought and their place in it; in that sense the separation between history of thought and theory development was by no means complete. As well as presenting his *General Theory* (1936) in contradistinction to the prevailing theory, Keynes also located it in relation to the work, for example, of Jean-Baptiste Say, Malthus, John Locke, and Hume. At the same time, Keynes emphasized the need for theory to fit the context. In the original drafts of the *General Theory*, he presented his monetary theory of production in terms of a stages theory of history, with the cooperative economy giving way to the entrepreneur economy (see Rotheim 1981). Keynes's focus on the history of economic

6. The word *knowledge* is used here not to refer to "true" knowledge, but to the knowledge carrying greatest weight, in the Keynesian sense of the term.

thought was thus only one aspect of a more generally historical approach. Sraffa, too, located his theory within IH (see Brewer, this volume). Indeed, the three key figures saw historical understanding as part and parcel of their economics, not as something separable.

History of Thought in Post-Keynesian Economics

While Keynes, Kalecki, and Sraffa were not unusual for their time in their awareness of, and interest in engaging with, the historical development of economic thought, the disciplinary context changed during the subsequent period in which post-Keynesian thought developed. But post-Keynesians retained a strong historical sense, in marked contrast with most of orthodox economics.[7] Joan Robinson (1979), for example, as well as locating her theory historically, displayed an awareness of historiographical issues. A. S. Eichner (1979) traced the influence from Keynes and Kalecki to later thought. Indeed, there have been several attempts to survey post-Keynesian economics, and the approach characteristically adopted is to trace post-Keynesian ideas in terms of the context of their development (see Harcourt and Hamouda 1988). John King's (2002) forthcoming history of post-Keynesian macroeconomics is an important development as it is the first comprehensive attempt to present a history starting with the father figures and then tracing the subsequent development of ideas as history, referring to context and authors' intentions.

All schools of thought have texts that refer to the development of the paradigm. But what is notable about post-Keynesian economics is that this is not confined to histories or surveys. It is also evident in the main post-Keynesian texts. P. Davidson (1972, 1994) makes explicit textual reference to the antecedents of post-Keynesian thought and specifically the different interpretations of Keynes. Similarly, P. Arestis (1992) and M. Lavoie (1992) refer extensively to older texts as they trace the different developments of ideas that underpin the theoretical structures they build up in their texts. These are not "histories of thought." Nevertheless, by relating ideas offered by a range of economists over the twentieth century, and drawing out those most relevant to what is seen as important for the present day, they are not simply "using" history of thought as

---

7. Reference to history of thought is also common in other heterodox schools of thought and in other social sciences, such as sociology and political theory.

something taken off the shelf. Nor can this practice be classified simply as HEA, as opposed to IH, as in sustaining a canon. While the context of the use made of history of thought is modern theoretical development, the way in which older works are referred to displays an awareness of the context in which they were written, and in turn can be said to contribute to our understanding of the texts.[8] Indeed many leading post-Keynesians publish history of thought as such, alongside work focusing more on modern theoretical development.[9]

The publication of Keynes's *Collected Writings* spawned a wide array of histories of Keynes's thought that are more clearly in the IH mold, tracing the development of Keynes's thought and the interrelations between the different pieces of work. This has been most notable in terms of both Keynes's philosophy as set out in the *Treatise on Probability* (1973) and its implications for his economics. Inevitably, debates have occurred over the representation of Keynes's thought, for example, how far there was continuity (see Carabelli 1995) and how far discontinuity (see Bateman 1987). There have been differences of opinion, too, on the applicability of this historical material to modern issues.[10]

Perhaps the best work to represent the relationship between post-Keynesian economics and the history of thought is Chick 1983. In this book, Victoria Chick discusses the development of the *General Theory* in Keynes's own terms, and in terms of the economic and intellectual context in which he wrote, and she discusses his macroeconomics in relation to modern macroeconomic problems. The very explicit attempt to enhance our understanding of Keynes's work by study of a text in the context in which it was written seems to point to IH. But the deliberate attempt to discuss Keynes in relation to modern problems— sometimes to demonstrate his relevance, sometimes to point out areas

8. An example is the new understanding of the precautionary motive for the demand for money, which differs from that stated by Keynes (1936) in the *General Theory*. But the development of this new understanding has led in turn to a new understanding of Keynes's work (see, for example, Runde 1994).

9. A recent example is Luigi Pasinetti's (2000) critique of neoclassical theory of growth and distribution, which offers a history of the development of ideas in the field. It contrasts notably with the companion article by Solow (2000), which provides a somewhat ahistorical account of the neoclassical theory of growth and distribution. The fact that Pasinetti's history is offered under the heading of "critique" may raise doubts among some as to its credentials as "intellectual history." Section 3 is designed to address this issue.

10. Anna Carabelli (1988) and Rod O'Donnell (1989) explicitly distanced their historical work from any direct application to modern economic issues, unlike Tony Lawson (1995) and Bill Gerrard (1995).

where Keynes's theory needs to be modified or developed along new lines—seems to accord more with history of economic analysis. But the exercise is something more than IH or HEA. As Chick (1983, vii) puts it herself:

> This is not a book in the history of economic doctrine as such, which is concerned with illuminating the author's point of view as brightly as possible on his own terms. I hope at several points to have done that, though I do not claim that this book reveals "what Keynes really meant." It is obviously important when reading anyone to use one's sympathy and intuition to understand him or her to the best of one's ability. That effort, and basic respect, is necessary even to make effective criticism. . . . The question of relevance ultimately dominates the book, whether evaluating Keynes's ideas vis-à-vis those of his predecessors and their modern representatives or the applicability of his ideas to the present.

Another exemplar is the two-volume exercise, organized and edited by G. C. Harcourt and P. Riach (1997), attempting to make up for the fact that Keynes never wrote the intended second edition of the *General Theory*. The contributors were asked to construct "accounts, based on whatever evidence was available and whatever speculation seemed reasonable, of what they thought Keynes would have written in, say, 1938 or 1939" (1:xiv) and also to outline developments from Keynes's own thought in the postwar period. This exercise clearly required a detailed understanding of Keynes's thought in the context in which it was developed and published. Indeed, since several contributors chose to write *as* Keynes, an unusual effort was made to understand both the intentions and context of Keynes. This part of the exercise was then combined with an account of postwar developments in thought inspired by Keynes, which required the capacity both to understand the significance of the changing context and to recognize where Keynes's theory needed modification and further development. This exercise is neither pure IH nor pure HEA.

Perhaps a particular example from this exercise might serve to explain further what is involved. The process of producing the contribution on endogenous money (Dow 1997) started from the conventional association of Keynes with an exogenous money supply assumption. Yet a more careful reading of the *General Theory*, approached from the perspective of the wider body of Keynes's work on money and banking, of the nature of the banking system at that time, and of the prevailing contemporary discussion of monetary policy, revealed a very different interpretation. This exercise, approached as history, was shown to have implications for modern economics, following an explicit discussion of how the environment has changed since the 1930s. In particular, Keynes's account of how money is generated was shown to have included a discussion of the liquidity preference of banks. This concept, adjusted in order to apply to a modern banking system, has now contributed to the modern debate over the relationship between liquidity preference theory and endogenous money theory.

Having attempted to demonstrate, through a brief account of the literature, the post-Keynesian approach to history of thought as integral to economics, we now consider further the reasoning behind the approach.

3. History of Thought and Post-Keynesian Methodology

This section explores what it is about post-Keynesian methodology that gives post-Keynesian history of thought its particular character.

The first issue is the very notion of a school of thought. Weintraub (1989) draws the distinction between methodology as an interpretive activity (which is integrally related to the history of thought) and Methodology as the grounding of interpretation in some external principles-of-theory appraisal. The issue of the role of methodology in general in relation to history of thought in general has been widely debated (see, for example, Coats 2000, and the Backhouse [1992] and Weintraub [1992] exchange). But there is a specific issue when it comes to schools of thought. Weintraub identifies schools of thought such as post-Keynesianism, Marxism, and neo-Austrian economics as engaging in Methodology when they juxtapose their theories to those of the mainstream orthodoxy, because they are applying to orthodox economics appraisal criteria that are external to that approach. These criteria are seen to color post-Keynesians' reading of the history of thought.

Post-Keynesians see themselves explicitly not as offering an analysis with the aid of some absolutist external Methodology, but rather from the perspective of an *alternative* methodology. It is a preferred alternative, and reasons are given for that preference that derive from practice, but there is no claim to demonstrable truth. It is a matter of paradigms, where each paradigm develops its own vision of reality. Inevitably this vision colors interpretation of text as well as context. But this does not preclude post-Keynesians from the interpretation of texts from alternative paradigms according to the visions of reality underpinning those paradigms. Thus, for example, T. Lawson (1997) aims to clarify neoclassical economics in terms of its context and intentions. It could be argued that, nevertheless, he is offering an interpretation from a critical-realist perspective. But because of the social structure of the discipline and the social nature of knowledge, any historian of thought has some methodological priors that conform more or less closely to some paradigm or another. Indeed, as we have seen, the very notion of a sharp divide between IH and HEA is itself methodologically laden.

It was the formation from the 1960s and 1970s of a grouping of post-Keynesians around various institutional arrangements that indicated the emergence of a distinctive school of thought. It was characteristic, particularly of the early post-Keynesian texts, to explain how post-Keynesianism differed from the prevailing orthodoxy. This was necessary not least because the methodology of the orthodoxy, backed up by Whig history of thought, carried the strong implication that the market in ideas had already identified the best approach. Starting from Keynes's own expressions of differentiation from the orthodoxy prevailing in his time, these markings-out of post-Keynesian territory proceeded with an account of how thought had developed since then, with an awareness of changing context. Since the differences were ontological and epistemological, it is not surprising that the arguments should be expressed at these levels as well as at the level of practice. If practice is embedded in a particular ontology and epistemology, then to refer to these levels is not going "outside" practice. This is an insight that owes much to the historical study of Keynes's own theory of knowledge under uncertainty, but that also appears in the more general historiography literature (Arouh 2000).

While methodological awareness was always evident in post-Keynesian economics, the analysis of methodology has increased immeasurably since the reissuing of Keynes's *Treatise on Probability* in 1973. The reissue provoked an extensive study of Keynes's epistemology, in the context in which he developed it, and seeing how it underpinned his approach to economics, post-Keynesians were able to build up a coherent account of their own ontology, epistemology, and methodology. Recognizing the difference in the modern context from that in which Keynes was writing, much of this literature considers how best to develop post-Keynesian methodology in a modern environment. As J. Pullen (1998) points out with respect to Malthus, so also with Keynes, the carrying forward of ideas to address practical modern problems can even be in tune with the original intentions of the author.

Post-Keynesian economics adopts a historical method in the sense that, since the purpose of theory is seen as informing practical issues, a preference is expressed for theory designed to fit the context at hand. Since social systems (both individual behavior and institutional structure) evolve, it is quite likely that theory will be different for different circumstances. Studying different (historical) contexts and the theories developed to address them helps economists to build up the judgment necessary for developing theories appropriate to new contexts.

Theory choice involves trade-offs: post-Keynesians trade off elegance and certainty of conclusions against the capacity to mold theory to different realities. By focusing on a context rather than an axiomatic structure, post-Keynesians choose to employ a range of methods that are not necessarily formally commensurate in order to build up some knowledge (with uncertainty reduced as far as possible). It is this plurality of method that lends post-Keynesianism its diversity; it is a conscious methodological choice, with the choice of methods constrained only by the shared ontology of the school of thought.[11]

This epistemology colors the role of the history of thought in post-Keynesian economics in a variety of ways. First, history of thought is no more separable as an activity than econometrics, for example. Second, by building up knowledge of past debates, modern economists enhance their understanding of the significance of the post-Keynesian line of thought. Third, history of thought plays a constructive part by informing modern economists of the choice of methods and theories made by their forebears in different circumstances. The wider the knowledge of other contexts, the greater the capacity to develop the art of choosing methods and theories appropriate to the problem at hand.

The epistemological implication is that it is not the purpose of economics to identify lawlike behavior to underpin theories for widespread application; some theories may suit some contexts well but not others. Theories are indirect knowledge held with uncertainty about an economic environment conditioned by the presence of uncertainty. Theory

11. Other heterodox schools of thought also tend to adopt pluralism of method. But because each school is defined by its ontology, the range of methods employed differs from school to school.

does not inevitably progress but may be identified as taking "wrong turn-ings" (from the perspective of a particular paradigm). Judgments may be expressed about theories as being more or less suited to a particular con-text, and good reasons presented for these judgments, without any claim to absolute truth.

From this perspective, the historian of thought is no different from anyone else in approaching a body of work from some perspective or other. The best that can be done is for the historian of thought to make that perspective explicit so that his or her own texts may be read accord-ingly. It need not be the author's perspective. Thus, for example, Esther-Mirjam Sent's (1998) account of Sargent's work provided an assessment according to Sargent's own criteria—but there was a range of possible criteria that could have been applied. But there is no such thing as pure description. There are numerous debates in the history of thought, since, no matter how good the intentions of the historian, there is no neutral ground from which to survey the scene. Even among contemporaries of the author under study there may well be different interpretations ac-cording to their differing perspectives (see, for example, Dow 2002).

Interpretation plays its part in the creation of the reality we study. The substantive, epistemological role of history of thought in post-Keynesian economics has been addressed by Chick (1999) in her commentary on Niebyl 1946. In the context of the development of classical monetary theory, Karl Niebyl points to the three interconnected levels at which history is important: the history of production, the history of institutions, and the history of ideas. In the area of monetary theory all three can be seen to play an active part in reality: ideas shape institutions, which shape production, which shapes ideas, and so on. Thus the thought about which histories are written is not simply the end product of the intentions and context of the author—it goes on to affect real economic develop-ments.

The way in which history of thought is written may influence how economists understand reality (see Weintraub 1991). Further, in a social system, epistemology itself can actually change the reality we study. In modern times, for example, the thinking behind the Maastricht Treaty has had real consequences for institutions and economic developments. Niebyl shows how problems arise when the three levels get out of phase—when institutions are introduced to suit a reality that no longer exists, for example. Thus, while it is important to consider the genesis of ideas in their context, the ideas then take on a life of their own, which requires further study. These ideas taken out of context, perhaps by subsequent theorists, still constitute the subject matter of the history of thought.

One substantive implication of the specification of post-Keynesian epistemology and methodology[12] is that it serves to define the school of thought. This kind of specification is a retrospective exercise, trying to tease out from the relevant texts what it is that post-Keynesians have in common. It involves application of new knowledge about Keynes's philosophy, explored particularly in the light of new developments in economic methodology (see Lawson 1997). While this might seem to be a clear indication of HEA rather than IH, it exposes in fact the problematic nature of the very concept of "modern" frameworks, as applied to history. It is not just that many modern ideas are reinventions of older ideas—and history of thought can serve to tease this out (see, for example, Dow forthcoming). But it is further that a new framework of ideas can sometimes help us, *as historians*, to see new facets of well-thumbed texts by enhancing our understanding of the historical context.

4. Conclusion: The Future Role of History
of Thought for Post-Keynesians

It might be thought that, once the historical texts have been thoroughly pored over and the definitive histories written, post-Keynesians will in the future pay less active attention to the history of thought. After all, it is a relatively young approach, which may now be said to be maturing nicely. Post-Keynesianism has gone through the stage of differentiation from the orthodoxy in terms of content, and in terms of methodology, has had its history documented, and could now be said to be free to get on with addressing modern issues of theory and policy.

But the distinctive post-Keynesian approach is such that post-Keynesian analysis will continue to be imbued with history. It is not just a matter of locating post-Keynesianism in relation to other approaches, but a matter of how knowledge relevant to policy issues is constructed. If theory is particular to context, then the more we know of different historical contexts and the theories developed to apply to them, the better able we will be to develop theories to apply to new contexts as they emerge.

12. See Dow 1998 and Dow 2001 for fuller expositions.

Post-Keynesian history of thought is thus something other than what is entailed in the dualistic application of the categories of IH/HEA, or methodology/Methodology. It is an attempt to understand the history of ideas in terms of the context in which they developed, but with the goal of informing modern theory development. Post-Keynesian history of thought is not history for its own sake.

But even history for its own sake cannot escape bringing *some* perspective to bear on interpretation. Indeed, the modern history of science literature discourages any ambition to identify the one true interpretation of any text. Historians of thought who are not post-Keynesians may not accept a post-Keynesian interpretation of a text because of a difference in perspective. But that in itself does not rule out post-Keynesian history of thought as history—confined to the concepts and concerns of the period of the text. Rather it should invite debate and generate further enlightenment for all concerned to be aware of readings of texts from a wider range of perspectives. The advocacy of IH, however, is said to require the "standards" of history to be applied to this exercise, separating it from the conduct of economic analysis. But it is important to recognize that there is debate among historians themselves over standards, just as in any discipline, including mathematics.

The key issue is how far history of thought is separable from economics, an issue highlighted by Peter Boettke's distinction (this volume) between producing and consuming history. It seems to be the integration of history of thought into post-Keynesian economics that for some is a major source of misgiving. It must be recognized that a separation from economics is, historically, an aberration. The norm before the ahistorical formalism that came to dominate in the second half of last century was for history of economic thought to be integral to economics. But in any case, if history of thought is to be used as input to modern economics, the lack of any basis for definitive, externally validated interpretation cannot be ignored. What is picked off the history shelf embodies some interpretive perspective or other. The discipline of history is no more immune from differences of perspective than is economics. Indeed, it is important for the basis for different interpretations to be brought to the surface, examined, and debated.

It is particularly important for post-Keynesians to have a well-reasoned historical interpretation of texts, backed up by a detailed knowledge of the context and intentions of the author, if history of thought is to contribute case studies to future theoretical development. Nor is it reasonable to associate such a view with dilution of standards; as we have seen, the specification of particular standards is contestable. For post-Keynesians, history of thought is not just an intellectual exercise; it really matters for modern economics, and the design of policy and institutions, that history of thought is done well. To advocate instead that the construction of histories be excised from economics, with the task of interpretation devolved to others, is to risk further undermining the liberal intellectual project as far as economics is concerned.

References

Arestis, P. 1992. *The Post-Keynesian Approach to Economics*. Aldershot: Elgar.
Arouh, A. 2000. Canon and Heresy: Religion as a Way of Telling a Story of Economics. In *The Canon in the History of Economics: Critical Essays*, edited by M. Psalidopoulos. London: Routledge.
Arrow, K. J., and F. H. Hahn. 1971. *General Competitive Analysis*. Edinburgh: Oliver and Boyd.
Backhouse, R. E. 1992. Rejoinder: Why Methodology Matters. *Methodus* 4.2:58–62.
Bateman, B. W. 1987. Keynes's Changing Conception of Probability. *Economics and Philosophy* 3:97–120.
Blaug, M. 1990. On the Historiography of Economics. *Journal of the History of Economic Thought* 12.1:27–37.
Carabelli, A. 1988. *On Keynes's Method*. London: Macmillan.
———. 1995. Uncertainty and Measurement in Keynes: Probability and Organicness. In Dow and Hillard 1995.
Chick, V. 1983. *Macroeconomics after Keynes*. Oxford: Philip Allan.
———. 1999. Karl Niebyl's Methodology: Classical Monetary Theory in Historical Context. Paper presented to the History of Economic Thought Conference, Glasgow, September.
Coats, A. W. 2000. The Historiography and Methodology of Economics: Some Recent Contributions. Paper presented to the HES Meeting, Vancouver, July.
Davidson, P. 1972. *Money and the Real World*. London: Macmillan.
———. 1994. *Post Keynesian Macroeconomic Theory*. Aldershot: Elgar.
Dow, S. C. 1997. Endogenous Money. In Harcourt and Riach 1997.
———. 1998. Post Keynesianism. In *Handbook on Methodology*, edited by J. B. Davis, D. W. Hands, and U. Maki. Cheltenham: Elgar.
———. 2001. Post Keynesian Methodology. In *The New Guide to Post Keynesian Economics*, edited by R. Holt and S. Pressman. London: Routledge.
———. 2002. Interpretation: The Case of David Hume. *HOPE* 34.2:399–420.
———. Forthcoming. Historical Reference: Hume and Critical Realism. *Cambridge Journal of Economics*.

Dow, S. C., and J. Hillard, eds. 1995. *Keynes, Knowledge, and Uncertainty.* Aldershot: Elgar.

Eichner, A. S, ed. 1979. *A Guide to Post-Keynesian Economics.* London: Macmillan.

Gerrard, B. 1991. Keynes's General Theory: Interpreting the Interpretations. *Economic Journal* 101:277–87.

———. 1995. Probability, Uncertainty, and Behaviour: A Keynesian Perspective. In Dow and Hillard 1995.

Halevi, J., and P. Kriesler. 1991. Kalecki, Classical Economics, and the Surplus Approach. *Review of Political Economy* 3.1:79–92.

Harcourt, G. C., and O. Hamouda. 1988. Post Keynesianism: From Criticism to Coherence? *Bulletin of Economic Research* 40.1:1–33.

Harcourt, G. C., and P. Riach, eds. 1997. *The "Second Edition" of the General Theory.* Vols. 1 and 2. London: Routledge.

Hume, D. [1740] 1938. *An Abstract of a Treatise on Human Nature.* Reissued with an introduction by J. M. Keynes and P. Sraffa. Cambridge: Cambridge University Press.

Kalecki, M. 1990–97. *The Collected Works of Michal Kalecki.* Vols. 1–7. Oxford: Clarendon Press.

Keynes, J. M. 1933. *Essays in Biography.* London: Macmillan.

———. 1936. *The General Theory of Employment, Interest, and Money.* London: Macmillan.

———. 1973. *A Treatise on Probability.* In vol. 8 of *Collected Writings.* London: Macmillan, for the Royal Economic Society.

King, J. E. 2002. *A History of Post Keynesian Economics 1936–2000.* Cheltenham: Elgar.

Lavoie, M. 1992. *Foundations of Post-Keynesian Analysis.* Aldershot: Elgar.

Lawson, T. 1995. Economics and Expectations. In Dow and Hillard 1995.

———. 1997. *Economics and Reality.* London: Routledge.

Lucas Jr., R. E. 1980. Methods and Problems in Business Cycle Theory. *Journal of Money, Credit, and Banking* 12:696–715.

Minsky, H. P. 1990. Sraffa and Keynes: Effective Demand in the Long Run. In *Essays on Piero Sraffa: Critical Perspectives on the Revival of Classical Theory,* edited by K. Bharadwaj and B. Schefold. London: Unwin Hyman.

Niebyl, K. H. 1946. *Studies in the Classical Theories of Money.* New York: Columbia University Press.

O'Donnell, R. 1989. *Keynes: Philosophy, Economics, and Politics.* London: Macmillan.

Pasinetti, L. L. 2000. Critique of the Neoclassical Theory of Growth and Distribution. *Banca Nazionale del Lavoro Quarterly Review* 53:383–432.

Pullen, J. 1998. Comment on Waterman: The Last Sixty-Five Years of Malthus Scholarship. *HOPE* 30.2:343–52.

Robinson, J. 1979. Foreword to Eichner 1979.

Roncaglia, A. 1995. On the Compatibility between Keynes's and Sraffa's Viewpoints on Output Levels. In *Income and Employment in Theory and Practice*, edited by G. C. Harcourt, A. Roncaglia, and R. Rowley. New York: St Martin's Press.

Rotheim, R. J. 1981. Keynes' Monetary Theory of Value (1933). *Journal of Post Keynesian Economics* 3:568–85.

Runde, J. 1994. Keynesian Uncertainty and Liquidity Preference. *Cambridge Journal of Economics* 18.2:129–44.

Sent, E.-M. 1998. The Evolving Rationality of Rational Expectations: An Assessment of Thomas Sargent's Achievements. Cambridge: Cambridge University Press.

Skinner, A. S. 1965. Economics and History: The Scottish Enlightenment. *Scottish Journal of Political Economy* 32:1–22.

Solow, R. M. 2000. The Neoclassical Theory of Growth and Distribution. *Banca Nazionale del Lavoro Quarterly Review* 53:349–82.

Sraffa, P, ed. 1951. *The Works and Correspondence of David Ricardo*. Cambridge: Cambridge University Press.

Tully, J., ed. 1988. *Meaning and Context: Quentin Skinner and His Critics*. Oxford: Oxford University Press.

Waterman, A. M. C. 1998. Reappraisal of "Malthus the Economist, 1933-97." *HOPE* 30.2:293–334.

Weintraub, E. R. 1989. Methodology Doesn't Matter, but the History of Thought Might. *Scandinavian Journal of Economics* 91.2:477–93.

———. 1991. Surveying Dynamics. *Journal of Post Keynesian Economics* 13.4:525–43.

———. 1992. Roger Backhouse's Straw Herring. *Methodus* 4.2:53–57.

———. 1999. How Should We Write the History of Twentieth-Century Economics? *Oxford Review of Economic Policy* 15:139–52.

Winch, D. 1998. The Reappraisal of Malthus: A Comment. *HOPE* 30.2:353–63.

The Use and Abuse of the History of Economic Thought within the Austrian School of Economics

Peter J. Boettke

> Nobody should believe that he will find in Smith's *Wealth of Nations* information about present-day economics or about present-day problems of economic policy. Reading Smith is no more a substitute for studying economics than reading Euclid is a substitute for the study of mathematics. It is at best an historical introduction into the study of modern ideas and policies.
> —Ludwig von Mises, "Why Read Adam Smith Today?" (1953)

> Essays on the history of economic thought are to be appreciated not only purely as history. No less important is the fact that they enable us to re-examine the present state of economic theory in the light of all attempts earlier generations made for their solution. In comparing our point of view with past achievements and errors we may either detect flaws in our own theories or find new and better reasons for their confirmation.
> —Ludwig von Mises, "The Economic Point of View" (1960)

In an examination of the paradoxical situation that characterizes the study of the history of economic thought within the economics profession, Mark Blaug (2001) points out that those attracted to the serious

The financial assistance of the J. M. Kaplan Fund is gratefully acknowledged. I would like to thank the students in my ECON 881 course at George Mason University for comments and criticisms of the argument developed in this essay, as well as Keith Jakee for comments and criticisms on an earlier version. Research assistance from J. Robert Subrick and Peter Leeson is gratefully acknowledged. In addition, I would like to acknowledge the comments of an anonymous referee and the editor on an earlier version. The usual caveat applies.

study of economics are usually of one of two types of mind.[1] One is
drawn to economics either because it affords the application of technical mastery in mathematics or because one is of a philosophical bent
and is concerned with the policy relevance or the social philosophical
relevance of the discipline.[2] If, Blaug conjectures, one is attracted to
economics for philosophical reasons, then the history and evolution of
ideas move to the center of scholarly attention. On the other hand, if
one is more mathematically inclined, then the study of the history of
economic thought is viewed as not vocationally useful. The majority
of economists are of the mathematical bent; however, there is a small
(but vocal) minority who are of the philosophical bent. The history of
economic thought as a subfield within economics provides an intellectual "home" for these economists. As Blaug (2001, 147) points out, "It
is a striking fact that conferences in history of economic thought attract Austrians, Marxists, Radical political economists, Sraffians, institutionalists and post-Keynesians in disproportionate numbers, all non-
neoclassicals or even anti-neoclassicals who have no place else to go
to talk to scholars outside their own narrow intellectual circles." History of economic thought has become an intellectual haven for heterodox economists (see tables 1 and 2).[3] Blaug further speculates that the

1. Paradoxically, while history of economic thought has almost completely fallen out of
the curriculum of graduate education in economics, interest in the history of economics as
a research focus has expanded as measured by articles published in specialized journals, attendance at regular meetings in the field, and so forth. Unfortunately, the implicit economics
within Blaug's article remains at the level of private preferences. His argument is ultimately that
economists' preferences should be different, and if he is persuasive economists would study the
history of ideas. But the paradox is really a collective action problem. The study of the history
of economic thought has social benefits for the economics profession, but the private actor
calculations within the economics profession do not align; PMB < SMB. As in any collective
action problem, the solution—if one is to be found—will be found in institutional arrangements
that align PMB with SMB. However, the institutions of the economics profession are resistant
to change. So ultimately, one comes back to Blaug's point about changing the preferences of
economists as the solution.
2. This "two types of mind in economics" thesis by Blaug recalls the distinction made by
Amartya Sen between economics as an engineering science and economics as a branch of moral
philosophy (see Sen 1987). Sen argues that in the trade-off between engineering and philosophy
modern economics has been impoverished by its exclusive attention to the engineering side of
the discipline.
3. Tables 1 and 2 examine the publication history of *HOPE* and the *Journal of the History
of Economic Thought* (*JHET*) with regard to the Austrian school of economics. Slightly more
than 5 percent of the articles in *HOPE* over the years, and 6.8 percent of the articles in *JHET*
over the last decade, have been written either by or about Austrian economists. This figure is
not disproportionately large in itself, but in comparison with articles published in other fields

foundation for heterodoxy can be found in a certain type of mind and style of thinking about economic issues, which provides common ground among the heterodox despite their many differences.

This factual situation within the history of thought community in economics has been a cause of concern for many intellectual historians of economics. The reason for the concern is the potential misuse of the history of economic thought by the ideologically or methodologically dispossessed within the economics profession. The subfield of the history of economic thought ought to uphold high intellectual standards: standards that meet those set in the field of intellectual history (and history of science) in general. A legitimate contribution to the history of economic thought is made not by people who simply engage arguments historically, but instead by people who write original intellectual history. The fact that history of thought meetings attract the dispossessed is in fact an undesirable situation because it reflects an unwillingness by scholars within the field to insist on rigorous standards. Just because someone is identified with a heterodox group of scholars in economics (say, Austrians) and tends to engage arguments historically doesn't mean that the history of thought community should embrace that person. Instead, whether a particular member of a school of thought considers himself or herself a historian of ideas should be irrelevant. What is at issue is whether the use of an argument found in, say, Friedrich Hayek's writings to resolve a contemporary policy problem, say, the transition problems in Eastern and Central Europe, should fit comfortably on the program at a history of thought meeting or be published in a history of thought journal. No doubt, this sort of writing could be seen as making a contribution to the subfield of Austrian economics. But isn't it a mistake to view it as a contribution to the history of economic thought? The answer is unequivocally "yes" for those who argue that the field of the history of economic thought would be best served by following the standards set in history of science and intellectual history.

I completely endorse the concerns about standards and the argument regarding what constitutes a contribution to the history of economics. However, I think the situation is a bit more subtle than this endorsement might imply. First, not all work in the history of economics need be in the style of intellectual history. There should be room for doctrinal

---

it does seem that Austrian economics is given more weight in this field than others within the profession at large.

Table 1 Articles in *HOPE* 1969–2000

Year	Number of Articles		
	Total	By Austrians	About Austrians
2000	33	0	0
1999	30	2	0
1998	26	2	0
1997	25	2	0
1996	30	1	2
1995	31	3	0
1994	34	2	0
1993	28	0	2
1992	37	1	1
1991	39	1	1
1990	42	1	1
Total, 1990–2000	355	15	7
Percentage, 1990–2000	—	4.2	2.0
1989	38	2	0
1988	35	2	2
1987	39	2	0
1986	37	5	1
1985	36	3	1
1984	33	2	0
1983	31	0	1
1982	34	0	0
1981	32	0	0
1980	32	1	0
Total, 1980–89	347	17	5
Percentage, 1980–89	—	4.9	1.4
1979	31	0	1
1978[1]	27	0	0
1977	25	1	0
1976[2]	24	1	0
1975	27	1	0
1974	27	0	0
1973	25	1	0
1972	29	1	0
1971	25	0	0
1970	20	0	1
1969	20	0	0
Total, 1969–79	280	5	2
Percentage, 1969–79	—	1.8	0.7

Table 1   continued

Year		Number of Articles	
	Total	By Austrians	About Austrians
Grand total, 1969–2000	982	37	14
Percentage, 1969–2000	—	3.8	1.4

1. Excluding the spring issue, which was devoted entirely to four chapters from an unfinished work by Jacob Viner on religious thought and economic society.

2. Excluding the spring issue, which was devoted entirely to an extended essay by Don Patinkin on Keynes's monetary thought.

Table 2   Articles in *JHET* 1989–99

Year	Articles	By Austrian Economists	About Austrian Economic Thought
1989	16	0	0
1990	14	0	2
1991	16	0	0
1992	17	2	0
1993	14	1	0
1994	15	1	1
1996	16	2	0
1997	15	1	1
1998	30	0	0
1999	20	0	0
Totals	190	9	4

Notes: Percentage of articles written by Austrians: 4.7. Percentage of articles about Austrian economic thought: 2.1. Percentage of total articles in *JHET* written by or about Austrian economists: 6.8.

exegesis. The history of the science of economics must be written, but doctrinal exposition also has a positive contribution to make. Second, within a community of scholars there must be both producers and consumers of the scholarly output. The history of economics community is a "thin market," and thus attracting consumers to the product is important to the survival of this research community. A significant segment of the consumer population will be those who want to engage arguments historically. Since progress in economics is ambiguous, the use of history of economic thought for contemporary theory assessment and construction is an invaluable exercise that should not be dismissed by those who

choose to focus their scholarly efforts on the production of original contributions in intellectual history.

I will attempt to develop this argument in the context of an examination of the uses (and abuses) of the history of economic thought within
the Austrian school of economics. The essay will build on the framework
for understanding the use of the history of economic thought that I developed in an examination of Hayek's writings (see Boettke 2001), but
that framework will be expanded to assess other writers in the Austrian
tradition. Those contributing to the Austrian school of economics (historically and currently) have disproportionately couched their contributions
within the guise of the history of economic thought. The "professional
sociology" for this penchant among Austrian economists is complicated
but relates to (1) the older manner in which authors prior to World War
II wrote theory and (2) the type of mind argument that can be found in
Blaug 2001, as already discussed. I will show that sometimes Austrians have used history of thought in an inappropriate manner, while in
many other cases the use of history of thought has been first-rate. Austrian economists have been both producers and consumers of the history
of economic thought. And just as producers and consumers in general
find, sometimes the product has been wanting, while at other times it
has been of high quality; similarly, sometimes they have been ignorant
consumers, while at other times they have been most intelligent. There is
nothing endemic to the Austrian school (as compared to any other school
or perspective) that ensures either good or bad production or consumption of the history of ideas. In the process of making my argument, I
will address and resolve the apparent tension in the use of the history of
thought as conveyed by the quoted material from Mises in the epigraph.

Austrian Economists and the History
of Political Economy

As the fate of the Austrian school of economics has waxed and waned
throughout the nineteenth and twentieth centuries, the use of the intellectual history of the discipline has always been part and parcel of this
particular approach to economic scholarship. To an earlier generation of
economists (say, those born in the nineteenth century), this just reflected
the way one did theory. Economic theory in the late nineteenth and early
twentieth century was much more akin in style and temperament to political philosophy and social theory. Theoretical advancement proceeded

by way of an analysis of the treatment of this issue or concept in the history of the discipline. Carl Menger ([1871] 1976; [1883] 1985), for example, set out to develop his own original contributions to economics and the social sciences but in so doing relied at points on commentary on the writings of Adam Smith, Jean-Baptiste Say, David Ricardo, and his other forebears in political economy (see, e.g., Menger [1871] 1976, 286–320). Eugen von Böhm-Bawerk ([1884–1909] 1959) is even a more obvious case, where his theories of capital and interest are developed in the context of extended critical commentaries of the theories of others before him. The Austrians were not the only thinkers who followed this style of reasoning in the early modern era of economics (postmarginalist revolution): Edwin Cannan ([1893] 1967) is an obvious example, but so are Jacob Viner ([1937] 1975) and Frank Knight ([1921] 1971). George Stigler ([1941] 1994) wrote his doctoral dissertation on the history of production theory. If you look at old Ph.D. oral exams, you will find questions on the history of economic doctrine alongside questions of a more technical nature.[4]

But economists educated after World War II do not think in these terms. The more scientific the discipline conceives of itself, the contention goes, the shorter its relevant history. This is because of the belief in continued progress in science, where bad ideas are weeded out and only good ideas survive.[5] What I am concerned about in this section is simply establishing that the Austrian economists educated since 1945 have continued the older practice of placing their contributions in the context of the subdiscipline of the history of economic thought.

Mises's bibliography (which continues to grow posthumously) contained, at the time it was compiled, 29 books and an estimated 270 articles and book reviews (Greaves and McGee 1993; Greaves 1995). Only 6 of his books and 9 of his 270 entries could count as exercises in history of thought. Mises's attitude toward the history of ideas was more in line with that of the modern theorist in economics, even though his works are interspersed with allusions to earlier writings and debates (often without appropriate citation) from an encyclopedic memory (e.g., Mises 1966). I will not count Joseph Schumpeter within the Austrian camp for this essay, although he could easily be so included. I raise his name only to

4. See, for example, Fritz Machlup's Ph.D. microeconomic study questions given to students at Princeton University in the 1960s, which are contained in an appendix to Gould and Ferguson 1980.

5. I challenge this belief in continued progress in economic science in Boettke 2000b, 2001.

point out that he, like his classmate Mises, supposedly wrote much of his monumental *History of Economic Analysis* (1954) from memory without either notes or immediate contact with his library.[6] Emil Kauder's work on *The History of Marginal Utility* (1966) and Karl Pribram's *A History of Economic Reasoning* (1983) could also be counted within the Austrian tradition, but neither contributed directly to the theoretical advancement of the school of thought in the process. In Hayek's bibliography, which includes 19 books, 14 edited volumes, and some 151 articles, are 4 published books that could be classified as works in the history of thought, 9 edited volumes in the field, and 29 published articles. Hayek was particularly fond of the biographical essay; seventeen of his twenty-nine articles are biographical in nature.[7] Hayek's interest in the history of thought is evident from the beginning of his career; Hayek [1927] 1937, for example, is an introduction to Hermann Heinrich Gossen's work, which Hayek contends anticipated the marginal utility revolution. Hayek (1933–36) introduced and edited *The Collected Works of Carl Menger*. He had also planned to write an intellectual biography on his distant cousin Ludwig Wittgenstein, but this endeavor was ceased because of difficulties in getting access to Wittgenstein's papers at that time. In addition, Hayek's teaching career included a lengthy period where he taught a course on the intellectual history of the liberal tradition at the University of Chicago, and a look at syllabi from his theory courses at the London School of Economics in the 1930s demonstrates how he attempted to integrate the evolution of concepts into an examination of contemporary theory.[8]

Murray Rothbard's (1995a, 1995b) last work was a two-volume history of economic thought.[9] In a bibliography compiled a few years before his death, Rothbard had at that time eighteen published books and more

6. Schumpeter is an important intellectual figure in economic thought and a colorful biographical character as well. His ideas continue to influence new generations of economists, and with the slogan "New Economy" some popular press outlets have even come to view Schumpeter and his idea of "creative destruction" as the concept of the age, as opposed to Adam Smith's "invisible hand." Schumpeter's intellectual relationship with his Austrian schoolteachers is a strained one, however, and as such I am not including him.

7. See the bibliography of Hayek's writings contained in Boettke 2000c (xxxviii–lv).

8. McCormick 1992 reprints many of the syllabi from the LSE.

9. Rothbard unfortunately passed away immediately before the publication of the first two volumes of the projected four-volume work. The first two volumes span antiquity to the brink of the marginalist revolution. I published a review essay on these volumes shortly after Rothbard's death, and that review essay should be read in part as an obituary to a lost icon within the Austrian tradition and as an appreciation of the novelty of the approach pursued in the book

than three hundred articles, notes, and book reviews published in journals, magazines, and newspapers. Ironically, Rothbard's writings contain only two books and twenty pieces within his articles that could be
counted as exercises in intellectual history of economics (this does not
include his major work in the history of thought). The majority of his
publications were libertarian political commentary or policy-relevant
discourse in economics (Gordon 1986). Rothbard also wrote more economic and political history than other writers in the Austrian tradition,
including a four-volume work on the history of the American Revolutionary period, *Conceived in Liberty* (1975–79), a book on the Great
Depression, *America's Great Depression* (1963), and his doctoral dissertation on the panic of 1819, which was subsequently published in
book form as *The Panic of 1819* (1962). Rothbard also wrote several
manuscripts on the "Progressive Era" and World War I, only a few of
which were published in his lifetime (e.g., 1972, 1989). A core notion
within Rothbard's system of thought was that ideas matter; his historical
work, therefore, has a large amount of intellectual history within it.

Israel Kirzner has written directly in the field of history of economic
thought throughout his career, including *The Economic Point of View*
(1960), *An Essay on Capital* (1966), and *Classics in Austrian Economics*
(1994). In fact, Kirzner has just completed an intellectual biography of
Ludwig von Mises.[10] Seven of the fourteen books he has either authored
or edited are directly related to the examination of the history of ideas.
Moreover, 29 of the 121 items listed in the latest published bibliography

---

(See Boettke 1995b). Prychitko's (1998a) review has more temporal and intellectual distance
from the Austrian camp and thus is more critical in its assessment of the Rothbard work.

10. Kirzner has titled that book *Ludwig von Mises: The Man and His Economics* (2001).
Kirzner has also officially announced his retirement from his post at New York University and
his intent to cease scholarly work in economics and social science to devote his energies to
religious study. So it appears that Kirzner will bookend his fertile career with two publications elaborating the Misesian system: *The Economic Point of View*, which examined the very
definition of the subject of economics from the classics through the neoclassical revolution
to Mises's development of praxeology, and *Ludwig von Mises: The Man and His Economics*,
which elaborates for the reader the essential insights to be gleaned through praxeology and
the rather intellectually heroic struggle that the man engaged in to advance his ideas. Kirzner,
in my opinion, is perhaps the greatest "scholar" that the modern Austrian tradition has had in
terms of the depth of his analysis and the seriousness with which he approached the study of
the Austrian tradition. His retirement will present a significant challenge to those working in
the tradition to pick up that standard he has set throughout his career.

of his writings (as of 1995) are history of thought pieces (see Boettke 1995c).[11]

In the 1970s there was a resurgence of interest in Austrian economics among a new generation of economists. These economists have almost to a person made contributions to the history of economic ideas. Karen Vaughn is a former president of the History of Economics Society (HES) and the author of *John Locke: Economist and Social Scientist* (1980) and *Austrian Economics in America* (1994). Another former HES president is Bruce Caldwell, who while avoiding the label *Austrian* has probably done more work on the history of Austrian economic thought than any of his contemporaries. Caldwell's editing on the Hayek *Collected Works* project has been first-rate (Caldwell 1995, 1997), and his various essays touching on the work of Menger (Caldwell 1990), Mises (Caldwell 1984), and Hayek (e.g., Caldwell 1988) are widely recognized within the economics profession at large as perhaps the best expositions of the system of thought within which these thinkers worked. Laurence Moss has also been a consistent contributor to the Austrian literature throughout the revival period and is a former president of HES as well. Moss's (1976) thesis was on Mountifort Longfield, a core contributor to the non-Ricardian English-language economists of the nineteenth century. In Rothbard's (1995a, 101–55; 485–87) history of thought work these non-Ricardians take center stage as precursors of the market process approach pioneered by the Austrian economists in the twentieth century.

Roger Garrison (1984, 1985, 2000) has couched his work as a historical reexamination of Austrian contributions to monetary and capital theory, and Don Lavoie's major work, *Rivalry and Central Planning* (1985), was published in the Cambridge University Press series "Historical Perspectives on Modern Economics," edited by Craufurd Goodwin. Lawrence H. White first advanced his rather radical position concerning competitive currencies within his Ph.D. thesis, which was subsequently published by Cambridge as *Free Banking in Britain* (1984) and contained a major reevaluation of the eighteenth-century debate between the banking school and the currency school (51–80). Mario Rizzo started his professional career contributing mainly to the literature in law and

11. Most of his articles since 1995 would qualify as history of thought. For example, in his last collection of articles, *The Driving Force of the Market* (2000), all seventeen pieces included would constitute contributions to understanding the historical significance of the Austrian School of Economics and in particular the ideas of Mises and Hayek. So the bibliography of his writings underreports his contributions to the history of economic thought.

economics, but he has also written articles throughout his career in the history of ideas, including works on Herbert Spencer (Rizzo 1999) as well as on Hayek (Rizzo 1990), Mises (Rizzo 1982), and the notion of causation in economic thought (Cowan and Rizzo 1996).[12] Gerald O'Driscoll's book *Economics as a Coordination Problem* (1977) is an assessment of Hayek's system of thought in the context of his debates in macroeconomics and on the price system. O'Driscoll also published works dealing with Adam Smith and Ricardo. O'Driscoll and Rizzo's *The Economics of Time and Ignorance* (1985) is advertised as a refinement and restatement of the modern Austrian argument, but the book proceeds in its stated task largely through an engagement with the discipline of political economy historically contemplated. Joseph Salerno has published numerous works on the French economists (1988), international monetary theory (1980), and the development of the Misesian tradition within the Austrian school of economics (1999). Steve Horwitz (1989, 1992, 1996, 1998, 2000), Dave Prychitko (1991, 1998a, 1998b), and myself (1989, 1990, 1992, 1993, 1995c, 1997, 2001; Boettke and Vaughn 2002) have also published several articles in *HOPE*, *JHET*, and *RHET&M*, as well as books negotiating debates within the history of economics from the early twentieth century.

In short, the empirical record seems to support Blaug's observation that Austrians contribute disproportionately to the subdiscipline of history of economic thought compared to other fields within economics (see tables 3 and 4).[13] The Austrians are a minority voice within the neoclassical tradition,[14] and as such, the Austrians as a school of thought

12. It may be significant to note that Rizzo earned his Ph.D. at the University of Chicago, and while Stigler was not his Ph.D. advisor, he did take the field in the history of economic thought, and his fellowship throughout graduate school was the Walgreen Fellowship, which Stigler supervised.

13. Twenty-five percent of the articles published in the *Review of Austrian Economics* (1988–2000) were of a history of economic thought nature. The *Quarterly Journal of Austrian Economics* (1998–2000) has published 17 percent in the field of the history of economic thought, and 19 percent of the articles in *Advances in Austrian Economics* (1994–98) were history of thought. Moreover, in the premier book series devoted to Austrian economic thought ("Foundations of the Market Economy," edited by Mario J. Rizzo and Lawrence H. White and published by Routledge) twenty books have appeared since 1990, five of which are explicit exercises in the history of economic thought. However, all but three of the books have considerable history of thought treatments within them.

14. By *neoclassical* I mean the shared understanding of universal explanation by way of marginal utility analysis, which I would distinguish from *Neoclassical*, where I mean the shared understanding that science is best done in economics through mathematical modeling and statistical testing. The term *Neoclassical* has an ambiguous meaning at best, as is now widely

Table 3 Articles in Journals Devoted to Austrian Economic Thought

Journal	Total Articles	History of Thought Articles
Review of Austrian Economics		
2000	11	3
1999	12	1
1998	9	2
1997	8	0
1996	14	1
1995	8	3
1994	9	5
1993	6	2
1992	8	3
1991	6	4
1990	7	0
1989	8	2
1988	8	3
Total	114	29
Quarterly Journal of Austrian Economics		
2000[1]	11	0
1999	13	2
1998	17	5
Total	41	7
Advances in Austrian Economics		
1998	11	1
1997	14	2
1996	8	2
1995	20	4
1994	15	4
Total	68	13

Notes: Percentage of total articles in the *RAE* in history of thought: 25.4. Percentage of total articles in the *QJAE* in history of thought: 17.1. Percentage of total articles in *Advances in Austrian Economics* in history of thought: 19.1.

1. Excluding issue 4.

---

recognized. The "problem" from an Austrian perspective of this ambiguity is that it simply reflects that the form an argument takes has in the modern practice of economics taken on a greater significance than the substance of the argument.

Table 4 Books in *Foundations of the Market Economy* series (1992–2001)

Author	Title	Primarily History of Thought	Considerable History of Thought Component
Kirzner	*The Meaning of Market Process*		✓
Thomsen	*Prices and Knowledge*		✓
Maclachlan	*Keynes' General Theory of Interest*	✓	
Dowd	*Laissez-Faire Banking*		
Lachmann (edited by Lavoie)	*Expectations and the Meaning of Institutions*	✓	
Machovec	*Perfect Competition and the Transformation of Economics*	✓	
Harper	*Entrepreneurship and the Market Process*		✓
O'Driscoll and Rizzo	*Economics of Time and Ignorance*		✓
Ikeda	*Dynamics of the Mixed Economy*		✓
Endres	*Neoclassical Microeconomics*	✓	
Chamlee-Wright	*The Cultural Foundations of Economic Development*		
Cowen	*Risk and Business Cycles*		✓
Lewin	*Capital in Disequilibrium*		✓
Kirzner	*The Driving Force of the Market*		✓
Sautet	*An Entrepreneurial Theory of the Firm*		✓
Garrison	*Time and Money*		✓
Horwitz	*Microfoundations and Macroeconomics*		✓
Dowd	*Money and the Market*		
Boettke	*Calculation and Coordination*		✓
Steele	*Keynes and Hayek*	✓	

believe that some intellectual mistakes have been made in the evolution of modern economics. To correct for that, they tend to engage arguments historically with the idea of resetting the development path of economic thought. Following this path, we may find dead ends in current trends of thought, which forces us to reconsider the earlier moments of choice and then imagine the path that could have been followed instead (see Leijonhufvud 1999).

As a final set of data points to confirm this emphasis within the Austrian tradition of engaging arguments historically, consider a cross-sectional analysis of the mean date of citation in articles published in the *Quarterly Journal of Austrian Economics* (*QJAE*) and *Review of Austrian Economics* (*RAE*) with that of the *Journal of Political Economy* (*JPE*) and the *Quarterly Journal of Economics* (*QJE*) in 2000. The average date of citation in the *JPE* is 1982.7, but this is biased downward by the publication in 2000 of a history of thought paper by William Grampp. The *QJE* average citation date is 1982.4, but this is also biased downward by the publication in 2000 of a set of reflections on the development of economics in the twentieth century, for example, William Baumol's piece on what we have learned since Marshall. Nevertheless, the comparison with the Austrian journals is very revealing considering the point I want to make. The average year of citation in the *RAE* is 1974.5, and the *QJAE* average year is 1951.4. The fact that the Austrians tend to present their arguments in a historically informed manner cannot be denied.

There Is a Lot of It, but Is It Good?

In their use of the history of economic thought, Austrian economists have tended to apply intellectual history in an instrumental, rather than an antiquarian manner.[15] Furthermore, they have tended to waffle between Whig and contra-Whig perspectives depending on where they

15. The terms *instrumental* and *antiquarian* are used in Boettke 2000b and 2001. *Instrumental* means for the purposes of contemporary theory, while *antiquarian* means for the purposes of historical accuracy. Karen Vaughn, Bruce Caldwell, and Laurence Moss are the main exceptions to this general description of work in the Austrian tradition, as their work in the field of history of economic thought has taken the form of historical reconstructions and doctrinal history. Vaughn and Moss, however, have published work utilizing the history of thought for contemporary theory construction. In particular, see Vaughn's (1999) intriguing paper on Hayek's implicit economics.

found themselves within the eyes of the profession.[16] Certainly in Böhm-Bawerk's reconstruction of economic knowledge it was a smooth linear transition from earlier error to logical corrections to himself. In Mises's mind, he was simply clarifying the implicit methodology, methods, and analysis of earlier writers, which culminated in the modern teachings of economics, which could be found in his writings. There is a definite Whiggish attitude conveyed in these writings of Menger, Böhm-Bawerk, and Mises—which means that their writings tend to be in the form of an older rational reconstruction. The arguments of precursors are appreciated only in the context of the successful advance of economic science as culminating in the writings of the author in question. Hayek also makes an instrumental use of the history of economic thought. However, in his published work we get both the Whiggish attitude, in his earlier writings in monetary theory and trade cycle theory, and the more contra-Whig, in his writings on socialism and social theory more broadly defined. As his theoretical work in business cycle theory grew in scientific stature, Hayek's presentation of his precursors in monetary and trade cycle theory were Whig in interpretive spirit. Theory is presented as a linear development where each step provides a piece of the puzzle and culminates in the mature monetary theory of the trade cycle as developed by Hayek. When his cherished nineteenth-century liberalism fell out of intellectual favor as the events of the early twentieth century unfolded, Hayek's work shifted to a more contra-Whig perspective. He was not persuaded by the arguments that challenged economic liberalism, so his research program took shape as an attempt to understand the errors that resulted in this intellectual detour (see Boettke 2000a).

I asked the students in my graduate seminar on Austrian economics what they considered to be the best and worst examples of the use of history of economic thought within the Austrian school.[17] They argued that

16. I use *Whig* and *contra-Whig* in the traditional meaning of these terms. Whig history is history as written by the victors, while contra-Whig is history as written by the losers. Again, see Boettke 2000b and 2001 for a clarification of the framework of analysis I am deploying.

17. I sent out a survey to Austrian economists in spring 2000 but did not get a sufficient number of replies to constitute a study. I don't know if the paucity of responses was a function of lack of interest, poorly designed question, or a lack of willingness to address the question in public. My graduate seminar (spring 2001) was focused on the question of assessing whether the value of the marginal product of Austrian economics is greater than zero with regard to modern economic theorizing. In other words, we engaged arguments historically to see whether all that was important in the Austrian tradition has already been absorbed into the main line of economic thinking.

the work of Lavoie ranked at the top, while that of Rothbard ranked at the bottom. The reason for this relative ranking was the ideological overtones in Rothbard's work, which some saw as forcing Rothbard to ignore key elements in earlier writers. One of the prime examples Austrian writers point to to demonstrate the importance of the history of thought for contemporary theorizing is Keynes's misunderstanding of the meaning of Say's law, as developed by Jean-Baptiste Say and John Stuart Mill. Because Mises and Hayek recognized the basic flaw in Keynes's interpretation of the law of markets, they were well suited to counter Keynes. But in Rothbard's treatment of John Stuart Mill there is no discussion of the latter's exposition of Say's Law. Because the younger Mill is less convenient for the ideological message that Rothbard champions, my students conjecture, his strong suits are to be ignored. In addition, they argued that Rothbard's treatment of Adam Smith is best viewed as a libertarian diatribe, rather than a careful examination of Smith's system. I, too, find Rothbard's treatment of Smith and Mill troublesome, but I also find his writing from a definite point of view to be actually refreshing and an aid to historical assessment rather than a hindrance.[18]

On the other hand, my students viewed Lavoie's reexamination of the socialist calculation debate as tackling an ideologically charged subject (the debate over socialism) in a most scholarly manner and demonstrating how the work of Lange and Lerner did not address the work of Mises and Hayek. Lavoie's work argued that the main protagonists in this debate talked past each other. In reexamining the debate, Lavoie highlighted the subtleties of the Austrian theory of the market process in contrast to the emerging neoclassical orthodoxy within which the model of market socialism was embedded. In the process, Lavoie's book is taken as the prime example of how studying history of economic thought can impact the development of modern theory.

18. Mark Skousen's *The Making of Modern Economics: The Lives and Ideas of the Great Thinkers* (2001)—which is an Austrian attempt to provide an alternative to Robert Heilbroner's *The Worldly Philosophers*—resurrects Smith as the central character in economic thought, as against the overrated status that Rothbard (and Schumpeter, I should add) attributed to Smith. Skousen is able to combine biographical detail (with a focus on scandal) and doctrinal history to present a narrative of the discipline with the central tension actually being the policy battle between Smith's invisible hand, Marx's radical socialist alternative to capitalism, and Keynes's interventionist demand management compromise between capitalism and socialism. Skousen writes from a definite perspective and one that is unapologetically triumphal with regard to laissez-faire.

The students did not name Kirzner's *The Economic Point of View* and *Classics in Austrian Economics*, but I would list them as perhaps *the* prime examples of doctrinal history within the modern Austrian school. Kirzner describes his work using the German term *dogmengeschichtlich*, that is, as a doctrinal reexamination. In judging the Austrian contribution to history of thought, however, it is important to stress that few writers have actually done the sort of historical research that is expected of contributions to intellectual history. The sort of criticisms that I mentioned in my introduction are relevant to the assessment of the modern Austrian contributions to the field. Austrians are primarily consumers of history of thought, not producers. What they produce are exercises in doctrinal exposition and reconstructions of an evolutionary story about economic theory, but not intellectual history, which situates thinkers in the broader intellectual and cultural climate within which they operate. The majority of work from writers in the Austrian tradition treats ideas as abstract and disembodied. No doubt arguments are historically engaged, but contextualizing arguments is not the goal of the Austrian work in history of thought. Instead, older ideas, like contemporary ideas, are examined for their logic and how they fit in the refinement of the basic concepts in economic science.[19]

Future work in the history of economic thought of the Austrian school would do well to follow the lead of Robert Leonard's forthcoming work on Oskar Morgenstern if the goal is production, rather than consumption, of intellectual history. Both Mises and Hayek await the sort of biographical analysis that has been directed at Keynes (e.g., Skidelsky 1983, 1992). Such work is much needed, as both Mises and Hayek are increasingly recognized as towering intellectual figures within the twentieth-century debates on economic theory and policy.[20] This work cannot, however, take on the tone it often has in the past of simply cheerleading for our lost intellectual heroes (e.g., Rothbard 1988). Instead, there must be a move to critical distance and an attempt to situate the thinker within his or her time and system of thought.[21]

19. Ironically, the Austrian style of history of thought work is very similar in style, if not Whiggish in spirit, to that of George Stigler (1965, 66). In particular, Stigler argues that history of thought can serve the purpose of setting forth the major steps in the development of theory, and thus can be justified by aiding our understanding of modern economics.

20. The biographies of Butler (1988) and Ebenstein (2001), while useful, fall short of this standard.

21. Strong ideological precommitment is not necessarily at odds with high standards in intellectual history. Malachi Hacohen's (2000) recent biography on Popper is a case in point,

Austrian economists who wish to contribute to the history of thought would do well to write better *history*. On the other hand, Austrian economists wishing to utilize the history of thought for contemporary *theory* construction should not shy away from their instrumentalist reading of history. Not only has this approach served economics well throughout its history, but the human sciences in general have mainly progressed through an extended dialogue between past and present.[22] It is a mistake to view economics as an empirical science in the same way we view the natural sciences and the applied disciplines of engineering science. The complex phenomena of the social world do not permit such an easy test of progress. Instead, the essential Austrian critique of scientism also implies a method of reasoning that is much longer in intellectual time horizon. It is not just a preference for more philosophical argument that leads one to appreciate the history of thought more, as Blaug suggests. Rather, it is the fact that we cannot escape from the philosophical, whether we care to admit it or not. All arguments bring on board philosophical presumptions, some of which are explicit, while most are implicit. Economics is a science, but a philosophical one, and as such one that has many "extended presents" (Boettke 2000b; Boulding 1971).

Conclusion

Doing history is different from engaging an argument historically. Very few economists within the Austrian tradition of economic scholarship have actually produced intellectual history, as opposed to using the history of thought in an instrumentalist fashion for contemporary theory construction, which is strongly represented within the Austrian literature. As the subdiscipline of history of thought regains its self-confidence in this age of disrespect for the history of ideas in economics, and insists once again on its own standards for original contributions, the Austrians

---

where one of his stated goals is to write to the academic Left and to save Popper from the Right. Nevertheless, Hacohen's work has been heralded as a significant contribution to intellectual history.

22. As Leijonhufvud (1999) has argued, the history of economics can be seen as a decision tree with many different branches. There is nothing predetermined, Leijonhufvud contends, about the way economics has developed; had the discipline taken a different turn in the past we would be doing a different economics today. The serious study of the history of economics can reveal the dead ends and lead us to reconstruct economics for contemporary theory development. Also see Boulding 1971 for an examination of how ideas from the past can remain part of our extended present for contemporary analysis.

will find it more difficult to publish in the pages of the leading outlets in the field by simply engaging arguments historically. The consumption of history of thought for theory construction will be directed toward the specialty journals in Austrian economics and classical liberal political economy. And this is how it *should* be. There are, however, good reasons why the history of thought community ought to value both the producers and consumers of intellectual history. For much of the value of knowledge of the past lies not in the intellectual pursuit of historical understanding but will be demonstrated in the ability to identify the intellectual profit opportunities that remain to be exploited.

The tensions evident in the opening quotes from Mises highlight the problem. History of thought for history's sake alone is something we should value as individuals, but only if we want to be learned scholars of economics, not because it helps us become better economists. Viewed instrumentally, however, the history of thought provides fertile ground for theory development by alerting us to the intellectual opportunities that exist in the reexamination of earlier writings. If, on the other hand, we limit our imagination to viewing history of thought as offering little to nothing in terms of contemporary theory construction, then the only recourse historians of thought will have in answering their colleagues' lack of interest is that the preferences of economists should change so that scholarship is given some modest ground in graduate education and that economists should pass a basic literacy requirement. This argument does not have legs, as the saying goes. It is imperative that economists who believe that economics has a useful past adopt a different argument. Of course, the writing of history is an important intellectual activity and should be respected; but that is why we have history departments. Economists don't need to be working on these issues, or at least this is the sentiment that I believe underlies my professional colleagues' puzzlement with my fascination with history of thought, and their boredom when in rare moments they are asked to contemplate an idea historically. Their boredom will disappear when we can show that superior ideas from the past have been lost to them because of the Whiggish presumption of efficiency in the exchange of ideas. The use of intellectual history by members of the Austrian school throughout the second half of the twentieth century was motivated by a recognition of the deleterious consequences of the efficiency presumption. For the most part, I have argued that the Austrians have been skilled doctrinal expositors of a tradition. Room for improvement remains within the Austrians as producers of good history, but as consumers of the intellectual history of modern economics to recast contemporary theory, many of the Austrian economists we have surveyed have demonstrated keen entrepreneurial alertness to intellectual profit opportunities for improved economic understanding that have hitherto gone unrecognized.

References

Blaug, Mark. 2001. No History of Ideas, Please, We're Economists. *Journal of Economic Perspectives* 15 (winter): 145–64.

Boettke, P. 1989. Evolution and Economics: Austrians as Institutionalists. *Research in the History of Economic Thought* 6:73–89.

———. 1990. *The Political Economy of Soviet Socialism: The Formative Years, 1918–28*. Boston: Kluwer Academic Publishers.

———. 1992. Analysis and Vision in Economic Discourse. *Journal of the History of Economic Thought* 14 (spring): 84–95.

———. 1993. *Why Perestroika Failed: The Politics and Economics of Socialist Transformation*. New York: Routledge.

———. 1995a. Publications of Israel Kirzner. *Advances in Austrian Economics* 2B:463–71.

———. 1995b. Review of Murray N. Rothbard, *An Austrian Perspective on the History of Economic Thought*. *Economic Affairs* (summer): 14–17.

———. 1995c. Why Are There No Austrian Socialists? Ideology, Science, and the Austrian School. *Journal of the History of Economic Thought* 17 (spring): 35–56.

———. 1997. Where Did Economics Go Wrong? *Critical Review* 11 (winter): 11–65.

———. 2000a. Which Enlightenment and Whose Liberalism: Hayek's Research Program for Understanding the Liberal Society. In Boettke 2000c.

———. 2000b. Why Read the Classics in Economics? *Library of Economics and Liberty*, 24 February. http://www.econlib.org/library/Features/feature2.html.

———, ed. 2000c. *The Legacy of F. A. Hayek: Politics, Philosophy, and Economics*. 3 vols. Aldershot, U.K.: Edward Elgar.

———. 2001. F. A. Hayek as an Intellectual Historian. In *Creating a Disciplinary Memory*, edited by Steve Medema and Warren Samuels, 117–28. New York: Routledge.

Boettke, P., and Karen Vaughn. 2002. Knight and the Austrians on Capital, and the Problem of Socialism. *HOPE* 34.1:155–76.

Böhm-Bawerk, E. [1884–1909] 1959. *Capital and Interest*. 3 vols. Indianapolis, Ind.: Libertarian Press.

Boulding, Kenneth. 1971. After Samuelson, Who Needs Adam Smith? *HOPE* 3.2:225–37.

Butler, Eamon. 1988. *Ludwig von Mises: Fountainhead of the Modern Microeconomics Revolution*. Brookfield, Vt.: Gower Publishing.

Caldwell, Bruce. 1984. Praxeology and Its Critics: An Appraisal. *HOPE* 16.3:363–79.

———. 1988. Hayek's Transformation. *HOPE* 20.4:513–40.

———, ed. 1990. *Carl Menger and His Legacy in Economics*. Durham, N.C.: Duke University Press.

———. 1995. Introduction. In *Contra Keynes and Cambridge*, vol. 9 of *The Collected Works of F. A. Hayek*. Chicago: University of Chicago Press.

———. 1997. Introduction. In *Socialism and War*, vol. 10 of *The Collected Works of F. A. Hayek*. Chicago: University of Chicago Press.

Cannan, Edwin. [1893] 1967. *A History of the Theories of Production and Distribution from 1776–1848*. New York: Augustus M. Kelley.

Cowan, R., and Mario Rizzo. 1996. The Genetic-Causal Tradition and Modern Economic Theory. *Kyklos* 49.3:273–316.

Ebenstein, Alan. 2001. *Friedrich Hayek: A Biography*. New York: St. Martin's Press.

Garrison, Roger. 1984. Time and Money: The Universals of Macroeconomic Theorizing. *Journal of Macroeconomics* 6 (spring): 197–213.

———. 1985. Intertemporal Coordination and the Invisible Hand: An Austrian Perspective on the Keynesian Vision. *HOPE* 17.2:309–19.

———. 2000. *Time and Money*. New York: Routledge.

Gordon, David. 1986. *Murray N. Rothbard: A Scholar in Defense of Freedom*. Auburn, Ala.: Ludwig von Mises Institute.

Gould, J. P., and C. E. Ferguson. 1980. *Microeconomic Theory*. Homewood, Ill.: Irwin.

Greaves, Bettina-Bien. 1995. *Mises: An Annotated Bibliography, 1982–1993 Update*. Irvington-on-Hudson, N.Y.: Foundation for Economic Education.

Greaves, Bettina-Bien, and Robert McGee. 1993. *Mises: An Annotated Bibliography*. Irvington-on-Hudson, N.Y.: Foundation for Economic Education.

Hacohen, Malachi Haim. 2000. *Karl Popper: The Formative Years, 1902–1945*. New York: Cambridge University Press.

Hayek, F. A. [1927] 1937. Introduction. In *Entwicklung der Gesetze des Menschlichen Verkehrs und der daraus fliessenden Regeln für menschliches Handeln*, by Hermann Heinrich Gossen. Berlin: Prager.

———. 1933–36. Introduction. In *The Collected Works of Carl Menger*. 4 vols. London: London School of Economics.

Horwitz, Steven. 1989. Keynes' Special Theory. *Critical Review* 3 (summer–fall): 411–34.

———. 1992. *Monetary Evolution, Free Banking, and Economic Order*. Boulder, Colo.: Westview.

———. 1996. Capital Theory, Inflation, and Deflation: The Austrians and Monetary Disequilibrium Theory Compared. *Journal of the History of Economic Thought* 18 (fall): 287–308.

———. 1998. Monetary Calculation and Mises's Critique of Planning. *HOPE* 30.3:427–50.

———. 2000. *Microfoundations and Macroeconomics: An Austrian Perspective.* New York: Routledge.

Kauder, Emil. 1966. *The History of Marginal Utility.* Princeton, N.J.: Princeton University Press.

Kirzner, Israel. 1960. *The Economic Point of View.* Princeton, N.J.: Van Nostrand.

———. 1966. *An Essay on Capital.* New York: Augustus Kelley.

———, ed. 1994. *Classics in Austrian Economics.* 3 vols. London: William Pickering,

———. 2000. *The Driving Force of the Market.* New York: Routledge.

———. 2001. *Ludwig von Mises: The Man and His Economics.* Wilmington, Del.: Intercollegiate Studies Institute Press.

Knight, Frank. [1921] 1971. *Risk, Uncertainty, and Profit.* Chicago: University of Chicago Press.

Lavoie, Don. 1985. *Rivalry and Central Planning: The Socialist Calculation Debate Reconsidered.* New York: Cambridge University Press.

Leijonhufvud, Axel. 1999. Mr. Keynes and the Moderns. In *The Impact of Keynes on Economics in the Twentieth Century,* edited by Luigi Pasinetti and Bertram Schefold. Cheltenham, U.K.: Edward Elgar Publishing.

Leonard, Robert. Forthcoming. *From Red Vienna to Santa Monica: Von Neumann, Morgenstern, and Social Science, 1925–1960.* New York: Cambridge University Press.

McCormick, Brian. 1992. *Hayek and the Keynesian Avalanche.* New York: St. Martin's Press.

Menger, Carl. [1871] 1976. *Principles of Economics.* New York: New York University Press.

———. [1883] 1985. *Investigations into the Method of the Social Sciences with Special Reference to Economics.* New York: New York University Press.

Mises, Ludwig. 1966. *Human Action: A Treatise on Economics.* Chicago: Henry Regnery.

Moss, Laurence. 1976. *Mountifort Longfield: Ireland's First Professor of Political Economy.* Ottawa, Ill.: Green Hill Publishers.

O'Driscoll, Gerald. 1977. *Economics as a Coordination Problem: The Contributions of Friedrich A. Hayek.* Kansas City, Kans.: Sheed Andrews & McMeel.

O'Driscoll, Gerald, and Mario Rizzo. 1985. *The Economics of Time and Ignorance.* Oxford: Basil Blackwell Publishers.

Pribram, Karl. 1983. *A History of Economic Reasoning.* Baltimore, Md.: Johns Hopkins University Press.

Prychitko, David. 1991. *Marxism and Workers' Self-Management.* Westport, Conn.: Greenwood.

————. 1998a. Catholicism, Calvinism, and the Comparative Development of Economic Doctrine: An Essay on the "Austrian" Perspective. *Research in the History of Economic Thought and Methodology* 16:241–58.

————, ed. 1998b. *Why Economists Disagree*. Albany, N.Y.: SUNY Press.

Rizzo, M. 1982. Mises and Lakatos: A Reformulation of Austrian Methodology. In *Method, Process, and Austrian Economics*, edited by Israel Kirzner. Lexington, Mass.: Lexington Books.

————. 1990. Hayek's Four Tendencies toward Equilibrium. *Cultural Dynamics* 3.1:12–31.

————. 1999. The Coming Slavery: The Determinism of Herbert Spencer. *Review of Austrian Economics* 12.2:115–30.

Rothbard, M. 1962. *The Panic of 1819*. New York: Columbia University Press.

————. 1963. *America's Great Depression*. Princeton, N.J.: Van Nostrand.

————. 1972. War Collectivism in World War I. In *A New History of Leviathan*, edited by R. Radosh and M. Rothbard. New York: E. P. Dutton.

————. 1975–79. *Conceived in Liberty*. 4 vols. New Rochelle, N.Y.: Arlington House.

————. 1988. *Ludwig von Mises: Scholar, Creator, Hero*. Auburn, Ala.: Ludwig von Mises Institute.

————. 1989. World War I as Fulfillment: Power and the Intellectuals. *Journal of Libertarian Studies* 9 (winter): 81–125.

————. 1995a. *Classical Economics: An Austrian Perspective on the History of Economic Thought*. Aldershot, U.K.: Edward Elgar Publishers.

————. 1995b. *Economic Thought before Adam Smith: An Austrian Perspective on the History of Economic Thought*. Aldershot, U.K.: Edward Elgar Publishers.

Salerno, J. 1980. The Doctrinal Antecedents of the Monetary Approach to the Balance of Payments. Ph.D. diss., Rutgers University.

————. 1988. The Neglect of the French Liberal School in Anglo-American Economics: A Critique of Received Explanations. *Review of Austrian Economics* 2:113–56.

————. 1999. The Place of Mises's *Human Action* in the Development of Modern Economic Thought. *Quarterly Journal of Austrian Economics* 2.1:35–65.

Schumpeter, Joseph. 1954. *A History of Economic Analysis*. New York: Oxford University Press.

Sen, Amartya. 1987. *On Ethics and Economics*. Oxford: Blackwell.

Skidelsky, Robert. 1983. *John Maynard Keynes: Hopes Betrayed, 1883–1920*. New York: Penguin Press.

————. 1992. *John Maynard Keynes: The Economist as Savior, 1920–1937*. New York: Penguin Press.

Skousen, Mark. 2001. *The Making of Modern Economics: The Lives and Ideas of the Great Thinkers*. Armonk, N.Y.: M. E. Sharpe.

Stigler, George. [1941] 1994. *Production and Distribution Theories*. New Brunswick, N.J.: Transaction Publishers.

————. 1965. *Essays in the History of Economics*. Chicago: University of Chicago Press.

Vaughn, K. 1980. *John Locke: Economist and Social Scientist*. Chicago: University of Chicago Press.

————. 1994. *Austrian Economics in America*. New York: Cambridge University Press.

————. 1999. Hayek's Implicit Economics. *Review of Austrian Economics* 11.1–2:129–44.

Viner, Jacob. [1937] 1975. *Studies in the Theory of International Trade*. New York: Augustus M. Kelley.

White, Lawrence. 1984. *Free Banking in Britain: Theory, Experience, and Debate, 1800–1845*. New York: Cambridge University Press.

The Marxist Tradition in the History of Economics

Anthony Brewer

There is a significant Marxist tradition in the study of the history of economics. Marx himself wrote extensively on his predecessors, albeit mainly in works that remained unpublished at his death. His approach has had a substantial impact in the field, particularly from the mid-twentieth century onward, although it may be fading now. It was, after all, Marx who introduced the name *classical* to describe Adam Smith, David Ricardo, and others, a usage that has become universal, and his interpretation has had a lasting influence on debates over the identification and characterization of classical economics.

The orthodox Marxist interpretation of classical economics focuses, as Marx did, on the labor theory of value and the notion of surplus-value.[1] After discussing Marx's own writings (and the rather special case of Marxist writings on Marx as a historical figure), I shall take Ronald Meek's work, and in particular his *Studies in the Labour Theory of Value* ([1956] 1973)[2] as exemplifying this approach. The publication in 1960 of Piero Sraffa's *Production of Commodities by Means of Commodities* launched an alternative approach, less obviously connected to Marx. Sraffa's book itself is a work of pure theory, but it led, as Sraffa must have intended, to a new reading of Marx and of the classical economists,

---

1. In a broader sense, Marx undoubtedly influenced the way we think about historical change. Space limitations force me to focus narrowly on the history of economics and, within that, to exclude areas such as the history of monetary theory.

2. I have cited the second edition of 1973, but the main text of that edition is a photographic reproduction of the 1956 edition.

which allowed the development of an essentially Marxist interpretation that is independent of the labor theory of value. It is mainly (but not exclusively) in this modified form that Marx's influence survives in the subdiscipline today.

This essay is a study of the line of interpretation that descends from Marx and its influence on thinking about the history of economics. For that reason, the title deliberately refers to the *Marxist tradition* rather than to *Marxism*. Some individuals writing in this tradition think of themselves as Marxists. Others do not. That is not very important. What matters here is the interpretative framework employed.

Marx as a Historian of Economics

Marx wrote a great deal about other economists, but there is a sense in which one could say that he made no attempt to study them histori-cally, in that he never attempted to understand earlier writers in their own terms. His approach was like that of a modern economist who prefaces an article with a survey of the existing literature and its shortcomings, as a preliminary to the original work presented. A historian of ideas, by con-trast, is "more concerned with a faithful reconstitution of developments over time than with current debates" (Clarke 1998, 129) and should aim to understand past writings in the context of their own time.

Marx's pattern of work is well known. He worked obsessively over the writings of his predecessors, going back to William Petty and before, copying out long sections of their work, commenting on it, and devel-oping his own ideas as he went. In the first instance, then, his reading of his predecessors was an integral part of his own self-education and of the construction of his own analysis. In his finished work, which here means primarily the first volume of *Capital*, he referred to earlier writers either to acknowledge the origins of particular ideas or to distinguish his own arguments from those of others and to argue the superiority of his own. But his treatment of other writers was in all cases subordinated to the development and presentation of his own theories. He saw the devel-opment of the subject as a process leading inexorably to himself. Any-thing that he could present as a step toward his own theory is praised, albeit in a rather patronizing way. It is, we are given to understand, a pity that Smith and Ricardo had not shown the insight and resolution needed to carry the argument through to its logical conclusion in Marx's own theory. With few exceptions, anything that does not fit the story is either ignored or dismissed.

If one were to assess Marx's treatment of his predecessors simply as history, it would rate badly, but it would be entirely unfair to criticize it in those terms. Marx did not aim to understand, say, Smith or Ricardo in terms of their own intentions and purposes,[3] and there is no reason why he should have tried to write that sort of history. *Theories of Surplus Value* and the rest should be read primarily for what they tell us about Marx, not about his predecessors.

There is no space here to discuss Marx's writings at length, but a brief discussion of his treatment of Smith will convey the flavor.[4] As a preliminary, I will set out some of the main points that Smith himself clearly considered important. On the first page of the introduction to the *Wealth of Nations*, he asserted that in "civilized and thriving nations" output is so great that "all are often abundantly supplied, and a workman, even of the lowest and poorest order, if he is frugal and industrious, may enjoy a greater share of the necessaries and conveniences of life than it is possible for any savage to acquire" ([1776] 1976, 10). In other words, the question Smith set himself was to explain the prosperity, not the hardships, of the working class. The benefits of the division of labor are a central plank in his explanation. He proceeded to discuss the market mechanism and the resulting tendency to natural (equilibrium) prices, and to explain how wages remain above subsistence in a growing economy. At a later stage in the argument he explained growth in terms of capital accumulation, arguing that accumulation, and hence growth, are normal, thus supporting the claim that wages are normally above subsistence. Arguments for free competition and discussions of policy issues are interspersed throughout the *Wealth of Nations*, leading up to a ringing endorsement of the "obvious and simple system of natural liberty."

Almost all of this vanishes in Marx's discussions of Smith. There is nothing very surprising about that—Marx mined Smith for what was useful to him, not to discover or expound Smith's own views—but what it does mean is that Marx's reading is not, and should not be presented as if it were, a valid historical reconstruction of the *Wealth of Nations*. At a detailed level, some of Marx's claims about Smith (and other writers) seem to me to be plainly wrong, in that Smith's text, on any reasonable reading,

3. He did link what they said, however, to class interests and the development of capitalism.
4. On Marx's treatment of Ricardo, see Steedman 1982.

simply does not say what Marx said it does. It should be remembered, of course, that *Theories of Surplus Value*, like most of Marx's other writings on the history of economics, was unfinished, and one has to expect errors and overstatement in a rough working draft. At a broader level, the point is not that Marx's reading of Smith (and other writers) was right or wrong in any absolute sense, but that it was heavily shaped by his particular priorities and his distinctive view of what is "correct."

It is worth noting that when Marx first came to economics, in 1844, he had already focused on classes and class conflict as a central issue and had identified the proletariat as the future revolutionary class. This much is clear from the introduction to his *Critique of Hegel's Philosophy of Right* (1970), published on its own in early 1844. He was possibly stimulated to start studying economics by Friedrich Engels's *Outlines of a Critique of Political Economy* ([1844] 1961), written in late 1843 and early 1844. It shows relatively little grasp of the subject and cannot be seen as a forerunner of Marx's economic analysis, but it foreshadows the prediction of growing class polarization that was to be a central theme of Marxism. The focus on classes and class conflict was not something Marx found in his economic reading but something he brought to it.

His earliest encounters with the economic literature are documented in the *Economic and Philosophic Manuscripts of 1844* (1961). The influence of Adam Smith is immediately obvious, but what needs to be stressed here is how selective and one-sided Marx was in what he took from Smith. He structured the document around the three categories of income corresponding to three classes—wages, profit, and rent—leading up to a short (and now very famous) discussion of estranged labor. His discussion of wages sets the tone: "The ordinary wage, according to Smith, is the lowest compatible with common humanity (that is a cattle-like existence)" (21). This is, of course, a travesty of what Smith said. Smith ([1776] 1976, 86–88) used the phrase "common humanity" in a passage defining the lowest possible wage and explaining that the wage would rise above this level in a growing economy. It is perfectly clear to any unbiased reader that Smith thought that all economies normally do grow (343–36) and hence that in reality the wage was set at quite a comfortable level, at least in England (99). I could give more examples, but the point here is not to condemn Marx for what he wrote in an early, unfinished work, but to show how single-mindedly he shaped to his own ends what he found in the writings of others.

Marx's most substantial writing on the history of economics is the unpublished manuscript subsequently edited and published as *Theories of Surplus Value* (1963–71), written in 1862–63 before the published version of volume 1 of *Capital* and before much of the material that was to go into volumes 2 and 3 had even been drafted. It is not at all a finished history but is deeply marked by Marx's process of self-education, with long digressions working out his own theory. For example, of the section that his editors singled out as a chapter on Adam Smith (1:69–151), more than half (107–50) is devoted to a digression on the exchange of products between different sectors of the economy, which has little or nothing to do with Smith or with the history of ideas.

Leaving out the digression mentioned above, the chapter on Smith deals primarily with value and with what Marx (but not Smith) called surplus-value. The tone is set at the start of the chapter with a claim that "Adam Smith expressly states that the development of the productive powers of labour does not benefit the labourer himself" (1:69). This is plainly false—as noted above, Smith had made the benefits of development to the common laborer the central theme of the *Wealth of Nations*. Marx supported his claim with a passage that actually says that workers had not received *all* the benefits, which is a very different matter.

Throughout the chapter, the emphasis is on Marx's own views, interspersed with a desultory commentary on Smith, sometimes claiming Smith's support, sometimes not, but with little or no attention to the structure or purpose of the *Wealth of Nations*. For example, Marx quoted Smith saying that rent and profit are deductions from the produce of labor and continued: "Adam Smith . . . describes rent and profit on capital as mere deductions from . . . the value of [the workman's] product, which is equal to the quantity of labour added by him to the material" (84–85). Nothing in Smith justifies the last clause, in which Marx read his own theory into Smith. Natural prices, in Smith's terms, are not proportional to labor embodied, as Marx well knew, and Smith ([1776] 1976, 71) had said, "In a civilized country there are but few commodities of which the exchangeable value arises from labour only."

Many more examples could be given, but one must suffice, from the chapter on "Ricardo's and Smith's theory of cost-price" in the second volume. "The basis from which [Smith] determines the natural rate of wages is," according to Marx (1963–71, 2:222), "the value of labour itself, the *necessary wage*," or (socially determined) subsistence, but Smith's chapter "contains not a word on the issue, the *natural price* of labour, but only investigations into the rise of wages above . . . the natural rate" (2:223). Here again Marx read his own theory into Smith. Smith's ([1776] 1976, 72) natural price was determined by the "ordinary or average" wage, and in a growing economy the ordinary wage is permanently above subsistence. That was precisely Smith's point. Marx (1963–71, 2:223–24) added a dismissive comment on "a piece of Malthusian population theory" before hurrying on. He was unwilling to recognize the simultaneous endogenous determination of wages and population growth in Smith because his politics compelled him to reject Malthusian population theory while claiming that Smith held a subsistence theory of wages. Insofar as classical economists held a subsistence theory of wages, it was of course squarely founded on Malthusian arguments (which go back long before Malthus). Smith did not hold a subsistence theory of wages because his Malthusianism was more sophisticated, not because he rejected population endogeneity.

Something should be said about the concept of "classical political economy" (or "classical economics"), a concept that originated with Marx. In *Capital*, Marx ([1867] 1961, 1:81) defined it thus: "Once for all I may here state, that by classical political economy, I understand that economy which, since the time of W. Petty, has investigated the real relations of production in bourgeois society, in contradistinction to vulgar economy, which deals with appearances only." This is not a very precise definition. As used by Marx it seems to include those writers whom he admired and could (selectively) read as forming a tradition of which he himself was the culmination, while excluding anyone he had reasons to condemn. Thus, Malthus seems to be excluded because his population theory was too explicit for Marx to sweep under the carpet as he did with Smith's rather similar position. Nassau Senior was evidently excluded because of his position on working hours, and John Stuart Mill because he was a living rival of Marx. (Marx treated Mill very shabbily, although it is unlikely that it worried Mill very much.) Marx was, of course, entitled to define *classical* as he chose, but his implicit definition is hard to justify. The term *classical economics* is now generally reserved for the school that derives from, and is based on, the *Wealth of Nations*.

Marx's attitude to demand and supply deserves further attention. He argued (1) that demand and supply could not explain natural prices, and (2) that the classical economists did not rely on demand and supply. The claim that the classical theory of natural prices is independent of demand

and supply is still maintained by some. Here is a relatively full and clear statement of it, for the case of wages:

> Classical political economy . . . soon recognized that the change in the relations of demand and supply explained in regard to the price of labour, as of all other commodities, nothing except its changes, i.e., the oscillations of the market price above or below a certain mean. If demand and supply balance, the oscillation of prices ceases, all other conditions remaining the same. But then demand and supply also cease to explain anything. The price of labour, at the moment when demand and supply are in equilibrium, is its natural price, determined independently of the relation of demand and supply. (Marx [1867] 1961, 537–38)

To a modern economist, this must appear nonsensical. Given supply and demand functions, the equilibrium condition that demand equals supply defines specific values for price and quantity. If the supply and demand functions satisfy certain conditions, the equilibrium will be unique.

None of this, however, was to be found in the literature that Marx knew. It is true that one can find an implicit understanding of the issues in, say, Richard Cantillon and Smith, but it was not spelled out, and it passed Marx by. A fuller and more formal statement of modern demand and supply analysis was emerging in the later years of Marx's life (for example, in William Stanley Jevons), but there is no sign that Marx was aware of it. In any case, the early marginalists presented their theory as if it were opposed to classical theories, and it was not until Alfred Marshall that the relation between demand and supply analysis and cost-based classical theories was clarified. In the literature Marx knew, "demand and supply" really was no more than an untheorized arm-waving backed at best by some vague notion of excess demand or supply as a cause of price changes. Marx's rejection of it was not unreasonable. No such excuse exists for those who repeat his claims today without setting them in their historical context.

To spell it out, the classical condition that returns should be equalized in all industries (allowing for different risks and the like) underlies the long-run supply curve (in Alfred Marshall's terms). If there are constant returns, the long-run supply curve is horizontal and the supply-side condition of equalization of returns can be seen as determining the equilibrium price, while the equilibrium quantity is determined by demand at the cost-determined price. If not, not. This digression is relevant to the history of economics insofar as it is claimed that classical price theory is distinctively different from its Marshallian successor. It is not.

Marxists on Marx

Before discussing the Marxist tradition in the history of economics more widely, I should say something about a very special case: Marxist writings on Marx himself. There is, of course, an immense literature on Marx, much of it by Marxists or by people heavily influenced by Marx. At the level of basic scholarship, a great deal has been done in uncovering and publishing his texts, establishing their chronology and their relation to each other, and so on. Marx left a mass of almost illegible material, so this is no small task. We now know perhaps more about Marx's working methods and the detailed development of his ideas than about any other writer.

If, however, we seek more than such basic factual material, the Marxist contribution to the study of Marx's ideas in their historical context is rather limited. Most Marxists, quite properly, read Marx as a basis on which to build, just as Marx did his predecessors. The interpretative principle to be applied in this case is: how can I read Marx so that his arguments are both logically consistent and relevant to the present day? This is almost the opposite of the interpretative principles used by an intellectual historian who must seek to understand a text in the context in which it was written, and who cannot start from any assumption that it is either correct or logically coherent. Much, perhaps most, of the literature on Marx's economics, however interesting and valuable in its own right, is therefore of little use to the historian of economics. It is, of course, entirely possible for an avowed Marxist to do good historical work on Marx, but relatively few have done so. This may be in part a matter of definition—anyone who seriously questions Marx's estimate of his own role and importance would not be counted as a Marxist.

Marxists and the History of Economics

After Marx's death in 1883, Marxist economics was slow to develop, and Marxist writing on the history of economics even slower. Volume 3 of *Capital* did not appear until 1894, and *Theories of Surplus Value* came out in installments, edited by Karl Kautsky, during 1905–10. Since Marx

had published little on economics after 1870, there was work to do to
update his theory to new conditions at the start of the twentieth century.
Two world wars, Stalin's terror in Russia, and the rise of fascism in Germany and Italy meant that original work on the history of economics
remained a low priority for Marxists. It was not until the second half of
the twentieth century that any substantial body of Marxist work in the
field emerged.

By then, eighty years after Marx's main economic writings, there was
an obvious problem: what was to be done about the history of economics
after Marx? With a few exceptions, Marxists have shirked this challenge.
There has been much Marxist criticism and discussion of "neoclassical"
economics but relatively little serious historical work by Marxists on developments after about 1830, apart from work on Marx himself and on
a few later Marxist or radical writers.[5] For Marxists, the history of economics still mostly consists of Smith, Ricardo, and Marx, plus a few
selected earlier figures such as Petty and the physiocrats (not coinciden-
tally, Marx's favorites).

I shall take Ronald Meek (1917–63) as my main example, because he
was among the first of the new generation of Marxist historians of economics, and because he was, by any standards, an outstanding scholar.
The Marxist tradition should be judged by its best representatives. Meek
made no secret of his aims. In writing his *Studies in the Labour Theory of Value* ([1956] 1973, 7) he wanted to convince others (as he had
failed to convince Joan Robinson in a long correspondence) that the labor theory of value was "good sense and good science" and "to persuade
sincere but sceptical non-Marxist economists that the intellectual quality
of the labour theory of value, and indeed of Marx's economic teaching as
a whole, had been seriously underestimated." The "genetic" (historical)
approach was a means to this end. His political position at the time can
be judged from a statement toward the end of the book: "I do not think
that in the long term it will be seriously disputed that Stalin's position
in history, both as political leader and as Marxist theoretician, is a very
great one" (284).

I shall concentrate, as I did for Marx, on Meek's treatment of Smith,
and in particular on the chapter on Smith in his *Studies in the Labour
Theory of Value*, a work that exemplifies both the strengths and the
peculiarities of his approach. Meek's treatment of Smith is cautious,

5. Howard and King 1989–92 is a splendid work but fits into the latter category.

thorough (on what it covers), and firmly based on the texts. One could always quibble about particular points of interpretation, but it would be rather pointless to do so. By the standards of basic scholarship and accuracy it is a fine piece of work. At the same time, Meek imposed Marx's agenda (or rather, his own reading of Marx's agenda) on Smith, in the sense that the focus is on Smith's treatment of the particular set of topics that Marx also stressed, while other parts of Smith's work are ignored. It is also clear throughout that Marx is taken as a benchmark. Where Smith can be said to have anticipated some conclusion of Marx he is patted on the head, and where he failed to take the line that Marx would later certify as correct his failure (as Meek sees it) has to be explained.

Meek's strategy in dealing with Smith was essentially to argue that he did not *reject* the labor theory of value, but rather (just) failed to reach it, mainly because of the baneful effect of his mistaken use of the labor-commanded measure of value. Smith (and Marx) knew that in a developed market system, prices are not proportional to embodied labor. What Meek had to maintain was that it was better to follow Marx in defining *value* as labor embodied and then "transforming" values into "prices of production" (Smith's natural prices) than to adopt Smith's approach, in which prices are derived directly from necessary input costs. Meek simply assumed that Marx is known to be right. Thus, that Smith asked whether prices are proportional to labor embodied, answered no, and "went straight on to enquire into the determinants of the 'natural' levels of wages, profits and rent without suspecting that he was thereby giving up the search for a value-principle which he had so brilliantly begun, illustrates that naïvety which in Marx's opinion constituted the 'great charm' of the *Wealth of Nations*" (Meek [1956] 1973, 81).[6] "The wonder is not that Smith failed to formulate the value problem in the same way as Marx, but that he managed to proceed as far as he did in the direction of Marx's formulation" (80). One could hardly ask for a clearer example of the way Meek took Marx as his benchmark.

Meek's discussion is shaped throughout by his Marxist agenda. Thus, he calls Smith's four-stages theory of history "materialist," adding that "in its formulation . . . by Smith, as well as its development by Marx . . . the labour theory of value was intimately associated with a materialist conception of history" (53). This is one of many statements that can

6. It is worth noting here that Meek retreated a little in the introduction to the second edition (xxix, written after the publication of Sraffa 1960; see the next section).

only appear as a rather fanciful non sequitur to anyone who does not start from a Marxist worldview. The four-stages theory is very different from Marx's historical materialism and is not at all closely associated with Smith's value theory, which was not in any real sense a labor theory of value anyway.

Meek makes much of Smith's emphasis on the division of labor, and hence on the exchange of products of different workers, translating this obvious truism into a claim that Smith saw value as "an attribute which was conferred on a commodity by virtue of the fact that it was a product of social labour" (62). Meek proceeds to argue that labor is therefore not only the "source" but the "substance" of value, before admitting that "Smith did not normally look at the matter quite this way" (63). The *normally* and *quite* in that sentence clearly function to imply that he might have done, and came close to doing so.

At the least, Meek argues, Smith had a cost-based theory of value that "has very little in common with those modern theories which attack the problem primarily from the side of demand" (77). The claim that classical theories are somehow different from demand and supply theories has been discussed earlier. On this particular instance of it, it is worth commenting that modern theories do not prioritize demand over supply or cost (remember Marshall's scissor blades) and that Smith did not ignore demand. There is, for example, a long and detailed discussion of the way increasing demand in a growing economy affects the relative prices of different agricultural products (Smith [1776] 1976, 234–46; see also Brewer 1995).

The approach adopted by Meek and other Marxist writers, in which the questions to be considered are defined by Marx while Marx's conclusions are taken as the benchmark against which his predecessors are judged, makes it almost inevitable that Marx will emerge, as he saw himself, as the culmination of the development of classical economics. If Marx's predecessors agreed with him on any point, then the agreement can be used to confirm his place in the classical pantheon, while disagreement shows that Marx was needed to put things right. Any line of thinking that points in a different direction (and there are many) is silently ruled out of consideration. The development of mainstream economics since Marx's time is marginalized and treated as an unfortunate mistake.

Sraffa and the Surplus Approach

The publication of Sraffa's *Production of Commodities by Means of Commodities* in 1960 led to a substantial shift in the way the history of classical economics was presented, both by avowed Marxists and by others. This in itself says something about the way history is done, since a strictly historical approach, placing past work in the context of its own time, could hardly be affected by the publication of a purely theoretical work containing no new historical information, more than a century after the period under consideration.[7]

The central element of *Production of Commodities by Means of Commodities* is a set of equations in which prices are such that the wage and the rate of profit are equalized across all industries. The physical coefficients of production are taken as given. As is well known, this set of equations is not enough to determine prices without the addition of one further relation describing the distribution between wages and profits, which could be a given profit rate (a possibility that Sraffa mentioned in passing) or a fixed real wage. Most (though not all) of Sraffa's followers have adopted the latter strategy. Sraffa (1960, v) himself said little about the motivation or use of this construct, beyond remarking that it was a return to the "standpoint . . . of the old classical economists from Adam Smith to Ricardo," but his colleagues and followers in Cambridge and elsewhere soon filled the gap. Sraffa's followers are now often called "neo-Ricardians," although their position has little in common with that of the historical Ricardo.

Although Sraffa mentioned only the classical economists "from Smith to Ricardo" in his introduction, there is little doubt that his thinking was deeply shaped by Marx. He said so himself: "Sraffa told us that he would not have been able to write *Production of Commodities by Means of Commodities* if Marx had not written *Capital* . . . the work of Marx strongly influenced him" (Dostaler 1982, 103; translation in Hollander 1998). Martin Bronfenbrenner (1989) and Pier Luigi Porta (1986a, 1986b; see also Dostaler 1986) have detected a Marxian influence on other grounds. Porta (1986b, 484) says that Sraffa disguised Marx "in Ricardian garb."[8] Samuel Hollander's (1998, 2000) conclusion

7. Sraffa's introduction to his edition of Ricardo and the edition itself are, of course, a different matter.

8. Porta and Dostaler differ over the relation between Marx and Ricardo but not, it seems, over the relation between Marx and Sraffa.

seems to me to get it about right: Sraffa's version of Ricardo does have a basis in the historical Ricardo, but in exactly that (narrow) subset of his writings that Marx focused on and in the set of problems relating to the determination of prices and profits that Ricardo and Marx shared.

What is the relevance of this to Marxism and to the history of economics? By the later twentieth century, the labor theory of value had become an embarrassing encumbrance. It was clear that Marx's solution to the transformation problem (the relation between prices and labor values) was inadequate and that the best way to proceed with converting labor values into equilibrium prices (Smith's natural prices, Marx's prices of production) was to throw away labor values and start from scratch, as Paul Samuelson had rather cruelly suggested. It is possible that Marx realized the weakness of his transformation algorithm and held back the completion of volume 3 of *Capital* for that reason.

Sraffa's price equations offered a possible way out. Meek, for one, seems to have seen it that way. In the introduction to the second edition of his *Studies in the Labour Theory of Value* ([1956] 1973), he reported that he had previously thought, like Marx, that Marxist theory required one to start with a theory of value and then derive a theory of distribution, so that the determination of values is prior to, and independent of, distribution. After Sraffa, he no longer thought that this was correct. Some "prior concrete magnitude" is needed, but this could be conceived in physical terms, as in Sraffa, "and it is possible to erect on this basis a theoretical system, not *essentially* different from Marx's, in which prices and incomes are mutually and simultaneously determined" (xxix). If Sraffa's theory is not essentially different from Marx, it can serve as a more rigorous replacement.

How can this help with the history of economics? There is clearly a sense in which it makes no difference at all. No one, I think, suggests that Marx, Ricardo, or Smith wrote down or even mentally formulated Sraffa's equations; so, if we seek to understand what past writers actually thought, Sraffa's work is irrelevant.[9] But the Marxist tradition does not work like that. Marxists start from Marx's theory, assessing Marx's predecessors in his terms, not theirs. What Sraffa did was to liberate Marxists, ex-Marxists, and others from the obligation to look for precursors

9. Some early-twentieth-century Marxists formulated the problem in essentially the same way as Sraffa. My point here is that the classics did not.

of Marx's labor theory of value, and to allow them to see the classics as precursors of Sraffa instead.

The key to this reading of the classics is the concept of surplus, that is, of output net of replacement of inputs and of some "necessary" wage for the workforce. This corresponds to Marx's "surplus-value" and to his corresponding concept of a (physical) "surplus-product." It was developed by various Marxist writers independently of Sraffa, notably by P. Baran (1957). Mark Blaug (1999) divides the surplus approach to the classics into a "soft" version, exemplified by Walsh and Gram 1980, which emphasizes the role of surplus as a source of accumulation, and a "hard" (Sraffian) version, which aims to quantify the story and to derive prices and income distribution from it. Both descend from Marx, but the hard version is closer to his obsessive concern with value and distribution.

Blaug argues cogently that the Sraffian approach could be regarded as a rational reconstruction of the classics but that it is grossly inadequate as a historical reconstruction. His arguments need not be repeated in detail here. My main concern is to ask how far the Sraffian approach can be seen as a continuation of the Marxist tradition. I should stress that what is under discussion is a particular tradition in the interpretation of the history of economics, not the motivation or political opinions of those who adopt it. There is no suggestion that Sraffians necessarily share Marx's views in other respects or consider themselves to be Marxists.

In the surplus approach, as outlined (for example) by Garegnani 1987 and by Kurz and Salvadori 1998, classical (and Marxian) economics is defined by the presence of a "core," which takes as given (1) the real wage, (2) the output of commodities, and (3) the technical conditions of production. Given these data, prices and profits could be determined using Sraffa-style equations. The classics, it is implied, posed Sraffa's problem (or a problem that could be solved using Sraffa's methods) even if they were unable to solve it satisfactorily.

Is the "core" identified above present in the works of Smith, Ricardo, and Marx? For Marx the answer is yes, at least up to a point. Items (1)–(3) provide the data required to derive labor values, the value of labor power, the rate of surplus value, and total surplus value. Ricardo, too, used data very like this in key chapters of the *Principles*, although elsewhere in the book he relaxed the assumption of a given subsistence wage and replaced it with Smith's more sophisticated view. Ricardo's wage theory is the focus of much debate between those who think a subsistence wage is an essential component of his theory and the followers of the "new view," who do not. It would not be productive to rehearse the arguments here. Smith clearly did not hold a simple subsistence theory of wages, and his above-subsistence wage cannot reasonably be seen as determined prior to the determination of surplus and of profits. Thus, for example, his explanation of the combination of high profits and high wages in new colonies clearly makes them joint results of land abundance. In all cases, however, the claim that the composition of output (item 2) is determined prior to the determination of income shares is clearly unreasonable. If constant returns could be assumed this might not matter, since (1) and (3) would be enough, but nonconstant returns in agriculture are essential to Ricardo, at least. The "core," then, represents (one part of) Marx quite well, Ricardo less well, and Smith rather poorly.

The word *core* cannot be regarded as neutral. It clearly implies that the core identifies the most essential or important elements in Smith, Ricardo, and Marx. If (a) importance is judged by relevance today, and (b) Sraffian theories are seen as current best practice, then one could agree. Heinz Kurz and Neri Salvadori (1998, xiii), for example, seem to take this view, since their "interest in the classical [read: Sraffian] approach is . . . not purely historical; we rather consider it as containing the key to a better understanding of a wide range of economic phenomena." Historians, however, should not accept (a), while the majority of practicing economists would reject (b).

From a historical point of view, does the "core" identified by the surplus approach properly represent the central concerns of Smith, Ricardo, or Marx as they or their contemporary readers saw them? For Marx the answer is a qualified yes. His real concerns, of course, were with the history of human society and the future overthrow of capitalism, but he saw the theories of value and surplus value as central to his contribution to economics. For Ricardo, the answer is less clear. He famously asserted that distribution was the "principal problem in Political Economy" ([1817] 1951, 5), but he may have meant that it was the main unresolved problem, not the most important in itself; and his main concern was not with the wage/nonwage division (the focus of Marx and of the surplus theorists) but with the division between rent and profit. Smith's avowed purpose was to explain the "wealth of nations," that is, the level of output, together with the relative success of developed commercial societies in raising the general wage level. His main aim was to explain things that the surplus approach treats as given. Other classical and pre-classical writers, from Petty to John Stuart Mill, are equally diminished by the imposition of an anachronistic Sraffian framework.

Conclusion

Marx was not very interested in what Smith or Ricardo intended to say or with their reasons for saying it. He was primarily concerned to develop his own theory, to place it in the most favorable light possible, and to provide it with a respectable pedigree. His followers have continued in the same vein. The surplus approach, I have argued, derives from Marx and presents essentially the same view of the history of economics, with Sraffa pricing replacing the labor theory of value. It is a mid-twentieth-century construction, of interest primarily as an element in the history of twentieth-century debates. It denies the real richness of the classical tradition by imposing an agenda that has little connection with the concerns of the classics themselves.

References

Baran, P. 1957. *The Political Economy of Growth*. New York: Monthly Review Press.
Blaug, M. 1999. Misunderstanding Classical Economics: The Sraffian Interpretation of the Surplus Approach. *HOPE* 31:213–36.
Brewer, A. 1995. Rent and Profit in the *Wealth of Nations*. *Scottish Journal of Political Economy* 42:183–200.
Bronfenbrenner, M. 1989. A Rehabilitation of Classical Economics. *Aoyama University Journal of International Political Economy* 13:35–41. Cited in Hollander 1998.
Clarke, P. 1998. *The Keynesian Revolution and Its Economic Consequences*. Cheltenham: Edward Elgar.
Dostaler, G. 1982. Marx et Sraffa. *L'actualité économique* 1–2:95–114.
———. 1986. From Marx to Sraffa: Comments on an Article by P. L. Porta. *HOPE* 18:463–69.
Engels, F. [1844] 1961. *Outlines of a Critique of Political Economy*. In Marx 1961.
Garegnani, P. 1987. Surplus Approach to Value and Distribution. In volume 4 of *The New Palgrave: A Dictionary of Economics*, edited by J. Eatwell, M. Milgate, and P. Newman. London: Macmillan.
Hollander, S. 1998. Sraffa in Historiographical Perspective: A Provisional Statement. *European Journal of the History of Economic Thought* 5:430–36.
———. 2000. Sraffa and the Interpretation of Ricardo: The Marxian Dimension. *HOPE* 32:187–232.

Howard, M., and J. King. 1989–92. *A History of Marxian Economics*. 2 vols. Hound-mills: Macmillan.

Kurz, H., and N. Salvadori. 1998. Introduction and Classical Political Economy. In *The Elgar Companion to Classical Economics*, edited by H. Kurz and N. Salvadori. Cheltenham: Edward Elgar.

Marx, K. [1867] 1961. *Capital*. Vol 1. English translation by S. Moore and E. Aveling. Moscow: Foreign Languages Publishing House.

———. 1961. *Economic and Philosophic Manuscripts of 1844*. Translated by M. Milligan. Moscow: Foreign Languages Publishing House.

———. 1963–71. *Theories of Surplus Value*. English translation by E. Burns, J. Cohen, and S. Rayazanskaya. 3 vols. London: Lawrence and Wishart; Moscow: Progress Publishers.

———. 1970. *Critique of Hegel's Philosophy of Right*. English translation by A. Jolin and J. O'Malley. London: Cambridge University Press.

Meek, R. [1956] 1973. *Studies in the Labour Theory of Value*. 2d ed. London: Lawrence and Wishart.

Porta, P. 1986a. Understanding the Significance of Piero Sraffa's Standard Commodity: A Note on the Marxian Notion of Surplus. *HOPE* 18:442–54.

———. 1986b. Understanding the Significance of Piero Sraffa's Standard Commodity: A Rejoinder. *HOPE* 18:479–84.

Ricardo, D. [1817] 1951. *On the Principles of Political Economy and Taxation*. Edited by P. Sraffa. Cambridge: Cambridge University Press.

Smith, A. [1776] 1976. *An Inquiry into the Nature and Causes of the Wealth of Nations*. Edited by A. H. Campbell, A. S. Skinner, and W. B. Todd. Oxford: Clarendon Press.

Sraffa, P. 1960. *Production of Commodities by Means of Commodities: Prelude to a Critique of Economic Theory*. Cambridge: Cambridge University Press.

Steedman, I. 1982. Marx on Ricardo. In *Classical and Marxist Political Economy*, edited by I. Bradley and M. Howard. London: Macmillan.

Walsh, V., and H. Gram. 1980. *Classical and Neoclassical Theories of General Equilibrium*. Oxford: Oxford University Press.

Afterword
A Pall along the Watchtower: On Leaving the *HOPE* Conference

Philip Mirowski

> All things that live long are gradually so saturated with reason that their
> origin in unreason becomes improbable. . . .
> Does the good historian not, at bottom, *contradict*?
> —Friedrich Nietzsche, *Daybreak*

Precisely because the experience of the 2001 *HOPE* conference was a
bit unnerving, I want to start out with a vote of thanks to Roy Weintraub and Craufurd Goodwin for coming up with the idea. Rarely have
we enjoyed the opportunity to talk seriously and openly about the future prospects and pitfalls of our chosen field. So occasions such as this,
where we collectively stare our predicament squarely in the face, are exceedingly scarce. It is even more rare to be confronted by the possibility
that the history of economics as a disciplinary identity is on its last legs.

Now, the one capacity that you might suspect is congenitally rare in
a collocation of historians is a well-developed ability to engage in fu-
turology. Economists as a group have never enjoyed high lifetime completion averages in the realm of prediction; and I suspect people who
have specialized in history are more inclined than most to avoid what
can only be considered a high-risk, low-return activity like prognosti-
cation. True to form, few attendees at this conference engaged in any
concerted reading of the tea leaves; more to the point, they tended to
avert their gaze when it threatened to precipitate. Rather, the overriding
impression I got from the papers and the conference was of a wistful sad-
ness and a vague premonition of disaster; maybe nothing so portentous

as shifting deck chairs on the *Titanic*, but perhaps something more like a fire sale before the Wal-Mart opens up down the block. Of course, for the younger participants at the conference, with more to fear and less commitment to the cause, glancing nervously in the direction of the lifeboats was an understandable reaction.

It never hurts to entertain the idea that the inexorable tide of history may not be raising all boats; but what I might have expected from self-identified historians located primarily in economics departments (although that is changing, too) would have been adoption of a more analytical approach to the predicament of the history of economic thought (HET), perhaps accompanied by a greater attempt to situate the prognosis in a larger context, be it that of the economics profession, or the larger university setting, or perhaps even larger cultural attitudes toward forms of legitimate research at the turn of the millennium. We did get some of that, especially from our European counterparts—and the contrasting health of the European and Japanese professions was one of the surprises of the conference—but I can't shake the feeling we did not really yet manage to get down to brass tacks. It doesn't help matters to suggest that the field has "always" been held in contempt (Blaug 2001); that's a prescription for paralysis and, anyway, is historically inaccurate, as I argue below.

As if it weren't enough to own up to the snubs and slights that are a daily penance for the historian of economics, I think we should also face up to the fact that there are in place some imposing structural obstacles in North America to the prospect of a flourishing program of research into the history of economics in the next millennium. Margaret Schabas (this volume) alludes to the first obstacle in her essay when she complains that the field is saddled with the designation *history of economic thought*. Most of us at some point in our career have had to endure some philistine calling what we do "economic history," but I doubt that the situation is ameliorated by opting for the opposite extreme of limiting the ambit of research to some disembodied "thought" thinking itself. Taking "thought" as our primary area of expertise is perhaps our first major stumbling block. The implied distinction between "thought" and everything else really only serves to reify and validate a sharp separation between "pure" and "applied" economics, a separation that only became firmly established in the economics profession in the 1930s to 1940s. Yet I have been vexed to discover at this late date how very little work has been done on the history of various practices of economic empiricism. (The recent rash of work on the history of econometrics, with few exceptions, has been the history of econometric *theory*.) Worse, this locution presupposes the existence of some Platonic form called "economic thought," nicely partitioned off from "sociological thought" or "culinary thought" or "religious thought" or "biological thought." Hence the very concept of an identity as a "historian of thought" has had real consequences in terms of the types of work previously attempted and the forms in which it is promulgated. As HET is now pushed out of economics departments, the very ontology of the subject matter suddenly grows more wobbly.

But our problems are not simply philosophical. Among historians in general, for instance, I think it is fair to say that practitioners of HET are frequently regarded as not quite cutting the mustard as *historians*. Most professional intellectual historians would frown upon someone reading a handful of superseded texts, ignoring the various citation clues deposited by the author, eschewing archival or contextual research, and then proceeding to write an essay expounding on the "true" meaning of the work as though it were transparently accessible to anyone who could read beyond a certain rudimentary level.[1] In some quarters, this is not considered history at all, but rote schoolroom explication de texte. Thus I think it is significant that while we had participants at this conference located in various departments outside of economics, we have not heard from a single one who resides in a history department. Opting to resemble orthodox economists far more than they seek to imitate historians in this fashion, with their economic "thought" traversing an abstract trajectory in a vacuum, the proponents of HET have alienated one of their natural core constituencies among the historians, without particularly gaining the respect or gratitude of economists.

This has some bearing on Craufurd Goodwin's claim that there is or was something like "HET for all the disciplines." Perhaps we move in different circles, but I don't detect that historians even acknowledge the existence of such a category. Look, for instance, at Novick 1988,

---

1. Perhaps I will be allowed one supporting quotation: "We historians, as a result of our training and inclinations, are professionally sensitized to the historicity of intellectual life: the extent to which the emergence of ideas and their reception are decisively shaped by surrounding cultural assumptions, social setting, and other elements of the total social context" (Novick 1988, 6). Economists, by contrast, are taught *not* to do this by their training. See, for instance, Myerson 1999.

which is an attempt to survey the twentieth-century American water-front, with a stress on intellectual history. There is no mention of Joseph Schumpeter, or Joseph Dorfman, or Mark Blaug, or anyone else recognizable as an HET author (although there is a passage on Robert Fogel and Stanley Engerman). Or contemplate how in their published work Dorothy Ross or Mary Poovey or Yuval Yonay or Emma Rothschild seem to go out of their way to avoid acknowledging the writings of our serried ranks. Or consult the *Journal of the History of Ideas* or *Journal of the History of the Behavioral Sciences* or *History of the Human Sciences* to savor the silence. The suggestion is that the supposed "classics" of HET may have been profoundly out of sync with historiographic trends for perhaps a century now, largely due to subordination to the economics discipline, and that the attempt to draw upon our fund of interdisciplinary credentials for respect or legitimacy in our hour of need is essentially bankrupt.

For a while, caught between the disdain of the historians and the contempt of their economist colleagues, historians of economics sought succor from their colleagues in the philosophy of science. That, for a while, seemed a more promising alliance. People who wandered into the history of economics probably did so out of a curiosity about the intellectual background, epistemic status, and ontological quiddity of economics, and in the 1960s it may have appeared that their concerns were being addressed by a working alliance being forged between the history and philosophy of science, which held out the enticing prospect of serious cross-fertilization. The third daunting obstacle to the future success of the history of economics is that these hopes have been sorely dashed in the interim (Hands 2001), with disenchantment with the Kuhnian version of the alliance having turned especially bitter of late (Mirowski 2001). The erstwhile Science Wars are merely symptomatic of this recent turn in academic culture.

But these are all eminently conceptual obstacles to a bright future for HET; I should be violating my own precepts if I neglected to point out that the material context of our activities also throws up a fourth obstacle to the continued flourishing of HET. This problem of the place of HET in the universities, and especially in the curriculum, has been raised by a number of papers at the conference; but parsed most explicitly by Brad Bateman and Roger Backhouse. People may make various claims for the salutary virtues of the study of history, but these are unavailing if we ignore the fact that the American and European university education is undergoing wrenching transformation as we speak. The way in which disciplines are organized, and the ways in which research is funded and conducted, and the relative status of pedagogy are being radically restructured from the older "Cold War" regime into the newer situation of competitive, globalized privatization (Mirowski and Sent 2002). Whatever pedagogical functions one may have believed a course in HET could have served in the older framework, historians of economics have yet to even begin to forge an accommodation with the newer regime. In some ways, this may be the most daunting obstacle facing historians in the new millennium. I shall therefore devote the rest of the essay to asking: Who might want the history of economics in the future?

History of Economics in the Modern Academic Landscape

How Disciplines Have Shed Their Histories

It would seem imperative to get clear on the changing role of self-histories in the evolving state of the sciences and the academic professions in general to begin to address the question at hand. Historians of science have pointed the way with careful consideration of their uneasy relationships with the fields they study (Reingold 1991; Thackray 1980; Dennis 1997). In short, and restricting our summary temporarily to the American context, the sciences only began to professionalize around the turn of the last century, and courses in the history of the individual disciplines (history of physics in physics; chemistry in chemistry departments; and so forth) were taught by practitioners within those disciplines with an amateur interest in intellectual history. These were offered explicitly to meet a demand to "humanize" what was often disparaged as a narrowly technocratic and vocational education by their opponents, the partisans of a "liberal education." In the first two decades of the century, history of science rested uneasily in the curriculum, often depending on the largesse of the odd amateur or bibliophile; it had "great difficulty in acquiring the cognitive and professional identities which mark an academic discipline" (Thackray 1980, 461). The career of George Sarton, the founder of the journal *Isis*, illustrates not the success of the discipline, but rather its shaky status within higher education and its lack of support from within the history profession.

This began to change around the 1930s, with historians recruited to take sides in the debate over whether science could be subject to planning, and entered a new and more stable academic phase in the 1940s. Most historians now trace the professionalization of the history of science, marked by its separation from "practitioner's history" and amateur incursions, to Harvard president James Conant's imposition of the General Education requirements at that university (Dennis 1997; Fuller 2000; Hershberg 1993). The issue that exercised Conant was the need to reconcile the apocalyptic products and authoritarian processes of "Big Science" with the political commitment to the superiority of democratic and egalitarian political structures in the Cold War. Conant and his lieutenant in "Nat. Sci. 4," Thomas Kuhn (that's right—the very same), started out from the premise that big science, like the atomic bomb, was here to stay; somehow ordinary citizens had to be brought to acquiesce in the wisdom of its existence even though they would never be able (due to incapacity or Cold War secrecy) to really understand how it worked. The pedagogical solution was to develop one image of science for the layperson and another, distinctly separate pedagogy for the tyro scientist. The layperson was to be cajoled into accepting an oversocialized conception of scientists so that they might believe (however wrongly) that dissension and disagreement were absent from legitimate science, and science, therefore, exhibited a self-organizing structure and unified valuation schema no matter what the cultural set-up. Further, it became imperative to reify a strong pure/applied distinction in order to deny that scientists bore any role or responsibility for the uses to which their discoveries were put—no more of Oppenheimer's hand-wringing about "discovering sin." Henceforward, grateful Harvard products would be satisfied that their tax dollars were being spent for who-knows-what arcane classified research, which might eventually result in such boons to mankind as Teflon and the Internet. While the Harvard general education course sought to inculcate the idea that all scientists deployed essentially the same "strategy and tactics" (Conant's terminology) from the seventeenth century to the present (the famous unique "scientific method"), with the newly professionalized historian of science running the drills, the alternative pedagogy for the budding tyro scientist would dispense with any history altogether.

I want to stress that Conant (and Kuhn) really did believe the doctrines they were promulgating and were not just cynically concocting convenient Cold War ideology. If science really was fully self-organizing and autonomous from the uses to which it was put, then there really was no need for the "humanizing" balm of history for apprentice scientists: they should just work the problem sets, fill in the lab books, and soak up the ineffable "tacit knowledge" of the scientific profession from their mentors. (Does this sound familiar? See Klamer and Colander 1990.) It is not frequently noticed that the Cold War reorganization of the university thus sought to *strengthen* boundaries between disciplines. Hence, in this program, history of science should be rescued from those prewar amateur practitioners (Kuhn never really liked "scientist's history" anyway) and plopped down in a new profession whose mandate was to acquaint nonscientists with the true nature of generic science and to convince them that it was best for a democratic polity to just fund scientists to the hilt but otherwise leave them alone. (The relationship of this description to the actual situation on the ground of military funding and organization of many sciences is best left for another time.) Practicing scientists may, as a consequence, end up with a warped view of what *really* happened in history—this was the "wicked" or Orwellian side of Kuhn's *Structure of Scientific Revolutions*—but in the final analysis, it didn't really matter. (This has some bearing on the opinion often expressed at the conference that famous economists would "appreciate" the labors of historians of economics, if only *historians* were a bit more subservient.)

So Kuhn really did turn out to be one of the most important figures in the postwar history of science, although not in the way most people originally imagined. By the 1960s, most natural sciences had shed their self-historians (modulo the odd Grand Old Man pontificating on the historical significance of his own work), gladly devolving that function to a newly professionalized history community. This was facilitated by all sorts of funding arrangements: the NSF developing separate programs in history of science and science education, foundation support, agencies such as the Smithsonian and NASA hiring their own historians, the Alfred Sloan Foundation commissioning biographies of Nobelists, and so forth. What is germane to the present issue is that the social sciences slowly imitated this model with a pronounced lag.

Most interwar social sciences treated their self-histories not as humanizing supplements to technical education, but rather as integral parts of their "theory" sequences. Graduate students in political theory read Plato, Machiavelli, and John Locke; graduate students in sociology read Émile Durkheim, Herbert Spencer, and Marx; graduate students in anthropology read Marx and James Frazer and Franz Boas and Bronislaw

Malinowski. One of the weaknesses of our own profession is that we do not adequately highlight that this was equally true in interwar economics, although Ross Emmett (1998, 144) has begun to rectify this situation with his work on the Chicago economics department. However, the ubiquitous science envy of the social sciences was another prominent feature of the postwar period, with many funding agencies and military patrons seeking to encourage what they perceived as the more "solid" scientistic tendencies within many of the social sciences. For instance, the Ford Foundation's initiative in "behavioral science" in the 1950s was an umbrella for encouraging a mélange of quantification, formalization, statistical hypothesis testing, and research focused intently on individuals as "part of an effort to dispel those notions of vagueness and reformism which so many laymen, including members of Congress, associated with social science" (Lyons 1969, 279). In effect, the patrons of social science sought to intensify a trend for the social sciences to imitate the natural sciences, both in research methods and in pedagogy. One seemingly minor aspect of this Cold War reengineering project was a notable movement in the newfangled "behavioral sciences" to jettison the older historical component of the graduate theory training sequence.[2] There were no such things as "hallowed classics" in the Conant-inspired construction of scientific pedagogy; only instrumentalist techniques (usually conflated with mathematics *tout court*): students don't need to *think* so much as subordinate themselves to their mentors and then go forth and *do* science. This trend has proceeded to a greater or lesser degree in all the American social sciences down to the present day.

But the situation for the historians of social science did not turn out to be completely symmetrical with that of historians of the natural sciences. The latter were professionalized with a particular pedagogical function in view, albeit one aimed not so much at scientists but rather at the general populace. In some cases, although not all, they even merited a separate department within the university, a sure sign of having ascended to postwar legitimacy. When economics and the other social sciences jettisoned their history components, there existed no commensurate alternative role for them to occupy, and therefore no structural

2. As an example, the disdain of Cowles members Jacob Marschak and Tjalling Koopmans for those attempting to include a doctrinal historical component to research is covered in Mirowski 2002 (chap. 5). Perhaps some future historian will more directly explore how history was banished from individual major economics departments. When that happens, some of the more "liberal" reputations of famous twentieth-century economists will have to be revised.

encouragement for a commensurate process of professionalization. This goes some distance in explaining the relative distance still maintained between the historians of science and historians of economics, as well as the impressions of the field of HET being stranded between history and economics. It also provides a contrasting diagnosis of the possibility of an alliance of history of economics with the history of science to that offered by Margaret Schabas in this volume.

Why Be a Historian?

I should like to briefly address the challenge that Roy Weintraub threw out at the conference, namely, to entertain the idea that our economist colleagues are right: specifically, that we do not "belong" in an American economics department. I shall respond to it by turning to a suggestive article written by a historian of science.

Paul Forman (1991) has a nice article where he suggests that historians of science must have different ideals and standards than the scientists they write about. He writes that science (and, I would add, mathematics and economics) holds out to its members the prospect of personal transcendence: they submit to the moral authority and autonomy of their professional identity, and in return, they get to see their lives as one part of a quest or world-historical process: the search for their bequeathed notion of truth, or perhaps the improvement of the welfare of mankind. "The critical historian—understanding that scientific knowledge is socially constructed, partly within and partly outside the scientific discipline—must instead focus either on social problems of science or on science as a social problem. . . . Both are characterized by an implicit repudiation of transcendence" (83). The best they can aspire to is independence from the value system of the objects of their study.

This has direct consequences for what appears to be the dominant model of doctoral theses that still aspire to some historical content, namely, three essays, of which two contain "good orthodox economics," while perhaps a third comprises a historical essay. If Forman is correct, then doesn't this hybrid attempt to help the student get a job actually stifle the intellectual development of the historian of economics?

Liberal Education, Cold War Education, and Privatized Distance Education

Brad Bateman has stood out as someone who has been willing not only to publicly defend the place of HET in the pedagogy of undergraduates, but also to question the "research university ideal" that has come to dominate graduate economics training. Further, he has also explored the coincidence of the decline of moral education with the rise to dominance of neoclassical economics in the American context (Bateman 1998). I am sympathetic to all these themes but would like to suggest that the problem is not specific to economics; rather, it is a function of the two great waves of innovation in American higher education: one dating from just after World War II, and the other really only getting underway in the 1990s.

The slow eclipse of liberal education is indeed one of the main determinants of the fortune of the history of economics in America. Liberal or moral education was the premier model of pedagogy in America up through the first third of the twentieth century. Various educational reformers like James Conant and Karl Compton of MIT, as well as the Ford and Rockefeller Foundations, wanted to thoroughly revamp education in the direction of meritocracy, technical expertise, and the closer integration of teaching and research roles through stratification of graduate and undergraduate curricula. Many innovations growing out of wartime, like overhead charges on research grants, research assistantships, the SATs (another Conant brainchild), and much else, transformed the way universities were run, or at least universities that wanted to hop aboard the government gravy train. As mentioned before, the effect of these Cold War innovations was to raise the barriers between disciplines and further encourage specialization. These institutions became vast assembly lines, offering students an impressive but ill-organized smorgasbord of "credit hours" often taught by graduate students, and with "requirements" largely structured around instrumental technique taught to large sections. By definition, those colleges and universities that hewed to the liberal education ideal, the Grinnells and Bowdoins and Oberlins and Williamses of the world, in effect opted out of the rankings race and could not expand at the rate of the newer "megaversities." (No wonder your average student at a "top 5" graduate program looks upon a job in a liberal arts college with disdain!) It was outlandishly costly to "sit on a log with Adam Smith," and in any event, it got in the way of the real output of the modern university, which was research. In the Cold War model, HET was just another elective, like public finance or the novels of Jane Austen. This model did not spread immediately to Europe but now is slowly becoming more and more the norm.

Yet I might suggest it would be misguided to pine after the older liberal model, because in turn the Cold War model has been concertedly dismantled in the more recent past. The Cold War model depended heavily on regular and substantial government subsidies and subventions, which started to melt away with the cessation of the Cold War. Instead, politicians began to promote universities as growth poles in economic development, and incentives too numerous to enumerate were put in place to encourage privatization, first of research and now of the education process itself. Parenthetically, the Internet innovations surveyed by Ross Emmett in this volume are a big part of this incipient model of pedagogy. Suppose someone does eventually manage to automate a course in the history of economics, complete with streaming videos and flashy graphics and full-text searchable databases of "the classics," as indeed many forward-looking educational institutions are presently encouraging their faculty to do.[3] It will then rapidly become de rigueur to (1) quickly nail it down as intellectual property, (2) license the software out to other universities, and (3) hire gypsy unfaculty to "teach" the course for three grand a pop. I leave it to the imagination of my audience what effect this will have on the future demand for the history of economics.

I fear that all three models will continue to coexist in the near future: a few liberal arts colleges will survive as niche markets for children of the rich, a few big research universities will find their way to live off private research contracts and wealthy alumni, but the vast majority of students will enjoy privatized virtual universities via (terrible euphemism) "distance education." Perhaps the role of HET in the liberal education model could not then be the really pressing issue.

Who Pays, and What Constitutes Value for Money?

Nevertheless, following up on the theme of this conference, the germane questions are who has paid for economics, and who might pay for history of economics? There is much less research by historians into this

---

3. For a glimpse of the future, visit the business school Web site of Professor Michael Rappa: digitalenterprise.org/about.html.

issue than one might hope, given that it would seem a natural inquiry for trained economists. The person with his finger on the pulse of this issue is indeed Craufurd Goodwin, both in Goodwin 1998 and in his article for this volume. In the former, he surveyed four postwar patrons: higher education, government, business, and foundations. I might slice his lineup a little differently, given, as above, that I think the structure of higher education was itself a Cold War phenomenon of government provenance; that "government" was not a monolithic player, but really should be subdivided into the military and the rest; and that the shift from foundations as purveyors of research initiatives to the military is the major theme in the postwar history of science policy in America. Nevertheless, what is really needed in the history of economics are studies of how much smaller but significant units of economics were and are funded: say, who paid for the National Bureau of Economic Research and why; the relative role of the Ford Foundation and the Air Force at RAND; the way in which the Cowles Commission was weaned off near-total dependence upon Alfred Cowles; who paid for the founding of CORE at the University of Louvain in Belgium; the role of various think tanks (Smith 1991); and so forth. Once we have a better handle on which patrons fertilized which sorts of economics, we might be better equipped to make realistic assessments of who might want to subsidize future versions of the history of economics.

For the nonce, the conference left us with some suggestions as to client groups who might still wish to devote a modicum of resources to promote HET as a component of their own agendas; but the stark truth is that no one could manage enthusiasm for the idea that the history of economics will be supported for its own sake in the foreseeable future. Indeed, as this appears, it seems likely that the popularity of the movie *A Beautiful Mind* based on Sylvia Nasar's life of John Nash (1998) will have raised this issue in even more stark terms, with journalists and infotainment content providers making a play to displace any serious academic history of the modern discipline. Perhaps the lesson we should take from this is that the discussion of the banishment of history from economics should be widened out beyond the narrow circle of attendees at the Duke conference.

References

Bateman, Bradley. 1998. Clearing the Ground: The Demise of the Social Gospel Movement. In Morgan and Rutherford 1998.

Blaug, Mark. 2001. No History of Ideas, Please, We're Economists. *Journal of Economic Perspectives* 15:145–64.

Dennis, Michael. 1997. Historiography of Science. In *Science in the Twentieth Century*, edited by J. Krige and D. Pestre. Amsterdam: Harwood.

Emmett, Ross. 1998. Entrenching Disciplinary Competence: The Role of General Education and Graduate Study in Chicago Economics. In Morgan and Rutherford 1998.

Forman, Paul. 1991. Independence, Not Transcendence, for Historians of Science. *Isis* 82:71–86.

Fuller, Steve. 2000. *Thomas Kuhn: A Philosophical History for Our Time*. Chicago: University of Chicago Press.

Goodwin, Craufurd. 1998. The Patrons of Economics in a Time of Transition. In Morgan and Rutherford 1998.

Hands, D. Wade. 2001. *Reflection without Rules*. New York: Cambridge University Press.

Hershberg, James. 1993. *James Conant*. New York: Knopf.

Klamer, Arjo, and David Colander. 1990. *The Making of an Economist*. Boulder, Colo.: Westview.

Lyons, Gene. 1969. *The Uneasy Partnership*. New York: Russell Sage.

Mirowski, Philip. 2001. What's Kuhn Got to Do with It? *History of the Human Sciences* 14:97–111.

———. 2002. *Machine Dreams: Economics Becomes a Cyborg Science*. New York: Cambridge University Press.

Mirowski, Philip, and Esther-Mirjam Sent, eds. 2002. *Science Bought and Sold*. Chicago: University of Chicago Press.

Morgan, Mary S., and Malcolm Rutherford. 1998. *From Interwar Pluralism to Postwar Neoclassicism*. Supplement to volume 30 of *HOPE*. Durham, N.C.: Duke University Press.

Myerson, Roger. 1999. Nash Equilibrium and the History of Economic Theory. *Journal of Economic Literature* 107:1067–82.

Nasar, Sylvia. 1998. *A Beautiful Mind*. New York: Simon & Schuster.

Novick, Peter. 1988. *That Noble Dream: The Objectivity Question and the American Historical Profession*. New York: Cambridge University Press.

Reingold, Nathan. 1991. *Science American Style*. New Brunswick, N.J.: Rutgers University Press.

Smith, James Allen. 1991. *The Idea Brokers*. New York: Free Press.

Thackray, Arnold. 1980. The Pre-History of an Academic Discipline: History of Science in the U.S., 1891–1941. *Minerva* 18:448–73.

Contributors

Roger E. Backhouse is professor of the history and philosophy of economics at the University of Birmingham, U.K. He has written *The Penguin History of Economics* (Penguin, 2002) and *The Ordinary Business of Life: A History of Economics from the Ancient World to the Twenty-First Century* (Princeton University Press, 2002), and he edited (with Jeff Biddle) *Toward a History of Applied Economics* (Duke University Press, 2000). He is one of the editors of the *Journal of Economic Methodology*.

William J. Barber, Andrews Professor of Economics Emeritus at Wesleyan University, served as a roving commentator at the conference. His books include *From New Era to New Deal: Herbert Hoover, the Economists, and American Economic Policy, 1921–1933* (Cambridge University Press, 1985) and *Designs within Disorder: Franklin D. Roosevelt, the Economists, and the Shaping of American Economic Policy, 1933–1945* (Cambridge University Press, 1996). He is also the general editor of *The Works of Irving Fisher* (14 vols.), published by Pickering & Chatto.

Bradley W. Bateman teaches writing and economics at Grinnell College. He is the author, most recently, of *Keynes's Uncertain Revolution* (University of Michigan Press, 1996).

Mark Blaug is visiting professor at the University of Amsterdam and Erasmus University Rotterdam. He is the author of numerous books and articles in the history and methodology of economics. He is executive editor of the *Journal of Economic Methodology*.

Peter Boettke is the deputy director of the James M. Buchanan Center for Political Economy, Department of Economics, George Mason University. He is the author of *Calculation and Coordination: Essays on Socialism and Transitional Political Economy* (Routledge, 2001), *Why Perestroika Failed: The Politics and Economics of Socialist Transformation* (Routledge, 1993), and *The Political Economy of Soviet Socialism: The Formative Years, 1918–1928* (Kluwer Academic, 1990). He is also the editor of the *Review of Austrian Economics*.

Anthony Brewer is professor of the history of economics at the University of Bristol and currently head of the department of economics. He has written extensively about Marx and Marxist economics, although his main research focus now is on eighteenth-century economics.

Derek S. Brown is a graduate student in the Department of Economics at Duke University. He began studying the history of economic thought as an undergraduate with Bradley Bateman at Grinnell College. While still searching for his niche in the history of economics, he retains a teaching and research interest in the subject, particularly in applied economics. He is presently working on an empirical dissertation in health economics.

José Luís Cardoso is professor of economics and history of economics at the Technical University of Lisbon, Portugal. He has published several articles and books on the history of Portuguese economic thought in a comparative perspective. His research interests also include economic history and the methodology of economics. He is the general editor of the series *Classics of Portuguese Economic Thought* and coeditor of the *European Journal of the History of Economic Thought*.

John Davis is professor of history and philosophy of economics at the University of Amsterdam and professor of economics at Marquette University. He is the author of *Keynes's Philosophical Development* (Cambridge University Press, 1994), *The Theory of the Individual in Economics* (Routledge, forthcoming), editor with Wade Hands and Uskali Mäki of the *Handbook of Economic Methodology*, and editor of the *Review of Social Economy*.

Ghislain Deleplace is professor of economics at the University of Paris 8, director of the economics laboratory of that university, and member of the editorial board of the review *Cahiers d'économie politique*. His main fields of interest are the history of monetary thought and the history of the international monetary system. His books include *Private Money and Public Currencies* (M. E. Sharpe, 1994; written with Marie-Thérèse Boyer-Xambeu and Lucien Gillard), *Money in Motion: The Post Keynesian and Circulation Approaches* (St. Martin Press, 1996; edited with Edward J. Nell), and the advanced textbook *Histoire de la pensée économique: Du "royaume agricole" de Quesnay au "monde à la Arrow-Debreu"* (Dunod, 1999).

Sheila Dow is professor of economics and head of the Department of Economics at the University of Stirling. She has worked previously as an economist with the Bank of England and the government of Manitoba, and has also taught in Canada. She has published extensively in the history and methodology of economic thought, money and banking, and regional finance. Her latest book is *Economic Methodology: An Inquiry* (Oxford University Press, 2002).

Ross B. Emmett is currently the John P. Tandberg Chair and Associate Professor of Economics at Augustana University College in Camrose, Alberta. His primary area of research has been the economics and social philosophy of Frank H. Knight. More recently, he has begun the Chicago Economics Oral History Project, which will eventually lead to a history of economics at the University of Chicago. He will become an associate professor at James Madison College at Michigan State University, starting in the 2003–2004 academic year.

Evelyn L. Forget is professor of economics working in the Faculty of Medicine of the University of Manitoba, Canada. Her research interests include health economics and the history of economic thought. Recent books are *The Social Economics of Jean-Baptiste Say: Markets and Virtue* (Routledge, 1999) and *A Biographical Dictionary of Women Economists* (Edward Elgar, 2000), which she edited with Robert Dimand and Mary Ann Dimand.

Ted Gayer is assistant professor of public policy at Georgetown University. From 1999–2001, he was a Robert Wood Johnson Scholar at the University of California, Berkeley. Much of his research examines environmental regulatory policy, with specific emphasis on estimating the benefits of risk reduction and the effects of risk information on risk perceptions. He has also conducted research on the regulatory discrepancy for light trucks versus cars, and the implications this has toward traffic fatality risks. His work on the history of economic thought (published in the *Journal of Economic Literature*, *HOPE*, and the *Journal of the History of Economic Thought*) has examined the communication and assessment difficulties that existed during the emergence of mathematical economics in the mid-twentieth century.

Craufurd D. W. Goodwin is James B. Duke Professor of Economics at Duke University and editor of *HOPE*. He is interested in the relationship between the history of economic thought and the history of art. A recent book by him is *Art and the Market: Roger Fry on Commerce in Art* (University of Michigan Press, 1998). Along with Neil De Marchi, Professor Goodwin edited the 1999 *HOPE* conference volume, *Economic Engagements with Art* (Duke University Press).

Aiko Ikeo is a professor at Waseda University, Tokyo. She teaches contemporary social sciences and comparative economic thought at the graduate level. Currently, she spends most of her time preparing for undergraduate courses on issues such as the philosophy of social science in the global context. She believes that economics is the most internationalized social science owing to its extensive use of mathematics. She edited *Japanese Economics and Economists since 1945* (Routledge, 2000) and *Economic Development in Twentieth Century East Asia* (Routledge, 1997), and has published a series of papers discussing Japanese economics in the international context.

Albert Jolink is associate professor of history of management and economics at Erasmus University Rotterdam and director of the Erasmus Center for History in Management and Economics. He is the author of *The Equilibrium Economics of Léon Walras* (1993) and *The Evolutionist Economics of Léon Walras* (1996) and is currently working on a book on Jan Tinbergen.

Matthias Klaes is a lecturer at the University of Keele. His research interests are the economy of knowledge, and history and methodology of economics. He is managing editor of the *Journal of Economic Methodology*. Recent publications include "*Begriffsgeschichte*: Between the Scylla of Conceptual and the Charybdis of Institutional History of Economics" (*Journal of the History of Economic Thought*, 2001) and "Psychological and Social Elements in a Theory of Custom" (*AJES*, 2002).

John Lodewijks is an associate professor in the School of Economics at the University of New South Wales, Sydney, Australia. He has been head of the Department of Economics (1994–97), editor of the *History of Economics Review* (1991–99), and Director of the Centre for South Pacific Studies (1993–99). His research interests are in the history of economics and developing economies.

Maria Cristina Marcuzzo is a full professor in the history of economic thought and presently head of the Department of Economics at the University of Rome, "La Sapienza." She has worked on classical monetary theory; her published works on that subject include *Ricardo and the Gold Standard: The Foundations of the International Monetary Order* (Routledge, 1997; written with Annalisa Rosselli), *Monetary Standards and Exchange Rates* (Routledge, 1997; edited with Lawrence H. Officer and Annalisa Rosselli), and articles in *Economica, Revue d'économie politique*, and *Cahiers d'économie politique*. She has also written on the Cambridge School of Economics (*The Economics of Joan Robinson* [Routledge, 1996; edited with Luigi L. Pasinetti and Alessandro Roncaglia]) and articles in the *Cambridge Journal of Economics*, the *Review of Political Economy*, and *HOPE*.

Stephen Meardon is a junior professional at the Research Department of the Inter-American Development Bank. His research is in the history of economic thought, geographical economics, and international trade and development. Among his recent publications are "Eclecticism, Inconsistency, and Innovation in the History of Geographical Economics," which appeared in the 2000 *HOPE* supplement *Toward* *a History of Applied Economics* (Duke University Press; edited by Roger E. Backhouse and Jeff Biddle), and "Modeling Agglomeration and Dispersion in City and Country: Gunnar Myrdal, François Perroux, and the New Economic Geography" (*American Journal of Economics and Sociology*, vol. 60, no. 1, 2001).

Steven G. Medema is Chancellor's Professor of Economics and executive director of the Center for the Study of Markets and Government at the University of Colorado at Denver. His research interests include law and economics, public economics, and the economic role of government in the history of economic thought. His recent books are *Economics and the Law: From Posner to Post Modernism* (Princeton University Press, 1997; written with Nicholas Mercuro) and a collection of Lionel Robbins's lectures (*A History of Economic Thought: The LSE Lectures* [Princeton University Press, 1998; edited with Warren J. Samuels]). Professor Medema also serves as editor of the *Journal of the History of Economic Thought.*

Philip Mirowski is Carl Koch Professor of Economics and the History and Philosophy of Science at the University of Notre Dame. He is author of *Machine Dreams: Economics Becomes a Cyborg Science* (Cambridge University Press, 2002), *The Effortless Economy of Science?* (forthcoming), and *More Heat Than Light: Economics as Social Physics, Physics as Nature's Economics* (Cambridge University Press, 1989), and the editor of *Science Bought and Sold: Essays in the Economics of Science* (with Esther-Mirjam Sent; University of Chicago Press, 2002) and *The Collected Economic Works of William Thomas Thornton* (1999). He has recently become personally acquainted with the sorts of professional hostility to history discussed in this volume.

Annalisa Rosselli is professor of economics and of the history of economic thought at the University of Roma Tor Vergata, Italy. Her current research interests are the Cambridge school, the history of monetary theory, and gender economics.

Shauna Saunders is a graduate student in the Department of Economics at Duke University. Her dissertation research examines the public and private funding of the nonprofit arts sector. She was introduced to her first love—the history of economics—by Margaret Schabas while an undergraduate in Toronto.

Margaret Schabas is professor of philosophy at the University of British Columbia and is the author of *A World Ruled by Number* (Princeton University Press, 1990) and *Nature in Classical Economics* (University of Chicago Press, forthcoming).

Bertram Schefold is professor of economic theory at Johann Wolfgang Goethe Universität, Frankfurt am Main, Germany. He has published books and articles on the modern revival of classical economic theory, in particular on Piero Sraffa and joint production, on the economics of energy, and, as the editor of the series *Klassiker der*

Nationalökonomie, on fifty path-breaking works in the history of economic thought. He is past president of the European Society for the History of Economic Thought. For details see much-magic.wiwi.uni-frankfurt.de/Professoren/schefold/.

Esther-Mirjam Sent is associate professor in the Department of Economics at the University of Notre Dame as well as Faculty Fellow in the Reilly Center for Science, Technology, and Values at the same institution. She is the author of *The Evolving Rationality of Rational Expectations: An Assessment of Thomas Sargent's Achievements* (Cambridge University Press, 1998), which was awarded the 1999 Gunnar Myrdal Prize of the European Association for Evolutionary Political Economy, and the editor, along with Philip Mirowski, of *Science Bought and Sold: Essays in the Economics of Science* (University of Chicago Press, 2002).

E. Roy Weintraub (Duke University) was trained as a mathematician although his professional career has been as an economist. In recent years his research on the history of the interconnection between mathematics and economics in the twentieth century has helped shape the understanding of economists and historians. He is the author of several books and the editor of two others, and he has published a number of articles in professional journals and edited volumes.

Index

AAAS. *See* American Association for the Advancement of Science (AAAS)
Abstract (Hume), 324
Accounting and Science (Powers), 210
Advancement of Learning (Bacon), 229
Advances in Austrian Economics, 347n. 13
AEA. *See* American Economic Association (AEA)
The Affluent Society (Galbraith), 179
The Age of Uncertainty (Galbraith), 179
Agrégation, 113, 116, 121
Akama, Michio, 169
Alabama, University of, 295
Alborn, Timothy, 211
Alfred Sloan Foundation, 384
Allais, Maurice, 116
Alvey, James, 159
American Association for the Advancement of Science (AAAS), 219

American Economic Association (AEA), 29, 37, 253
Committee on Graduate Education in Economics (COGEE), 29, 37, 47
Job Openings for Economists (JOE), 304–5, 310
American Heritage Virtual Archive, 250
Americanization, 12
American Scientist, 219
America's Great Depression (Rothbard), 345
Amzalak, Moses B., 138
Andrew W. Mellon Foundation, 248, 249
Annals of the Society for the History of Economic Thought, 169
Antiestablishment movements, Italy, 105
Anti-Semitism, 184–85
Archival resources on-line, 249–50
Arena, Richard, 130
Arestis, Philip, 228, 325
Arguelles, José Canga, 138
Aristotle, 85

Arrow, Kenneth, 132, 289, 290, 322
ArXiv.org e-Print archive,
    Los Alamos National
    Laboratory, 251
Ashley, William, 216
Ashworth, William, 211
"Ask the Professor" service, 257
Aspromourgos, Tony, 156, 157
ASSA. *See* North American Allied
    Social Science Associations
    (ASSA)
Association Charles Gide, 111, 120
Astronomy, history of, 212
Attanasio, Orazio, 290
Auckland, University of,
    156, 159, 161
Australia and New Zealand, 10
    Auckland, University of,
        156, 159, 161
    Curtin University, 158
    History of Economics Review,
        154–56, 191, 192
    history of economic thought,
        154–64
        Kalecki, influence of, 160
        Keynes, influence of, 159–60
        Marshall, influence of, 160
        nature and character of, 159–62
        research, 157–58
        universities, 158–59
    History of Economic Thought
        Society of Australia
        (HETSA), 154, 159, 160, 191
        conference, 161
        HETSA Bulletin, 154
        membership, 154–55, 157
    Melbourne, University of, 156
    New Zealand Economics
        Association Conference, 159
    Sydney, University of,
        156, 158
Austrian Economics in America,
    346

articles in journals devoted to
    Austrian economic thought,
    348
*Foundations of the Market
    Economy* series, *349*
Misesian tradition, 347
Austrian School of Economics,
    337–60
    history of political economy and,
        342–50
    Whig perspectives, 350–51,
        353n. 19, 355
Autobiography and biography,
    226–44. *See also* Life
    writing
Autobiography (Mill), 231
Avalon Project, 248

Babbage, Charles, 211
Backhaus, Jürgen, 126, 127
Backhouse, Roger E., 9, 79–97,
    229, 280, 381
Bacon, Francis, 229
Bagehot, Walter, 231
Baloglou, C., 127
Barber, William, 3
Barre, Raymond, 121
Barthe, Roland, 264, 265n. 2
Basalla, George, 219
Bateman, Bradley W., 10, 17–34,
    73, 240, 304, 381, 387
Baumol, William, 350
Bayles, Pierre, 229
*Beautiful Mind: A Biography of John
    Forbes Nash* (Nasar),
    228, 235, 389
Behavioral science, 385
Bentham, Jeremy, 170, 184
Berkeley Electronic Press, 253
Bernal, John Desmond, 217, 218
Besomi, Daniele, 254
*Biblioteca de Econonomistas
    Aragoneses*, 140

Biddle, Jeff, 275
Binswanger, Hans Christoph, 127
*Biographical Dictionary of
Dissenting Economists*
(Arestis and Sawyer), 228
*A Biographical Dictionary of
Women Economists*
(Dimand et al.), 228, 236
Biography, 226–44. *See also*
Life writing
intellectual history as, 230
literary, 238–39
Birth of Economics (Uchida), 172
Blaug, Mark, 186, 211
Austrians, on, 347
conference commentator, as, 3
*Economic Theory in
Retrospect*, 181
interviews, collections of, 229
Netherlands, HET in, 148–53
types of mind, on, 337–38
Boettke, Peter J., 8, 337–60
Böhm, Stephan, 130
Böhm-Bawerk, Eugen von, 149,
343, 351
Bombach, G., 127
Bonnot de Condillac, Étienne, 213
Boulding, Kenneth, 179, 208
Bowen, H. R., 35
Boxmind.com lectures, 254–55
Brantlinger, Patrick, 210
"Breaking Away" (Schabas),
209, 217, 220
Breit, W., 229
Brewer, Anthony, 8, 361–77
Britain, 79–97
attraction of non EU students,
79
careers
academic, 80
HET, 88–93, *94*, 96–97
questionnaire on, 96–97
centralization, 80

Centre for History and Economics,
95
changes in higher education, 79
Conference of Heads of
University Departments of
Economics (CHUDE), 82
Faculty of Economics and Politics,
95
grades, 80–81
Higher Education Funding Council
for England (HEFCE), 80
historian of economics,
defined, 90n. 32
history of economic thought
age, initial steps by, *93*
age structure of historians, *89*
career paths by cohort, *94*
career patterns, *92*, *93*
careers in, 88–93
fringe subject, HET as, 85
future of, 79–97. *See also lines
throughout this topic*
heterodoxy/orthodoxy
of historians, *90*, 91
introductory courses, 86
levels and trends in teaching,
83
number of Ph.D.s, *92*
outlook, overall, 93–95
place of, 82–88
questionnaire on careers, 96–97
questionnaire on HET teaching,
95–96
reasons for working on HET, *91*
staffing levels, *84*, 88
undergraduate education of
historians, *89*, 90
*History of Economic Thought
Newsletter*, 253
homogenization within higher
education, 79–82
London School of Economics,
95, 344

(*continued*)
  research assessment exercise
    (RAE), 80–82, 93
    response to questionnaire, 83–88
    staffing levels, *84*, 88
  Royal Economic Society, 80
  Scottish Higher Education Funding
    Council (SHEFC), 80
  survey of British historians of
    economics, 88–93
  United States, comparisons, 80
British Columbia, University of, 218
British Higher Education Funding
  Council, 11
British Medical Journal, 234
Broman, Tom, 211
Bronfenbrenner, Martin, 181, 372
Brookings Institution, 182
Brown, Derek S., 9, 27, 31, 239
  graduate training in economics,
    298–308
  job market, on, 36
Brown, Vivienne, 233
Buckingham, University of, 81n. 8
Bürgin, A., 127
Burns, Arthur, 182
Business cycle theory, 351
Business of Alchemy (Smith), 210–11

Cahiers d'économie politique,
  118, 120
Cairns, John Elliot, 161
Cajori, Florian, 216
Caldwell, Bruce, 206, 346, 350n. 15
California Digital Library, 250
Cameralists, 125
Campomanes, Pedro de, 137
Canaan, Edwin, 343
Cantillon, Richard, 367
Cantor, Geoffrey, 228
Capital (Marx), 165, 365
  classical political economy
    concept, 366

influence of, 372
  publication of, 368
  subtitle, 103
  transformation algorithm, 373
Caravale, Giovanni, 220
Cardoso, José Luís, 11, 137–47,
  190–207
Careers. *See also* Employment
  Britain
    academic careers, 80
    HET, 88–93, *94*,
      96–97
    questionnaire on,
      96–97
  Italy, 105
  liberal education and,
    24–25
Carlyle, Thomas, 248
Carnegie Foundation, 19
Carnegie-Mellon University, 292
"Cartesian Economics" (Soddy),
  216
Center d'Études Prospectives
  d'Économie
    Mathématique Appliquées à
    la Planification
    (CEPREMAP), 117
Centre for History and Economics,
  95
CGP. *See* Commissariat Général du
  Plan (CGP)
Chalmers, Thomas, 214
Chambers, Ephraim, 229
Chapple, Simon, 160, 161
Chicago, University of, 344, 385
Chichilnisky, Graciela, 295, 296
Chick, Victoria, 280, 326–27
CHIMES. *See* Erasmus Center for
  History in Management and
  Economics (CHIMES)
Christensen, Paul, 209
Chronicle of Higher Education,
  23, 304, 310

CHUDE. *See* Conference of Heads of University Departments of Economics (CHUDE)
Clark, David, 160
Clásicos del Pensamiento Económico Espanol, 139
Clásicos del Pensamiento Económico Vasco, 140
Classical political economy, 366–67
Classics in Austrian Economics (Kirzner), 345, 353
Coats, A. W., 62, 161, 209
COGEE. *See* Committee on Graduate Education in Economics (COGEE)
Cohen, I. Bernard, 209, 210, 215
Colander, D., 36
Cold War, 218, 256, 382–84
education and, 387–88, 389
Colecçao de Obras Clássicas do Pensamento Económico Português, 139
Coleman, William, 162, 217
Collected Works (Hayek), 346
Collected Writings (Keynes), 326
Colmeiro, Manuel, 138
Colombia University, 295
Commissariat Général du Plan (CGP), 115
Committee on Graduate Education in Economics (COGEE), 29, 37, 47
Committee on the Status of Women in the Economics Profession (CSWEP), 71
Commodification versus freedom, 294–97
Commons, John R., 181
Complete Works on the History of Economics (Kobayashi), 172
Compton, Karl, 387
Comte, Auguste, 230

Conant, James, 383, 387
Conceived in Liberty (Rothbard), 345
Condorcet, Marquis de, 213
Conference of Heads of University Departments of Economics (CHUDE), 82
Contemporary World and Welfare State, 171
Copyright, 249
CORE, founding of, 389
Core, presence of, 374–75
"Core" journal standards, 74–75
Cost, notions of, 104
Council on Economic Advisers, 182
Council on Economic and Fiscal Policy (Japan), 174
Cournot, Augustin A., 168, 212
Course of Positive Philosophy (Comte), 230
Cowles, Alfred, 389
Cowles Commission, 389
Creation of Economic Science (Hirata), 172
Creativity, 238
Credentialing
History of Economics Society meetings, role in process, 72–75
Creedy, John, 156, 161
Cremaschi, Sergio, 209
Critical historian, 386
Critique of Hegel's Philosophy of Right (Marx), 364
Croom Helm, 157
Cults, 184–85
Curtin University, 158
Cyclopaedia (Chambers), 229

Darmstadt conference 2001, 131
Darwin (Desmond and Moore), 228
Dascal, Marcelo, 209

Das Kapital (Marx). *See Capital*
    (Marx)
Daston, Lorraine, 210
Davidson, P., 325
Davis, John, 10, 62–76, 151
Daybreak (Nietzsche), 378
Debreu, Gérard, 116
Deleplace, Ghislain, 10,
    110–124
Demand and supply,
    367–68
De Marchi, Neil, 151, 211, 219,
    273, 287
Depression era, 345
Descartes, 212
Description of a Chart of Biography
    (Priestley), 230
Desmond, Adrian, 228
Development, Geography, and
    Economic Theory (Krugman),
    17
Dictionary of Scientific Biography
    (Gillespie), 213
Dictionary of the History of Economic
    Thought, 169
Dimand, Mary Ann, 228, 236
Dimand, Robert, 209, 228, 236
Distance education,
    387–88
Divisia, François, 116
Dogmengeschichtlich, 353
Dogmenhistorische Ausshuß,
    126–27
Donoghue, Mark, 161
Donovon, Arthur, 228
Dorfman, Joseph, 180
Dow, Sheila C., 8,
    319–36
Drake, Stillman, 217
Duke University Press. *See also*
    History of Political Economy
    (HOPE)
Internet, 254

Dupré, John, 290
Durkheim, Émile, 214

Eagly, Robert, 65
EBSCO Information Service,
    249, 250
EconLit, 201
Econometrica, 216
Economía y Economistas Espanoles,
    140
Economic and Philosophic
    Manuscripts of 1844 (Marx),
    364
Economic Doctrine and Method
    (Schumpeter), 172
Economic Mind in American
    Civilization (Dorfman), 180
The Economic Point of
    View (Kirzner),
    345, 353
"Economic Point of View"
    (Mises), 337
Economics as a Coordination
    Problem (O'Driscoll), 347
Economics Letters, 295
The Economics of Time and Ignorance
    (Rizzo), 347
The Economics of T.R. Malthus
    (Endres), 161
Economic Theory in Retrospect
    (Blaug), 181
Economist, 295
Economists' Papers Project, 250
Edge of Objectivity, 214
Edgeworth, F. Y., 324
Edinburgh School, 267
Edison, Thomas, 233
Effective demand, principle
    of, 101
Ehime University, 169
EH.Net, 251, 255, 257
Eichner, A. S., 325
Einstein, Albert, 213

EJHET. See European Journal of the History of Economic Thought (EJHET)
Ekelund, Robert B., Jr., 209
Electronic Society for Social Scientists (ELSSS), 202–3n. 3
Elgar, Edward, 162, 198
ELSSS. *See* Electronic Society for Social Scientists (ELSSS)
E-mail lists, 246–47
Eminent Victorians (Strachey), 231
Emmett, Ross, 7, 8, 245–60, 385, 388
Employment. *See also* Careers
  finding employment, 36, 275–76
    discussion on, 309–14
    HET graduate studies and, 303–7
  liberal arts colleges, North America, 22
Encyclopédie (Diderot and d'Alembert), 229
Encyclopedia of Economic and Business History, 255
Encyclopedia of Political Economy, 162
Endres, Tony, 156, 159, 161
Energy and Empire: A Biographical Study of Lord Kelvin (Smith and Wise), 228
Energy and Entropy (Brantlinger), 210
Engels, Friedrich, 213, 364
Engerman, Stanley, 381
England. *See* Britain
E-Print, 251
Equiano, Olaudah, 273, 274, 281
Erasmus Center for History in Management and Economics (CHIMES), 152

ESHET. *See* European Society for the History of Economic Thought (ESHET)
Essay Concerning Human Understanding (Locke), 238
An Essay on Capital (Kirzner), 345
Essays in Biography (Keynes), 227, 238, 324
Essays in Persuasion (Locke), 238
Essays (Schumpeter), 216
Establishment of the System of the "Wealth of Nations" (Kobayashi), 172
Europe, 10, 12
European Journal of the History of Economic Thought (EJHET), 191–92
  commercial behavior, 204
  editorial responsibility, separation from production, 200, 201
  editors and publisher, relations, 203
  on-line, 252
European Society for the History of Economic Thought (ESHET), 129–131, 133
  Newsletter, 253
Exemplary Economists, 236

Faculty of Economics and Politics, 95
Fatal Vision (McGinness), 296–97
Federal Reserve Bank, 183
Federal Reserve Board, 182
Fetter, Frank, 65
Feynman, Richard, 228
Figured account of history of economics, 265–69
Fischer, Stan, 306
Fisher, Irving, 213
Fitzgibbons, Athol, 160, 195
Fleming, Grant, 161
Fogel, Robert, 381

Foley, Vernard, 217
Ford Foundation, 385,
    387, 389
Forget, Evelyn L., 7, 8, 226–44,
    309–16
Forman, Paul, 386
Forum Financial Group, 295
Foucault, Michael, 228
Foundations of the Market Economy
    series, 349
France, 10, 110–24
    academic recruitment procedures,
        113–14, 115
    agrégation, 113, 116, 121
    agrégation externe, 113, 115, 121
    agrégation interne, 113, 121
    Association Charles Gide,
        111, 120
    Center d'Études Prospectives
        d'Économie
        Mathématique Appliquées
        à la Planification
        (CEPREMAP), 117
    civil servants, university professors
        as, 113
    Commissariat Général du
        Plan (CGP), 115
    four-year programs, *112*
    grandes écoles, 114, 115, 116
    history of economic thought (HET)
        analytical view of HET, 118, 120
        consensus about tools, 122
        controversies about
            fundamentals, 122
        cultural conception of HET, 119
        endogenous view of HET, 118
        evolution of economic
            thinking, 116–17
        facts about HET, 110–17
        forecasting, 120–23
        four-year programs with
            HET, *112*
        generational effect, 121–22

institutional environment
    of HET, 114–16
Keynesian economics, 117
modern theory, link between
    HET and, 120
1960's, 116–17
present situation, 110–24
Sraffian economics, 117
two attitudes toward, 118–20
weight of HET, 111–14
Institut National de la Statistique
    et des Études Économiques
    (INSEE), 115
levels of graduation, 111
maîtres de conférences, 113
professeurs, 113–14
Revue économique, 113, 117
Revue d'économique politique, 113
universities, 114
World War II, aftermath, 116
Frängsmyr, Tore, 210
Franklin, Benjamin, 237
Free Banking in Britain (White), 346
Friedman, Milton, 185
Fronsperger, Leonhard, 129

Gadamer, Hans-Georg, 270
Galbraith, John Kenneth, 179
Garegnani, Pierangelo, 101
Garfield, James, 25–26
Garrison, Roger, 346
Gayer, Ted, 9, 27, 35–61, 73
Gehrke, Christian, 130
General Theory of Employment,
    Interest, and Money (Keynes),
    101, 165, 324,
    326–28
Genesis and Geology
    (Gillespie), 213–14
Genius: The Life and Science of
    Richard Feynman (Gleick),
    228
German Historical School, 170

Germany, 10, 125–36, 369
    cameralists, 125
    Dogmenhistorische Ausshuß,
        126–27
    European Society for the History of
        Economic Thought (ESHET),
        129–31, 133, 253
    history of economic thought
        (HET), 125–36
        Darmstadt conference 2001, 131
        European Society for the History
            of Economic Thought
            (ESHET), 129–31, 133
        pure theory, advance of, 125
        research and teaching, 126–29
    Klassiker der Nationalökonomie,
        131
    Verein für Socialpolitik, 126
    Verstehende Nationalökonomie,
        128–29
Ghosh, R. N., 161
Gillespie, Charles C., 213–14
Gleick, James, 228
Globalization, 12–13
Global privatization regime, 294
Goethe, 127
Goffe, Bill, 253
Golinski, Jan, 281
Goodwin, Craufurd D., 9, 11,
        161, 312
    HES meetings, 65
    "Historical Perspectives on
        Modern Economics," 346
    HOPE, view from, 179–89
    HOPE conference, aftermath,
        380, 389
    new audiences, on, 240
    student, supervision of, 274, 275
Gordon, D. F., 35
Gordon, Kermit, 182
Gossen, Herman Heinrich, 344
Grabiner, Judith, 210
Grades, Britain, 80–81

Graduate studies, history of economic
        thought, 35–61
    degree students are exposed to HET
        (questionnaire), 38–48, 58–59
    department chairs' responses,
        43–44
    evaluative/speculative responses,
        47, *48*
    HET courses, information about,
        42–45
    required core courses, 42–45
    students, information on, 45, *46*
    survey response, *40–41*
    employment, finding, 303–7,
        309–14
    extracurricular activities and,
        301–3
    faculty members that have taught
        doctoral HET (questionnaire),
        49–57, 59–61
    changes in attitude, 55
    course offerings, *53–54*
    courses, information about,
        52–55
    evaluative/speculative responses,
        55–57
    information about HET
        professors, 49–52, *50*
    primary or minor fields of
        interest, 51
    students, information
        about, 52–55
    North America, 35–61
Graduate training in economics,
        288–308. *See also*
            specific topic
    COGEE. *See* Committee on
        Graduate Education in
        Economics (COGEE)
Grampp, William, 350
Grattan-Guinness, Ivor, 209
Graunt, William, 215
Gray, Alexander, 216

Great Britain. *See* Britain
Great Depression, 345
Green, Roy, 160
Grice-Hutchison, Marjorie,
    139, 143
Groenewegen, Peter, 10, 154,
    156–58, 160, 161, 228
Gruber, Howard, 217
Gruson, Claude, 116
Guala, Francesco, 209
Guerlac, Henry, 216

Haberler, Gottfried, 181
Hacking, Ian, 210, 278
Hacohen, Malachi, 353n. 20
Hagemann, H., 127
Hahn, Frank, 322
Halevi, Joseph, 160
Halévy, Élie, 214
Halley, Edmund, 215
Hamilton, Earl J., 139
Hankins, Thomas, 227
Harcourt, Geoffrey,
    10, 156, 158, 160, 327
Harrison, Frederick, 230
Harrod, Roy, 254
Harvard Institute for International
    Development, 295
Harvard University, 383
Harvard University Press, 11
Hay, Rod, 247–48
Hayek, Friedrich, 338
    analysis of, 353
    articles on, 347
    bibliography, 344
    business cycle theory, 351
    Collected Works, 346
    cult following, 184
    ranking by graduate students, 352
    writings of, 342, 344
HEA. *See* History of economic
    analysis (HEA)
Heertje, Arnold, 229

*HEI. See History of Economic Ideas
    (HEI)*
Heilbroner, Robert, 180, 240,
    255, 352n. 18
Henderson, James, 209
Hennipman, Pieter, 150
*HER. See History of Economics
    Review (HER)*
Herbert, Robert F., 209
Heresy, 183–84
Herschel, John, 211
HES. *See* History of Economics
    Society (HES)
HET. *See* History of economic
    thought
Heterodox traditions, 8
    Austrian School of Economics,
        337–60
    HOPE 2001 conference, aftermath,
        378–90
    Marxist tradition, 361–77
    post-Keynesian tradition, 319–36
Hetherington, Norriss, 211
HETSA. *See* History of
    Economic Thought Society of
    Australia (HETSA)
Hicks, John, 254
Higher Education Funding Council
    for England (HEFCE), 80
Hirata, Kiyoaki, 172, 173
Hiroshi, Mizuta, 170
Hishiyama, Izumi, 170
Historians, practitioners of HET as,
    380
History and Critical Dictionary
    (Bayles), 229
*History and Present State of
    Electricity* (Priestley), 230
History of economic analysis (HEA),
    320–23
History of Economic Analysis
    (Schumpeter), 172, 180, 344
History of Economic Ideas (HEI), 191

A History of Economic Reasoning (Pribram), 344
History of economics. *See specific topic*
History of Economics in Germany, 129
History of Economics Review (HER), 154–56, 191, 192
current research, 195
on-line, 252
symposia, 199
History of Economics Society Bulletin, 191
History of Economics Society (HES), 2, 12
Committee on the Status of Women in the Economics Profession (CSWEP), 71
conferences, *66*, 378–90
e-mail lists, 246–47
first annual meeting, 64n. 1
founders, 65
meetings, role in history of economics as subdiscipline, 62–76
change in participation, 67–72
conferences, *66*
credentialing process, role of meetings, 72–75
locations of meetings, *66*
number of presentations per conference, *69*
number of sessions per conference, 68n. 4
organization of meetings, 65
programs from 1978 to 2000, review of, 67–72
women, presentations by, 71
officer of, 346
presidents, *66*
programs from 1978 to 2000, review of, 67–72

2001 HOPE conference, 2–12
aftermath, 378–90
History of Economic Theory: Classic Contributions (Niehans), 127
A History of Economic Thought: The LSE Lectures (Robbins), 17
History of economic thought (HET)
articles, 1969–2000, *340–41*
Australia and New Zealand, 154–64. *See also* Australia and New Zealand
Britain, 79–97. *See also* Britain
formation of, 213
France, 110–24. *See also* France
Germany, 125–36. *See also* Germany
graduate studies, North America, 35–61
degree students are exposed to HET (questionnaire), 38–48, 58–59
faculty members that have taught doctoral HET (questionnaire), 49–57, 59–61
historians, practitioners of HET as, 380
Italy, 98–109. *See also* Italy
Japan, 165–75. *See also* Japan
life writing, prospects for, 239–40
Marxist tradition, 361–77
methodology, 328–32
narrative and, 226–44
Netherlands, 148–53. *See also* Netherlands
post-Keynesian tradition, 319–36
future role of history of thought, 332–34
history of thought, 320–28
methodology, 328–32
role and nature of HET, 320–23

(*continued*)
   publication and research, *HOPE*
      view of future, 179–89
      beyond academe, 179–80
      cults and, 184–85
      disciplines, HET for, 180–81
      economics manors, 181
      graduate students, 181
      heresy and, 183–84
      liberal arts, 180
      policymakers, HET and, 182–83
      pursuit of HET for own sake,
         185–86
      roots, return to, 185
      subdisciplines, HET in, 181–82
      technology and ideology, HET
         as refuge from, 183
   Spain and Portugal, 137–47.
      See also Spain and Portugal
   types of mind in economics,
      337–38
   Wisconsin, University of, database,
      217
*History of Economic Thought
   Newsletter*, 253
History of Economic Thought Society
   of Australia (HETSA),
   159, 160, 191
   conference, 161
   HETSA Bulletin, 154
   membership, 154–55, 157
*History of European Thought in
   the Nineteenth Century*
   (Merz), 217
The History of Marginal Utility
   (Kauder), 344
History of Modern Economics
   (Sugimoto), 172
History of political economy
   Austrian School of Economics and,
      342–50
History of Political Economy (HOPE)
   history of, 190–91

   on-line, 252
   science, history of as history of
      economics, 209
   view of future, 179–89
      cults and, 184–85
      disciplines, HET for, 180–81
      economics manors, 181
      graduate students, 181
      heresy and, 183–84
      liberal arts, 180
      policymakers, HET and, 182–83
      pursuit of HET for own sake,
         185–86
      roots, return to, 185
      subdisciplines, HET in, 181–82
      technology and ideology, HET
         as refuge from, 183
A History of Political Economy
   (Ingram), 215
*History of Post-Keynesian
   Macroeconomics* (King), 159
History of science, history of
   economics as, 208–25
History of Science Society,
   211–12, 219
History of the Inductive Sciences
   (Whewell), 230
History of thought, 320–28
   founders of post-Keynesian
      economics, 323–25
   generally, 325–28
Hollander, Samuel, 102, 161,
   218–19, 372–73
Holmes, Larry, 228
Hong, Sungook, 211
*HOPE. See History of Political
   Economy (HOPE)*
HOPE 2001 conference, 2–12
   aftermath, 378–90
Hopkins, Mark, 25–26
Horwitz, Steve, 347
Hueckel, Glenn, 203n. 6
Hume, David, 213, 230, 321, 324

Humphrey, Thomas, 183
Hutchison, Terence, 4–6

Ibanez, C. U., 229
Iberian Association of the History of
    Economic Thought, 137, 146
Iberian countries. *See* Spain and
    Portugal
Idaho, University of, 250
IH. *See* Intellectual history
Iida, Kanae, 170
Ikeo, Aiko, 10, 165–75
"In Defence of Biography"
    (Shapin and Thackray),
    227–28, 235
Ingram, John Kells, 215
Ingrao, Bruna, 209
INSEE. *See* Institut National
    de la Statistique et des Études
    Économiques (INSEE)
Institute of Fiscal Studies, 139, 140
Institut National de la Statistique et
    des Études Économiques
    (INSEE), 115
Intellectual curiosity, 21–22
Intellectual history, 320–25
    Austrian School, 354, 355
Inter-American Development Bank,
    312
*The Interesting Narrative of the Life
    of Olaudah Equiano or
    Gustavus Vassa, the African,
    Written by Himself*, 273
International Congress of the History
    of Science
    Bucharest meeting, 218
International issues. *See also*
    specific country
    Australia and New Zealand,
        154–64
    Britain, 79–97
    France, 110–24
    Germany, 125–36

Italy, 98–109
Japan, 165–75
Netherlands, 148–53
Spain and Portugal, 137–47
Internet, 245–60
    archival resources on-line, 249–50
    copyright and, 249
    current research, on-line archives,
        250
    digital projects, 254–56
    e-mail lists, 246–47
    on-line journals, 252–53
    on-line text archives, 247–49
    teaching prospects and, 256–57
    Web sites and their addresses,
        258–60
Interpretation, 331
Isis, 214–18, 382
Italy, 10, 98–109
    antiestablishment movements, 105
    careers, 105
    economics as HET, 98–109
        academic strength, necessity for,
            107–8
        American and British approach,
            differences, 102
        career strategies, 105
        changes in influence, 105–6
        cost, notions of, 104
        legitimate contribution, defined,
            98
        Marx, influence of, 102–4
        past economists, 101
        past ideas and authors,
            relationship with, 103
        Sraffa, influence of, 100, 102–4
        subdisciplines, 106–7
        survival of HET, 107
        textual exegesis approach,
            99–100

Jackson, Miles, 211
Japan, 10

(*continued*)
Council on Economic and Fiscal
Policy, 174
history of economics, 165–75
connections with, 171
Cournot, influence of, 168
education, 165–68
forecasting, 173–74
graduate level, 167–68
high school level, 165–66
JHSET, 167, 168–71
Keynes, influence of, 165, 167,
170
Marshall, influence of, 166, 170
Marx, influence of, 165, 169,
170, 172
Mill, influence of, 167, 169
pre–World War II, 168
respected works, 171–73
Smith, influence of, 165, 167,
169, 170, 172
Sraffa, influence of, 170
undergraduate level, 166–67
Walras, influence of, 168
Japanese Society for the History
of Economic Thought
(JSHET), 167, 168–71
Ministry of Education and Science,
167
Science Council, 171
unemployment, 166
Japanese Society for the History
of Economic Thought
(JSHET), 167, 168–71
*Annals of the Society for the
History of Economic Thought*,
169–70
*Dictionary of the History of
Economic Thought*, 169–70
German Historical School, 170
meetings, 168
membership, 168
SHET (mailing list), 169

Jevons, William Stanley, 194, 212,
213, 324, 367
*JHET. See Journal of the History
of Economic Thought (JHET)*
JHSET. *See* Japanese Society
for the History of Economic
Thought (JSHET)
Job market. *See* Employment
Job Openings for Economists (JOE),
304–5, 310
John Bates Clark medal, 295
*John Locke: Economist and Social
Scientist* (Vaughan), 346
John Maynard Keynes (Skidelsky),
228
Jolink, Albert, 148–53
Jones, Evan, 156
Jorland, Gérard, 209, 211
Journalism, lawsuits, 296–97
Journal of Economic Education, 253
Journal of Economic Literature, 1
Journal of Economics and Finance,
253
Journal of the History of Biology, 212
*Journal of the History of
Economic Thought (JHET)*,
4, 191, 194
articles, 1989–99, *341*
commercial behavior, 204
editorial responsibility, separation
from production, 200
editors and publisher, relations, 203
on-line, 252
symposia, 199
*Journal of the History of the
Behavioral Sciences*, 212
Jovallanos, Gasper M. de, 137
JSTOR, 249–251

Kalecki, Michal, 160, 195
founder of post-Keynesian
economics, 323, 324
influence of, 325

Kates, Steven, 156, 161
Kauder, Emil, 344
Kautsky, Karl, 368
Kautz, Julius, 125
Kaye, Joel, 211
Kerr, Ian, 162
Kerr, Prue, 160
Keynes, John Maynard, 99, 179, 217
  biography, 228, 353
  Collected Writings, 326
  criticisms of, 157
  cult following, 184
  effective demand, principle of, 101
  Essays in Biography, 227, 238, 324
  *General Theory of Employment,
    Interest, and Money*, 101, 165,
    324, 325–28
  Harrod, Roy, correspondence, 254
  influence of
    Australia and New Zealand,
      159–60
    France, 117
    Italy, 105, 108
    Japan, 165, 167, 170
    Netherlands, 151
    Spain and Portugal, 145, 146
  interventionist demand
    management, 352n. 18
  political audience, 182
  post-Keynesian economics.
    See Post-Keynesian tradition
  research on, 194–95
  science, history of, 213
  theory of expectations, 322
  Treatise on Probability, 326, 329
  work on, 104
King, John, 156, 159, 161, 325
Kingsland, Sharon, 209
Kirzner, Israel, 345–46, 353
Klaes, Matthias, 9, 239,
    263–71, 299
Klamer, A., 36
Klant, J., 151

Klassiker der Nationalökonomie, 131
Klein, Judy, 209, 219
Knight, Frank, 52, 247, 343
Kobayashi, Noboru, 170,
    172, 173
Koerner, Lisbet, 211
Koizumi, Prime Minister Junichiro,
    174
Koopmans, Tjalling, 385n. 2
Koyré, Alexandre, 210
Kraus, J. X., 127
Kregel, J., 229
Kriesler, Peter, 156, 160
Krüger, Lorenz, 210
Krugman, Paul, 180
Krugman, Paul R., 17, 173, 275–78,
    280, 282
Kuhn, Thomas, 211, 228, 293
  The Road since Structure, 1
  science, history of, 212
  science, on, 383–84
  *The Structure of Scientific
    Revolutions*, 214, 384
Kurz, Heinz D., 130, 161

Lakatos, Imre, 211
Latour, Bruno, 210
Lavoie, Don, 346, 352
Lavoie, M., 325
Lavoisier, Antoine, 213, 214
Lavoisier (Donovon), 228
Lawson, T., 329
Lawsuits, 295–97
Learned helplessness, 313
*Lecture Notes on Advanced
  Theory of Value*
  (Sraffa), 103
Leeson, Robert, 155, 162
Legitimate contribution, defined, 98
Leijonhufvud, Axel, 354n. 22
Leonard, Robert, 209, 219
Leontief, Wassily, 157
Levy, David, 248

Liberal arts
colleges. *See* Liberal arts colleges,
North America
publication and research, *HOPE*
view of future, 180
Liberal arts colleges, North America,
17–34
careers and liberal education,
24–25, 303–4
definition, 19 20
elite colleges, list of, 32
employment, nature of, 22
future for history of economic
thought, 26–27
history of economic thought,
reason for success of, 21–25
ideal college concept, 25–26
intellectual curiosity, 21–22
"nonprofessional" nature of,
20n. 10
Ph.D. programs, 29–30
"policy studies," 27
"political economy," 27
rankings, 18–19
research, 31
small colleges, 20
subdisciplines, 17–18
success of, 18–19, 21–25
teaching environment, 23, 29
Liberal education, 387–88
Life of Adam Smith (Ross), 228, 233
*Life-Study: Experiencing
Creative Lives* (Progoff),
237, 240
Life writing, 226–44
challenge of, 227–34
forms of, 235–39
history of economic thought,
prospects for life writing,
239–40
science biography, 228–30
Limoges, Camille, 209
Lindqvist, Svante, 210

Lippi, Marco, 100–101
List, Friedrich, 172
Littleboy, Bruce, 160, 195
Lives of the Laureates
(Breit and Spencer), 236
Locke, John, 213, 238, 324, 346
Lodewijks, John, 10, 11,
154–64, 190–207
History of Economics Review, 192
Loeb, Jacques, 214
London School of Economics, 95, 344
Longfield, Mountifort, 346
Los Alamos National Laboratory, 251
Louvain, University of, 389
Lucas, Robert, 322
*Ludwig von Mises: The Man and His
Economics* (Kirzner), 345n.
10
Luxemburg, Rosa, 324

Maas, Harro, 209
Maastricht, 151
MacDonald, Jeffrey, 296–97
Mahl, Bernd, 127
Mahoney, Michael, 211
Mäki, Uskala, 209
Making of America digital project,
248
*The Making of Modern Economics:
The Lives and Ideas of the
Great Thinkers*, 352n. 18
Malinvaud, Edmond, 116, 132
Malthus, Thomas Robert,
194, 212, 324
Chalmers on, 214
methodology and, 330
population theory, 366
Mandeville, Bernard, 129
Marcuzzo, Maria Cristina, 10, 98–109
Marjolin, Robert, 116
Marschak, Jacob, 385n. 2
Marshall, Alfred, 52, 145, 161, 324
biography, 228

criticisms of, 157
cult following, 184
influence of
  Australia and New Zealand, 160
  Japan, 166, 170
  Netherlands, 151
research on, 194
Sraffa and, 103
Marx, Karl, 22, 28, 161
Capital. See Capital
Cold War and Marxism, 218
core, presence of, 374–75
*Critique of Hegel's Philosophy
  of Right*, 364
cult following, 184
*Economic and Philosophic
  Manuscripts of 1844*, 364
influence of, 28
  Italy, 102–4
  Japan, I overwrote something!!,
    165, 169, 170, 172
Marxist tradition, 361–77
  historian of economics, Marx as,
    362–68
  history of economics, Marxists
    and, 368–71
  Marxists on Marx, 368
  Sraffa and, 372–76
Mill and, 366
reproduction schemas, 324
research program, 105
Russia, study of, 132
science, history of, 213
Smith, Adam, discussions on,
  363–67
theories of, 100–101
Theories of Surplus–Value,
  103, 172, 364, 365, 368, 374
universal law of production, 100
Massé, Pierre, 116
*Maynard Keynes: An Economist's
  Biography* (Moggridge), 228
Mazane, Kazuo, 170

McFarlane, Bruce, 160
McGinness, Joe, 296–97
McLure, Michael, 162
McMaster University Archive in
  the History of Economic
  Thought, 247–49, 257
Meardon, Stephen, 239, 299
  editorial for HES list, 254
  employment, 312
  narrative, 272–83, 303
Measures, 104
Medema, Steven G., 11,
  190–207
Medicine, history of, 234
Meek, Ronald, 361, 369–71, 373
Mehrling, Perry, 182
Melbourne, University of, 156
Ménard, Claude, 217
Menger, Carl, 128, 343, 344, 351
Merz, Theodor, 217
Mesmer, Antoin, 237
Methodology, history of thought,
  328–32
Michael Faraday (Cantor), 228
Michigan, University of
  Project Gutenberg, 249
  Text Initiative, 249
Middleton, Roger, 229
Military, 294
Mill, John Stuart, 161
  Autobiography, 231
  Blaug, compared, 181
  influence of, Japan, 167, 169
  Marx and, 366
  obscurity, 194
  political audience, 182
  ranking by graduate students, 352
  science, history of, 212
Millmow, Alex, 156
Ministry of Education and Science
  (Japan), 167
Minnesota, liberal arts colleges, 18,
  32–33

Mirowski, Philip, 161
  conference commentator, as, 3
  correspondence regarding,
    289–291
  HOPE conference, aftermath,
    378–90
  More Heat Than Light, 211
  price theory, 182
  science and, 209, 218, 219
Mises, Ludwig von, 337
  analysis of, 353
  articles on, 347
  political economy and,
    343–44
  ranking by graduate students, 352
  writings of, 345–46
Mississippi Scheme, 256
Miyazaki, Saiichi, 170
Modern academia
  historian, reasons to be, 386
  self-histories, changing role,
    382–86
  types of education, 387–88
  value for money, what constitutes,
    388–89
Moggridge, Don, 228
Moore, Gregory, 161
Moore, James, 228
Moore, Walter, 228
More Heat Than Light
  (Mirowski), 211
Morgan, Mary S., 151, 209,
    211, 219
Morgenstern, Oskar, 353
Morrell, Jack, 210
Morrison, Margaret, 211
Moss, Laurence, 346, 350n. 15
Mosselmans, Bert, 209
Motives, 104
Myrdal, Gunnar, 277, 278
  *Political Element in the
    Development of Economic
    Theory*, 281

underdeveloped countries,
    aid to, 282

Nagai, Yoshio, 170
Napster, 251
Narrative and history of economic
    thought, 226–44
Nasar, Sylvia, 228, 235,
    240, 389
Nash, John Forbes,
    228, 389
National Bureau of Economic
    Research, 389
"The Natural History of Industry"
    (Chalmers), 214
*Natural Images in Economic
    Thought* (Mirowski), 209
*The Natural Sciences and the Social
    Sciences* (Cohen), 210
Negishi, Takashi, 166, 170
Neoclassical, meaning of,
    347–48n. 14
Netherlands
  Erasmus Center for History in
    Management and Economics
    (CHIMES), 152
  history of economic thought
    (HET), 148–53
    post–World War II period,
      150–51
    present situation,
      151–52
    pre–World War II period,
      149–150
  Maastricht, 151
  Rotterdam School of Economics,
    149, 152
  Tilburg University Economics
    Department, 149, 151
Neu, John, 217
*Never at Rest: A Biography of Isaac
    Newton* (Westfall), 228
New Atlantis (Bacon), 229

*The New Calendar of Great Men:
Biographies of the 558
Worthies of All Ages and
Nations in the Positivist
Calendar of Auguste Comte*
(Harrison), 230
"New Economy," 344n. 6
New Lights upon Economics
(Sugimoto), 172
New School History of Economic
Thought Web site,
255, 257
Newton, Isaac, 228
New Zealand, 10. *See* Australia
and New Zealand
New Zealand Economics Association
Conference, 159
Niebyl, Karl, 331
Niehans, Jürg, 127
Nietzsche, Friedrich, 378
*Night Thoughts of a Classical
Physicist* (McCormmach),
238–39
North America, 10
graduate studies, history of
economic thought, 35–61
History of Economics Society
meetings, role of, 62–76
liberal arts colleges, 17–34
North American Allied Social Science
Associations (ASSA), 68
Nye, David, 233–34
Nyland, Chris, 161

Oakley, Allen, 156, 160
O'Donnell, Rod, 156, 160
O'Driscoll, Gerald, 347
Oehlers, Alfred, 159
O'Hara, Phil, 162
Ohio, liberal arts colleges, 18,
32–33
On-line journals, 252–53
On-line text archives, 247–49

*On the Methodology of Economics
and the Formalist Revolution*
(Hutchison), 4–6
*On the Principles of Political
Economy and Taxation*
(Ricardo), 374
"On the Progress of Quantification in
Economics" (Spengler), 217
*Outlines of a Critique of Political
Economy* (Engels), 364
Owen, R., 170

Page, Frank, 295, 296
The Panic of 1819 (Rothbard), 345
Pareto, Economics, and Society
(McClure), 162
Paris, University of, 117
Pasinetti, Luigi, 101, 130, 326 n.9
Patinkin, Don, 254
Pearson, Heath, 128
Pechman, Joseph, 182
*Peterson's Graduate Programs in the
Humanities, Arts, and Social
Sciences, 2000*, 38
Petridis, Ray, 154, 160, 161
Petty, William, 194, 213, 215, 362,
366, 369
Peutinger, Conrad, 129
Phaedrus (Plato), 268n. 12
Ph.D. programs
credentialing, 74
departmental rankings, 74
history of economic thought. *See*
Graduate studies, history of
economic thought
liberal arts colleges,
North America, 29–30
Ph.D. institutions, generally, 73–75
Phillips, Bill, 162
Physiocrats, 104, 194, 217, 219, 369
"Pilgrim's Progress: Male Tales
Told during a Life in
Physics" (Traweek), 301

Plasmeijer, H., 203n. 6
Plato, 268n. 12
Playfair, John, 230
Poincaré, Henri, 214
Poirer, Jean-Pierre, 211
Pôle d'Histoire de l'Analyse et
    des Représentations
    Économiques, 248
Policymakers, HET and, 182–83
"Policy studies," 27
"Political economy," 27
*Political Element in the Development
    of Economic Theory*
    (Myrdal), 281
Poovey, Mary, 381
Population theory, 366
Porta, Pier Luigi, 130, 372
Porter, Theodore, 6–7,
    209–11, 220
Portugal. *See* Spain and Portugal
Post-Keynesian tradition, 319–36
    history of thought, 320–28
    founders of post-Keynesian
        economics, 323–25
    future role of history of
        thought, 332–34
    generally, 325–28
    methodology, 328–32
    interpretation, 331
    role and nature of HET, 320–23
    writing style, 331–32
Powers, Michael, 210
Pribram, Karl, 344
Prices, 365, 367
Priestley, Joseph, 230
Privatized distance education, 387–88
Probabilistic Revolution
    (Krüger et al.), 210
*Production of Commodities by
    Means of Commodities*, 361,
    372
Productivity Theory of Friedrich List
    (Kobayashi), 172

Professionalizing history of
    economics. *See* History of
    Economics Society (HES)
Progoff, Ira, 237, 240
"Program for the Whig History of
    Economic Science"
    (Samuelson), 274
Project Gutenberg, 249
Project Muse, 252
Publication and research
    active readers, defined, 200
    authors, challenges for,
        196–99
    autobiography, 226–44
    biography, 226–44
    challenges for future, 196–207
    disciplinary identity, 205–7
    gatekeeper function of editor, 194
    genres, 193
    history, 190–91
    history of economic thought
        (HET), *HOPE* view of future,
        179–89
    cults and, 184–85
    disciplines, HET for,
        180–81
    economics manors, 181
    graduate students, 181
    heresy and, 183–84
    liberal arts, 180
    policymakers, HET and, 182–83
    pursuit of HET for own sake,
        185–86
    roots, return to, 185
    subdisciplines, HET in,
        181–82
    technology and ideology, HET
        as refuge from, 183
    history of science, history of
        economics as, 208–25
    Internet, role of, 245–60
    life writing, 226–44
    narrative, 226–44

publishers, challenges for, 202–5
readers, challenges for, 200–2
specialist journals, role of, 190–207
state of the art, 193–94
Pullen, John, 154, 156, 158, 330

*Quantifying Spirit in the Eighteenth
  Century* (Frängsmyr), 210
*Quarterly Journal of Austrian
  Economics (QJAE)*, 347n. 13,
  350
*Quarterly Journal of Economics
  (QJE)*, 350
Quesnay, François, 168, 170, 217
  tableau économique, 173
Quetelet, Adolphe, 215

RAE. *See* Research Assessment
  Exercise (RAE)
RAE. *See Review of Austrian
  Economics (RAE)*
Rashid, Salim, 209
Recktenwald, Horst Claus, 127
Recollections of Eminent Economists
  (Kregel), 236
Redman, Deborah, 209
RePEe. *See* "Research Papers in
  Economics" (RePEe)
Research. *See* Publication and
  research
Research Assessment Exercise
  (RAE), 11, 80–82, 93
  response to questionnaire, 83–88
  staffing levels, *84*, 88
*Research in the History of
  Economic Thought and
  Methodology (RHET&M)*,
  190–91
"Research Papers in Economics"
  (RePEe), 251
Research university ideal, 387
Review of Austrian Economics (RAE),
  347n. 13, 350

Revue économique, 113, 117
Revue d'économique politique, 113
Riach, P., 327
Ricardo, David, 99, 179
  classical, description as, 361
  comparative advantage theory, 165
  core, presence of, 374–75
  criticisms, 362–63
  Hollander's work on, 102
  Japan, influence, 165, 170
  obscurity, 194
  political economy and, 343
  *On the Principles of Political
    Economy and Taxation*, 374
  Sraffa's version of, 324,
    372–73
  work on, 104
  *Works and Correspondence
    of David Ricardo* (Sraffa), 324
Riskin, Jessica, 211
Rivalry and Central Planning
  (Lavoie), 346
Rizzo, Mario J., 346–47
The Road since Structure (Kuhn), 1
Robbins, Lionel, 17, 181
Robertson, Dennis, 123
Robinson, Joan, 325, 369
Robinson, Mike, 203n. 6
Rockefeller Foundation, 387
Romano, Richard, 209
Roman/Stoic tradition, 321
Roscher, Wilhelm, 128, 129
Ross, Dorothy, 381
Ross, Ian Simpson, 228, 233
Rosselli, Annalisa, 10, 98–109
Rothbard, Murray, 344–45, 346, 352
Rothschild, Emma, 381
Rotterdam School of Economics,
  149, 152
Roy, René, 116
Royal Economic Society, 80
Rudwick, Martin, 217
Rusnock, Andrea, 211

Russia, 295, 296, 369

Salerno, Joseph, 347
Samuels, Warren, 65
Samuelson, Paul, 128, 132, 232, 273
    Marx, on, 373
    "Program for the Whig History of
        Economic Science," 274
    Whig history, 6
Samuelson, Robert, 180
Sargent, Thomas, 289, 291
Sarton, George, 214–16, 382
Saunders, Shauna, 9, 27, 31, 36, 239,
    288–308
Sawyer, Malcolm, 228
Say, Jean-Baptiste, 114, 157,
    161, 324
    political economy and, 343
    ranking by graduate students, 352
    Say's Law, 352
Scazzieri, Roberto, 130
Schabas, Margaret, 7–8, 13, 27,
    208–25, 312, 379, 386
Schaffer, Simon, 210, 211
Schama, Simon, 239
Schefold, Bertram, 10,
    125–36
Schmoller, Gustav, 127
Scholarly Publishing and Academic
    Research Coalition (SPARC),
    202n. 2
School of Salamanca, 143
Schrödinger (Moore), 228
Schumpeter, Joseph A., 139, 211
    cult following, 184
    Essays, 216
    History of Economic Analysis,
        172, 180, 344
    history of economic analysis,
        231–32
    "New Economy," 344n. 6
    political economy and, 343
Schweber, S. S., 217

Science
    biography, 229
    history of as history of economics,
        208–25
Science and Polity in France at the
    End of the Old Regime
    (Chalmers), 214
Science Council of Japan, 171
Science in History (Bernal), 218
Science in Sweden (Frängsmyr), 210
Scotland
    history of economic thought,
        90n. 30, 321
Scottish Higher Education Funding
    Council (SHEFC), 80
Self-histories, changing role, 382–86
Séminaire Aftalion, 117
Sempere y Guarinos, Juan, 138
Sen, Amartya, 185
Senior, Nassau, 194, 366
Sent, Esther-Mirjam, 9, 209, 219, 239
    correspondence, 284–94
    personal experiences of,
        284–97, 299
    Sargent, account of work, 331
    Simon, Herbert and, 289, 292–94
Shapin, S., 227–28, 235
Sheets-Pyenson, Susan, 228
Shionoya, Yuichi, 170, 171
Shleifer, Andrei, 295
Shortland, Michael, 228
Silk, Leonard, 180
SilverPlatter
    WebSPIRS, 249, 250
Simon, Herbert, 185, 289, 292–94
Skidelsky, Robert, 228
Skinner, Andrew, 130
Skousen, Mark, 352n. 18
Smith, Adam, 22, 26, 52, 179,
    232, 273
    analysis of, 194
    astronomy, history of, 212
    biography, 228, 233

Chalmers on, 214
classical, description as, 361
core, presence of, 374–75
criticisms, 362–63
early mathematical concepts in
    Germany, 127
influence of, 28, 31
    Japan, 165, 167, 169, 170, 172
    Netherlands, 151
Isis, in, 217
market coordination system, 322
Marx and, 363–67
Meek on, 369–70
political audience, 182
political economy and, 343
ranking by graduate students, 352
science, history of, 213
Scottish education tradition, 321
studies on, 172
surplus value, 374–75
Theory of Moral Sentiments,
    273, 274
*Wealth of Nations. See Wealth of
    Nations*
"Why Read Adam Smith Today?"
    (Mises), 337
Smith, Crosbie, 228
Smith, Pamela, 210–11
Smith, Robert S., 139
Snowdon, B., 229
Soaring Eagle: Alfred Marshall
    (Groenewegen), 228
Social Science Research Network,
    251
Social Sciences Citation Index,
    11, 201, 202
Society for the History of Economic
    Thought (ESHET), 2
Society of American Archivists, 250
Soddy, Frederick, 213, 216
Söderqvist, Thomas, 238
Sokal, Michael, 238
Sombart, Werner, 125

South America, Iberian
    colonies, 144
Spain and Portugal, 137–47
    arbitrismo, 144
    *Biblioteca de Econonomistas
        Aragoneses*, 140
    *Clásicos del Pensamiento
        Económico Espanol*, 139
    *Clásicos del Pensamiento
        Económico Vasco*, 140
    *Colecçao de Obras Clássicas do
        Pensamento Económico
        Português*, 139
    *Economía y Economistas
        Espanoles*, 140
    history of economic thought
        (HET), survey, 137–47
    Iberian Association of the History
        of Economic Thought,
        137, 146
    Institute of Fiscal Studies, 139, 140
    Keynesian economics, 145, 146
    Marshallian economics, 145
    mercantilist economic literature,
        143–44
    School of Salamanca, 143
    South America, colonies, 144
    Universidade do Porto,
        140–41, 146
    Universidade Técnica de Lisboa,
        140
    Walrasian economics, 145
SPARC. *See* Scholarly Publishing
    and Academic Research
    Coalition (SPARC)
Spary, Emma, 211
Specialist journals, role of,
    190–207
Specialization, 313–14
Spencer, Herbert, 215, 347
Spencer, R., 229
Spengler, Joseph J., 65, 181, 217
Spiegel, Henry, 211

Spiethoff, Arthur, 125
Sraffa, Piero
  cult following, 184
  Hume and, 324
  influence of
    France, 117
    Italy, 100, 102–4
    Japan, 170
  Lecture Notes on Advanced Theory
    of Value, 103
  Marxist tradition, 372–76
  post-Keynesian tradition, 323
  Production of Commodities by
    Means of Commodities
    (Sraffa), 361, 372
  research program, 105
  surplus approach, 372–76
  Works and Correspondence of
    David Ricardo, 324
SSCI. See Social Sciences
    Citation Index
Stanford Encyclopedia of Philosophy,
  255
Stein, Herbert, 180
Steps of Social Recognition (Uchida),
  172
Steuart, James, 172, 321
Stigler, George, 181, 343, 353n. 19
Stoa, 127
Strachey, Lytton, 226, 231, 238
Streißler, Erich, 128
The Structure of Scientific
  Revolutions (Kuhn), 214, 384
Studies in the Labour Theory of Value
  (Meek), 361, 369, 373
Study of the Ending of Mercantilism
  (Kobayashi), 172
Sturn, Richard, 130
Sturt, Charles, 156
Subdisciplines, 17–18
  HET in, 181–182
  History of Economics Society
    meetings, role of, 62–76

Italy, 106–7
  liberal arts colleges, North
    America, 17–18
Sugihara, Shiro, 170
Sugimoto, Eiichi, 172
Sumner, James, 210
Supplement to the Encyclopaedia
  Brittanica, 230
The Surgions Mate (Woodall), 263
Sur l'homme (Sarton), 215
Surplus. See Marx, Karl; Smith,
  Adam; Sraffa, Piero
Sydney, University of, 156, 158
Szenberg, M., 229

Tableau économique, 173
Taieb, Paulette, 248
Takahashi, Seiichiro, 173
Takashima, Zenya, 173
Takenaka, Heizo, 174
Tanaka, Hiroshi, 171
Tanaka, Shoji, 170
Tanaka, Toshihiro, 170
Tarascio, Vincent, 65
Tasmania, University of, 162
Textual exegesis approach,
  99–100
Thackray, Arnold, 210, 227–28, 235
Theories of Surplus–Value (Marx),
  103, 172, 364, 365, 374
  publication of, 368
Théories économiques, 120
Theory of expectations, 322
The Theory of Games and Economic
  Behavior, 8
Theory of Moral Sentiments (Smith),
  273, 274
Thornton, Henry, 161
Thünen, Johan Heinrich von, 127
Tilburg University Economics
  Department, 149, 151
Times Higher Education Supplement,
  310

Tinbergen, Jan, 150
Tomaselli, Sylvana, 211
Torrens, Robert, 182
Training, historian of economics, 273–75
Traweek, Sharon, 301
Treatise on Probability (Keynes), 326, 329
Tribe, Keith, 229
Trust in Numbers (Porter), 210
Tugan-Baranovsky, Mikhail, 324
Tulane University, 250
Turgot, Anne-Robert-Jacques, 213, 214
2001 HOPE conference. *See* HOPE 2001 conference
Types of mind in economics, 337–38

Uchida, Yoshihiko, 172, 173
Uchitelle, Louis, 180
UNEAJ. *See* Union of National Economics Associations in Japan (UNEAJ)
Unemployment, Japan, 166
Union of National Economics Associations in Japan (UNEAJ), 168
United Kingdom, 12
Universidade do Porto, 140–41, 146
Universidade Técnica de Lisboa, 140
University of New England, 154
U.S. News and World Report, 39

Values of Precision (Wise), 210
Vane, H., 229
Vaughan, Karen, 346, 350n. 15
Veblen, Thorstein, 179
cult following, 184
Verein für Socialpolitik, 126

Verstehende Nationalökonomie, 128–29
Vickers, Douglas, 161
Viner, Jacob, 181
Virginia, University of
Electronic Text Center, 248–49

Wages, 363–67
Wales, history of economic thought, 90n. 30
Walker, Donald, 218–19, 220
Walras, Léon, 168, 184, 213
Walrasian economics, 145
Warsh, David, 180
Waterman, A. M. C., 320, 324
Wealth of Nations (Smith)
central theme, 365
classical economics, 366
described, 337
introduction to, 363
Japan, influence, 165, 170, 172
Meek's treatment of, 370
streetlight, provision of, 273
Weber, Max, 125, 132
Web sites and their addresses, 258–60
WebSPIRS, 249, 250
Weintraub, E. Roy, 1–14, 98, 161, 273
correspondence regarding, 292
discussion of, 272–83
methodology, distinctions, 322
Wesleyan University, 295
Westfall, Richard S., 218, 228
Whewell, William, 212, 230
Whig perspectives, 350–51, 353n. 19, 355
White, Hayden, 239, 281
White, Lawrence H., 346, 347n. 13
White, Mike, 156, 160

"Why Read Adam Smith Today?"
(Mises), 337
Williams College, 25–26,
275–76, 306
Winch, Donald, 180
Wisconsin, University of,
217, 218
Wise, Norton, 210,
211, 228
Wittgenstein, Ludwig, 344
Wood, John Cunningham, 154, 157,
161–62
Woodall, John, 263
Wooders, Myrna, 295, 296
Woolf, Harry, 216–17
Works and Correspondence of David
Ricardo (Sraffa), 324

The Works of Carl Menger
(Hayek), 344
The Worldly Philosophers
(Heilbroner), 180,
352n. 18
World of "Das Kapital"
(Uchida), 172
World War I, 345
World War II, 116, 369

Yale Law School, 248
Yeo, Richard, 228
Yonay, Yuval, 209, 381
Young, Robert, 217, 237

Zirkle, Conway, 217
Zuidema, Jan, 150